1995

Glory Bound

D1019321

Sports and Entertainment
Steven A. Riess, *Series Editor*

Glory Bound

Black Athletes in a White America

David K. Wiggins

 Syracuse University Press

Permission to reprint the following essays is gratefully acknowledged:
"Victory for Allah: Muhammad Ali, The Nation of Islam, and American Culture," in *Muhammad Ali: The People's Champ*, ed. Elliott J. Gorn. Copyright © 1995 by the Board of Trustees of the University of Illinois. Used with permission of the University of Illinois Press; "The 1936 Olympic Games in Berlin: The Response of America's Black Press," *Research Quarterly for Exercise and Sport* (Sept. 1983), 283–92. *RQES* is a publication of the American Alliance for Health, Physical Education, Recreation and Dance, 1900 Association Drive, Reston, Va. 22091; "The Notion of Double-Consciousness and the Involvement of Black Athletes in American Sport," in *Ethnicity and Sport in North American History and Culture*, ed. George Eisen and David K. Wiggins, 133–53. Reproduced with permission of Greenwood Publishing Group, Inc., Westport, Conn.; "The Play of Slave Children in the Plantation Communities of the Old South, 1820–1860," *Journal of Sport History* 7 (Summer 1980), 21–39; "Peter Jackson and the Elusive Heavyweight Championship: A Black Athlete's Struggle Against the Late Nineteenth-Century Color-Line," *Journal of Sport History* 12 (Summer 1985), 143–63; " 'The Future of College Athletics Is at Stake:' Black Athletes and Racial Turmoil on Three Predominantly White University Campuses, 1968–1972," *Journal of Sport History* 15 (Winter 1988): 304–33; "Wendell Smith, the *Pittsburgh Courier-Journal* and Campaign to Include Blacks in Organized Baseball, 1933–1945," *Journal of Sport History* 10 (Summer 1983): 5–29; "Isaac Murphy: Black Hero in Nineteenth-Century American Sport, 1861–1896," *Canadian Journal of History of Sport and Physical Education* 10 (May 1979): 15–33; "The Year of Awakening: Black Athletes, Racial Unrest, and the Civil Rights Movement of 1968," *The International Journal of the History of Sport* 9 (August 1992): 188–208.

The paper used in this publication meets the minimum requirements of American National Standard for Information Sciences—Permanence of Paper for Printed Library Materials, ANSI Z39.48-1984. ∞™

Library of Congress Cataloging-in-Publication Data
Wiggins, David Kenneth, 1951–
        Glory bound : black athletes in a white America / David K.
    Wiggins.—1st ed.
            p.   cm.—(Sports and entertainment)
        Includes bibliographical references (p.   ) and index.
        ISBN 0-8156-2733-5 (cloth : alk. paper).—ISBN 0-8156-2734-3
    (pbk. : alk. paper)
        1. Afro-American athletes—History. 2. Sports—United States—
    History. 3. Discrimination in sports—United States—History.
    4. Afro-American athletes—Social conditions. I. Title.
    II. Series.
    GV583.W545   1994
    796'.089'96073—dc20   96-46218

Manufactured in the United States of America

To my parents, Lurline and Gene L. Wiggins,
who attended all of my games and gave me every advantage

David K. Wiggins is a professor in the Department of Health, Fitness, and Recreation Resources at George Mason University. He is editor of *Sport in America: From Wicked Amusement to National Obsession* and coeditor of *Ethnicity and Sport in North American History and Culture.* His numerous articles have appeared in such journals as *Quest, Journal of Sport History, Research Quarterly for Exercise and Sport,* and the *International Journal of the History of Sport.*

Contents

Illustrations

Acknowledgments

I am indebted to a number of people for their help and encouragement in the completion of this book. Jeffrey Sammons urged me to publish my essays so that they would become more readily available to scholars and the general public. He also has provided insights into race relations and sport that have influenced other academicians working in the field. Steven Riess has always been very supportive of my work, offering cogent comments and important suggestions on many of the essays. Through his various editorships and his own scholarly work, he has contributed greatly to the growth of sport history as an academic discipline. Patrick Miller also encouraged me to put together this collection. He has given me sage advice, has been extremely helpful in reviewing my work, and has become a good friend and trusted colleague. I know of no one who is more generous with his time and has such a love for history and the sharing of ideas. I owe special thanks to Donald Mrozek, Ronald Smith, Elliott Gorn, Randy Roberts, Stephen Hardy, Bruce Bennett, James Henderson, and Dr. Calvin Sinnette for their comments and various suggestions on many of the essays in this book. I am also greatly indebted to Susan Pufnock, my editorial assistant, who always gives generously of her time and is the consummate professional. This collection would have been impossible to put together without her assistance. Lastly, I would like to thank Brenda, Jordan, and Spencer for their unwavering patience and support. The three of them are all special and have made my life so much more fulfilling.

Introduction

This collection of essays recounts the involvement of black athletes in American sport. Written at various stages during my nearly seventeen years in academia, the essays in this collection, ten of which have been previously published, have been kept substantially in their original form with the exception of selected footnotes which have been slightly altered to reflect the most current research literature. My intent in putting this collection together is to make the essays more readily available to scholars who have an interest in sport, race, and civil rights issues. I believe the essays provide insights into the experiences of African American athletes not always found in other secondary works. For one thing, the essays are based on a variety of different sources, including little known materials emanating from the African American community. I have employed materials ranging from slave narratives and black newspapers to black autobiographies and personal memoirs. At the time the essays first appeared, they tackled subjects not previously examined by other academicians, emphasizing the role of sport in the black community, interrelationships between black and white athletes, and the effect of racial discrimination at the various levels of sport.

I first became interested in the history of African American athletes as a beginning graduate student at San Diego State University during the early 1970s. The increasing amount of media attention given to African American athletes, the growing number of academic studies being completed on various aspects of black life and culture, and the emergence of sport studies as a legitimate area of scholarship within departments of physical education all combined to spark my interest in the black athlete's past. My initial attempt to write seriously about the history of African American athletes was a term paper I completed for a graduate course taught by the late Reet Howell. Although I cannot recall the exact title of the paper, I do remember Dr. Howell's liberal use of her red ink pen and strong suggestion to delimit my topic and establish a consistent theme.

I also remember, even at that early stage of my career, how few scholarly articles and books had been written on the African American experience in sport. Other than a smattering of studies in certain academic journals and a few popular books, the secondary literature on African American athletes was limited in scope and often devoid of serious analysis and interpretation. Although this made my aforementioned term paper that much more difficult to write, it also meant that those of us interested in the subject had a plethora of possible topics to select from and the opportunity to both expand the body of knowledge and forge new directions in research. One could choose from a number of possible areas of investigation, including studies that examined the individual exploits of African American athletes, the role of sport among free blacks and slaves in early nineteenth-century America, and the participation patterns of African American athletes in both segregated and predominantly white organized sports programs over the last several decades.

The almost limitless opportunities to do research on African American athletes served me well while I was working toward my Ph.D. in Sport History at the University of Maryland between 1975 and 1979. Under the tutelage of my major advisors, Marvin H. Eyler and Joan Hult, I began to probe the African American athletes' past with increased vigor. For my doctoral dissertation, I examined the recreational and sporting activities of slaves living on southern plantations during the first half of the nineteenth century.[1] The dissertation would prove to be a valuable educational experience for me and have a significant influence on my subsequent publications, including the eleven essays that comprise this book. I learned how time-consuming historical research can be and how difficult it sometimes is to locate primary source material on African Americans, particularly about slaves who were not permitted to read or write. I also learned about the importance of writing style, the need to delimit a topic, and the difficulty in organizing vast amounts of historical material. Perhaps most important, I learned how arduous yet stimulating it is to reconstruct the past and account for the differing motives of individuals based on incomplete and sometimes conflicting evidence.

One of the chapters in my dissertation was devoted to the play of slave children. After several rewrites and additional research, it was published under the title, "The Play of Slave Children in the Plantation Communities of the Old South, 1820–1860," in the *Journal of Sport History*. This essay, which is the first chapter in part 1, "From Plantation to Playing Field," chronicles the play of slave children, attempting to determine the role that various games and sports served for the younger slaves living on southern plantations during the antebellum period. Depending to a great extent on the slave narratives edited by George P.

Rawick (a WPA project) and well-known secondary works written by such scholars as John W. Blassingame, Eugene D. Genovese, Leslie H. Owens, and Thomas L. Webber, the essay's thesis is that slave children were able to realize a much needed sense of community with other children and adults of the plantation through play activities.

A number of criticisms of the essay have been made by academicians, including my reluctance to ask more questions of the evidence and my uncritical approach to the works of Eugene D. Genovese and other scholars of the slave experience.[2] I generally think these criticisms are well founded. My major regret, however, is that I conducted the study without having a more thorough grasp of the secondary literature on play and play theories. The essay would have been enhanced significantly if the experiences of slave children had been placed more squarely in the context of the literature on play emanating from anthropology, psychology, sociology, and various other disciplines. Fortunately, two subsequent studies have examined the play of slave children more fully within the context of play theory. Both Bernard Mergen's *Play and Playthings: A Reference Guide* and Wilma King's *Stolen Childhood: Slave Youth in Nineteenth-Century America* critically explore certain aspects of the play of slave children with an awareness of play theory as it relates directly to games, role reversal, and modeling.[3]

My second essay is a study of the famous jockey Isaac Murphy that was initially published in 1979 in the *Canadian Journal of the History of Sport and Physical Education*. I first became interested in Murphy after reading about him and other prominent black jockeys in John Rickards Betts's classic work, *America's Sporting Heritage, 1850–1950*.[4] I was fascinated by Betts's description of the most well-known of the group of black riders that dominated the jockey profession in post-Civil War America and proceeded to search for as much information as possible about his life and career. The research I conducted on Murphy was especially satisfying because it allowed me to examine such wonderful periodicals as the *Spirit of the Times* and *National Turf Register* in the Rare Book Room of the Library of Congress and the voluminous material on horse racing in the Keeneland Library in Lexington, Kentucky. The most frustrating aspect of my work on Murphy was trying to get inside the mind of this famous jockey to determine his thoughts regarding his profession, racial discrimination, and a host of other matters. As is the case with some of the other early black athletes, there are no extended interviews, personal reminiscences, or autobiographies to determine Murphy's personal value scheme or motivations.

I am unaware of any other scholarly work that focuses exclusively on Murphy. While an occasional piece on Murphy has appeared in more popular magazines and books, no academicians have turned their attention specifically to him or any of the other great black jockeys that distinguished themselves in horse racing during the latter half of the nineteenth century.[5] In fact, the only other scholarly books of note on late nineteenth-century African American athletes are Andrew Ritchie's *Major Taylor: The Extraordinary Career of a Champion Bicycle Racer* and David W. Zang's *Fleet Walker's Divided Heart: The Life of Baseball's First Black Major Leaguer.*[6] These excellent biographies recount the lives of two well-known African American athletes who experienced both triumphs and the pangs of racial discrimination in their respective sports during a period marked by deteriorating racial conditions and legalized segregation.

The final essay in part 1 is a biography of Peter Jackson, a boxer from the West Indies, who captured the Australian heavyweight championship and eventually traveled to America seeking a fight with the famous "Boston Strong Boy," John L. Sullivan. Originally published in 1985 in the *Journal of Sport History,* the essay required me to examine unfamiliar sources, learn as much as possible about the sport of boxing, and become aware of the differing racial climates in Australia, Great Britain, and the United States during the late nineteenth century. I received wonderful support in my research from Bill Schutte, who welcomed me into his home in Whitewater, Wisconsin, and allowed me unrestricted access to his many documents and photographs of Jackson and other nineteenth-century boxers.[7] It would have been impossible to complete the essay on Jackson without Schutte's generosity. In part 2, "Civil Rights and the Quest for Equality," I include essays that detail African American athletes' efforts to overcome racial prejudice in both sport and American society. In "The 1936 Olympic Games in Berlin: The Response of America's Black Press," I examine several of America's leading black newspapers to determine their reaction to the involvement of African American athletes in perhaps the single most important sporting event in history. Originally published in 1982 in the *Research Quarterly for Exercise and Sport,* the essay details the response of black newspapers to the proposed boycott of the Games, the triumphs of Jesse Owens and other African American athletes, and the influence these triumphs had on America's black community. For this essay I was awarded the first of my two research writing awards from the Research Consortium of the American Alliance for Health, Physical Education, Recreation, and Dance.[8] The most lasting result for me, however, was the tremendous amount of respect I came to have for black newspapers and the work they did on behalf of civil rights. The black press, through the work of a group of talented writers, helped shape public opinion in the African American community while at the same time fighting to eliminate racial discrimination both within and outside of sport.

One of the most gifted writers in the black press was Wendell Smith, the subject of chapter 5. In an essay originally published in 1983 in the *Journal of Sport History,* I discuss Smith's role as a sports writer for the *Pittsburgh Courier-Journal* and the part he played in Branch Rickey's signing of Jackie Robinson to a baseball contract with the Brooklyn Dodgers. Until my recent publication dealing with Muhammad Ali's relationship to Elijah Muhammad and the Black Muslims, I always believed the piece on Smith was my best work in terms of organization, writing style, and interpretation. Unfortunately, I have also always believed that the essay was one of my least appreciated pieces—partly a result, no doubt, from the fact it was published at about the same time as Jules Tygiel's seminal work, *Baseball's Great Experiment: Jackie Robinson and His Legacy.*[9] My other disappointment is that no other scholars have seen fit to write about Smith or the other black sportswriters who contributed to the desegregation of predominantly white organized sport. Such legendary sportswriters as Sam Lacy, Romeo Dougherty, A. S. "Doc" Young, Joe Bostic, and Rollo Wilson all await their biographers and full recognition from an American public unaware of their many accomplishments.

Chapter 6 is an essay on African American athletes and the civil rights struggle in 1968. Originally published in the *International Journal of the History of Sport,* the essay recounts such events as Muhammad Ali's legal battles over his conviction on draft evasion, the Harry Edwards-led boycott of the Mexico City Olympic Games, and the numerous racial confrontations involving African American athletes on predominantly white university campuses during one of America's most tumultuous years. This essay gave me special satisfaction because it allowed me to recall many of the events I read about and observed on television as a high school student in California. I remember quite vividly how impressed I was with the stand taken by Muhammad Ali against the United States government, the courage exhibited by Tommie Smith and John Carlos on the victory stand in Mexico City, and the uproar and fear caused by disgruntled black college athletes on predominantly white university campuses. If I were to do the essay over again, I would recount in more detail how the revolts of African American athletes in 1968 fit into the larger civil rights movement and write more specifically about black women athletes. I write virtually nothing about black women athletes in this essay and offer only a cursory analysis of their contributions to sport in the other essays that comprise this book. This is, fortunately enough, an area of study that has been taken up by such noted scholars as Susan Cahn, Cindy Himes Gissendanner, and Martha Verbrugge.[10]

Chapter 7 is an essay that delineates the revolts of African American athletes at the University of California, Berkeley; Syracuse University; and Oregon State University during the latter part of the 1960s and early 1970s. Originally published in 1988 in a special issue I edited on "The Black Athlete in American Sport" for the *Journal of Sport History,* the essay was enormously challenging to write because I attempted to describe both the similarities and differences among the three revolts.[11] One of the criticisms made of the essay is that it does not include any personal interviews with the principals involved in the racial disturbances at the three universities. I agree that personal interviews would have greatly enhanced the essay. It is important to note, however, that I was involved tangentially in the racial confrontation involving African American athletes at Oregon State University. I was a member of Dee Andros's all-white recruiting class of 1969 and played for Gene Hilliard, the black coach brought in to help ease racial tension following the "Fred Milton Affair." I was also one of the thirteen members of Oregon State's baseball team that asked for Gene Tanselli's resignation as coach, a decision that was terribly difficult for me to make as a nineteen-year-old college student who had always been taught to respect those in authority.

The last chapter in part 2 is an essay on Muhammad Ali that was originally presented as a paper during a 1992 symposium at Miami University of Ohio and recently published in Elliott J. Gorn's *Muhammad Ali: The People's Champ.*[12] This essay will always have special meaning for me because Ali was in attendance at the symposium and listened attentively as I attempted to talk, with some authority, about his involvement with Elijah Muhammad and the Nation of Islam. To say I was a bit anxious speaking about Ali's association with the Nation of Islam while he was sitting no more than twenty feet in front of me would be a gross understatement. But I came out better for the experience and actually ended up eating dinner and socializing with Ali and the other presenters following the symposium. The opportunity to be in the presence of the champ was a highlight of my professional career, as it was for the other participants in the symposium who had also grown up watching the great heavyweight perform his magic in and out of the ring.

The first chapter of part 3, "Race Relations and the Ideology of Sport," is an essay that analyzes the historical debate over alleged black athletic superiority. This essay, originally published in 1989 in the *Journal of Sport History,* was not a work I approached lightly or without some trepidation. In fact, I waited ten years before writing it. It took me that long to gain the confidence and feel comfortable enough with the research literature to write on a topic that elicits the most visceral responses from individuals of both races. I am thankful I ultimately decided to write the essay because I believe it provides insight into racialist thinking, sport, and deep-seated stereotypes so prevalent in American society.

The essay, however, has drawn some criticism and in some circles perhaps can even be considered controversial. The historian Jeffrey Sammons, while praising the essay as "a remarkable piece of scholarship," takes exception to my statement in the last paragraph that the "spirit of science necessitates . . . that academicians continue their research to determine if the success of black athletes is somehow the consequence of racially distinctive chromosomes." Sammons notes that this conclusion of mine "alerts us that the most well-meaning can fall prey to the traps set by the misguided, sometimes malicious, intentions of race thinkers."[13] Sammons's criticism is well taken and, if I were to rewrite the essay, I would eliminate much of what I wrote in the last paragraph. I do believe, as I imply throughout the essay, that the repeated attempts to draw a link between great performances of black athletes and innate physical abilities has resulted from feelings of white superiority and justification for various forms of racial discrimination.[14]

Chapter 10 is an essay that was originally published in a book I co-edited with George Eisen, *Ethnicity and Sport in North American History and Culture*.[15] Taking as my theme W. E. B. Du Bois's notion of double-consciousness as expressed in his famous work *The Souls of Black Folk*, I provide an historical examination of the African American athlete's participation in sport. I have always considered this essay more of a primer than anything else, hopefully providing readers with a cogent analysis of the experiences of African American athletes at various levels both within and outside the black community. I thought a great deal about my own racial background while writing this essay. Although I had always been sensitive to being a white academician studying black culture, the nature of this essay seemed to heighten that sensitivity. Could I, as a white academician, accurately assess the life experiences of African American athletes and determine their feelings about being both black and American? As a white academician, could I ever really understand the trials and tribulations experienced by African American athletes? These questions, of course, are as old as historiography itself and ultimately can only be answered by the readers of the essay. These are also questions that have become less important to me as time goes by. I realize now that the best work on African American athletes has more to do with academic preparation, sense and sensibilities, and knowledge of the black experience than it does with the racial origins of the author.

The book's final chapter, the only one that has not been previously published, deals with Edwin Bancroft Henderson, an African American educator, civil rights activist, and writer I have termed "The Father of Black Sport History." Although his accomplishments were many and extraordinarily diverse, the essay deals exclusively with Henderson's voluminous publications on the history of African Americans in sport.

Conducting the research for this essay was a wonderful experience, primarily because it allowed me to canvass once again the manuscript materials in the Moorland-Spingarn Research Center at Howard University and to make contact with some of Henderson's friends and family. I exchanged several letters with Bruce L. Bennett, a well-known physical educator and historian of physical education and sport who became a good friend of Henderson's during the latter stages of his life. Perhaps most important, I had several conversations over the phone and a meeting of approximately an hour and a half with Henderson's youngest son, James. Having traveled from Tuskegee, Alabama, where he is a professor of plant physiology and biochemistry at Tuskegee University, to Northern Virginia for a visit with family and friends, James Henderson took time out from his busy schedule to talk with me in my office about his father. I am so glad he did. I gathered information about his father that does not appear in written materials and had the unique opportunity to learn firsthand about the extraordinary Henderson family.

David K. Wiggins

Fairfax, Virginia
July 1996

Part One

From Plantation to Playing Field

1

The Play of Slave Children in the Plantation Communities of the Old South, 1820–1860

Most of the earliest studies done on Southern plantation life portrayed slaves as people without a culture, without philosophical beliefs, and without educational instruments of their own.[1] Historians often viewed slaves as barbarians to be civilized; as perpetual children at best, and animals at worst. As such, it was assumed that slaves held no strong values or convictions and that they were without a coherent culture or social organization of their own. To suggest that slaves were capable of molding or fashioning their own particular life-style was inconceivable. The more current research, however, has altered our perceptions of what the "peculiar institution" was really like. Many scholars now assert that slaves were capable of creating their own "unique cultural forms" largely free from the control of whites. Regardless of how cruel the plantation became for slaves, their struggle for survival never became so severe that it destroyed their creative instincts or prevented them from establishing their own personal way of life. The distinguishing elements of their culture—superstitions, religion, recreation, music, folktales, and language—allowed the slaves a degree of individual autonomy and self-respect. While slaves recognized the superior power that whites held as a group, they resisted the total assimilation of white culture.[2]

The play of slave children between the years 1820 and 1860 makes clear that they were similar to adult slaves in recognizing their uniqueness and separate identity as a group. Play was essential to slave children because it was one means through which they learned the values and mores of their parents' world. Play became a means by which cultural traits were preserved from one generation to the next. Like all young people, slave children liquidated some of their problems and relieved themselves of worries and anxieties by talking about and dramatizing

3

the things which disturbed them. Through play, slave children were also able to realize a much needed sense of community not only with other children of the plantation but with the adult slaves as well. Most importantly, the play of slave children makes apparent that they generally considered themselves, as recently noted by Thomas L. Webber, as a familial group, with similar life-styles, similar concerns and problems, and a mutual need to support one another no matter what the circumstances. Despite individual suspicions and hostilities, slave children recognized each other as a distinct group with a shared experience and a common approach to life.[3]

Some of the best evidence available about slave life is the series of slave narratives edited by George P. Rawick.[4] This nineteen-volume work, sixteen of which contain interviews prepared by the Federal Writers Project between 1936 and 1938, nonetheless has some inherent problems. Since approximately two-thirds of the slaves were eighty or more years of age at the time they were interviewed, not only is there a concern about failing memories but also the question of whether longevity was the result of unusually good rather than typical treatment as slaves. Most of them were also recalling the experiences of their childhood, a period before the worst features of slavery were normally felt, and were likely, therefore, to give a more favorable picture of the institution. In addition, the biases, procedures, and methods employed by the predominantly southern white interviewers can be justly criticized. On the other hand, these narratives, as muddled and contradictory as they are, represent the voices of the inarticulate masses that scholars are always bemoaning. In spite of their imperfections, they are not much different from any other types of historical sources. Historians simply have to use caution and discrimination when using the interviews. And naturally they should make use of all the skepticism their trade has taught them if they expect to come up with an honest interpretation. The narratives are certainly a most valuable piece of information on black history in America and should not be neglected. They contain evidence and answers for just about every kind of question that could be asked about life under slavery. For this particular study on the play of slave children they are the single best source available.

Slave children held a rather precarious position in the plantation community. For six days a week, while their parents were in the fields toiling under the hot sun or attending to chores in the "big house," slave children were generally left alone to raise one another. Exempted from routine labor until sometimes as late as fourteen or fifteen years old, a certain portion of the slave child's early life was spent in nurturing those younger than themselves and performing such chores as carrying water to the field hands, cleaning up the yards, fetching wood, tending the family garden, and feeding the livestock. The slave children's existence, however, was not all work and no play. On the contrary, when not engaged in their light tasks, they spent much of their time in the simple pleasures of eating, conversing, and playing with their companions.[5]

Hardly anything was more enjoyable for the older slaves than roaming the fields and woods within the borders of their home plantation. Like all young people, slave children loved to explore the world around them. It helped them to discover their particular strengths and weaknesses and enabled them to cope with situations and events appropriate to their size and stamina. Acie Thomas spent much of his childhood roaming over the "broad acres" of his master's plantation with other slave children. "They waded in the streams, fished, chased rabbits and always knew where the choicest wild berries and nuts grew."[6] "On Sundays we'd strike out for the big woods and we'd gather our dresses full of hickory, walnuts, and berries," recalled Fannie Yarbrough from Texas. "I was jes' lying' here dreamin' 'bout how we use to go to the woods every spring and dig the maypop roots."[7]

The younger children did not have the privilege of wandering about the plantation. During the day parents expected their younger offspring to restrict their play activities to within the borders of the plantation nursery, slave quarters, or "big house."[8] Estrella Jones said the younger children on her master's Georgia plantation were allowed to play anytime "as long as they didn't wander away from the quarters."[9] It was much the same way on Ann Hawthorne's plantation in Texas. "We done our playing around that big house," recalled Hawthorne, "but that front gate we mustn't go outside dat."[10]

The children frequently had the opportunity to visit their peer group on neighboring plantations. Parents usually did not mind if their children traveled to a nearby plantation, as long as they returned before nightfall. The slave children living on smaller plantations were especially anxious to make these excursions, since it was often the only chance they had to play with children of their own age group. "The patteroles never bothered the children any," remembered the Arkansas slave Allen Johnson. "And there wasn't any danger of them running off. It was all right for a child to go in the different quarters and play with one another during the daytime just so they got back before night."[11]

Older slave boys, and less frequently the girls, willingly contributed to the welfare of their family by hunting and fishing with their fathers during the evening hours. Exemption from field labor at night gave fathers and their children an opportunity to augment their diet by trapping small game and catching fish in nearby streams. They realized a much needed feeling of self-worth by adding delicacies to the family table. Often prevented by their masters from contributing to their families' material welfare, slaves relished the chance to hunt and angle for food. Maybe most important, slave men found these two activities particularly satisfying because it allowed them the opportunity to teach their children the intricacies involved in hunting and fishing. There were not many activities in the plantation community where slave fathers and their children could share in the excitement of common pursuits. They both enjoyed the camaraderie and spirit that characterized these occasions.[12] "My old daddy partly raised his chilluns on game," remembered Louise Adairs of North Carolina. "Mighty lot of fun when we could go with em."[13]

Like that of most young people, the play of slave children consisted of both traditional games passed down from the older to younger children and those "improvised on the spot."[14] Phyllis Petite of Texas said they used to play a game called "skeeting" when the lake would freeze over in the winter time. "No, I don't mean skating," recalled Petite. "That's when you got iron skates and we didn't have them things. We just get a running start and jump on the ice and skeet as far as we could go, and then run some more."[15] An ex-slave from Tennessee remembered playing a game they called "Smut." "We played it just like you would with cards only we would have grains of corn and call them hearts and spades, and so forth and go by the spots on the corn."[16] Charlie Davenport played a variety of the more traditional games on his Mississippi plantation. "Us played together in de street what run de length o' de quarters," remembered Davenport. "Us tho'owed horse shoes, jumped poles, walked on stilts, an' played marbles."[17] Chana Littlejohn played mumblety-peg, hopscotch, and "jumpin' de rope" when she was growing up on her small North Carolina plantation.[18]

The most popular group activities of the slave children, especially the girls, were "ring games" or "ring dances," accompanied by a variety of songs and riddles. There were infinite variations in these games, but the general procedure was to draw a ring on the ground, ranging from fifteen to thirty feet in diameter, depending on the number of children engaged in the dancing ring. The participants would congregate within the ring and dance to different rhythmic clappings.[19]

Often during their ring games the children would berate the whites in song:

> My old mistress promised me,
> Before she dies she would set me free.
> Now she's dead and gone to hell
> I hope the devil will burn her well.[20]

Or they would comment on their particular fears and anxieties:

> Run nigger, run.
> De patteroll git you!
> Run nigger, run.
> De patteroll come!
> Watch nigger, watch.
> De patteroll trick you!
> Watch nigger, watch.
> He got a big gun![21]

Many of the games played by children of the slave quarters had definite educational implications. Through the playing of games, slave children were often able to learn simple skills of literacy. "I learned some of the ABC's in playing ball with the white children," remembered Mattie Fannen of Arkansas.[22] Anna Parkes, who lived on a large plantation in Georgia, remembered nothing about special games except "Ole Hundred." "Us would choose one and that one would hide his face against a tree while he counted to a hundred. Then he would hunt for all the others. They would be hiding while he was counting. We learned to count a playing Ole Hundred."[23]

Much of the life of slave children consisted of role-playing and reenacting those events that were most significant for them.[24] Like all young people they wished to be grown-up and yearned to be wanted, needed, and a useful part of the grown-up world. It was natural for them to recreate that world using themselves as the leading characters. There were several distinguishing features about the imitative play of slave children. First, they did not necessarily reenact those events found most enjoyable by the adult slaves. Second, they normally re-enacted events they had witnessed and heard of rather than experienced. Third, they usually imitated the social events of their own people and not those of the planter's family. Last and perhaps most important, the evidence strongly suggests that slave children attempted to relieve particular anxieties and fears through the medium of imitative play. By reenacting certain events, they attempted to master specific problems that they were not able to resolve realistically.

Slave children were not necessarily unique in their imitative play, but rather in the social events they chose to emulate. The frequency with which they conducted simulated church activities, funerals, and auctions shows the importance that slaves attached to these three "cultural affairs." Benny Dillard, who lived on a Georgia plantation that contained over fifty slaves, remembered "the best game of all was to play like it was big meeting time. . . . We would have make believe preachin' and

baptism'. When we started playing like we were baptizing them we thro-
wed all we could catch right in the creek, clothes and all, and ducked
them."[25] Dinah Perry of Arkansas remembered how they made arrangements for a grand funeral. "We marched in a procession singing one of
our folks funeral hymns," recalled Perry. "We stopped at the grave under
the big magnolia tree by the gate, and my sister Nancy performed the
ceremony."[26] Abe Livingston of Texas remembered playing the game of
"Auction" on his "Massa's" plantation. One of the children would become the auctioneer and conduct a simulated slave sale.[27]

Two games that were played repeatedly by slave children were different variations of "Hiding the Switch" and "No Bogeyman Tonight." In
the first activity the players hunted for a switch that had been concealed
by one of the children. Whoever found it ran after the others, attempting
to hit them. In the latter game one of the children assumed the role of an
evil spirit and attempted to frighten the others. The girls found these
games as popular as the boys. Julia Banks of Texas said they used to "get
switches and whip one another. You know after you was hit several times
it didn't hurt much."[28] Rachel Harris of Arkansas remembered playing
"No Bogeyman Tonight" with the white children. "One would catch the
others as they ran from behind the big trees. Then whoever he caught
would be boogerman, till he caught somebody else."[29]

One historian of slavery feels these two particular games were means
through which children assisted themselves in coping with their fear of
"whippings" and "evil spirits."[30] This is certainly a plausible explanation. Slave children who had witnessed the "floggings" of their parents
or heard the frightening stories of ghost-like "spirits" could be expected
to engage repeatedly in these games if it assisted them in lessening their
fears. But this is only one of the possible interpretations. In these two
games the children appeared to represent to themselves concretely those
puzzling events they did not actually experience. The children may have
been exploring their innermost feelings and emotions through a graphic
representation. Or they may have been overtly "going over" two bewil-
dering events in an attempt to confirm a vague memory. In other words,
there was a need to physically reenact "whippings" and "ghost stories"
in order that their obscure features could be remembered more easily.
Finally, slave children possibly participated in these two games simply
for the excitement and sudden fear they wrought. Like most children,
they found a certain satisfaction in voluntarily exposing themselves to
dangerous situations and inflicting what Roger Callois calls "a kind of
voluptuous panic upon an otherwise lucid mind."[31]

Slave children played many different ballgames. One of the distinctive features of these games was their simple organization, which was no
doubt part of the reason why children of the slave quarters found them

so popular. There were seemingly very few rules in their ballgames or those of their white counterparts. Simplicity of this type was necessary because of the slave children's personal level of social maturity and their inability to continually acquire "sporting" accoutrements. "Shinny was de thing dat I like the best," reminisced Hector Godbold of South Carolina, "just had stick wid crook in de end of it en see could I knock de ball wid dat." [32] Tom Johnson, also of South Carolina, "played lots of games, like rolly hole. There are two holes and you try to roll a ball in one hole." [33] Hanna Davidson of Kentucky remembered playing the game of "Anti-Over." Six of us would stay on one side of the house and six on the other side," recalled Davidson, "then we'd throw the ball over the roof. If you'd catch it you'd run around to the other side and hit somebody then start over." [34]

Older slave boys often mentioned playing "baseball." The available evidence does not specify the rules that were used or the number of players that made up a team. In all probability, the games they usually played were the various modifications of "rounders" and "townball" engaged in by white southerners. [35] The most popular game of these boys throughout the South was marbles. It was a game that required very little playing gear. A match could be arranged anytime two boys came together who were anxious to demonstrate their "shooting" abilities. The playing of marbles, furthermore, appeared to be one activity in which slave boys could experience a temporary feeling of "power." The collection of marbles was one instance in which they could acquire objects of material worth, no matter their monetary value. "Us boys played marbles," recalled James Southall of Tennessee. "I got to be a professional. I could beat em all." [36] Charles Coles of Maryland said that he "had many marbles and toys that poor children had then" and that his "favorite game was marbles." [37]

Slave boys, and less frequently the girls, challenged members of their peer group to impromptu contests that would test their physical prowess. They delighted in seeing who could run the fastest, jump the highest, throw the farthest, swim the longest, and lift the heaviest objects. "Athletic" accomplishments were a source of great pride for slave children. The ability to perform well in physical contests usually guaranteed them the respect of their impressionable young playmates. One of the fastest ways for them to attain a degree of status and the recognized leadership of their peer group was to be successful on the playing field. "Because of my unusual strength and spirit I would let none of them beat me at any game," remembered Robert Ellett of Virginia. "I was best of the young boys on the plantation." [38] Sam Stewart, who lived on a large plantation in North Carolina, recalled that the little boys "near my own age were playmates and companions and accepted me as their natural leader and chief. By the time I was eight years old, I could shoot, ride, fish, and swim with anyone."[39]

The more sportive slave boys enjoyed placing a wager or two in their game playing. They were especially fond of shooting craps and playing cards but would place bets on just about any activity that was conducive to gaming. To elude the eyes of their virtuous parents as well as those of their concerned master they often had to resort to the woods or some other secluded spot. Because they had little to gamble with, their stakes consisted of any objects they attached special importance to. William Ballard and the other slave children used to play hide-the-switch, marbles, and several other games on their South Carolina plantation. But "later on some of de nigger boys started going to the woods to play cards and gamble."[40] "De only game I ever played wuz marbles," remembered John Smith of North Carolina. "I played fer watermelons. We didn't hab any money so we played fer watermelons."[41]

The play of slave girls differed in some respects from that of the boys. There were very few games the girls did not play or at least attempt to play during their childhood.[42] Their most frequent activity was "jump rope."[43] A great deal of their time was spent playing with "dolls" and keeping "house."[44] Maybe most important, slave girls had a particular fondness for dances, parties, and other social entertainments. They repeatedly expressed, like other members of the slave quarters, a desire to be among their own people engaged in group activities. In recollections of the girls' various play activities, there comes through a sense of mutual affection and a spirit of kinship among all the slaves. Phoebe Anderson of Georgia remembered that she would "go fishin down on the creek and on Saturday night we'd have parties in the woods and play ring plays and dance."[45] Caroline Bevis of South Carolina said that when she was a little girl she "would play anti-over in the moonlight but enjoyed most the parties and dances on the plantation."[46]

Slave children spent very little of their leisure time in combative activities. There are occasional references to boxing and wrestling in the slave narratives, but the children generally preferred to engage in more gentle pursuits.[47] Physical abuse of one child by another was considered unjustifiable and a veritable threat to the general well-being of the group. Like their parents, slave children apparently viewed themselves as a distinct body with common concerns, problems, and life-styles. They recognized the need to remain together as a familial group, regardless of the particular circumstances. The point here is not that slave children never fought each other, but rather that they understood that their mutual advantage required them to care for each other and to refrain as much as possible from foolish "skirmishes."[48] John Brown stated that he and his friends saw no wrong in cheating, lying, and fighting "so long as we were not acting against one another."[49] Susan Davis Rhodes, who lived as a slave in North Carolina, said that "People in my day didn't know book learning but dey studied how to protect each other, and didn't believe in fightin' each other."[50]

One of the significant features about the play of slave children was the apparent absence of any games that required the elimination of players. Even the various dodge ball and tagging games played by the children contained designed stratagems within their rule structure that prevented the removal of any participants. Despite the personal animosities and jealousies that individual slave children might have had towards one another, there seemed to be a mutual affection between the mass of children that precluded the elimination of any players in their games. One of the fears in their daily life was that members of their family —father, mother, brothers, sisters, grandparents, uncles, aunts, nieces, nephews—could be indiscriminately sold or hired out at any time. Possible separation from their loved ones was frequently a source of great uneasiness and apprehension for those slave children who were old enough to realize their social position in the plantation community.[51] Their "frivolous" play life was one area of their existence in which they could be assured that their companions would not be suddenly removed or excluded from participating. The lack of elimination in the slave children's games, moreover, can possibly be accounted for by some basic values generally held by members of the slave quarters community. A "survival of the fittest" or "natural selection" mentality did not normally characterize slave society. At the center of the slaves' social philosophy was a necessary belief in cooperation and community spirit. There was little room in the slaves' world for ruthless rivalry, unrestrained competition, and unprincipled domination. Personal conquest and individual success was certainly prevalent in their society but was considered much less important for survival than the belief in group solidarity and a sense of loyalty to fellow members of the slave quarters. Ma Eppes of Alabama remembered playing "Snail Away Rauley" all the time. "Us would hol' han's an' go 'roun' in a ring, gittin' faster an' faster an dem fell down was not out de game but would have, tah ge' back in line."[52] Moses Davis of Arkansas recalled that in playing "Ant y Over" they "would get six on one side of de house and six on de other. When somebody got hit we would just start the game over again."[53]

Occasionally the slave children were permitted to continue their play at night. They longed for the close of day because it meant they could frolic with their parents and other adult slaves—free from the continual surveillance of the planter and his family. The children loved to congregate outside the cabins and listen to some "learned" old slave relate tales of Africa, gather around a blazing fire to dance and sing songs, accompany the more gamesome men on raccoon and possum hunts, travel with their family to a nearby plantation for a dance or corn-shucking, or simply stay around the slave quarters and "cut capers" with the other children. Pet Franks of Mississippi remembered playing "Hide-de switch" and "Goose and Gander" in the daytime. "Den at nighttime when de moon was shinin' big an' yaller, us'd play ole molly bright. Dat was what us call de moon. Ud'd make up stories 'bout her."[54] Jane Simpson, who lived on a small plantation in Missouri, recalled that "de white folks didn't want to let de slaves have no time for der self, so de old folks used to let us children run and play at night, while de white folks sleep and dey watch de stars to tell about what time to call us in and put us to bed, 'fore de white folks know we was out."[55]

Slave children also eagerly looked forward to Saturday afternoons, Sundays, and various holidays because it was an opportunity for them to participate in family and community activities or merely play with their friends and relatives. These moments were prized by all members of the slave quarters, not simply as periods free from labor but as times when slaves could be with one another. These were ideal times for children to become familiar with the organization, the customs, and the leaders of their community. Through their mutual experiences they learned how their community made common decisions, organized clandestine meetings, provided for common recreational activities, and organized itself to be as free as possible from the strictures of their overseer or master. Unable to spend extended periods of time with the children because of a heavy work schedule, slave parents took advantage of these moments to play with and talk to their children. These interactions were extremely important to the children in determining their personality and the particular way in which they viewed the world.[56] "One of de recreations us chilen had in dem days was candy pulling at Christmas times," reminisced Hemp Kennedy of Mississippi. "We all met at one house an' tol' ghost stories, sung plantation songs, as' danced de clog while de candy was cookin'."[57] "Christmastime was when slaves had their own fun," said the Georgia slave Jefferson Franklin Henry. "They frolicked, danced, run races, played games, and visited around, calling it a good time."[58]

Slave children not only played among themselves but frequently participated in the same games and played together in a relative degree of social equality with the white children of the plantation. Some planters did attempt to prevent their children from playing with the children of the slave quarters for fear that they would be "corrupted."[59] Their attempts to circumscribe the play of their children, however, usually proved futile. The white children of the plantation earnestly sought the friendship of the slave children their own age and thoroughly enjoyed

Slave children and their families looked forward all year to the Christmas holidays because it allowed them some respite from constant toil and an opportunity to socialize with one another. This woodcut depicts a "Plantation Frolic on Christmas Eve." Courtesy of the Library of Congress.

the opportunity to frolic in the slave quarters. In fact, through the playing of games, slave and white children would often develop friendships that lasted a lifetime (although those relationships usually existed only between the white children and one or two blacks who became body servants or occupied some special station in the plantation community). "I belonged to ole Massa Harry ebber sin' he was married," recalled an exslave from Virginia. "He an' me was jes' about of an age, an' tended him all his life. I allers 'tended to him when he was a boy, am' went out hunting, shooting, and trapping wid him all over the place." [60] "I hunted and fished with the slave children," responded Edward Pollard, the son of a Virginia slaveholder. "I have wrestled on the banks of the creek with him, and with him as my trusty lieutenant I have filibustered all over my old aunts dominion." [61]

Much of the leisure time of slave and white children was spent getting into mischief and helping each other out of difficult situations. Hand in hand, they would go about pilfering the plantation hen house and performing no small amount of reciprocal trading. There are also numerous examples of white children helping their slave playmates avoid punishments or assisting them in a variety of subtle ways. "Me and young master had the good times," recalled Jack Cauthern of Texas. "He was nigh my age and we'd steal chickens from old Miss and go down in the orchard and barbecue 'em."[62] Matilda Daniel said they surely did some "devilish" things on her Alabama plantation. "We hid red pepper in old Black Bob's chewin' bacca, an' you ought to seed de faces he made. Den we tuken a skunk dat us little white an' black debils katched an' turn him loose in de slave quarters."[63]

Notwithstanding those occasional friendships, a caste system frequently operated within the "play world" of the slave and white children just as it did in the everyday affairs of the plantation community. Older slave children in particular were often forced to assume a subservient position in their game playing. Many of the white children of advanced age were anxious to assume their position as "superiors." Candis Goodwin of Virginia remembered that when the war first started they would "play Yankee an' Federates, 'course de whites was always the 'Federates. They'd take us black boys prisoners an' make b'lieve dey was gonna cut our necks off; guess dey got dat idea f'om dere fathers."[64] Amelia Thompson Watts, who lived on a relative's Louisiana cotton plantation in the summer of 1832, described a scene that also illustrates the caste distinction between slave and white children:

> One of the negro boys had found a dead chicken and we arranged for a funeral. The boys made a wagon of fig branches, and four of them as horses. We tied a bow of black ribbon around the chicken's neck and covered him with a white rag and then marched in a procession singing one of the quaint negro hymns, all the white children next to the hearses marching two by two, and the colored children following in the same order.[65]

Many white children loved nothing better than to torment the slave children, and even the adults, by simulating the role of an overseer or master of a large plantation in their imitative play. Soloman Northup, who labored on a number of southern plantations, recalled the ten or twelve-year-old son of a despotic slaveholder who had no trouble in picking up all his father's habits. "Mounted on his pony," said Northup, "he often rides into the field with his whip, playing overseer, greatly to his father's delight."[66] Frederick Law Olmsted, while traveling through Texas, observed the play of a planter's son that illustrates this point:

> This gentleman had thirty or forty negroes and two legitimate sons. One was an idle young man. The other was already eight years old a swearing tobacco chewing young bully and rufian. We heard him whip-

ping his puppy behind the house and swearing between the blows, his father and mother being at hand. His tone was an evident imitation of his father's mode of dealing with his slaves. "I've got an account to settle with you; I've let you go about long enough; I'll teach you who's your master, there; go now God damn you, but I haven't got through with you yet.[67]

Slave children were not always on the receiving end of such foolish mocking and harassment. Those children of the slave quarters who were clever enough to outwit the white children did not hesitate to return personal insults. Some planters even encouraged these rebukes, because they did not always appreciate seeing their children become tyrants. A slave from Tennessee recalled how they "teased" the white children:

> They didn't allow us to even look at the white children. I 'member we used to slip and play with 'em anyway. About a mile from the house there was a lane, and we would git all the chillen together and play with them down in that lane where our white folks couldn't see us' then we would make 'em skit home! We say 'ya'll gwan now, here come the white folks; he, he, he. We would drive 'em home and tell 'em ole master would whip them if they saw us with 'em. . . . Next morning we would go and get 'em and play with 'em again. We would tell 'em we was better'n than they was, he, he, he.[68]

This feeling of confidence, which shows through the account, was a theme throughout the slave narratives and the other black folklore. In fact, slave children normally thought of themselves not only as morally superior to white children but as superior on a physical level as well. Whereas most slave children thought of themselves as skillful "athletes," their white counterparts were generally felt to be less competent physically—unable to dance, run, jump, or throw! The white children were so inept they were hardly able to tie their own shoes or comb their own hair. "We was stronger and knowed how to play, and the white children didn't," recalled Felix Heywood of Texas.[69] Remembering life under slavery in South Carolina, Josephine Bauchus concluded that "white folks couldn' dance no more den dey can dance dese days like de colored people can."[70]

One of the most striking differences between the play of slave and white children was the type of equipment used in their game playing. In contrast to the planters' children, who were normally able to purchase their own toys, the children of the slave quarters either made their own playthings, obtained various toys that their fathers had crafted, or acquired hand-me-downs that the white children no longer found usable. Hanna Davidson of Kentucky said that "the kids nowadays can go right to the store and buy a ball to play with. We'd have to make a ball out of yarn and put a sock around it for cover."[71] Sam McAllum of Mississippi didn't "recollect any playthings" they had "'cept a ball my young marster gimme,"[72] Letita Burwell, the daughter of a Kentucky planter, remembered they "early learned that happiness consisted in dispensing it, and found no greater pleasure than saving our old dolls, toys, beads, bits of cake, or candy for the cabin children, whose delight at receiving them richly repaid us."[73]

The white children of the plantation engaged in many of the same activities as their slave counterparts. For example, Lanty Blackford, the son of a wealthy Virginia planter, played with his friends in a variety of activities that Brian Sutton-Smith refers to as central-person games.[74] These are games in which one child plays against the rest of the group. Some of the more popular ones among slave and white children were different variations of "Goosie, Goosie, Gander," "Pig in the Pin," "I Spy," "Base," Hide-and-Seek," "Blind Man's Bluff," and "Fox and Hounds." In addition to these games, the white children in Blackford's neighborhood also engaged in some organized activities such as boating, swimming, fishing, hunting, and wrestling. The children, furthermore, often reenacted different situations from southern life in their play. They were particularly fond of participating in mock military drills, court trials, and political debates.[75] Interestingly enough, what was apparently lacking in the white children's play world were any games of chance. The admonitions they received from their parents quite possibly discouraged the children from playing these games or at least discussing them openly. Still, in comparison to the slave children they seemed to favor those games that principally required the skill and effort of the performers.[76] The emphasis on these particular kinds of games seems to reflect the particular cultural focus of the white southerners more than anything else. The research on play has shown that games emphasizing physical prowess are usually the main determinants in achieving sucess.[77] The planters of the Old South certainly embraced these values. Consequently, through the playing of those games that required a degree of physical prowess, the white children of the plantation were possibly learning that the outcome of particular endeavors was a result of the amount of effort that was expended and that other factors were basically superfluous. On the other hand, slave children could be expected to find gambling and other games of chance particularly enticing. Survival to the slave was not necessarily contingent upon the skill and effort one put forth, but rather upon a variety of other uncontrollable factors—not the least of which was indiscriminate luck.[78]

The white children of the plantation not only placed a great deal of emphasis on the amount of effort expended in their games but were also concerned about the specific manner in which they were played. In many instances they seemed more interested in the mode of play than in the outcome of the game itself. In other words, white children were not simply concerned about the effort expended in their games, but found it necessary that they achieve their desired results in a deliberately stylized way.[79]

It is evident that slave children, like their parents, viewed themselves as a special kind of people and took pride in expressing their peculiar style in many of their play activities. It was often a way to assure themselves of their own self-worth, the medium through which they established lifelong friendships, and the manner in which their individuality was asserted and maintained. Their play life consisted almost solely of informal and oftentimes improvised games that could be arranged any time two children came together who were eager to have some fun. Whether they did it deliberately or not, slave children often learned from each other how to play games. Generally left alone to raise each other, slave children typically had ultimate control as to what they did or did not play. Despite occasional attempts to restrict slaves from playing with their own children, southern slaveholders did not normally concern themselves with the types of games played by slave children. The majority of "proprietors" did allow their slaves a somewhat extended childhood in hopes they would attain the degree of health necessary to become "efficient" workers. However, this prolonged childhood did not include any formal program of games or exercise designed to improve the fitness of the slave children. In fact, the majority of planters generally did not pay much attention to the slave children's physical well-being until they were old enough to join the regular plantation work force. In their way of thinking, freedom from strenuous labor was all that was needed to ensure a "hearty" adult slave. Paradoxically, exemption from work and opportunities for play were probably more influential in the development of a potentially more self-reliant and spirited adult slave.

Like most young people, slave children realized a great deal of pleasure from participation in various play activities. It was often the medium through which they learned the values and mores of the adult world. By simulating those events characteristic of the grown-up world, slave children were able to understand the complicated world about them and perceive the differences that normally existed between a master and his servants. The evidence also suggests that through various play activities slave children were able to relieve themselves of the fear and anxiety that normally characterized the lives of most of the children. By participating in certain amusements, they apparently attempted to overcome particular problems that they were not able to resolve realistically.

A theme that frequently appeared in the narratives was the feeling of black supremacy exhibited by many slave children in their various play activities.[80] Apparently, only at a certain point in their lives did slave children come to realize fully that they were "servants" and that their white companions held a more exalted position in the plantation community. Many did not recognize the difference until they were separated from their white playmates and sent out to the field or up to the "big house" to begin their life of labor. On some plantations the slave children learned the difference when one of their family members was suddenly sold or hired out; or when the planter or overseer superseded their parents' authority in some way. Other slave children learned the difference almost immediately if they were forced to call a white baby "Young Massa" or "Young Misses."[81] Still others immediately recognized the difference when they were forced to assume an obsequious position in their game playing or were excluded from participating altogether. Quite possibly, before their realization that they occupied an inferior position in the plantation community, slave children were unaware of the usual decorum that normally existed between the races and therefore were probably more inclined not to comply with the desires of their white playmates. Of course, simply sharing in the excitement of various play activities probably did much to create temporary feelings of equality and fellowship between the children. It is when people are mutually involved in uninhibited merrymaking that intrinsic differences are most often disguised. The joy and pleasantry of the moment possibly helped erase some of the disparities that existed between the children. Furthermore, slave children could assume almost any attitude they wished because there were very few adults around to keep watch over their every move. In any event, whatever the reasons for the slave children's feelings of superiority, they frequently thought of themsleves as being more energetic dancers, better hunters, faster runners, and more imaginative in all their game playing. The white children were often portrayed simply as clumsy fools who were decidedly prosaic in their play activities.

Not only did slave children often exhibit a marked feeling of superiority but they also realized a much needed sense of community with other slave members through various play activities. In fact, the joy they found in play seemed to be accounted for, more than anything else, by the group solidarity and fraternal spirit this activity brought forth. The slave children eagerly looked forward to play because it gave them opportunities to frolic and socialize with their peer group under comfortable conditions. The fellowship attained during these occasions seems especially significant because it furnished individual slave children with a feeling of security they might not experience under any other circumstances. Moreover, the constant reinforcement, common language, and strong positive sanctions that normally characterized these events helped to succor the slave children in their struggle to discover their personal identities.[82]

This did not mean that slave children ever felt any sense of community with the white children and their family. It is true that mutual enjoyment of various play activities did much to develop friendships among the children. But simply sharing in the excitement of popular pastimes was never enough to erase the intrinsic differences between the children. To develop a true feeling of community requires at least a common life-style, common interests and problems, or a common philosophical approach to the world. It would be misleading in terms of history to say that participating in several of the same play activities was responsible for developing these sentiments between the children—even for a brief period of time. This is not to say that mutual participation in play activities did not temporarily eliminate the usual propriety between the races—only that play was insufficient to develop a sense of community between two people with such different world views.

Finally, the singular style of the slave children's various games, as noted by Dickson Bruce, cuts deep into the heart of one of the basic differences between slave and white society, specifically, their differing notions about the concepts of work and play.[83] Planters seemed to think of play primarily in contrast to work, whereas the dichotomy between these two activities was not quite as discernible in slave society. Relatively speaking, southern slaveholders, like many people in today's world, frequently judged the worthiness of individuals by the amount of effort they expended in their work. They viewed labor as being both a necessity for survival and a virtue in its own right. This did not mean that the Protestant work ethic characterized the southern planters' personal value scheme. On the contrary, they realized that hard work was inevitable to achieve success but not if it meant abstinence or an unrealistic devotion to one's calling. The southern slaveholders certainly did enjoy living it up. Their reputation as a fun-loving and frolicsome society is bascially an accurate one. On the other hand, most planters considered play as generally trifling in the sense that it was immaterial to survival, should be engaged in by gentlemen only in the most organized and refined fashion, and ought to be exclusive in nature and devoid of any frivolous public displays.

Slaves seem to have had a much different view of work and play than their masters.[84] They certainly did not place the same kind of emphasis on work or judge the personal worth of individuals by the successful completion of their regular plantation tasks. The slaves' sense of accomplishment was identified with the family unit and measured primarily by the successful maintenance of the familial order of the household. They realized the necessity of working long and difficult hours during planting and harvesting seasons but expected to work considerably less during other seasons. They did not understand the incessant need for labor and resisted what they felt was senseless work. In other words, for the slaves work was generally not the basis for evaluating their personal integrity and character of their being. Conversely, play was one activity in which slaves could realize a certain degree of dignity and could affirm and sustain their unique existence. They could withstand bondage much more easily when allowed to participate with fellow slaves in a variety of play activities.

2

Isaac Murphy

Black Hero in Nineteenth-Century American Sport,
1861–1896

In the latter half of the nineteenth century, African Americans participated regularly in several sports at various levels of competition. They hunted and fished, established baseball teams, played golf and tennis, handled gamecocks, fought in the boxing ring, and rode horses at various racetracks around the country. Black athletes usually played among themselves, but they also competed with whites. Black pugilists boxed white fighters, black baseball players frequently competed against white athletes, and blacks rode against white jockeys. White athletes held stereotypical notions about their black counterparts, but it was apparent that the majority of whites were not threatened by interracial competitions, until the last decade of the century.[1]

Riding horses became a means of social and economic mobility for members of disadvantaged social groups. Diminutive young black men, first as slaves and then later as freemen, rode regularly at various racetracks in the United States. Fourteen of the fifteen jockeys in the first Kentucky Derby in 1875 were black. The most outstanding of the late nineteenth-century black jockeys was Isaac Murphy, who achieved a national and even international reputation. Indeed, many turf experts believed that Murphy was the finest jockey in the country between 1880 and 1890. Contemporary writers referred to Murphy as "The Colored Archer," after the famous English jockey Fred Archer.[2] Many people believed it would have been more appropriate, in view of their comparative achievements, to refer to Archer as the "White Murphy."[3]

Throughout his brief career, Murphy rode nearly every famous horse in the land, and won every major race except the Futurity, which always eluded him. He was the first jockey ever to win three Kentucky Derbies, was victorious in four American Derbies, and won the famous Latonia

Derby five times. Murphy was also the winning jockey in the celebrated match race between Salvator and Tenny at Sheepshead Bay in 1890. During his career he had an amazing winning percentage of 44 percent, being victorious on 628 of 1,412 mounts.[4]

In 1955, nearly sixty years after his death, Murphy was honored for his many accomplishments by being the first jockey elected to the National Racing Hall of Fame in Saratoga Springs, New York.

Murphy was born Isaac Burns in 1861 on the farm of David Tanner in Fayette County, Kentucky. After the death of his father, Murphy's mother immediately moved the family to Lexington to live with her father, Green Murphy, who was the town's bell ringer and auction-crier.[5] Noting his small stature, Murphy's mother and grandfather decided to apprentice him as a prospective jockey in the fall of 1873. According to legend, the first horse Murphy was put on, a yearling named Volcano, threw him quickly. After much persuasion he was coaxed into re-mounting and for the next two years exercised and rode horses under the tutelage of the Williams and Owing Racing Stable.[6]

In 1875, Murphy, riding under his legal name of Burns, rode his first race aboard a horse named Lady Greenfield, which ran unplaced at a meet in Louisville.[7] Shortly thereafter, at the request of his proud grandfather, who had great hopes for his grandson's future as a jockey, Burns changed his name to Murphy.[8]

Murphy's career was very short, but brilliant and lucrative. At the height of his fame, he was reported to have made between $15,000 and $20,000 a year.[9] This was an enormous sum when one considers that most of the other top jockeys were not making more than $5,000 yearly. Murphy's financial standing afforded him many opportunities and privileges denied other blacks of the period. While most members of his race were barely able to carve out a living, Murphy was purchasing lavish clothing and being accompanied by a personal valet during the racing season.[10] He owned property in some highly desirable white neighborhoods in Lexington and as far away as Chicago. He owned his own stable of horses, which he rode in local races around Lexington.[11] Murphy and his wife also organized elaborate social entertainments. In fact, it was said that Murphy entertained more often than "any black man in the South, if not in the whole country." [12]

Murphy appears to have handled the white world quite well. But it was only on a very superficial level and only then in business transactions or other job-related affairs. Murphy's inner circle of friends and other close social relationships were primarily with members of his race. In fact, Isaac "always kept place with the Negro," said Nate Cantrell, a black trainer from the Chicago area and a close friend of Murphy's. "He ate with the Negro, slept with the Negro, then got up and worked for the white man." [13]

According to many contemporary authorities, Murphy had no superior as a rider. He was admired particularly for his sense of pace, steady hands, and marvelous seat. For instance, L. P. Tarelton, a former owner of the famed Fleetwood Stable, believed Murphy was the finest judge of pace ever seen in a saddle.[14] Broad Church, a respected sporting journalist, called Murphy the best jockey he had ever seen. "Murphy is a capital man on a rouge," explained Church, ". . . a good deal the best we have."[15] The turf historian Walter Vosburgh also described him as the finest jockey he had ever seen. Murphy was "an elegant specimen of manhood," Vosburgh wrote, "strong, muscular, and as graceful as an Apollo. He sits in his horse like a centaur."[16]

In the judgment of many turf experts, the only fault in Murphy's riding was a tendency to draw his finishes too fine. Many whites criticized him unduly for apparent sensationalism and grandstand finishes.[17] The *New York Tribune* in 1889 made the following comment on this habit of his:

> He has a penchant for gallery finishes, the temptation to draw it fine not infrequently overmastering his judgement and causing him to lose on the post races at the mercy of his mounts. In order to shine at his brightest Murphy wants to be mounted on a horse about forty pounds better than any other horse in a race. This enables him to lounge along in the rear of the field till he strikes the homestretch and comes in range of the clear vision of admires in the grand stand . . . then letting his mount move up and get his nose in front of the leader he proceeds to hold it there in a most artistic way till both horses pass the judges. It is the height of Murphy's ambition to ride such a finish.[18]

L. P. Tarelton believed these criticisms were totally unfounded. Murphy had no vanity and was not interested in grandstand finishes. "Such impressions," Tarelton argued, "were created by the very excellence of his riding, which enabled him to win even by a nose when others would have failed entirely."[19] Murphy answered his critics by simply saying: "It is hard to be told you ought to have won further off when I had to hold my breath to win as I did."[20]

Murphy's wide-reaching fame resulted not only from his superior riding skills but also from his gentlemanly behavior and character. In his most successful years, he added much-needed stature to a sport that was thoroughly drenched with improbity and characterized by jockeys who lacked any kind of morals. A major concern in horse racing during the eighties and nineties was the suspicion that races were not properly conducted. Crooked racing continually plagued the tracks around the country. Jockeys would pull up their own mounts.[21] Owners would regularly bet against their own horses and then order their jockey to lose the race. Bookmakers often bribed jockeys to "throw" races. The jockey Billy Donohue, for instance, was notorious for pulling his mounts and accepting bribes. He never even bothered to deny that he threw races or pulled horses.[22] Similarly, the jockey Billy McDermott amassed a fortune by his devious methods. Suspiciously, he won an unusually high percentage of bets on horses that seemingly had no possible chance of winning.[23] One historian even cited a humorous case of a rider who tried to increase the speed of his horse by using an "electric saddle."[24]

What differentiated Murphy from other jockeys was his reputation for complete honesty. It was so well recognized that Murphy could not be corrupted that few people had the audacity to ever suggest wrongdoing to him. Murphy would, if he suspected dishonesty on the part of a stable, return the owner's colors and refuse to ride; or he would simply notify the judges of his suspicions. It was also said that Murphy would not place bets or have others bet for him.[25] For example, one observer noted that "Isaac could have made enough to buy a blue grass farm if he would have agreed to lose on Falsetto in the Kenner Stakes of 1879."[26] But he refused the gambler's wages and guided Falsetto home to victory.

There are several possible explanations for Murphy's apparently unfeigned honesty. First, some people attributed it to the lessons in character development he received from his earliest trainer, Eli Jordan, and one of his first employers, Mrs. Hunt Reynolds. Of the latter a contemporary newspaper wrote that "it is to the refining influences of her household that Murphy owes his good breeding and his fine moral character."[27] Second, Murphy's religious convictions perhaps restrained him from committing any dishonorable acts. He was a devout member of the first black Baptist church in Lexington.[28] Third, it is conceivable that Murphy made so much money legitimately that crooked offers were not tempting. For example, he once tried to convince a notoriously unscrupulous jockey that it was easier to make money by being honest and obeying the rules. "Stoval, you just ride to win," explained Murphy. "A jockey that will sell out to one man will sell out to another. Just be honest, and you'll have no trouble and plenty of money."[29] Finally, it is quite possible that Murphy knew a black man was the number one suspect in any unprincipled dealing. It would be foolish, therefore, to try anything the least bit suspicious.[30]

Murphy first came into national prominence in 1879 when in the red and white colors of the Reynolds Stable, he rode Falsetto in the stake races for three-year-olds. He rode Falsetto to victory in the Phoenix Hotel Stakes, was second to Lord Murphy in the Kentucky Derby, and then came back to win with him in the Clark Handicap at Louisville.[31] Murphy then journeyed east with Falsetto and at Saratoga Springs defeated the noted Spendthrift in the Travers and Kenner Stakes.[32] These two races marked a turning point in his career. "It was when Falsetto and Murphy journeyed east," explained the *Thoroughbred Record,* "and defeated Spendthrift . . . that the fame of both horse and rider became world wide."[33] It was also in 1879 that Murphy experienced his single most successful day as a jockey. On the Fourth of July in Detroit he rode the entire card of four winners. He almost repeated the feat at St. Louis that year by winning three of four races at the meeting. The only race he failed to win was the one in which he had no mount.

During the next four years, Murphy rode many "cracks" and captured his share of important derby events. In 1880 he managed to win eleven out of thirty-five races, despite the fact that Falsetto and some of the other powerful horses of the Reynolds Stable had been sold. The following season Murphy rode Checkmate to victory at Saratoga Springs, winning the Saratoga Cup, the Excelsior Stakes, and the Grand Prize of Saratoga. In 1882 he rode Checkmate to victory in Louisville, winning the Dixiana and the Swigert Stakes; won the Brewers Cup in St. Louis; captured the Distillers Stakes in Lexington while aboard Creosote; and rode Ben Or to victory in Chicago in the Board of Trade Handicap, the Welter Stakes, and the Summer Handicap. The year 1883 brought Murphy 51 winning mounts out of 133 races.[34] He never lost a race that year while riding Leonatus or General Harding. He also rode Lida Stanhope to victory in the prestigious Louisville Cup that year.

After spending six years with the Reynolds Stable, he left them and signed on with Ed Corrigan, the famous California turfman, for the 1884 and 1885 seasons.[35] It was while he was under the employ of Corrigan that Murphy experienced his greatest successes. During those years he rode such famous horses as Freeland, Modesty, Irish Pat, and Pearl Jennings, as well as a host of others. In 1884, Murphy rode Modesty to victory in the first American Derby at Washington Park in Chicago.[36] During the same year he won his first of three Kentucky Derbies aboard Buchanon.[37] In 1885 the Corrigan Stable headed the jockey club's list of winners with seventy-five victories. Murphy gained thirty-three of those victories, most notably on Freeland in two of that gelding's victories over the great mare Miss Woodford. For years the racing contingents from the West had engaged in an intense rivalry with the older racing establishments from the East.[38] The triumphs of Freeland did much to bring a measure of respectability to the racing men from the West. In two out of three of the races, Murphy on Freeland outmaneuvered one of the East's best jockeys, James McLaughlin on Miss Woodward.[39] In the same year Murphy won his second consecutive American Derby aboard Volante.[40]

In 1886, Murphy, who had become dissatisfied with the money he was receiving from the Corrigan Stable, signed a contract to ride for another Californian, Ed Baldwin. It was a significant turnabout in Murphy's career since it was the first time he had switched employers because of a contract dispute. Often referred to as the "Poor Owner's Friend," Murphy was credited by sports writers with never seeking mounts that simply guaranteed large financial rewards.[41] He had the reputation of being willing to ride for an owner regardless of salary. This reputation, however, seems to have been accurate only for a portion of his career. Before 1886 he did not realize his own worth and significance to the sport. Slow to recognize the many opportunities that his fame began to make available, the modest Murphy was quick to accept offers disproportionate to his ability. Apparently satisfied with just making a living as a jockey, he often accepted the first proposition offered him. But his signing with Baldwin confirmed that Murphy had begun to appreciate his skills and to start to accept the best financial offers regardless of owner. Like the professional athletes of today, Murphy began to engage in disputes with his owners while attempting to negotiate a salary commensurate with his skills and popularity.

Murphy's most famous race came on June 25, 1890, at Sheepshead Bay in a match race between two horses named Salvator and Tenny.[42] Murphy rode Salvator, and Tenny's jockey was "Snapper" Garrison, Murphy's toughest contemporary. The match was as much between the jockeys as between the horses. People had debated for a decade as to who was the best jockey in the country, the "Colored Archer" or the great white rider, "Snapper" Garrison. More than 25,000 customers packed the Coney Island Track when the big day came. "Newspapers sent their page one byliners abetted by staff artists to depict the event in line drawings."[43] It was certainly one of the most talked about and exciting races of the last half of the nineteenth century. In terms of popularity and interest, it was comparable to the famous North-South Match races between Eclipse and Sir Henry in 1823, and Fashion versus Peytona in 1845. Murphy came out victorious, coolly holding Salvator together for a decision by half a head over Tenny under the wildly driving Garrison. Rarely had there been a better display of Murphy's level-headed judgment of pace. In 1890 Murphy also won his second Kentucky Derby aboard Riley.[44]

Murphy's last great triumph was his Kentucky Derby victory in the 1891 classic.[45] Riding the great Kingman, Murphy was able to win by a length over the well-known mare Balgowen. It was the first time that a jockey had won back-to-back Kentucky Derbies.

Murphy's life from this point on is a story of fallen greatness. Although he won the Kentucky Derby in 1891, he was to win only five more races that year. In 1892 he rode six winners in only forty-two races; in 1893 he rode four winners in thirty races; in 1894 he had no wins at all to his credit; and in 1895 he won only once in twenty trials.[46]

Isaac Murphy partying with friends at a clambake sponsored by the newly formed Salvator Club in August 1890. Courtesy of the Keeneland Library, Lexington, Kentucky.

Throughout his career Murphy had to struggle to get down to proper racing weight. During the off season, he would balloon to 130 or 140 pounds, then try to reduce to his riding weight of 105 as the season opened.[47] His body became ravaged by the rigors of "making weight" at a time when scientific dieting methods were unknown. Murphy's procedure for losing excess weight was simply to go without food and take extended walks for several days before a race. This reducing process contributed to the undermining of his health and left him prey to illness. For example, Murphy became so sick at Saratoga Springs in 1885 that he was hardly able to ride. "That Murphy . . . was a sick man is well known," reported a contemporary sporting journal. "He had traveled a great deal between Saratoga and Monmouth and moreover in reducing to ride Bluewing before the Select Stakes he had become debilitated to an extent that his stomach refused food."[48]

Murphy's weight problem was certainly not unique. Many of the larger jockeys had to go through various privations during the racing season in order to keep their weight down. For instance, James Mc-

Laughlin, one of Murphy's chief rivals, was unable to fill many of his
engagements because of his inability to lose weight.[49] Similarly, a famous
turfman said that it would not surprise him if one of America's "foremost
riders did not jump off the Brooklyn Bridge some day." "Why," he said,
"I have seen him get off his horse in such a weak condition after the
finish of a race that the attendants would have to support him from
falling, and all this weakness caused by reducing."[50] It comes as no
surprise that the jockeys of this period had difficulties in keeping their
bodies at a proper weight. As was previously mentioned, they were ignorant of any types of dieting methods, other than starving themselves to
death. Also, the scale of weights had not been raised sufficiently to keep
the heavyweight jockeys eligible to ride.[51] The riders, furthermore, did
not have the advantage of an extensive winter racing season that today's
jockeys enjoy.[52] Obviously, it was much more difficult to stay in shape
when they had a lengthy off-season.

Not wanting to subject his body to the strenuous wasting regimen,
Murphy gradually began to limit the number of races he would compete
in. By 1887, he was riding only about one-third as often as Ike Barnes,
Ed Garrison, and some of the other leading jockeys.[53] Eventually, the
only races he competed in were the important derby events. There was
even talk after 1887 that Murphy would not ride for any particular
stable so that he would not have to constantly be reducing.[54]

Besides his nagging weight problems, Murphy began to drink exces-
sively. Why he drank is a difficult question to answer because of the lack
of evidence. But it was certainly not a case of a star athlete who begins
to drown his sorrows after realizing his talents are fading and his career
is about to come to a close. Ever since the beginning of his career, turf
experts had suspected that Murphy had drinking problems. On numerous occasions it was believed he had been under the influence of alcohol
during races. But until 1890 the racing establishment did not take action
against the famous jockey. They were reluctant to punish the otherwise
model jockey, possibly because they could not prove his guilt but more
importantly because they believed he needed champagne to give him
added strength while reducing.[55]

The critical turning point in Murphy's career came during a race at
Monmouth Park on August 26, 1890. He was charged with drunkenness
while aboard a horse named Firenzi.[56] Ironically, this was only two
months after his great triumph on Salvator. The *New York Times* gave
this report of the incident:

A popular idol was shattered at Monmouth Park yesterday. That Isaac
Murphy, who has always been considered the most gentlemanly as well
as the most honest of jockeys, would have made such an exhibition of

himself as he did was past belief. He rode Firenzi in the Monmouth Handicap, and that he did so was alone the reason for the ridiculous way in which she was beaten, finishing last in a field of horses that she should have defeated with but little trouble.[57]

Murphy repeatedly argued that he was not drunk but was weak from losing weight. Several turfmen came to his defense and the theory was put forward that he had been drugged.[58] But the managers of Monmouth Park felt otherwise, charging Murphy with drunkenness and suspending him for the rest of the racing meeting.[59] In retrospect it appears that the evidence against Murphy in this particular incident was not based on fact and that his suspension was undeserved. He had suffered so much, both physically and mentally, that he often appeared to lose his intense desire to ride. Reports from Lexington said that he was in such terrible condition he would never ride again.[60] "Isaac Murphy is in a feeble condition at his home in Lexington," reported a contemporary sporting journal. "What ever it may have been that caused his illness on that unfortunate day when he rode Firenzi . . . he has never been himself since then. . . . It is doubtful if he ever rides again."[61]

Murphy's ensuing years as a jockey were not very productive ones. He frequently expressed a desire to simply stay at home and train his own horses.[62] His weight problems were forcing him to consider retirement from the saddle. His personal habits were also robbing him of his magnificent skill as a horseman. "It is not so very long ago since Isaac was among the topnotchers," explained Broad Church in 1891, "but for reasons pretty well known he has lost his grip. The procession seems to have left him in the rear."[63] Another sportswriter echoed the same sentiments that year stating: "His drinking propensities in a large measure has brought about his ruin. His once great abilities are no more."[64]

Perhaps the major reason for Murphy's sudden decline in success was that he was experiencing, like other black athletes, the effects of this country's intolerance of interracial sports during the last decade of the nineteenth century. By the 1890s social pressures and Jim Crow laws were beginning to eliminate blacks from organized sports. "Strict and inviolable segregation practices" were causing the cessation of black-white athletic contests. Black athletes were discovering that the idea of equality on the playing field was largely a myth. They were facing the same type of discrimination in sports that they were experiencing in other walks of life. Sports simply mirrored prevailing social attitudes and provided an inadequate safety valve in the field of race relations.[65] For example, "in the early 1890s" cyclists in New Orleans threatened to withdraw "from the League of American Wheelmen because it admitted black members in the North."[66] The "Boston Strong Boy," John L. Sullivan, refused to cross the color line and fight the great black boxer Peter Jackson. "I will not fight a negro," explained Sullivan in 1892. "I never have, and never shall."[67] Similarly, "Gentleman" Jim Corbett, after fighting Jackson in a sixty-round draw in 1891, refused to fight him a second time. His manager proclaimed, "Corbett will never meet Jackson again. We are against fighting negroes any more."[68] "White baseball players threatened to boycott white teams if they competed with blacks." Bud Fowler, George Stovey, Moses Walker, and other black stars eventually were forced to create their own supposedly equal professional baseball leagues.[69] Black jockeys, moreover, were disappearing from the larger and more famous racetracks.[70]

The treatment accorded Murphy after the Monmouth incident was anything but gracious. If he lost a race he was accused of either being drunk or not putting forth an all-out effort. For example, his employer for the 1892 season, Frank A. Ehret, refused to put him on any important mounts. Ehret accused him of being an incompetent drunk who did not ride to win.[71] Murphy believed he had been unjustly treated by the Ehret Stables. He asked to be severed from the Ehret organization and attempted to receive monetary compensation for all the mounts he was refused. Horse racing's Board of Control, in a decision that reeked with racial overtones, denied Murphy his due compensation. Obviously distraught over the Board's decision, he vowed never to come east again to ride. "I am disgusted with the way they treated me in the east during the summer," explained Murphy. "When I won it was all right, but when I lost . . . they would say 'there that nigger is drunk again.' I tell you I am disgusted and soured on the whole business."[72]

By 1893, Murphy was spending most of his days at his Lexington home with his wife. Most of his time was spent in training his own horses, but he would occasionally ride in a local race. Also, to the regret of many of his admirers, Murphy tried his hand at acting, agreeing to go on stage in a horse play. One of the sporting journals of 1894 reported:

> Isaac Murphy, the whilom great jockey, is about to go on stage, having made an engagement with the manager of "The Derby Winner." The latter is a horse play now performing in the west and is booked for Lexington next week. There are seven thoroughbreds engaged in the play, Freeland being one of them and as Murphy used to ride the great son of Longfellow years ago, he was selected as a drawing card to pilot Freeland once more in the fierce contests on the stage.[73]

To see Murphy as nothing more than a freak in a side show was a difficult thing to accept for those who had followed his magnificent career.

Murphy was also suspended for the second time in his career at the Latonia Races of 1894. Again he was charged with possible drunkenness and suspended for the whole meeting.[74]

Murphy himself was very aware of his fallen greatness and the sudden disappearance of his former skills. But like many great athletes at the end of a fading career, he made last efforts at recapturing his once splendid talents. "I think I will go down to New Orleans," Murphy told Broad Church in 1895, "and maybe I can make a reputation once more."[75] But his dream was shattered. In his two races there, Murphy came in last both times.[76] Several months later, still not convinced that his talents had vanished, Murphy rode unplaced in a race at the old Kentucky Association Track.[77] It was the last race of his career. Murphy died of pneumonia on Lincoln's birthday in 1896, at the age of thirty-five.[78] It was less than five months after his last race.

It is not possible to make sweeping generalizations when discussing Murphy's career. His remarkable achievements and the many accolades he received from contemporaries during the early part of his career are seemingly in direct contrast to the more ignoble feature of his character exhibited during the last few years of his life. In other words, his career, like his character, appeared to be divided into two inconsistent halves. Before 1890, Murphy was lauded by many as the greatest living jockey. His winning percentage, number of major victories, and overall riding ability were unmatched by any of his peers. He was the winning jockey in one of the most important match races of the nineteenth century. After 1890, however, Murphy's career took a strange downward turn. No longer was he recognized as the country's outstanding rider. He was suspended for apparent drunkenness while riding in a race. He was thwarted in several desperate comeback attempts. Brokenhearted, he finally returned home to Lexington, where he lived out the remaining few months of his life.

Yet it is not entirely accurate to divide Murphy's career and character into two entirely different parts. His life was as free from vice during the last six years as during the first six years of his career. At no time did Murphy lose control of his gentlemanly manner. His cardinal sin was a fondness for alcohol, a personal problem that became generally known only after the Monmouth Park incident. Most importantly, Murphy never lost his sense of pride or love of racing, only the inability to transcend certain racial barriers and recapture his former skills.

It is impossible to measure the effect that Murphy had on horse racing or on other blacks. Despite his many successes, he never reflected on what it meant to be black and a major sportsman. He was always too unassuming for that. Yet it was unique to have a black man achieve the degree of fame and fortune that Murphy realized. Obviously, his marvelous physical skills contributed heavily to his enormous popularity. Still there were other jockeys, black and white, with commensurate skills, who never equaled his popularity or had such a hold on the public's imagination.

The acceptance of Murphy was partially a result of the racing establishment's general attitude toward black jockeys. For approximately thirty-five years after the Civil War, the jockey profession was considered suitable for the black man's abilities. In other words, to ride horses for a living was nothing more than "nigger work." White riders generally did not challenge the black jockeys' preeminence because of the stigma attached to working at the same job as a black. To work in the same occupation as a black was to acquire the particular characteristics whites generally imputed to blacks. Therefore, blacks often monopolized such work as jockeys, caterers, bathhouse keepers, tailors, butchers, coachmen, barbers, and delivery boys. Most of these jobs required little capital and depended on white customers. Furthermore, these particular occupations were closely identified with work done on the antebellum plantation, where blacks had originally learned them. Slaves had been exploited as jockeys by the southern planter. The position of a black who rode for a wealthy racing stable in the post-Civil War years was quite similar to that of a slave who rode for his master. The black jockeys were simply hirelings who rode primarily for someone else's benefit. Paradoxically, the stigma of "nigger work" greatly enlarged the black jockey's economic and social opportunities. Only during the 1890s, when white jockeys formed "anticolored unions" and virtually drove black riders off the tracks, did the jockey profession attain its current "respectability."

Perhaps the secret of Murphy's popularity was simply that he recognized the expectations of others. The racing establishment appreciated black jockeys who conformed to its cultural tastes and mores. Murphy had the singular ability to embrace the standards of the white man without sacrificing his own racial identity. It was so important for him to gain acceptance and recognition that he was often compelled to wear two hats, one white and one black. Most importantly, he achieved his enormous popularity because he was one jockey that everyone knew could be trusted. He was instrumental in establishing credibility in the jockey profession. He was admired by racing fans all over the country for his complete honesty. He became the symbol for everything that was pure and clean in horse racing.

Murphy most certainly had an individual style, and his flair was unmatched, even during the uneventful last years of his life. Whatever ingredients go into making a legendary sporting figure, Murphy had them. It is significant that he be honored as one of the first black athletes to achieve national and even international fame. Lastly, it should be remembered that Murphy met standards of performance and style that were the model for a generation. "I'm as proud of my calling as I am of my record . . . and I believe my life will be recorded as a success, though the reputation I enjoyed was earned in the stable and saddle. It is a great honor to be classed as one of America's great jockeys."[79]

3

Peter Jackson and the Elusive Heavyweight Championship

A Black Athlete's Struggle Against the Late Nineteenth-Century Color Line

Peter Jackson was full of optimism when he arrived in San Francisco in the spring of 1888. At the urging of the local sportswriter W. W. (Bill) Naughton, Jackson had made the nearly 9,000-mile trek from Australia in hopes of securing matches with America's leading boxers and ultimately wrestling the world's heavyweight championship from the "Boston Strong Boy," John L. Sullivan. Jackson's arrival was anxiously looked forward to by West Coast sports fans who had read nothing but glowing reports about the boxing exploits of the man Australians admiringly referred to as the "Black Prince." Jackson had ascended swiftly to the top of the pugilistic ladder in Australia by defeating the country's top fighters, including Tom Lees for the heavyweight championship in 1886. The word out of Australia was that Jackson was a great boxer. No one could stay in the ring very long with the talented black boxer and expect to survive. His enormous size, superior reach, and lightning-quick hands had proved too much for even the best of the Australian fighters.

Unfortunately, Jackson's stay in America did not bring about the unconditional success he and his ardent admirers had hoped for. Instead it was a period in Jackson's career that coupled great triumphs with personal frustrations and disillusionments. Although he would establish himself as perhaps the most famous black athlete of the late nineteenth century, he would be denied the one thing he coveted most in life—fighting for the world heavyweight title. Like most black athletes of the period, Jackson could not transcend the increasing American intolerance of interracial sports.[1] Despite several lucrative offers, Sullivan repeatedly

34

refused to cross the color line and fight Jackson. Sullivan's successor to the crown, James J. Corbett, cleverly avoided giving Jackson a match after he became champion in 1892. Corbett's conqueror, Bob Fitzsimmons, did the same thing—adamantly refusing to enter the ring with the talented black boxer. The fact that Jackson was never given the opportunity to fight for the world's title raises several questions. How did Jackson respond to having the color line drawn against him? Was the racial discrimination faced by Jackson any different from that endured by other black athletes during the latter half of the nineteenth century? Was Jackson treated differently in America than he was in Australia and England?

Jackson's early years differed from those of most children. Born in the village of Frederiksted on the island of Saint Croix, Virgin Islands, on July 3, 1861, Jackson emigrated to Australia with his parents when he was twelve. His father had become disenchanted with sailing the waters of the Caribbean as a fisherman and decided to seek employment elsewhere. But by the time Jackson was fifteen, his parents had tired of Australia and returned to their native land. The adventurous young Jackson stayed behind and became a sailor for American ship owner, Clay Callahan. He never saw his parents again. When he finally returned to Saint Croix, some twenty-one years later, his parents had already passed away. The only remaining members of his family were a brother and two sisters whom he never met.[2] Nonetheless, staying in Australia helped Jackson's career, because it was while under the employ of Callahan that he got his first taste of boxing. Both a highly successful businessman and a boxer of some note in Sydney and its environs, Callahan took an immediate liking to Jackson. He was enamored of the skills Jackson exhibited in several of their informal boxing matches and in bouts Jackson had arranged with other crew members. In Jackson, Callahan saw a quiet and unassuming young man who possessed everything necessary to become world champion someday. Besides extraordinary athletic ability, Jackson possessed those character traits normally thought to be lacking among members of his race. He was a bright, hardworking, ambitious man—and, perhaps more than anything else, a man with a great heart.

Callahan proved his respect for Jackson's talents by taking the fledgling black fighter to Sydney and introducing him to Larry Foley, the most famous man in Australian boxing. A smallish but rugged man, Foley was perhaps the person most responsible for the enormous popularity of boxing in Australia during the late nineteenth and early twentieth centuries. Shortly after defeating Abe Hickey for the Australian championship in 1879, Foley retired from the prize ring and became a distinguished boxing instructor at his White Horse Saloon in Sydney. Foley's saloon was one of the first great centers of prizefighting in Australia, only to be surpassed in popularity by the Sydney Amateur Athletic Club and the

Melbourne Athletic Club in the early 1890s. Boxers, young and old, famous and not so famous, came from the most distant parts of the country to seek Foley's advice and train under his watchful eye. To many fighters, training under his tutelage was indispensable to their future success in the ring.[3]

Jackson's life changed dramatically the day he and Callahan arrived in Foley's saloon. His days as a sailor were over. Foley took one look at Jackson and decided to take him on as a pupil. Other than a couple of fighters he had seen as a young boy growing up in New South Wales, Foley had never laid eyes on someone so perfectly built to be a boxer. Though still in his late teens, Jackson was already a superb figure of a man, molded on such perfect lines that it was difficult to believe that so slender-looking a body actually tipped the scales at close to two hundred pounds. His wide shoulders, deep chest, slim waist, and long arms and legs were so beautifully balanced on his six-foot-quarter-inch frame, that his appearance suggested, in the words of the English boxing authority W. S. Doherty, "an idea of some splendid glossy-coated thoroughbred racehorse."[4]

Jackson was brought along very slowly. He spent upwards of two years in Foley's saloon learning everything he possibly could about the sport. His training proved particularly beneficial because he had the luxury of going head-to-head with some of boxing's future stars, many of whom would figure prominently in Jackson's career. Also receiving their boxing education in Foley's saloon at the time were the eventual world champion Bob Fitzsimmons and such outstanding performers as Frank Slavin, "Young Griffo" (Albert Griffiths), and Jim Hall. Like all good trainers, Foley was careful to teach the standard techniques and fundamentals of the noble science to Jackson without insisting that his black protégé adopt a precise style. Foley, who had learned some of the finer points of the sport from the famed English fighter Jim Mace during Mace's visit to Australia in 1877, stressed a defensive style of fighting that placed a premium on the short left jab and punches emanating straight from the shoulder. Jackson, for his part, took to the prize ring like a duck to water. He was a natural. During his sparring sessions, the rest of the boxers in Foley's basement gymnasium would invariably stop in the middle of what they were doing and gather around the ring to gape at Jackson's graceful moves and magnificent style. His arrow-like straightness of figure while fighting, his lightness of foot for so big a man, and the precision of his left hand were beautiful to watch. The feints, cross-counters, and sidestepping that were marked features of his coming fights were already in evidence.[5]

By 1882, Foley began to match Jackson in a series of fights that would ultimately result in his becoming Australia's heavyweight cham-

Peter Jackson always struck an impressive pose and was perfectly built to be a fighter, circa 1890. Courtesy of Bill Schutte.

pion. In the summer of that year, Jackson fought a four-round draw in Sydney against Jack Hayes, a good but forgettable local fighter. In a return match two months later, Jackson overwhelmed Hayes in a seven-round knockout. Just a few weeks after the second Hayes fight, Jackson kayoed Sam Britain, a bullish heavyweight from New South Wales, in the sixth round. In December, Jackson scored his biggest triumph yet, a three-round victory over Mick Dooley, the doughty and herculean young New South Welshman who had devoured his previous opponents. Jackson fought two intensely physical bouts with Bill Farnan, the hard-hitting blacksmith from Victoria whose slugging style of fighting was reminiscent of the former English champion Tom Sayers. Unfortunately for Jackson, he was knocked out by Farnan in the third round of their first bout in Melbourne and had to settle for a draw with Farnan in a return match in the same city just one month later. Devastated by his lack of success against Farnan, Jackson spent the next two years in Foley's saloon honing his skills and occasionally fighting in exhibition matches. He was thoroughly determined to become his adopted country's recognized champion. Finally, on the evening of September 25, 1886, his dream of capturing the Australian championship became reality when he defeated the spirited Victorian boxer Tom Lees in a grueling thirty-round fight in

Foley's saloon. Certainly one of the more written about fights in Australian history, the victory over Lees was the culmination of four years of intense training by Jackson and convincingly proved that he was one of boxing's brightest stars.[6]

Jackson's elation following his victory over Lees was short-lived. Despite his willingness to fight all comers, Jackson quickly found out that it was, indeed, lonely at the top. He simply could find no one to fight. Why? First of all, there were only a handful of fighters in Australia at the time who stood a chance in the ring with Jackson. Former opponents such as Hayes, Britain, Dooley, and even Farnan, would have been outclassed by the Jackson of 1886. Secondly, Jackson and Frank Slavin, perhaps the most legitimate contender for the crown, could never come up with a mutually agreeable location in which to fight. Slavin would consent to a match with Jackson only if it were held in Melbourne, while Jackson was just as adamant that the fight be held at Foley's saloon in Sydney. The two boxers would not get together until some five years later when they fought a much celebrated match at the National Sporting Club in London. Lastly, Jack Burke, the popular boxer known as the "Irish Lad," repeatedly refused to cross the color line and fight Jackson. He asserted that he did not want to injure his reputation by fighting a black boxer. Burke's decision was just one small example, of course, of the kind of racism that had existed in Australia for years.[7] Jackson handled his first taste of discrimination in much the same way he did similar situations later on his career. Instead of hiding his true feelings behind a facade of passive acquiescence, Jackson denounced Burke for his actions and repeatedly challenged him to a fight. He pursued Burke with an aggressiveness that belied his basically easygoing and cheerful nature. His assailing tactics were probably best illustrated by the challenge he hurled at Burke immediately after Burke's exhibition match with Larry Foley in 1887. Before Burke left the arena and the crowd began to disperse, Jackson stepped to the side of the ring and angrily challenged Burke: "He says he [Burke] draws the color-line. Well, John L. Sullivan, who also draws the color-line, says he has no objection to meeting a colored fighter in private. If Mr. Burke is of the same way of thinking, I will gladly meet him tonight, tomorrow or any day he might select in a cellar barn or any private room he chooses to name, and will wager him 1,000 pounds on the result."[8] Jackson's little speech did nothing to change Burke's mind. The veteran white fighter simply glared at Jackson, said nothing, and quickly found his way out of the arena.

While Burke's unwillingness to fight frustrated Jackson, it made his decision to leave Australia that much easier. With no one to fight in his adopted homeland, Jackson set sail for America aboard the steamship *Alameda,* arriving in San Francisco in early April 1888. Accompanying him on the trip were the Australian lightweight boxers Paddy Gorman and Tom Meadows.[9] The arrival of the three boxers in San Francisco was significant because they represented the initial wave of Australian fighters that invaded America in hordes during the last decade of the nineteenth century. Following closely behind the Jackson contingent, many of them settling in San Francisco, were such prominent Australian fighters as Bob Fitzsimmons, George Dawson, Jim Hall, Abe Willis, Joe Goddard, Jim Barron, Steve O'Donnell, Tom Tracy, Billy Smith, Jim Ryan, "Young Griffo," Billy Murphy, Jack Hall, George McKinzie, and George Mulholland.

Jackson was lured to America by the opportunity for financial gain and the chance to fight the world heavyweight champion, John L. Sullivan. Like the Eastern European athletes who have recently immigrated to this country, Jackson viewed America as the place where his potential could be fully realized and his fortunes made. He was encouraged to make the move by W. W. Naughton, the noted San Francisco sportswriter. Not that he needed a great deal of prodding, but Jackson had some mixed emotions about leaving Australia. Having become a darling of the sporting crowd, he was treated quite well in Australia. He also realized that American blacks were not treated much better than their counterparts in Australia and sometimes even worse. Ultimately, however, the chance to gain wealth and prestige overshadowed Jackson's fears.

Jackson's first two months in San Francisco were taken up primarily by visits to some of the city's famous sporting establishments. He called upon the sporting men from such noted organizations as the Olympic Club, the Golden Gate Athletic Club, and the California Athletic Club (CAC). He soon became closely associated with the CAC, becoming its professor of boxing almost immediately after his arrival in the city. The club sponsored four of Jackson's most important fights and became one of America's most influential boxing organizations during its relatively brief seven-year history. Organized in 1886 by a Southern California native, Sam Matthews, and Jack Seymour, an Englishman who had been closely identified with pedestrian sports in Australia, the CAC was perhaps the first organization in America where Queensberry glove contests were regularly staged. With a membership that exceeded 1,700 by 1890, the CAC included some of the most influential men in San Francisco.[10]

Jackson had difficulty in arranging matches during his first days in San Francisco. No one dared to get into the ring with him until Con Riordan, boxing instructor at the Golden Gate Athletic Club, finally agreed to an exhibition match on June 4. Held at Jack Hallinan's Cremorne Garden, the fight with Riordan was Jackson's coming-out party. This was the first opportunity for San Francisco's sporting element to see the much ballyhooed black boxer in action, and Jackson did not disappoint them. In front of a crowd of about 1,500, Jackson flashed the skills that had made him one of Australia's most famous fighters. Those in attendance had nothing but praise for his abilities. It was the general consensus following the bout that Jackson was the cleverest boxer ever seen in the city. "Fear alone," said one of the spectators, "will prevent Sullivan from meeting Jackson." [11]

The local sporting press was so impressed with Jackson's efforts against Riordan that they immediately began clamoring for a fight between him and Joe McAuliffe, the San Francisco fighter considered one of the finest heavyweights on the West Coast. McAuliffe was a logical choice to fight Jackson. He had amassed an impressive ring record, defeating in succession such noted boxers as Dick Matthews, Mike Brannan, Paddy Ryan, and Frank Glover. Unfortunately, McAuliffe refused to cross the color line and fight Jackson. Despite repeated efforts to induce him to fight, McAuliffe steadfastly stuck to his decision not to fight Jackson. He had never fought a black man before and he was not about to start now. [12]

Unable to arrange a bout with McAuliffe, Jackson was forced to fight George Godfrey, the well-known black boxer from Boston. Jackson was not overly enthusiastic about the match. He understood that a victory over a good but noncontending boxer like Godfrey would not bring him any closer to a championship fight. In spite of this, Jackson agreed to the match with Godfrey for a purse of $2,000 and the "colored heavyweight championship of the world." He had been in America for nearly five months without fighting a major bout and desperately needed a match to hone skills already grown rusty from inactivity. Perhaps most importantly, Jackson needed the money. He had to recover some of the expenses he incurred on his trip from Australia and the money he had freely spent in San Francisco. [13]

The Jackson-Godfrey match came about through the efforts of the CAC and took place on August 24. None of the experts gave Godfrey much of a chance against Jackson. He was simply not as good as the black Australian. Clearly approaching the end of his career at the age of thirty-six, Godfrey owned a respectable but less than spectacular fight record. Like Sam Langford and other black boxers of the early twentieth century, Godfrey was compelled, because of economic reasons, to fight some of the same black boxers over and over again. His most recent opponent had been McHenry Johnson, a little-known black boxer he had fought three times previously. Perhaps Godfrey's most famous fight was one he never fought. Legend has it that John L. Sullivan, just before capturing the world heavyweight title from Paddy Ryan, once entered the ring with Godfrey in Boston, only to have the match interrupted by the police. [14]

It was apparent from the moment the two boxers entered the ring on the night of the fight that Jackson outclassed Godfrey. Wearing his customary blue stockings, soft leather heelless shoes, and white tights, Jackson towered over his opponent, and Godfrey was never able to overcome Jackson's reach advantage. There were moments when Godfrey landed some forceful punches, but most of his blows fell far short. Jackson hit his opponent with alarming regularity in the first ten rounds, sending Godfrey to the floor with an uppercut in the second round. By the beginning of the fourteenth round, Godfrey probably wished he was anywhere but in the ring with Jackson. Jackson relentlessly followed him around the ring, raining him with blows that caused blood to flow freely from his nose and mouth. Godfrey tried to hold him up with his right hand and hit him with left jabs. Finally, in the middle of the nineteenth round, Godfrey murmured, "I give in," saying later that he had "no desire to be killed." [15]

Jackson's defeat of Godfrey was significant because it caused Joe McAuliffe to have a change of heart. Initially refusing to meet Jackson on account of his color, McAuliffe was now doing everything he could to get Jackson into the ring. His sudden decision to cross the color line did not stem from any altruistic reasons, but was strictly a career move. McAuliffe was pragmatic enough to know that despite his hatred for blacks he would have to fight Jackson if he were ever to be considered a legitimate contender for the heavyweight title. There was a little bit of irony in all of this, of course. While Jackson continued to be denied the opportunity to take part in a championship bout, boxers like McAuliffe often improved their chances or actually earned the right to fight for the title because of their performances against the black Australian. [16]

Jackson was obviously delighted that McAuliffe finally decided to cross the color line. It would be the first time since his arrival in America that his abilities would truly be tested. As it turned out, Jackson passed his first test with flying colors. Though a 2 to 1 underdog, Jackson convincingly defeated McAuliffe at the CAC on December 28. At no point in the contest was Jackson in serious trouble. In fact, he simply toyed with McAuliffe for most of the fight. He had no difficulty in ducking McAuliffe's powerful right and administering counterpunches to the face and body of the well-built white boxer. The fight ended about halfway through the twenty-fourth round, when Jackson delivered a left hook to McAuliffe's stomach and immediately followed it up with a straight right between the eyes. The badly beaten McAuliffe fell near the ropes with his knees doubled under him and was counted out amid cheers from many of the spectators. [17]

The American public reacted to Jackson's victory over McAuliffe as it would throughout most of his career. His triumph almost immediately earned him hero status among the black community. Blacks from all over the country regarded Jackson with the greatest admiration for what he had accomplished in the ring with McAuliffe. For the black man in American society, Jackson, perhaps more than any other athlete of his day, symbolized unbridled aggression. While most black men of the period were taught to hold back and camouflage their normal masculine assertiveness, Jackson was openly expressing his aggressive impulses against white boxers. To be sure, Jackson typically assumed a defensive style in his fighting and was careful not to dole out undue punishment to white fighters. But he fought with a kind of fury that let blacks vicariously share his uninhibited masculine drive.[18]

Perhaps no black community reacted more enthusiastically to Jackson's triumph than the one in San Francisco. One local newspaper noted that the city's black population had "not had such a jubilee since Mr. Lincoln signed the Emancipation Proclamation." Every black man who had been waiting outside the CAC clubroom rushed back home immediately after the conclusion of the fight and spread the glad tidings. The word around town after the bout was that anyone who employed a black man "got mighty little work out of him." Those blacks who had placed bets on the fight "jingled coins in their pockets" and for "once were disposed to dispute the superiority of any race other than their own." The black waiters in the restaurant of the luxurious Palace Hotel neglected their customers, supposedly doing nothing but discussing the fight. Groups of them "stood about chuckling" and "letting the hungry men sit and curse the hotel and all in it." Easily the most demonstrative and revealing reaction occurred in the early morning hours after the fight when some hundred blacks gathered on Market Street and began parading up and down the well-known thoroughfare, rejoicing in Jackson's victory.[19]

Interestingly, some whites praised Jackson's victory over McAuliffe as much as blacks did. The defeat of McAuliffe provided one of the first real opportunities to discover how whites felt about Jackson, and generally their reactions were quite favorable. Tellingly, many of the post-fight comments of the white press were centered as much on Jackson's positive character traits as on his boxing abilities. Jackson possessed those personal qualities deemed suitable for members of his race. While never explicitly stating it, the white community believed that other blacks would do well to emulate him. In public, Jackson often assumed a deferential mask and shaped his feelings in the direction he thought whites wanted them to be. He ordinarily adopted an ingratiating and compliant manner with members of the majority race. Even in his dress, noted several commentators, Jackson was rather conservative in comparison to other prominent blacks of the period.[20]

The irony in all of this was that Jackson was anything but submissive. He could become combative when encountering discrimination, even though it might temporarily negate the quiet reticence on which he mostly relied. On more than one occasion he got into street fights after whites hurled racial slurs at him. In the end, Jackson was prepared to stand on his dignity as a West Indian and protest American discrimination on his own behalf. Accustomed from infancy to standing up for his rights, Jackson did not hesitate to be forceful and more enterprising than many contemporary native black American athletes.

Jackson wandered aimlessly for nearly three months after the McAuliffe match, having no immediate fight plans and repeatedly refusing to grant McAuliffe a rematch. He divided most of his time equally among the CAC, Joe Dieves' Road House, and the various entertainment districts of San Francisco. Jackson established a well-deserved reputation as someone who enjoyed a night on the town partying with friends and, occasionally, a bevy of beautiful, if not altogether virtuous, females. Like many others in his profession, he was a big spender and heavy drinker, and during the evenings he haunted the many saloons located on Morton Street near Union Square. In the end Jackson seemingly squandered his winnings on booze and women. His generous nature and love of a good time did not allow him to do otherwise.[21]

Jackson's nearly three-month layoff came to an end when he agreed to fight Patsy Cardiff, the "Peoria Giant," at the CAC on April 26, 1889. The West Coast sportsmen did not expect the bout to be a particularly difficult one for Jackson, and they were right. Cardiff, who had gained a degree of notoriety for a match he had fought against John L. Sullivan some two years earlier in Minnesota, was able to withstand Jackson's onslaught for ten rounds before finally admitting defeat. Jackson was never in serious trouble during the fight, repeatedly scoring with combination punches that left the tall and muscular Cardiff badly battered.[22]

Jackson decided to leave San Francisco shortly after his fight with Cardiff and traveled East, seeking matches with legitimate title contenders. Increasingly frustrated in San Francisco, Jackson hoped for better luck in such boxing-rich metropolitan areas as Chicago and New York. He embarked on his trip sometime in May 1889. Traveling with him were some of the most prominent men in boxing. Sam Fitzpatrick, the former Australian boxer who guided the careers of several outstanding fighters, including Jack Johnson, went along as Jackson's trainer. Jackson's sparring partner was Tom Lees, the man he had defeated for the Australian Championship in 1886. W. W. Naughton was along, covering the trip for his newspaper. The final member of the contingent was Charles "Parson" Davies, a Chicago sporting man who had recently become Jackson's personal manager. Davies was widely known as both a promoter of pedestrian races and a manager of fighters. A shrewd and resourceful businessman, Davies recognized Jackson's moneymaking potential. He believed Jackson could be as big a drawing card as one of his former fighters from Boston, John L. Sullivan.[23]

Jackson and his friends arrived in New York City after a trip of approximately three months that was marked by an occasional exhibition match and an endless round of partying. Jackson was in New York for barely two weeks before he decided to leave the country at the urging of "Parson" Davies. Jackson's journey to London in the latter part of August 1889 came as no big surprise to insiders in the fight game. Almost everyone knew that Jackson had his sights set on Jem Smith, the former champion of England, probably best known for his 106-round bout against Jake Kilrain in 1887. Talk of a fight between Jackson and Smith had been brewing for some time, even before Jackson's match with George Godfrey. Negotiations between the two men resurfaced almost immediately after Jackson's victory over Joe McAuliffe. But on both occasions Jackson and Smith had prior commitments that precluded their making a match.[24]

Almost immediately upon his arrival in London, Jackson arranged a bout with Smith at the famous Pelican Club.[25] It was one of his shortest but finest fights, and he may never have been more impressive as a boxer. Standing some four inches taller than his opponent, Jackson moved effortlessly around the ring from the first moments of the bout. Smith, on the other hand, looked like "a cart horse beside a thoroughbred." In the opening round Jackson avoided most of Smith's blows and landed his own punches whenever and wherever he pleased. In the second round, Smith found things even more difficult. Jackson began to force the fight, battering Smith from one end of the ring to the other. Smith spent most of his time covering up and clinging to the ropes with his right hand for support. Finally, with about one minute left in the round, Smith caught Jackson around the waist, threw him heavily to the ground, and used his left, as one Australian tabloid described it, "to smite Jackson in a part of the body which may be hinted at but not named in newspaper phraseology." Not surprisingly, Jackson got up rather slowly. But it did not matter. The officials, Lord Clifford and the legendary marquis of Queensberry, immediately jumped into the ring and awarded the fight to Jackson amidst the cheering of the wildly partisan crowd.[26] The fight that had received so much advance publicity was over after just two rounds.

Jackson's victory over Smith was important because the sporting public began clamoring louder than ever for a contest between Jackson and John L. Sullivan. There were a considerable number of organizations throughout America that offered to stage a fight between the two celebrated heavyweights. Some of the offers were not worth the paper they were written on, but many were legitimate proposals that involved great sums of prize money. The CAC, for instance, offered to host a Jackson and Sullivan match sometime in the spring of 1890 for a purse of $15,000. The Santa Cruz Athletic Club did even better than that, offering a purse of $30,000 for the fight. Both the Erie County Athletic Club in Pennsylvania and the Seattle Athletic Club matched the $30,000 offer of the Santa Cruz Athletic Club. Perhaps the most intriguing proposal was received from a group of men from San Francisco and Nevada who offered to stage the fight in the middle of Lake Tahoe. The proposal called for a fight to the finish without gloves and was to take place, so as to ensure that the authorities would not interfere, on a specially constructed barge anchored on the state line.[27]

Jackson was so encouraged by the various proposals that he decided to discontinue the exhibition tour he was currently making through Europe and return to the United States in the latter part of January 1890. He should not have altered his plans. His hasty return to America only left him open to more frustration and disillusionment at the hands of Sullivan. The champion refused to accept any of the offers. While experiencing great delight in dangling the carrot in front of Jackson by occasionally expressing his willingness to fight, Sullivan never had any real intentions of getting into the ring with the black Australian. As he would do throughout the remainder of his career, Sullivan declined to meet Jackson on account of his color. If Sullivan could have arranged a fight with a less talented black boxer for the same kind of prize money that was being offered, then perhaps he would not have drawn the color line quite so tightly. In fact, William Muldoon, Sullivan's manager, told the boxing historian Nat Fleischer years later that he had kept Sullivan from making a match with Jackson because he wanted to "save [Sullivan] the humiliation of being defeated by a Negro."[28]

The failure to arrange a bout with Sullivan did not exactly shatter Jackson's career. If anything, he was more in demand than before he had left for England. The defeat of Smith had enhanced his reputation as one of the world's great boxers. The most visible indications of Jackson's enormous appeal were the many accolades and tributes that were handed out to him by the black community in the months immediately following his return to this country. Black Americans were absolutely ecstatic over Jackson's most recent accomplishments. The black press could not say enough about him. Such influential newspapers as the *New York Age*, the *Indianapolis Freeman*, the *Cleveland Gazette*, and the *St. Paul Western Appeal* praised Jackson as a race hero of unparalleled proportions. His performances in the ring were reminiscent of those given by Tom Molineaux, Bill Richmond, and other great black boxers of the past.[29] In virtually every city Jackson visited, the local black community went wild

with excitement over his presence and would honor him with a testimonial dinner. New York's Harlem Unique Club, for instance, honored
Jackson with a banquet in January 1890, and similar dinners were organized for him in Baltimore, Washington, D.C., Philadelphia, Chicago,
St. Louis, Boston, and Indianapolis.[30]

Ironically, this attention was being lavished on Jackson during one
of the most emotionally distressing periods of his career. Sullivan's continuing refusal to fight for the championship was beginning to exact its
toll on Jackson. While he valiantly tried to maintain an air of confidence
during his public appearances, Jackson was obviously dejected about the
way he was treated by Sullivan. He was developing the sadness and the
intimacy with misery that were to become so much a part of Isaac Murphy, Sam Langford, and other outstanding black athletes who confronted racial discrimination around the turn of the century. Melancholy
rather than happy-go-lucky was now a more accurate way to describe
Jackson.

Jackson's frustrations could easily be seen in his boxing performances during 1890. He was rather listless in a five-round victory over
Gus Lambert in Troy, New York, in March and only slightly more impressive in his triumph over "Denver" Ed Smith in Chicago a couple of
months later. In October, Jackson fought one of the worst fights of his
career against Joe Goddard in Melbourne, Australia. Although the bout
was officially recorded as an eight-round draw, Jackson probably deserved to lose the fight. A native of New South Wales who had just begun
his professional boxing career, Goddard battered the black Australian as
no other fighter ever had. Jackson's heart was simply not in the bout. He
almost appeared to welcome the punishment doled out by Goddard,
repeatedly dropping his hands and sticking out his chin as if to dare
Goddard to hit him.[31]

Jackson's spirits were temporarily revitalized when he was able to
arrange a fight with James J. Corbett in San Francisco for May 1891.
The fight was held at the CAC, the winner to receive an unprecedented
$10,000 purse. Jackson's match with Corbett was one of the most thor-
oughly discussed fights in the last half of the nineteenth century. The
fascination that many people had with the bout stemmed from several
different reasons. First of all, Jackson and Corbett were both local fighters with enormous popular appeal. Corbett was born and raised in the
city and had already shown unlimited potential. Jackson had spent most
of his time in San Francisco, and had cultivated a loyal following among
the city's black and white residents. Second, the fight took on added
significance because it matched the most gentlemanly and scientific white
fighter of the age with his black counterpart. Corbett and Jackson represented a new breed of fighter. They both fashioned themselves as men of

honor who relied on ring generalship rather than the mauling tactics of old-time fighters like Sullivan. Last, and perhaps most important, most people in boxing assumed that the winner of the bout would be the logical choice to fight Sullivan for the heavyweight championship. To get at Sullivan, Corbett was willing to overcome his own abhorrence of blacks and fight Jackson this one time because a victory over the black Australian would almost guarantee him a title shot. A triumph over Jackson, combined with his previous wins over such boxers as Joe Choynski, Jake Kilrain, and Dominick McGraffrey, would just about seal a championship fight for Corbett.[32]

The fight did not live up to its advance billing. It was a painfully slow affair, with both men cleverly feinting, ducking, and jabbing each other for some sixty-one rounds before the referee, Hiram Cook, decided that no useful purpose would be served by allowing the fight to continue. It was apparent from the outset that Jackson and Corbett had great respect for each other's boxing abilities and that each was content with lying back and letting the other be the aggressor. Round after round was fought without one solid punch being landed on either side. At moments during the bout, the two fighters livened up things a bit, but for the most part they moved around the ring like two dancers performing a waltz. W. W. Naughton noted that about midway through the bout people began leaving the arena and the remaining spectators "stretched themselves out on the vacated benches and went to sleep."[33]

The fight between Jackson and Corbett had different effects on the careers of the two participants. For Corbett, simply staying in the ring with his celebrated opponent for sixty-one rounds greatly enhanced his reputation as a boxer and gave him immediate credibility among influential people in the sport. His rather lackluster performance against Jackson was conveniently forgotten, and he now became almost everyone's choice to fight Sullivan for the heavyweight championship. As for Jackson, it was the consensus of most sporting men that the black fighter had just about reached the end of his boxing career. Jackson was simply not the same man who had so handily defeated such fighters as George Godfrey, Patsy Cardiff, Joe McAuliffe, and Jem Smith. At no time during the fight did he exhibit the physical skills he had become famous for.[34]

No one was more frustrated over the outcome of the fight than Jackson. Friends said they had never seen him so despondent after a bout. His frustrations, interestingly enough, were not directed at Corbett, or at Hiram Cook for his decision to call the fight a draw, but at himself. Always critical of his performances in the ring, Jackson was particularly chagrined at the way he had fought Corbett. Outweighing his less experienced opponent by some thirty pounds, Jackson knew it was a fight he should have won.[35]

In truth, Jackson was blinded to the reality of the situation. Corbett was just as responsible for the poor fight as he was. Even more unusual, however, was that Jackson never voiced any complaint about Corbett's sudden emergence as the number one contender for the heavyweight crown following their fight. Surely he must have been upset by the fact that Corbett was now being touted as the top challenger for Sullivan's title, based on a limited number of fights, however impressive some were. Corbett obviously had great talent, yet there was nothing in his boxing record to indicate that he was more worthy of a shot at the championship than Jackson himself. Like a host of other boxers, Corbett had gained a big reputation by limited fighting. In the words of San Francisco's *Daily Examiner*, "it is not what he [Corbett] has done but what people believe he can do that makes him a famous fighter."[36]

Perhaps one of the reasons for Jackson's uncustomary silence was that he simply believed that no good purpose would be served by voicing his complaints at this time because a fight between Corbett and Sullivan was inevitable. He would simply bide his time and challenge the winner of that particular contest. More likely, though, Jackson may have been reluctant to acknowledge that the boxing establishment had exerted any negative discriminatory influence over his life. While on one level Jackson was always painfully aware of the insensitivity and the discriminatory practices of the boxing profession, on another level there was the opposite tendency—a determination not to see. Jackson sometimes acted as if the boxing establishment had done nothing to curtail his career, even in the face of such realities as Sullivan's continuing refusal to fight him and the fact that he was constantly being passed over for title shots by less deserving boxers like Corbett. The apparent reason for Jackson's blindness was that he desperately wanted to believe that the men in boxing were immune to racism and that advancement in the profession was based strictly on merit. By deluding himself this way, Jackson could be assured that his efforts would be duly rewarded and that it was just a matter of time before he was given a chance at the title. In other words, he could feel that he had some control over his own destiny and that his future did not hinge on racial discrimination and the personal whims of individuals in the fight game.[37]

Jackson remained in San Francisco for some nine months following his fight with Corbett, passing his time in the usual fashion. If he was not drinking and playing cards with the boys at Joe Dieves' Road House, he was out combing the streets looking for female companionship. To supplement his always depleted pocketbook, Jackson became an entrepreneur of sorts and opened a saloon that catered to the city's sporting fraternity. He was anything but a businessman, however, and after a short time sold the saloon to two acquaintances. Occasionally Jackson would drag himself into the gymnasium for some exercise. But as in most interludes between his fights, Jackson paid very little attention to those activities that contributed to physical fitness.[38]

Jackson left San Francisco in February 1892 for a return trip to England. No one had to persuade him to go back. Most of the arrangements had already been made for a fight between him and his old nemesis, Frank Slavin, for some time in the early spring. From a personal standpoint, this was perhaps the most important fight of Jackson's career. He and Slavin had been bitter rivals ever since their early days in Australia when they were both students of Larry Foley's. The two fighters never got along, and for good reason. The two men were constantly competing for the affections of their former mentor, and it led to several heated confrontations through the years. Also contributing to the bad blood between the two Australian heavyweights was the fact that Slavin was an unabashed racist who rivaled Corbett and Sullivan in his hatred of blacks. He had proudly stated on several occasions that he would never let a black man beat him. If all this were not enough, Jackson and Slavin had made the mistake of falling in love with the same girl. At one time or another, both fighters were involved with Josie Leon, the beautiful niece of a wealthy Jamaican planter. Jackson and Slavin had come to blows over the girl at least three times during their careers, the most notorious a twenty-minute brawl at Foley's White Horse Saloon in 1883. Neither one of them had anything to show for their efforts because Miss Leon eventually ran off and married someone else.[39]

There was obviously a great deal at stake, then, when Jackson and Slavin met at London's National Sporting Club[40] on the night of May 30, 1892. Boxing promoters, journalists, and various members of London's ruling class jammed the club's recently constructed 1,300-seat gymnasium in Covent Garden to witness the fight between the two bitter antagonists. It was immediately apparent upon their entry into the ring that Jackson and Slavin were a study in contrasts. Slavin, who was dressed in dark blue knee breeches, light blue stockings, and russet shoes, was a formidably built man whose rough-hewn figure bespoke strength rather than grace. He had a large, hairy chest and hairy arms; smoldering, deeply sunken eyes; and a black handlebar mustache that covered up his always truculent frown. Jackson, on the other hand, wore white drawers, white socks, and dark leather shoes. His beautifully proportioned bronzed body suggested more balance and style than brute strength. His smiling face could easily be seen under the still not too familiar glare of the club's new electric chandeliers and through the dense cigar smoke that began to hang in a haze under the paneled ceiling.

The fight was everything that boxing fans had expected and more. Chroniclers of the sport have repeatedly ranked it as one of the most viciously contested fights ever held in England.[41] From the moment they first emerged from their respective corners, Jackson and Slavin went after each other like two ravenous alley cats grappling over a leftover piece of food. The fight was virtually even through the first three rounds, with each boxer landing a number of telling blows on his opponent. In the fourth round, however, the tide began to shift in Jackson's favor. Jackson kept throwing stinging jabs until Slavin's left eye was nearly closed, his right cheek was marked with a gash three or four inches in length, and his lips looked like "two big lumps of bladder." Slavin was able to regroup somewhat and landed several significant punches over the next few rounds, but Jackson continued to batter him so severely that his face became nearly unrecognizable. Finally, in the tenth round Jackson settled the question as to who was the superior boxer. Taking advantage of every possible opening, Jackson rained blow after blow on Slavin's damaged face and eye. The white boxer became a pathetic figure, his head loosely flopping about as he wandered aimlessly around the ring. The fight ended with about one minute left in the round when the courageous Slavin fell helplessly to the floor. He had let the unthinkable happen—he had lost to a black man.[42]

Jackson's victory over Slavin greatly increased his already enormous popularity among the English public. He mingled freely with a broad segment of English society, treated more like a prince than a black boxer. He was welcomed into the charmed circle of the finest men's clubs and learned associations, and he became a well-known figure in London's most fashionable public places. Members of some of England's most famous families vied with one another for Jackson's friendship. The fifth earl of Lonsdale, for instance, president of the National Sporting Club and one of Victorian society's most celebrated sportsmen, was a friend and supporter of Jackson. Famous for his gray side-whiskers, nine-inch cigars, and gardenia buttonhole, the intensely individualistic Lonsdale was perhaps the man most responsible for arranging the bout between Jackson and Slavin.[43]

Jackson was obviously delighted with and appreciative of the kind treatment he received from polite society in England. In fact, ever since his bout with Jem Smith in the latter part of 1889, Jackson had repeatedly complimented the English on their hospitality and contrasted his freedom from insult in that country with his experience of discrimination in America. Why Jackson was apparently treated differently in England is a difficult question to answer with any certainty. Not unexpectedly, many Englishmen took a rather patronizing attitude towards Jackson. He was their pet. He was someone to pat on the back and play with. The English, however, seemed to react more sharply to differences of class than to racial differences. Late nineteenth-century Englishmen were certainly color-conscious, but unlike Americans in being more inclined to treat a black gentleman like Jackson as a gentleman. Through his social connections and his ability as a boxer, Jackson had both the position to command respect and the money to pay his way. He gained the friends, influence, and training in the social graces to make him an acceptable visitor in distinguished circles. His success rested upon his ability to conform to conventions of appropriate behavior. In manner, speech, dress, confidence, and in his own social ease, Jackson was eminently qualified and therefore accepted in the finest circles of English society. Jackson had been raised in a West Indian home where English customs, notions of etiquette, and social behavior had been adopted and followed for more than a century. He had not only been taught to regard himself as a member of one of the oldest British colonies but was also proud to think of himself as a British subject.[44]

After spending some five months socializing with England's privileged classes and fighting an occasional exhibition match, Jackson suddenly decided to return to America in the latter part of October 1892. The reason for his unexpected departure was to seek a rematch with Corbett, who just one month earlier had defeated John L. Sullivan for the heavyweight championship.[45] Shortly after his arrival back in the United States, Jackson, through his manager, "Parson" Davies, challenged the newly crowned champion to a fight. His proposal was simple enough. He wanted to fight Corbett for a side wager of $20,000, the contest to take place at a "mutually agreed upon club no sooner than six to ten months from the date [February 10, 1893] of this challenge." Corbett agreed to Jackson's offer but with the stipulation that his acceptance would be void if he was first able to arrange a match with Charlie Mitchell, a full-time crook and part-time boxer from England. Corbett and his manager, William Brady, desired a match with Mitchell above all others. Corbett felt obligated to give Mitchell first shot at the title because the Englishman was the first boxer to lay down a challenge, a representative of Mitchell's having approached him with an offer immediately after his victory over Sullivan. Corbett also noted that a fight with Mitchell would be financially more rewarding and generate a great deal more interest among the sporting public. The majority of Americans, said Corbett, would rather see Mitchell "thrashed than any man living." Tellingly, Corbett was quick to point out that his decision to give Jackson second billing was not based on the latter's race. He told a group of reporters in Minnesota "that he had no objection to fighting Peter Jackson because he is colored. I think he is a credit to his profession."[46]

Corbett's choice of an opponent did not sit well with Jackson and "Parson" Davies. They were appalled by the champion's actions and let the sporting public know exactly how they felt. Jackson said he had no intention of being Corbett's "lackey" and refused to travel around the country begging for a fight. Davies was even more pointed than Jackson in his assessment of Corbett. In several scathing newspaper editorials, Davies admonished Corbett for avoiding a match with his boxer. The only reason Corbett wished to fight Mitchell, Davies maintained, was to get back at the Englishman for some unkind remarks he had made about him at the Bowery Theater in New York City the previous spring. Unlike Jackson, Mitchell had never won any kind of championship nor distinguished himself as a legitimate contender for the crown.[47]

By the latter part of February 1893, Jackson had temporarily given up on Corbett and, like his antagonist, went on the stage. After much persuasion Jackson agreed to join L. R. Stockwell's Theatrical Company in San Francisco and play the role of Tom in *Uncle Tom's Cabin*. Jackson entered into this project rather reluctantly, agreeing to take part only after being convinced by Davies that a great deal of money could be made if the play was successful. His apprehension stemmed from the fact that he knew absolutely nothing about acting and was not eager to learn. While quite worldly in many ways, Jackson was like most members of his profession in that his total commitment to boxing had failed to prepare him for other kinds of work. As it turned out, Jackson's fears were well founded. He was totally inept as an actor, and, after a trip of approximately three months through such principal American cities as Portland, Seattle, Salt Lake City, Chicago, and Milwaukee, the play closed amidst less than enthusiastic reviews. It was an experience Jackson would have liked to forget.[48]

Jackson's dreadful stage experience was soon blotted out, because in April 1894 he and Corbett finally arranged a bout. The two boxers placed a $20,000 stake wager with Will J. Davies of Chicago, agreeing to meet sometime during the last week in June at a "responsible club north of Mason and Dixon's Line."[49] However, no sooner had Jackson and Corbett made their stake wager with Davies than a bitter argument broke out between the two fighters over the exact location of their proposed bout. Two clubs made legitimate offers for the fight, but for various reasons Jackson and Corbett could never come to any agreement. In May the National Sporting Club of London offered a purse of $15,000 for the fight. While Jackson was willing to accept the offer, Corbett refused it. Corbett believed, among other things, that he would not be treated fairly by the club since some of its most influential members were friends of Jackson's. He insisted that the fight be held at the Duval Athletic Club in Jacksonville, Florida, but Jackson was adamantly opposed to the Florida club's offer, having always made it clear that he would never fight in the South, where he could not expect fair treatment.[50]

The verbal sparring match between Jackson and Corbett finally came to a conclusion on August 13, 1894, when the two fighters came face to face for the first time to discuss their differences at the Grand Union Hotel in New York City. Until then, Jackson and Corbett had communicated almost completely through the press, and each boxer welcomed the opportunity to present his side of the story personally. Corbett instigated the meeting through William Brady, contacting Jackson in July while on a theatrical tour of Europe, and asked for a conference upon his return to America. Jackson willingly accepted Corbett's overture and hurriedly made his way east from San Francisco. The meeting between the two boxers was not pleasant. In a cramped hotel room about twelve feet long and ten feet wide, Jackson and Corbett stood so close that at times their noses were not more than six inches apart. They spoke to each other in the most combative way. Corbett reiterated that he would not fight in England under any circumstances. He insisted that the bout be held in America and that it be a fight to the finish. Jackson angrily responded by calling Corbett a bluffer. To show his sincerity, Jackson offered to give Corbett an American referee if Corbett would go to England. But Corbett stubbornly refused the proposition. Finally, after about twenty minutes of wrangling, the two boxers decided further discussion was fruitless and angrily stalked out of the room. The much talked about rematch between Jackson and Corbett would never materialize.[51]

Some of the most influential people in boxing criticized Corbett for the way he treated Jackson. W. W. Naughton argued—and perhaps correctly so—that Corbett was avoiding the match until Jackson had physically deteriorated to the point where he would no longer be a serious challenger. The *Referee,* Australia's foremost sporting tabloid, castigated Corbett for his "underhanded" dealings with Jackson.[52] The fact remains, however, that Corbett made an offer that Jackson refused to accept. As badly as Jackson yearned to be heavyweight champion he was no different from Corbett in wanting the bout to be fought on his terms. He was simply unwilling to swallow his pride and consent to the various stipulations set down by Corbett. The champion had already passed him over to fight the less deserving boxer Charlie Mitchell and made him wait an unreasonable amount of time before seriously discussing a match. Considering such things, Jackson was not going to let Corbett dictate to him where and when the fight should take place.

Although Jackson certainly had good reason to be unhappy with Corbett, he was probably acting against his better judgment in not agreeing to fight in the South. He was not exactly in an ideal bargaining position. Corbett was, after all, heavyweight champion of the world and therefore had the upper hand in any dealings with prospective opponents. Jackson was at Corbett's mercy, not the other way around. Equally disadvantageous to Jackson was the fact that other than the Jacksonville Athletic Club and the National Sporting Club, virtually no organization was willing to sponsor a title fight between a black fighter and a white one. For instance, the Olympic Club of New Orleans, one of America's most renowned boxing organizations, made no attempt to arrange a match between the two fighters. The sportsmen in that city had decided shortly after the featherweight championship bout between George "Little Chocolate" Dixon, a black, and Jack Skelly on September 6, 1892, that they would never sponsor another interracial bout. Unfortunately for Jackson, the idea of an interracial bout, particularly one for the heavyweight title, was becoming repugnant to the majority of white Americans. The world heavyweight championship had come to symbolize the Anglo-Saxon belief in racial superiority, and to allow Jackson to fight for the exalted title would have posed a challenge to this belief, one of the basic underpinnings of American society. A black man might be allowed to fight for a title in the lower divisions but not in the heavier divisions, because these were, in the words of Randy Roberts, "the championships that mattered."[53] The bigger the fighters physically, the more important the contest, and the more crucial it was that a black and a white boxer not be allowed in the ring on terms of equality.

The inability to arrange a fight for the heavyweight championship was a stultifying experience for Jackson. In some ways, he was less fortunate than many of the other well-known black athletes of the late nineteenth century because he was unable to reach the pinnacle of his profession. Such star athletes as Isaac Murphy, Moses "Fleetwood" Walker, and Marshall "Major" Taylor, were able, however temporarily, to reach the top of their particular sports. Murphy captured the Kentucky Derby three times, Walker played Major League baseball with the Toledo Mudhens, and Taylor captured the National Cycling Championship twice. Like these athletes, Jackson was caught between two worlds, in neither of which he really belonged. Because he relied on the boxing establishment for his position and material rewards, he was separated somewhat from his origins. Yet no matter how great his achievements, he was still black. Even when he did triumph in the ring, he often received only half-hearted praise from the American public, not the glory he might have expected. Jackson lived in a continual state of agonizing ambiguity, a condition he found progressively difficult to deal with.

Following his meeting with Corbett at the Grand Union Hotel, Jackson decided to return to England, where he stayed for most of the next three years. Shortly after his arrival Jackson began to fight a series of exhibition matches with David St. John, the mammoth heavyweight boxer from Ireland. Despite challenges from such fighters as Frank

Slavin, Peter Maher, Frank Craig, and Charlie Mitchell, Jackson was content to travel through Europe sparring with St. John. When not on tour, Jackson was either conducting boxing classes at the Harmony Club in London or, more likely, partying with friends until all hours of the night. He was drinking more than ever now, and word out of London was that "almost any afternoon between 4 and 5 o'clock" he could be seen staggering down the Strand. Physically he was not the same man who had so convincingly thrashed Frank Slavin at London's National Sporting Club just a few years earlier. Alcohol had swollen his face and clouded his eyes. His body was marked by a certain flabbiness and laxity of movement that were uncharacteristic of him in his earlier days. Friends of Jackson remarked that his hands shook when lifting a glass and there was a curious "halt now and then in his speech."[54]

In September 1897 a thoroughly worn-out and restless Jackson grew weary of England and once more returned to San Francisco. Unfortunately, he did not receive a particularly cordial welcome in the city he considered his American home. Jackson quickly found out how fleeting fame is and how America's racial lines had hardened when he was denied a room at the well-known Baldwin Hotel, an establishment where he had frequently stayed during his previous sojourns in San Francisco. When Jackson arrived in the city, he went directly to the Baldwin, registered, and was assigned a room. However, after visiting with some friends that evening, Jackson discovered that his registration and baggage had been moved to a room in the hotel annex across the street. He was absolutely livid and complained vehemently to the hotel management, but to no avail. The proprietor denied that the color line had been drawn, explaining that the room in the annex was the only one available. Although Jackson was obliged to accept the room for the night, he subsequently secured other accommodations across the bay in Oakland, where there was a much larger black population. The man who had "dined with Earls, hobnobbed with dukes and shaken hands with royalty" felt the pangs of discrimination in a city whose racial climate was generally considered to be mild in comparison to other parts of the country.[55]

Jackson had been in the Bay Area for about six months when he arranged what was to be the last major fight of his career—against Jim Jeffries, the burly Southern California native who would later become world champion. He made the match only after Tom Sharkey, the whilom pride of the American Navy and future challenger for the heavyweight championship, drew the color line and refused to fight him. At this point in his career, Jackson would have been better off if Jeffries had also drawn the color line. He was humiliated by the heavy-hitting white boxer in a three-round bout on March 22, 1898, at San Francisco's Woodward Pavilion. Jackson gave a terrible performance; the few blows he landed had no effect on Jeffries. The hardest punch he threw all night was when he accidently tripped over his own feet at the end of the first round and inadvertently struck Jeffries on top of the head. Jeffries, for his part, seemingly tried not to inflict undue punishment on Jackson. He had too much respect for the veteran to treat him any other way. The three knockdowns Jeffries scored were caused more by Jackson's ineptness than by any punches Jeffries had thrown. The sight of Jackson moving helplessly around the ring was particularly sad for the legion of fans who had followed him faithfully throughout his career. They preferred to remember him as the lightning-quick black boxer he had been, not this sluggish and overweight fighter who was too helpless to answer the bell for the fourth round.[56]

Jackson stayed in San Francisco after his fight with Jeffries just long enough to say goodbye to old friends and then traveled north to Victoria, British Columbia. He hoped a change of residence would alter his luck, but he was wrong. After five months in Victoria, Jackson came down with viral pneumonia, which brought him close to death.[57] To recuperate from his nearly fatal illness, Jackson decided to return home to Sydney in March 1900 and take advantage of Australia's warmer climate. Jackson received a hero's welcome in a country generally considered one of the most racist in the world. While never completely able to escape his homeland's abhorrent practices of racial discrimination, Jackson was almost universally admired by Australians not only for his boxing triumphs but also for his embodiment of qualities Australians found so worthy in their sport heroes. Jackson symbolized the very essence of English sportsmanship that was adopted and rigorously applied in Australia. He was modest and unselfish; and, above all else, he was an athlete who played by the rules. He never threw a fight, never made excuses for a poor performance, and never took advantage of an inferior opponent. In short, he was a hero to many Australians precisely because he never transgressed the Victorian rules of good sportsmanship.[58]

During his first days back in Australia, Jackson appeared to be on the road to full recovery. He regained enough strength to give boxing exhibitions as he traveled throughout different parts of the country with the Fitzgerald Brothers Circus.[59] Toward the end of the year, however, Jackson was stricken with sciatica, a condition which caused debilitating pain in his lower back and hips. No sooner had Jackson recovered from the sciatica when he was stricken with tuberculosis. At his doctor's request, Jackson traveled to the small town of Roma and entered the local sanitarium. He probably would have been better off staying in Sydney. Despite the close care he received, Jackson grew steadily worse. He died quietly in the arms of his close friend, the black comedian Ernest Hogan, on the evening of July 13, 1901. He was only forty years old.[60]

The cause of Jackson's death was officially listed as tuberculosis. It was a broken heart, however, that was probably most responsible for bringing on his premature aging and early death. Jackson's failure to reach the pinnacle of his profession and fight for the heavyweight championship was a saddening experience. It was apparent that certain whites in the fight game had locked arms against him and that he lived in a society that often viewed his success with hostility. Ironically, Jackson sometimes appeared to be held back by an inner command to be anonymous. Despite his numerous triumphs in the ring, he was never completely comfortable with success and never liked to draw attention to himself. Even while pursuing Corbett, he continually shied away from the publicity and notoriety that inevitably came to an athlete of his stature. While he was highly skilled in the social graces and liked to enjoy himself, Jackson was always quick to guard his privacy. He liked to be alone much of the time, away from fans and the hangers-on of the boxing world.

In the final analysis, Jackson cannot be considered simply an innocent victim. He made some choices in his career that contributed to his inability to arrange a title fight. His decision not to fight Corbett in the South and his preference for staying in England for long periods of time cannot be passed off as inconsequential. If the heavyweight championship was his primary goal, and undoubtedly it was, then Jackson committed some tactical mistakes that a black man in late nineteenth-century America simply could not afford to make. Nevertheless, Jackson's failure to arrange a title fight did not stop him from becoming the nineteenth century's most internationally renowned black athlete. In varying degrees, he was a hero to both blacks and whites in Australia, America, and England. Jackson was frequently ignored and often discriminated against, but he was always deep in the consciousness of Sullivan, Corbett, other members of the boxing profession, and the sporting public.

Part Two

Civil Rights and the Quest for Equality

4

The 1936 Olympic Games in Berlin

The Response of America's Black Press

There has been a great deal written about the Modern Olympics since they began over eighty years ago, but none of the Games have received as much attention as those held in Berlin in 1936. The Nazi Olympics have held a particular fascination for scholars who seemingly never tire of writing about Jesse Owens, Adolf Hitler, and the other individuals who occupied a central role in the Games that year. It seems odd, however, that no one has examined the view of America's black press on this subject, particularly because the Games were marked by a worldwide discussion of Germany's racial policies, and some of the outstanding athletic performances of the Games were turned in by black Americans. The secondary accounts of the 1936 Games have essentially been based on the descriptions given by the dominant white press. The results, of course, are accounts taken from a predominantly white perspective.[1] This essay is concerned with the role of the black press and its coverage of the 1936 Olympic Games. How did the black press view the proposed boycott of the Games? What type of coverage did they give the games themselves? In the view of the black press, what ramifications would the success of black athletes have on the rest of black America.

Since its inception, the black press has always given wide publicity to any campaign by a black individual or group for racial equality. In fact, the black press has traditionally served as the agency responsible for disseminating news among the black community that primarily concerned themselves. Except for news of crime and scandal—or an occasional item concerning some individual black prominent in a cultural field—white papers have traditionally given limited coverage to those activities engaged in by black Americans. The black press is often the only satisfactory source available to the black reader for information

61

about his or her own racial group. Functioning as a sounding board for thoughts and feelings in the black community, it frequently reports in great detail racial incidents regarded by the white press as too insignificant to print. In addition, the black press has often been the initial and sometimes the only instrument to bring to the attention of the black population stories of success by members of its race.[2]

The *Baltimore Afro-American, Chicago Defender, Indianapolis Recorder, New York Age, New York Amsterdam News, Philadelphia Tribune, Pittsburgh Courier-Journal,* and *St. Louis Argus,* were some of the most influential and widely circulated black newspapers in the United States (The *Defender* and *Courier-Journal* are still two of the most influential black newspapers in the country). Their circulation totaled almost 315,000 by the time the Games began in 1936, with the *Chicago Defender* alone accounting for 82,000.[3] The *Defender,* along with the *Pittsburgh Courier-Journal, Baltimore Afro-American,* and *New York Age,* were nationally distributed weeklies with five-figure circulations and several editions—local, regional, and national. The remaining papers were weeklies distributed only in their particular cities, with sales that ranged from approximately 14,000 to 30,000. All of the papers, whether nationally or locally distributed, were read almost exclusively by blacks. Most whites had little exposure to black newspapers and hence were virtually unaware of their content.[4]

The black press gave front-page headlines to the athletic achievements of America's black stars in the 1936 games. With the possible exception of the second Max Schmeling–Joe Louis heavyweight boxing match in 1938, no single sporting event received such broad coverage in the black press during the 1930s as did the Berlin Olympics. In the opinion of the black press, the success of Jesse Owens and the other black athletes had significant ramifications for the rest of black America —both positively and negatively. The Games made it clear to the black press that America's black colleges, unlike predominantly white universities, were failing to produce any outstanding athletes in track and field. Not one athlete from a black college made the American Olympic Team, and it angered many black newspaper writers and editors, who believed that black colleges were failing to produce great athletes because of their lack of equipment and facilities. On the positive side, the success of black athletes had shed serious doubt on Hitler's tenets of Aryan racial superiority. It would be difficult for anyone to believe in the Nazi racial philosophy after watching the performances of America's black athletes. In addition, the controversy that came about over Germany's treatment of minority groups was apparently gratifying to the black press because it made a number of people aware of racial prejudice who might not otherwise have been. In no way were the Games responsible for sweeping improvements in race relations, but they did apparently broaden the perspective of some whites in regard to black Americans. Lastly, and perhaps most importantly, the black press believed that the triumphs of black athletes in the Berlin Games should be an incentive to black Americans to do everything they could to strive for success in other fields of endeavor. It would be detrimental to their very existence if black Americans permitted themselves to be stereotyped as athletes and nothing more, merely because of the triumphs of black athletes in the 1936 Games.

The Proposed Boycott

Almost from the moment Adolph Hitler came to power in 1933, a discussion began among the various amateur sport leaders around the world as to whether the eleventh Olympiad should be held in fascist Germany.[5] These men were deeply troubled by the Nazi party, now powerful, which not only blamed the downfall of Germany on Jews and communists, but also maintained notions that were blatantly anti-internationalist and racist even in the area of sport. Should the Games be held in a totalitarian state that denied Jewish athletes the opportunity to participate in organized sport, and that on several occasions, especially during the 1932 Games in Los Angeles, had suggested that blacks not be allowed to participate in the 1936 Games? The athletic organizations in the United States were particularly sensitive about the matter and discussed the various issues regularly.[6] Their basic argument centered around the question of whether the United States could participate in the Berlin Games and still maintain this country's own ideals of fair play and equality for all athletes. Apparently, the Amateur Athletic Union (AAU) believed it should not, because this most powerful of all American amateur sport bodies passed a clear resolution in November 1933 declaring that the United States should not compete in the Games if the situation in Germany did not change for the better.[7]

The initial response of the black press was one of amazement. Its leaders were disheartened that such a concerted effort was being made by sport organizations in the United States to ensure that minority groups were being treated fairly in Germany, while little or no effort was being made in this country to guarantee that black athletes were given freedom of opportunity. They believed it was hypocritical for American Olympic officials to demand that Germany treat Jewish athletes fairly when nothing was being done to curtail discrimination against black athletes at home.[8] The *Chicago Defender* found it especially disconcerting that Avery Brundage, then president of the AAU, advised Germany that an American team would not be sent to the Games unless Germany removed its restrictions on Jews.[9] Brundage was the same man who, a year earlier at the Los Angeles Games, had done nothing to see that Jimmy Johnson and Tydye Pickett were restored to the American team, which had unjustly dismissed them because of their color.

The black press was quick to point out that it did not condone the atrocities of the Nazi government but was simply interested in receiving assurances that black athletes would be treated fairly during their brief stay in Germany.[10] For example, the NAACP vehemently denounced the attacks on minority groups in Germany and in July 1933 at its national meeting in Chicago passed a resolution calling upon the American members of the International Olympic Committee (IOC) to secure an immediate and unequivocal statement from the German government that no discrimination against blacks or other races in the 1936 Olympics would be tolerated.[11] Similar to the resolution that would be passed by the AAU four months later, it stipulated that "if assurances were not forthcoming the Games should be transferred to another country."[12]

Even after supposed assurances, the black press was still apprehensive about the kind of treatment black athletes would receive while in Berlin. Meanwhile, in the summer of 1934, Avery Brundage was dispatched by the American Olympic Committee to investigate the situation in Germany and, after a tour of the new totalitarian state, decided that its sports programs were in compliance with the spirit of Olympianism.[13] Relying heavily upon this favorable report, the AAU and IOC formally accepted Germany's invitation to participate in the eleventh Olympiad in Berlin—a decision to which the black press was not necessarily opposed, but one it approached with some skepticism.[14] The most disturbing factor was that Brundage's report expressed concern only about the treatment of Jewish athletes and said nothing specifically about the treatment of black participants. The black press was troubled that black athletes were not mentioned in the report because it was well known that the German government included blacks as well as Jews in its statewide discriminatory acts. It was not easy to forget, for example, that the official Nazi newspaper *Volkischer Beobachter* had editorialized on the occasion of the Los Angeles Olympics in 1932 that black athletes must be excluded from participating in the Berlin Games for fear that the "sacred grandeur of the Olympiad" would not be upheld.[15]

The fears expressed by the black press following Brundage's trip to Germany were virtually ignored by sports leaders in the United States, who by July 1935 were again embroiled in a heated debate over whether to send an American team to Berlin.[16] With the passing of the ill-fated Nuremberg Race Relations Laws, an extremely emotional debate over a possible boycott of the Games took place among American sports organizations between July 1935 and December 1935—a discussion that caused internal strife in the AAU. The deprivation of German Jews' rights as citizens caused a philosophical split among members of the AAU. One side, led by its president Jeremiah T. Mahoney, advocated a boycott of the Games, while another faction, under the leadership of Avery Brundage, favored participation. Each side spent considerable time and money securing support for its position. In an attempt to sway public opinion, both groups published pamphlets and expressed their views in radio interviews. There were a number of rallies and demonstrations staged, and pressure exerted from political groups, the majority of which argued nonparticipation. The most frequent argument in favor of a boycott was that American participation would mean at least tacit approval of the Nazi regime, which was diametrically opposed to the Olympic ideals of peace and equality. Those who favored participation believed that it was inappropriate for those in sport to interfere in a situation that was essentially a political matter, and therefore one that should be settled by political leaders.

It is important that the worldwide discussion of a boycott was followed very closely by the dominant white press in America.[17] Both white newspapers and popular periodicals devoted a great deal of column space to a presentation of the arguments for and against American participation in the Games. Almost daily between July and December of 1935, the actions of Avery Brundage, Jeremiah T. Mahoney (AAU president), Henri Baillet-Latour (IOC president), and other notable Olympic figures were discussed in the white press. The primary topic in these reports was Nazi discrimination against German Jews, and what was the most appropriate way for America to deal with such a delicate situation. Tellingly, there was rarely anything written in the white press describing the positions taken by blacks on the boycott issue. For example, the *New York Times* devoted just three small columns to a review of the opinions of black Americans on this subject, simply mentioning that the *New York Amsterdam News* and the NAACP were urging black athletes to boycott the Games.[18] There was never any real attempt to communicate the thoughts and feelings of those in the black community or to assess their philosophical position on the boycott issue. That task was left to the black press.

While the white press was stepping up its coverage of the boycott issue, black newspapers began receiving requests from a number of interested groups pleading with them to do everything they could to keep black athletes from participating in the Berlin Olympics. Just a month after the debates began, the Anti-Nazi Federation expressed to the *New York Amsterdam News* how glad they were to see that black athletes were being urged in that paper to boycott the Games.[19] While on brief speaking engagements in America, Madame Sonja Branting, a prominent attorney and teacher from Sweden, and Otto Katz, editor of two of that country's leading publications, implored the *Chicago Defender* to encourage readers to support a boycott and keep black athletes at home.[20] The American League Against War and Fascism opposed American participation in the Berlin Games and expressed to the *Pittsburgh Courier* its fear that "Germany's discrimination against racial minorities might extend to include the Negro Group."[21] Finally, Jewish Americans wrote a number of editorials to the black press describing the atrocities that Germany was inflicting upon minority groups and urged the newspapers to persuade black athletes not to compete in Berlin.[22]

Response of the Black Press

In spite of the pleas from various segments of society, there were divergent reactions from the black press concerning America's proposed boycott of the Games. Some black newspapers advocated a boycott, while the majority encouraged participation. Those newspapers arguing that American athletes should stay at home often used a rationale similar to that voiced by the pro-boycott wing of the AAU: To send a team to Germany would be an indication to the rest of the world that the United States gave at least implicit support to a regime that fostered racial discrimination and stood for everything that Olympianism opposed.[23] No doubt American race relations were not ideal. But the black newspapers supporting a boycott believed that despite the discrimination faced by blacks in America, advancements were continually being made, and that to contribute both moral and financial support to the Berlin Games would be a serious transgression because the German government, unlike the American one, was doing all it could to see that minorities were denied equality of opportunity. One of the boycott supporters, the *New York Amsterdam News,* wrote an open letter to Jesse Owens and other outstanding black athletes, pleading with them not to participate in the Games. "As members of a minority group," the *News* editorialized, "whose persecution the Nazis have encouraged, as citizens of a country in which all liberty has not yet been destroyed, you cannot afford to give moral and financial support to a philosophy which seeks the ultimate destruction of all you have fought for."[24] The *Cleveland Gazette* voiced many of the same concerns. Though admitting that the United States had much to answer for in the matter of racial discrimination, especially among black athletes in the South, the *Gazette* believed that this censure was justified. "Refusal to participate," said the *Gazette,* "would do untold good in helping Germany and the world to realize that racial bigotry must be opposed in its every manifestation."[25]

The belief that improvements were being made in race relations in America during this period was held even by those members of the black press who favored participation and has been reiterated by historians who have studied that period. Despite the interest of philanthropic whites in the Urban League and the Harlem Renaissance during the 1920s, it was during the 1930s that a definite change in the attitudes of white Americans became evident. The New Deal marked a turning point in American racial policies, even though its programs were not free of discrimination. Blacks shared in jobs, relief, and public housing, and black leaders, who benefited from the open sympathy of many highly placed New Dealers, held more prominent political positions than ever before. The humanitarian work of public figures like Eleanor Roosevelt and Secretary of the Interior Harold Ickes was part of the larger interest in the welfare of the underprivileged. Because the black vote had reached sizable proportions in northern cities, New Deal politicians of the North were forced to give more attention to black welfare. Significantly, the growth of the Congress of Industrial Organizations (CIO), which clamored for equal treatment of the races, aligned black and white workers for the first time since the Knights of Labor disbanded almost a half-century earlier.[26]

The recognition that race relations had improved in America, however, did not alter the attitude of the large majority of black newspapers, which expressed the belief that the talk of a boycott on the part of some black newsmen was rather naive and even foolish.[27] Certainly it was unwise counsel on the part of the black press to suggest that black athletes alone stay away from the Olympics in Berlin. Why single out Jesse Owens, Ben Johnson, Ralph Metcalfe, and the other black stars? If America were going to stay out of the Games, was it not logical that all American athletes should stay out?

The ideal way to combat Germany's racial policies, in the opinion expressed by most black newspapers, was to send black athletes to the Games and have them defeat the Nazi youths. There was no better way to lift the prestige of the "despised darker races and lower the prestige of the proud and arrogant Nordic."[28] Besides that, the preponderance of black newspapers repeated the argument that it was simply hypocritical for Americans to advocate a boycott of the Games on account of Hitler's racial policies, while themselves denying black athletes equality of opportunity. Again, the black press was quick to point out that it did not condone Nazi Germany's racial policies. Nor did it question the fact that some racial advancements had been made in the United States. But every argument that had been advanced against participation in the Berlin Olympics might with equal force be used against holding them in

America. For example, even though amateur track and field and professional boxing were generally open to black athletes, most sports in American society were still segregated, with no prospect of ever being otherwise. Not allowed to participate in organized professional baseball because of that sport's racial policy, blacks were forced to create their own separate leagues. Like professional golf's Caucasian clause, the "Gentlemen's agreement" by major league owners prohibited any black players—regardless of ability—from entering white organized baseball. Professional football allowed some black athletes to participate for a time, but by 1933 it had instituted a Jim Crow clause and become segregated. If a black wanted to participate in athletics at a major, predominantly white university, it would have to be at one of the institutions in the North, because no schools in the South permitted blacks as students. At a more informal level of sports competition, blacks in American society were still not permitted in many locations to make use of swimming pools, playgrounds, and other recreational facilities.[29]

That there would be differences of opinion in the black press over tactics to be followed in the boycott issue was not surprising considering the nature of black protest over the years. Traditionally, the primary assault of black protest in America has been aimed at segregation and discrimination; the primary demand has been for equal treatment with other citizens. However, a striking feature of black protest in the twentieth century has been the enormous amount of dispute within the black community over what strategies and tactics to employ to realize the goal of equality.[30] Similarly, the central thrust of all black newspaper coverage of the 1936 Games was against racial discrimination, but the decisions over tactics to combat the malady split the black press into two opposing groups. These factions did not divide neatly into "radical" and "conservative" camps but generally followed their own previously established political stances. Of the newspapers advocating a boycott, the *New York Amsterdam News* was the most vocal and insistent on nonparticipation. It ran a vigorous campaign and devoted a large amount of column space in an effort to see that black athletes stayed away from the Berlin Games.[31] Publications in favor of participation were led by the *Pittsburgh Courier-Journal,* perhaps the most influential of all black newspapers in America. The *Courier-Journal* published a series of editorials condemning those papers that favored a boycott, saving its most biting criticism for the *Amsterdam News,* which it believed was inappropriately influencing other members of the black press.[32] Interestingly, the *Courier-Journal* was the same publication that so strongly backed Joe Louis in his early career and that later would be most responsible for persuading Branch Rickey to sign Jackie Robinson to a major league baseball contract.[33]

Injustices and Inconsistencies

The organization that most often drew the ire of the black press for its handling of the boycott issue, particularly by those newspapers that favored participation, was the AAU.[34] The most powerful of American amateur sport bodies continually railed against the cruelties inflicted by the Hitler government but generally did nothing to improve the plight of the black athlete in America—with the possible exception of refusing to sanction track meets in the South because of that region's racial policy. In the words of the *Philadelphia Tribune,* "the A.A.U. shouts against the cruelties of other nations and the brutalities in foreign climes, but conveniently forgets the things that sit on its own doorstep."[35] The most frequently mentioned example of the AAU's injustice toward the black athlete was the decision to eliminate Jesse Owens's name from the list of finalists eligible for the 1935 Sullivan Award as the nation's outstanding amateur athlete.[36] After an outstanding season on the track, which included breaking three world records and tying another at the Big 10 Championships in Ann Arbor, Owens was originally nominated but then was denied the opportunity to win the coveted award by the AAU, which charged him with professionalism because of money he allegedly received while working for the Ohio State legislature. The black press denied there was any truth to those allegations and believed the AAU utilized them as a convenient means to deny the award to a black man. Tellingly, shortly after the award was given, Owens was absolved of any wrongdoing and given his amateur status back.[37]

The injustices of white America were plainly evident to this country's outstanding black athletes, but the majority of them made it clear in interviews given to the black press that they strongly approved of sending a team to Berlin.[38] Understandably, most black athletes believed that it would be unfair to deny them an opportunity to compete after they had devoted so much time and effort training for the Games. Like all competitive athletes, they yearned for the chance to exhibit the physical skills they had so diligently and carefully honed. For those black athletes who had previously competed in Germany, the talk of a boycott seemed particularly inappropriate, because they had been treated with nothing but kindness during their stay in that country. For example, Marquette University's Ralph Metcalfe told the *Chicago Defender* that he and the other American athletes were treated like royalty during their tour of Germany in 1933 and did not anticipate being treated otherwise in Berlin.[39]

Last, and perhaps most important, the large majority of black athletes were reluctant to clamor for a boycott out of sympathy for Jews when Jews had done nothing to improve the lot of black Americans. Merely identifying with the sufferings Jews had experienced was not enough to warrant a boycott of something as important as the Olympics, particularly when Jews made no protest about lynchings or other barbarities inflicted on black Americans.[40]

In truth, a strong undercurrent of anti-Semitism was evident among black Americans during the Depression years. Blacks in the United States did not easily buy into the idea that they suffered the same injustices or faced problems similar to those of Jews. Blacks seemed as caught up as American whites in the anti-Semitic movement that reached a high water mark in the United States during the mid-thirties.[41] In fact, it was not uncommon for members of the black community to lay much of the blame on Jewish Americans for the injustices they suffered during the Depression, particularly in the economic sphere. Black Americans were certainly not devoid of prejudice and the tendency to blame other people for those things they were most guilty of themselves; and nowhere was it more evident than in their scathing attacks upon Jewish Americans. They frequently stereotyped Jews and blamed them for everything from economic exploitation to murder.[42] In this context, it would have been surprising for any member of the black press to advocate a boycott of the Games out of sympathy for German Jews.

Decision to Participate

When it was finally decided at the AAU convention of December 6–8, 1935, to send an American team to Berlin, the leading members of the black press immediately responded by stating that any further opposition to sending the U.S. athletes abroad was senseless.[43] The small number of black newspapers that had previously advocated a boycott apparently heeded this advice, because nearly all of them decided in favor of participation by the early part of 1936.[44] Even the *New York Amsterdam News* finally agreed that it would be a serious mistake if the United States did not send a team to Berlin.[45] The endorsement by black newspapers took considerable pressure off the athletes themselves; all the black athletes who were expected to make the U.S. team had favored going to Germany. Judging by the favorable treatment they had received earlier while competing in Germany under the Nazi regime, they had no reason to believe that they would encounter any worse treatment in Berlin than they had experienced in American cities. Indeed, there were questions as to whether Hitler's hatred of non-Aryan peoples was at all representative of the German population. Even under a dictatorship it was difficult to suppress the graciousness of the German people. Most importantly, the Olympic Games should not be allowed to lapse because of any one individual. Not only did the Games potentially contribute to international goodwill, but they would also allow black athletes an opportunity to display their physical talents in front of the whole world. Although their success would not blot out racial prejudice, it would give black Americans a new sense of pride and a much needed feeling of importance. The black community in America desperately needed heroes to look up to and emulate.[46]

The Black Athlete's Ambiguous Position

The black press was extremely optimistic about the black athletes' chances for victory and consequently approached the upcoming Games with great anticipation.[47] It was evident to black newspapers that America would have to rely heavily on the performances of black athletes—particularly in track and field—if it was to be successful in Berlin. In fact, the black press realized that in spite of the discrimination faced by black athletes at home, there was never any question that they would be allowed to compete in the Games because America was too dependent on their talents to deny them that opportunity. If there was one thing that could momentarily transcend racial discrimination in America, it was the obsession for victory in international sport. The United States would not allow blacks to participate in most white organized sport yet thought nothing of putting their services to good use in Berlin. It was this kind of exploitation that caused the German press to categorize America's black athletes as "black auxiliaries" and prompted one influential black newspaper to comment that "Negroes in the United States are and are not. They are granted citizenship rights in some things but are denied citizenship rights in others—a kind of subsidiary existence."[48]

It was this attitude toward race on the part of American Olympic officials that was such a source of irritation to the black press.[49] Allowing black athletes to participate in the Olympic Games yet denying them access to most white organized sport in America was despicable—the worst kind of discrimination. The circumstances that black Olympians found themselves in were disturbing to the black press not only because of the insincere stance taken by American sport officials but also because those circumstances epitomized the dilemma that black Americans had to confront during the first half of the twentieth century. Like their white fellow citizens, black athletes wished to participate in the American social structure, but the injustices of sport leaders in the United States often forced them into an ethnocentric loyalty to the black race, which, as previously mentioned, resulted in the creation of separate leagues and conferences operated without white interference. Although the freedom to take part in some white-controlled sports held out hope for black athletes, the inability to share in other sports concomitantly obliged them to identify with an oppressed group. The enormous gap between ideal and practice in American sport was especially troublesome because it reminded black athletes of their precarious status—and of the fact that it often seemed conflicting to be both proudly black and loyally American. Black athletes were no different from other black citizens in that they exhibited an ethnic dualism, a constant longing to attain a full sense of their ethnicity while freely participating in American life.

The College Park Incident

It became increasingly obvious that the United States team would have to rely on black athletes to be victorious in Berlin, because by the time the Olympic trials were completed almost a score of them had made the American team—the largest number ever to represent the U.S.[50] During the Olympic trials, however, a racial incident occurred at a regional track meet in College Park, Maryland, that received as much coverage in the black press as any single event before the Games.[51] Black newspapers became incensed when four black athletes were indiscriminately banned from competing in this local Olympic tryout by Dorsey J. Griffith, chairman of the District of Columbia AAU. Allegedly basing the decision on his personal racial bias (according to the black press), Griffith wrote letters to Arthur A. Green, physical education director of the district YMCA, and John Burr, head of the Department of Physical Education at Howard University, explaining that the entry blanks they had submitted for their four athletes would not be accepted because there were no events included "for colored athletes, as they have their own championship."[52] If the two men had any complaints they should address them to William J. Bingham, chairman of the Olympic track-and-field committee. Completely disgusted with these conditions, Green and Burr immediately wired Bingham, vehemently protesting the decision made by Griffith and demanding that prompt action be taken to remedy the problem. Bingham made no effort to reinstate the four black athletes in the regional meet in College Park but ruled instead that they would automatically qualify for the semifinal tryouts to be held in Cambridge, Massachusetts, in late June 1936.

What infuriated the black press so much was that Bingham and the other American Olympic officials had skirted the real issues in the College Park affair and had again failed to utilize their influence to help stamp out the racial inequalities that pervaded the South.[53] Armed with the authority to demand that qualified blacks be allowed to compete in the regional trials, the heads of amateur sport were remiss, as far as the black press was concerned, in not disciplining Griffith for his actions and requiring that the four athletes be allowed to qualify regionally. Essentially, the American Olympic officials avoided the issue entirely by treating the black athletes as special cases, glossing over their difficulties in qualifying regionally. Olympic officials thus passed up the opportunity for a strong gesture against the racial injustices of organized sport in the South. Moreover, the decision to allow the four black athletes to participate in the semifinal trials without first qualifying in a regional meet was completely unfair to the white athletes, who were denied such privileges and had to qualify at each successive level. Black athletes did not need or want special treatment, but simply asked that they be given the same consideration afforded other athletes.

The frustration that black newspapers expressed over the racial incident at College Park was relatively short-lived because just over two months later the eighteen American blacks chosen for the Games arrived in Berlin. Accompanying the athletes, coaches, and other team officials were various members of the black press, including Robert L. Vann, editor of the *Pittsburgh Courier-Journal,* and William N. Jones, staff correspondent of the *Baltimore Afro-American,* who were making the trip to Germany to report on the eleventh Olympiad firsthand.[54]

The Games Themselves

America was represented by eighteen black athletes in all—twelve track-and-field performers, four boxers, and two weight lifters—when the Games finally began in Berlin on August 1.[55] As the black press had anticipated, black athletes performed magnificently in the Games, capturing six individual gold medals and accounting for 83 of America's 167 total points. All of the points scored by black athletes were in track-and-field events. Ohio State's Jesse Owens led the way with gold medals in the 100-and 200-meter dashes, the broad jump, and the 400-meter relay. Other winners included Marquette University's Ralph Metcalfe, who placed second to Owens in the 100 meters and ran on the victorious 400-meter relay team; Mack Robinson (Jackie Robinson's older brother), from Pasadena Junior College, who came in second in the 200 meters; Berkeley's Archie Williams, winner of the 400 meters; UCLA's James Luvalle, third-place winner at 400 meters; John Woodruff, from the University of Pittsburgh, who captured the 800 meters; Compton Junior College's Cornelius Johnson, who won the high jump; Owens's Ohio State teammate David Albritton, who came in a close second in the high jump; and Fritz Pollard, Jr., from the University of North Dakota, who placed third in the 100-meter hurdles.[56]

Jesse Owens, here with Ralph Metcalfe, the great sprinter from Marquette University, realized lasting fame for his triumphs in Berlin in 1936. The black press recounted his four gold-medal performances in great detail. Courtesy of the Moorland-Spingarn Research Center, Howard University.

The black press was elated with the accomplishments of all the black-track-and-field performers but saved its greatest adulation for Owens, who they believed had dealt a severe blow to the Nazi belief in Aryan supremacy.[57] To black newspapers, Owens's four-gold-medal performance was a cause for celebration among black Americans because it was not only one of the greatest athletic feats ever but also proof of what a black man could accomplish if given the opportunity. Owens was rightfully singled out because he did more to establish a sense of pride and feeling of self-worth among his people than any other black athlete who participated in the Games. Like Joe Louis, he was a worthy role model for black children: an athlete who set a positive example for other members of his race by living a virtuous life, he was symbolic of the black man who was able to overcome tremendous personal odds to achieve success and fame in his particular field.

Owens's triumphs were indeed magnificent, but of almost equal concern to the black press during the Berlin Games was the much publicized incident in which Adolph Hitler supposedly refused to shake hands with Owens and the other victorious black athletes.[58] The German sport historian Arnd Kruger has recently shown that Hitler's decision not to congratulate black athletes was not a blatant form of discrimination, as was most commonly believed, but actually resulted from an attempt by the Germans to avoid difficulties with the IOC.[59] During the first day of track-and-field competitions, Hitler took it upon himself to receive all the victorious athletes personally but committed an obvious blunder when he failed to stay and congratulate the winners of the high jump—the final event of the day, which lasted much longer than scheduled. Two of the three American medalists in the event were black athletes: the winner, Cornelius Johnson, and the second-place finisher, David Albritton. Upset about this apparent snub, the IOC president Baillet-Latour complained the next day to the German organizers, whereupon a fellow IOC member, Karl Ritter von Halt, a Nazi, agreed to request that Hitler "congratulate publicly either all or none of the winners."[60] Hitler chose the latter route and therefore did not shake hands with Owens after his 100-meter victory that day, or with any other subsequent winners in the Games.

The black press had no sympathy for Hitler and not unexpectedly viewed the Nazi leader's action as a case of overt racial discrimination. Hitler in their view was simply not able to cope with watching Owens and the other black athletes dominate the Games when he had vaunted his theories of Aryan racial superiority. After deriving the greatest pleasure from seeing Joe Louis fall at the hands of Max Schmeling two months earlier, Hitler watched in disbelief as his vaunted Aryans were defeated by black stars from America. To black newspapers, Hitler's discourteous behavior simply exhibited his true character as a man. In the words of the *Pittsburgh Courier-Journal,* "Hitler is an individual envious of talent, suspicious of high character, devoid of chivalry, bereft of culture, a cowardly effeminate, who proved incapable of being a gentleman even at the Olympic Games where prejudice and politics are traditionally taboo."[61]

While the black press viewed Hitler with much disdain, they thought better of the mass of German citizens, who were extremely courteous and hospitable to the visiting black athletes during their brief stay in Berlin.[62] Black newspapers were quick to point out that the Nazi policies of racial discrimination were clearly not shared by the German people in general. The black press also informed their readers with some pride that America's black athletes never gave the German citizenry an opportunity to treat them in any other fashion, because they all conducted themselves flawlessly throughout the Games.[63] In contrast to some of the participants, no black athletes from the United States were accused of any wrongdoing while in Berlin. None of them broke training rules or put themselves and their race on the spot by indulging in "midnight cocktail parties and early morning revelries to watch the sun come up."[64]

The Games officially came to a close on August 16. When the triumphant American athletes finally came home after a brief series of exhibition meets in Europe, they received the kind of welcome usually reserved for returning war heroes or political dignitaries.[65] After a ticker-tape parade through downtown New York, they were greeted by Mayor La Guardia in special ceremonies held at Randall's Island before a cheering crowd estimated at 5,000. As expected, the person who received the greatest fanfare was Owens, whom La Guardia singled out as the greatest of all Olympic athletes and an "American that all America should be proud of."[66] When he returned to his hometown of Cleveland in mid-September, Owens was given another parade and testimonial banquet to honor his outstanding performances in the Games. In the words of the *Chicago Defender*, it was a celebration "more ostentatious than the Armistice demonstration, and equaled only by the reception given Colonel Charles A. Lindbergh."[67]

The Games' Effect on Black America

An important question to ask at this point is, what effect did the success of this country's black athletes in Berlin have on the rest of black America? First of all, the 1936 Games made it patently obvious to the black press that America's black colleges were failing to produce any outstanding athletes in track and field like those from predominantly white universities.[68] Not one athlete from a black college made the American Olympic team. This was a source of great irritation to black newspapers, which believed black colleges simply did not have the equipment and facilities necessary to produce star performers. The failure to generate an athlete the caliber of Owens or Metcalfe was an indictment of black colleges, making it clear that in comparison to white universities they had insufficient funds to train their students properly.

If there was one result of the 1936 Games that the black press pointed to with the greatest pride, it was the success of the black Olympians in showing the world that the Nazi doctrine of Aryan superiority was untrue.[69] How could any person who believed in Nordic supremacy account for the numerous triumphs garnered by Jesse Owens and his black teammates? White science had confirmed over and over again that blacks were inferior, yet black athletes consistently prevailed over their white competitors in the Berlin Games.

Although they were terribly disturbed by Germany's racial policies, the black press appeared to welcome the controversy that arose during the Games over that country's treatment of minority groups. The mere fact that the question of race became a central issue and was debated openly by leaders around the world was itself beneficial to black America because it helped clarify the problem of racial prejudice in America.[70] The *Baltimore Afro-American* even remarked that the ostracism of Jewish athletes from organized sports in Germany was something that black athletes in America understood all too well, and that perhaps, with two minority groups affected instead of one, there would be hope for redoubled efforts toward wiping out the disgraceful practice.[71]

The discussion that took place concerning Germany's racial positions apparently did have some effect in lessening the apathy of white Americans toward racial issues, because by July 1936 there was an increasing number of editorials in the white press deploring the hypocrisy of American attitudes toward race.[72] In some ways the changes in white attitudes that began with the New Deal were accelerated by the Berlin Games. The Olympics of 1936 made thoughtful whites painfully aware of the contradiction in opposing Nazi racial philosophy while doing nothing about racism at home. In defending Germany's right to host the Games, the Nazi press had raised the issue of American racism in order to embarrass the United States in the eyes of the world. This ploy did not remove the contempt people felt towards Germany's own racial policies but did raise the consciousness of some whites who had not theretofore thought seriously about the plight of black Americans. Of course, there were other events taking place around this time—such as the revolution against Western imperialism in Asia and Africa, and the participation of new nonwhite nations in international councils—that benefited blacks and helped to liberalize American racial attitudes. But perhaps no event had such immediate impact in broadening the perspective of whites concerning America's racial policies as did the 1936 Olympics. Like other international sporting contests, the Berlin Games were most appropriate for raising such issues because of their visibility and the worldwide attention they commanded.[73]

On the other hand, the black press continued to maintain that all the hero worship was a temporary phenomenon and it would not take long before black athletes were again mired in anonymity and relegated to second-class citizenship.[74] The black press, aware that many black Americans looked upon the recent victories of black athletes in the Olympics as a major factor in the lessening of prejudice, cautioned its readers that the ramifications of the race question were much too complicated to be decisively affected by the success of isolated members of a victimized people. No doubt America's black athletes should be lauded for their accomplishments, but it should never be forgotten that no racial minority had ever solved its problems solely through the athletic prowess of its members. To black newspapers, athletics was clearly no solution to the problems of the race, because the political and economic dominance still remained in white hands. The only way to maintain a healthy black community and at the same time move into the mainstream of American life was to gain the competencies necessary to become professional people—financiers, politicians, and the like. However psychologically satisfying or however materially advantageous to a few, success in athletics was not a satisfactory solution to the problems of segregation and discrimination.[75]

Nonetheless, the black press believed the triumphs of black athletes in the Berlin Games should prove to be an incentive and impetus to every black in America to strive for success in all fields of endeavor.[76] The record-breaking achievements of black Olympians demonstrated in convincing style what blacks could accomplish if they were given a fair opportunity and proper facilities for training. There was little question that black Americans had to be better than their white competitors if they wished to achieve a semblance of equality and recognition for their work. But a great future lay ahead for black Americans if they would manage to "tap the huge reservoir of energy and talent at their disposal and refine and utilize it."[77] Why not explode once and for all the myth that blacks could excel only in the athletic arena? Why not produce a great number of "Owenses" in other professions? It would be detrimental to their very existence if black Americans allowed themselves to be stereotyped as athletes and nothing more, simply because of the success of black athletes in the Berlin Games.

The Olympic Games of 1936 were followed very closely by the black press and, as I have shown, was viewed as a significant event with far-reaching implications for black Americans. That black newspapers would devote so much column space to describing the accomplishments of Owens and the other black athletes was quite natural considering the enormous success they experienced in Berlin. The black press was extremely proud of the performances of black Olympians in front of Hitler and the Nazis (as well as the rest of the world) and was eager to make the black community in America aware of those accomplishments.

Nor could the success of black athletes in the Berlin Games be easily dismissed as inconsequential by the American black press. The significance of the Games lay in the fact that they heightened racial pride in the black community and simultaneously made whites more aware of the discrimination faced by minority groups. Admittedly, America's black Olympians would probably find on their return home that public buildings and hotels would still make them use the freight elevators; many restaurants would refuse to feed them; state and federally supported colleges would continue to refuse matriculation to athletes of their color; and theaters where pictures of their performances would receive the loudest applause would refuse to let the athletes see themselves in action, unless they retired to the galleries or some other designated room. Nevertheless, the performances of black athletes momentarily surmounted racial prejudice and therefore held out hope that the malady could someday be permanently rubbed out. This, in and of itself, was of cultural significance to America's black press.

5

Wendell Smith, the *Pittsburgh Courier-Journal*, and the Campaign to Include Blacks in Organized Baseball, 1933–1945

In his autobiography *I Never Had It Made*, Jackie Robinson wrote that he would be forever indebted to Wendell Smith, because it was Smith who had first recommended him to Branch Rickey as the man most suited to break the color barrier in white organized baseball.[1] As sports editor of the *Pittsburgh Courier-Journal*, the largest and perhaps most radical black newspaper in America, Smith told Rickey during a meeting between the two on April 17, 1945, that Robinson was one black player who had major league potential.[2] The meeting between Smith and Rickey was a significant one not only because it put Rickey on the trail of the talented shortstop of the Kansas City Monarchs, but because it represented a turning point in the nearly twelve-year campaign that the *Courier-Journal* had waged against the exclusion of blacks in America's "National Pastime." Since 1933 the Pittsburgh-based newspaper had written editorials, conducted interviews with white major leaguers, and written feature-length articles, all in an attempt to see that qualified blacks were allowed to compete in organized baseball. Led by the spirited and tenacious Smith, the *Courier-Journal* relentlessly hammered away at Commissioner Kenesaw Mountain Landis, club owners, field managers, ballplayers, and anyone else it felt was responsible for the ban on black ballplayers. By the time Smith had his meeting with Rickey in the spring of 1945, the *Courier-Journal* was recognized nationwide for its unrelenting campaign to end discrimination in organized baseball.[3]

While scholars have given much attention to the part played by Rickey and white sportscasters in ending discrimination in organized baseball, the role of Smith and the *Courier-Journal* in seeing that blacks

80

were allowed in the sport has heretofore been untold.[4] What is immediately apparent is that the black Pittsburgh paper was partly responsible for Rickey's decision to bring a black player into organized baseball. Although there were other black newspapers in the United State that participated in the campaign against lily-white baseball during the 1930s and the first half of the 1940s, it was the *Courier-Journal* that proved most effective in seeing that the game's racial barrier was finally lifted.[5] It had greater influence in helping break down the walls of discrimination partly because it had the largest circulation of all black newspapers in the country. When the paper initiated its campaign in 1933, its circulation figure approximated 46,000. By the time Robinson had signed his contract with the Dodgers some twelve years later, the *Courier-Journal's* circulation had risen to nearly 260,000—almost 100,000 more than its nearest competitor.[6] In addition to its large readership, the paper was particularly effective because it refused to relent in its call for complete equality in baseball and continued to remonstrate against discrimination in the game despite the efforts of friend and foe alike to restrain its protests. Even during those moments when integration seemed an impossibility, the paper maintained a lively interest in the plight of the black ballplayer and never stopped pressuring the baseball establishment. The *Courier-Journal* proved most effective in its campaign largely through the tireless efforts of Smith, who became obsessed with seeing that blacks were allowed in the game. Chester Washington, Alvin Moses, Rollo Wilson, and the other sports writers on the staff all took an active role in the campaign, but it was Smith who most doggedly fought for the inclusion of blacks in organized baseball.

The issue of allowing blacks in organized baseball did not become a popular topic of discussion in America's newspapers until the 1930s. One of the first attacks in the white press against the sports color line was made in 1931 by Westbrook Pegler of the *Chicago Tribune*.[7] Pegler wanted to know how baseball could possibly be considered the National Pastime when it was the one sport that excluded blacks from participating in it. He observed that great black athletes were allowed to compete in football, basketball, and track, yet were unjustly excluded from participating in baseball. While black collegiate athletes could compete and associate on an equal basis with white collegians, "professional ballplayers must be protected by a regulation which the magnates haven't the gall to put on paper."[8] Pegler was astonished that sports-minded Americans had not lashed out against the color line.

In 1933, Heywood Broun told the baseball writers at their annual dinner in New York that he saw no reason why blacks should not be allowed in the big leagues. Broun claimed that if Paul Robeson was good enough to win a place on the "mythical all-American" football team and

Eddie Tolan was allowed to represent the United States in the Olympic Games, then blacks were certainly capable of playing in the National and American Leagues. At the same dinner, Jimmy Powers, sportswriter of the *New York Daily News*, took a poll of some of the important baseball figures in attendance to determine their philosophical position on the issue. Of the six people polled by Powers, only John McGraw of the New York Giants openly objected to allowing blacks in the major leagues. Such notables as John Heydler, president of the National League; Colonel Jacob Ruppert, owner of the New York Yankees; and Gary Nugent, president of the Philadelphia Phillies all expressed a willingness to accept blacks in the big leagues.[9]

It was only after the stand taken by Broun and Powers at the baseball writers' dinner in New York that the *Courier-Journal* began its concerted drive to see that the color line was dropped in the National Game. It immediately began its campaign by conducting what it called the Big League Symposium.[10] The symposium, which was the brainchild of the paper's sports editor, Chester Washington, was set up to solicit the opinions of leading baseball men concerning the sport's exlusionary policies. The paper focused on appraising the various arguments given as to why blacks should or should not be allowed in organized baseball. Tellingly, most of the baseball executives who responded to the symposium denied that they had any objections to opening up organized baseball to black athletes, being reluctant even to admit that a color line existed in the game. John Heydler, the first respondent to the survey, had the audacity to say that baseball never excluded anyone on the basis of race, creed, or color. He noted that the only requirements for a major league player were great athletic ability and good character habits.[11] A similar comment was made by Gary Nugent, who claimed that baseball "catered to all races and creeds." Nugent had no objections to black players in the big leagues. The only question in his mind was whether black players had the ability to play in organized baseball.[12]

The four-month-long Big League Symposium run by the *Courier-Journal* was instructive in that it reminded the newspaper of organized baseball's racist policies. Allowing black athletes to participate in some white-controlled sports yet denying them the opportunity to take part in organized baseball was contemptible—one of the worst forms of discrimination. The situation that black ballplayers found themselves in was not irritating to the *Courier-Journal* merely because of the evasive position taken by baseball officials, but because it epitomized the dilemma that black athletes had to cope with during the first half of the twentieth century in America. Like their fellow citizens, black athletes wished to participate in American social life, but the injustices on the part of sport leaders in the United States reminded them of their dubious status and the fact that it was nearly impossible for them to be both a black and an American. Black athletes were no different from other black citizens in that they displayed an ethnic dualism, a continual longing to attain self-conscious manhood while freely taking part in American society.[13]

When the Big League Symposium ended in May 1933, the *Courier-Journal* was faced with the problem of what strategies it should employ to see that blacks were finally allowed in organized baseball. About the only option available to the newspaper at this point was to try to convince the baseball establishment that there were black athletes who possessed the physical abilities and "character habits" requisite to playing in the big leagues. Accordingly, the paper spent a great deal of time over the next five years praising the abilities of black players, comparing their talents with players in the big leagues, and recommending to baseball executives that they sign deserving black players. It was customary for the paper to send letters and telegrams to baseball's top brass, imploring them to hire black players, not only because it would improve the performances of their individual clubs, but because it would prove to be of benefit to them financially. Chester Washington, for instance, submitted what he called a "Roster of Stars" to Horace Stoneham, president of the New York Giants, in the fall of 1937. Washington told the Giant president that if he signed such black stars as Satchel Paige, Josh Gibson, Buck Leonard, and Cool Papa Bell, his club would be a more formidable opponent for the New York Yankees in next year's World Series. Washington added that all these players were available at very reasonable prices.[14]

The black Pittsburgh paper continued to send messages to baseball executives, knowing full well that these men were already very much aware of the outstanding skills of black players. The baseball establishment did not fail to notice the excellent performances of black ballplayers in the black leagues' annual East-West All-Star Game and the success these athletes experienced in a series of exhibition games against barnstorming major leaguers. The East-West Game, organized in 1933 by the Pittsburgh numbers king and tavern operator A. W. "Gus" Greenlee, was played each year at Chicago's Comiskey Park and brought together the greatest stars in black baseball.[15] This baseball classic was particularly important to the newspaper's campaign efforts because it was an event that showcased the talents of black athletes. In fact, a degree of optimism always ran through the pages of the newspaper at the time of the All-Star game because it was the one occasion when organized baseball took notice of those outstanding black players forced to perform in relative obscurity throughout most of the year.[16] Never attracting fewer than 20,000 fans, the East-West Game was always attended by a number of influential baseball executives and white newspapermen who regularly came away from the contests praising the abilities of black ballplayers. Not surprisingly, in Jim Crow America most of these men stopped short of suggesting that these black athletes had definite major league ability.

The outstanding performances turned in by black players in the East-West Classic served the *Courier-Journal*'s crusade very well, but not nearly as well as the victories garnered by black clubs in exhibition games against selected groups of major leaguers.[17] To lend more credence to its argument that many black players were comparable in ability to their counterparts in organized baseball, the newspaper was quick to point out the successes that black clubs experienced in games against barnstorming big leaguers. Examples of those games would include the victory garnered by the Kansas City Monarchs over Dizzy Dean and a group of major leaguers on October 20, 1934, or the win posted by Satchel Paige and the Pittsburgh Crawfords over the same contingent of players just one week later.[18] These exhibition games always brought forth a plethora of favorable comments from big leaguers concerning the abilities of black ballplayers. The person who was most vocal in his praise of black players and on more than one occasion advocated the inclusion of these athletes in organized baseball was Dizzy Dean. He told the *Courier-Journal* in 1935, for instance, that if the "big leaguers believed that they were better than the best Negro players they had another thought coming" and that he would like to organize an "All Star Sepia Club to go barnstorming and show the Nordics something."[19]

By the beginning of 1938, the *Courier-Journal* had stopped merely trying to persuade organized baseball of the big league potential of black players and began to advocate more radical procedures for ending discrimination in the National Game. The person most responsible for the shift in tactics was Wendell Smith, whom the newspaper had recently hired as a sports reporter. Born in Detroit, Michigan, on June 27, 1914, Smith had been a competitive athlete at both the high school and college levels. He participated in basketball and baseball at a local high school in Detroit and after graduation enrolled at West Virginia State College, where he was elected team captain in both sports. He received a bachelor's degree in education from that institution in 1937. The interest that Smith took in the campaign may have stemmed from the way he was treated as a young athlete. He reportedly experienced his first bitter taste of discrimination in sports at the age of sixteen, when he was unfairly dropped from an American Legion baseball team. Legend has it that Smith was finally restored to the team by his father's famous employer, Henry Ford. Later Smith experienced, like other athletes of his color, segregated living accommodations while on road trips. These incidents left an identifiable mark on him.

Disenchanted with what he considered the *Courier-Journal*'s rather conservative position on the baseball issue, Smith immediately began to lash out at the National Game for its racial policies.[20] In his column self-styled "Smitty's Sport Spurts," his first article on the baseball issue appeared in the paper's May 14, 1938, edition. Here Smith indicted black Americans for their continual economic support of major league baseball. He was sickened by the fact that blacks continued to flock to big league parks, spending their hard-earned money and applauding the exploits of white ballplayers. Organized baseball had made it perfectly clear that it did not want black ballplayers, yet black Americans persisted in upholding the "institution that places a bold 'not welcome' sign over its thriving portal." Maybe most disconcerting to Smith was the fact that black Americans were not patronizing their own ballparks, seemingly not caring if the black leagues survived or not. In spite of the outstanding teams and brilliant players in black baseball, most black Americans, he said, offered them no encouragement or, worse yet, completely ignored their efforts. "Oh, we're an optimistic faithful, prideless lot," concluded Smith, "we pitiful Black folk."[21]

Smith did not mean that black Americans should be content with their segregated leagues, nor that they should give up their struggle to see blacks allowed in the National Game. On the contrary, no one was more adamant than Smith in insisting that the color line be dropped from organized baseball. But along with the demand for equal opportunities in baseball, Smith was also calling for self-improvement, racial pride, and group unity among black Americans—appeals that he believed were appropriate complements to the campaign effort. Smith believed that blacks must do more than simply protest against segregation in organized baseball; they must also assume responsibility for seeing that black baseball was a thriving and healthful institution. Smith noted that American custom and tradition had forced blacks into segregated leagues, and while the *Courier-Journal*'s campaign had rightfully been directed toward breaking down this enforced segregation, he was convinced that segregation and discrimination would continue in organized baseball for the foreseeable future. Consequently, while Smith believed that the *Courier-Journal* should not flinch in its fight against discrimination in baseball, he insisted that the newspaper also encourage racial self-help and self-organization to insure that black baseball supplied what black athletes lacked because of segregation. Only such action would rekindle race pride, and without pride it would be impossible for blacks to have the unity and the foundation necessary for a successful long-range attack against discrimination in the National Game. In other words, Smith believed that black Americans had to identify positively with their own race before it would be possible for them to stage any effective campaign effort. The continual emulation of major league baseball by blacks was

A bespectacled and smiling Wendell Smith was dogged in his campaign to include African Americans in major league baseball. Reprinted by permission of GRM Associates, Inc., agents for The Pittsburgh Courier. *From the issue of June 2, 1965. Copyright © 1965 by* The Pittsburgh Courier; *copyright renewed 1993 by* The New Pittsburgh Courier.

effected only at the cost of frustration and disillusionment, which tended to undermine the self-reliance and confidence that Smith considered essential for ultimate integration of the sport.[22]

As part of his program of unity, Smith was proposing by the beginning of 1939 that black Americans organize a National Association for the Advancement of Colored People (NAACP) on behalf of the black ballplayer and attack the color line "until we drop from exhaustion."[23] Smith noted that blacks had been unable to make any progress as individuals; but, by being united into one large group, they could put more pressure on organized baseball to open its doors to black athletes. He believed the time had come when the black community in America should join forces and make a concerted stand on behalf of black ballplayers.

Like many other thoughtful blacks of this period, Smith was also beginning to prick the conscience of white America by pointing out the similarities between its treatment of blacks and Nazi Germany's treatment of minorities.[24] Smith took advantage of the unrest in Europe to tie his racial demands to the ideology for which World War II would be fought. He believed that this was the ideal time to persuade, embarrass, and shame the leaders of the great American Pastime into a more enlightened attitude towards the black athlete. Smith noted that baseball had always been flaunted before the world as a symbol of America's democratic process and belief in fair play. So, what better time to fight for the inclusion of blacks in organized baseball than while America was busily crying out against inhumane practices in other countries and shouting about freedom and democratic ideals? If black Americans must, wrote Smith, they should show the rest of the world that, compared with the demagogues of organized baseball, Hitler was not really so bad after all. The only difference was that his methods were a bit cruder.[25]

Shortly after announcing his plans for a NAACP on behalf of the black athlete, Smith conducted an exclusive interview with the president of the National League, Ford Frick. The interview with Frick, the first of many that Smith would conduct with the most influential men in organized baseball, was characterized by the kind of racist policies that black Americans were only too used to. Frick told Smith that organized baseball had always been interested in black athletes but had not used them because white Americans had not been educated to the point where they would accept them on the same standard as they did the white player. Frick said that major league baseball was like a newspaper in that it could not make changes until public opinion was ready for it. As an example, Frick noted that blacks would not be able to travel with a club during spring training or while playing in certain major league cities because southern hotels and other public places would not accommodate them. This situation would raise havoc within a ball club, Frick pointed out, because the only way a manager could develop team spirit was to keep his men together as much as possible.[26]

Frick's statements provoked Smith into conducting a succession of interviews with eight managers and forty players in the National League to determine their position on the race issue. These interviews culminated in a series of articles in the *Courier-Journal* between July 15, 1939, and September 2, 1939, entitled "What Big Leaguers Think of Negro Baseball Players."[27] This was the most ambitious project yet undertaken by Smith, and the interviews were illuminating. Of all the men that Smith talked to, only Bill Terry, manager of the New York Giants, expressed the belief that blacks should continue to be barred from organized baseball. All other managers told Smith that they would use black athletes if club owners and league officials permitted it, and all the players interviewed expressed the hope that they could someday play alongside a black ballplayer. For example, Leo Durocher, manager of the Brooklyn Dodgers, told Smith that he would sign a black player without hesitation if he thought it would help his ball club. "However," said Durocher, "the decision as to whether or not they shall play is not up to the managers but the ball club owners."[28]

The interviews conducted by Smith did not bring about any visible reaction from organized baseball's top executives but did occasion a lengthy discussion among thoughtful black Americans over the eventual plight of black baseball. The favorable comments from major league coaches and players elicited some veiled concerns among black Americans that they had not heretofore expressed publicly. Would the entrance of black players in organized baseball automatically spell doom for the Black American and National Leagues? If the black leagues were not eliminated, would they then simply be used as training grounds for black players before their entry into organized baseball? Like Smith himself, many people in the black community believed it was their duty to protest organized baseball's racial policies. But in addition to protest, many of these same people expressed the belief that even if the color barrier were dropped in major league baseball, it was still feasible and advisable that black Americans maintain the black leagues to promote their own interest in the sport. Many black Americans believed that it was absolutely necessary to maintain the quality of the black leagues so that they could testify to black talent and enterprise. Even if the outstanding black athletes were signed to major league contracts, it was still the responsibility of black Americans to ensure that their leagues were of sufficient quality so as to continue to supply employment for the largest number of black players. Whereas Smith advocated self-help and racial unity primarily as a means to break down discrimination in the National Game and to guarantee for blacks those opportunities they lacked because of segregation, many black Americans seemed just as concerned with maintaining a certain degree of self-organization after the color line was broken. In no case did black Americans, even those who were staunch supporters of integration in organized baseball, ever forget their connection with an oppressed people. Because of the enormous gap between ideal and practice in organized baseball, most blacks, while wanting to be a part of that institution, found it desirable to preserve their separate leagues, which operated with very little white inference.[29]

Smith responded to these concerns by pointing out that he was no different from most black Americans in wanting to maintain separate leagues once the color line had been broken in the major leagues. But he could not guarantee that black baseball would continue to survive once organized baseball had been integrated. In truth, Smith was so involved with the campaign for integration that the future status of the black leagues was not foremost in his mind at this time. In an apparent attempt, however, to reassure fearful black Americans, Smith predicted that the desegregation of the major leagues would prove to be beneficial to black baseball in every way. Smith noted, for example, that organized baseball would have to compensate black baseball in some way for the players they signed from those leagues. As a result, wrote Smith, organized baseball would "add money to the pocket of the Negro owners, thereby enabling him to improve his ball club and build for the future."[30] In retrospect, Smith was rather naïve and overly optimistic in forecasting what the future might hold for the black leagues once organized baseball had been integrated. The entrance of blacks into the major leagues, of course, would eventually result in the demise of the always financially unstable black leagues.

While Smith was at work conducting interviews and discussing the prospects of black baseball, the *Courier-Journal* busily reported the criticism increasingly levied against organized baseball's racial policies by socially conscious white Americans. During the late 1930s there was a ground swell of protest in the white community over baseball's color line, and the newspaper was anxious not only to make its readers aware of the protests but also to commend white citizens for their courageous stand. The paper reported in 1938, for instance, that the American Youth Congress had passed a resolution censuring organized baseball for their exclusion of black players.[31] In 1939, the *Courier-Journal* praised Senator Charles Perry of New York City for the resolution he introduced in the New York State Legislature expressing disapproval of major league baseball's racial policies.[32] In the same year the paper lauded Jimmy Powers for the campaign he had been waging in the *New York Daily News* against racial discrimination in the National Game. The newspaper reported that Powers had recommended in his *Daily News* column that, instead of worrying about minorities in foreign lands, some attention should be given to the black ballplayer in America.[33] In 1940 the paper noted that a group of sports editors from various college newspapers in New York had passed a resolution condemning discrimination against black players by major league baseball.[34] It was also in 1940 that the New York Trade Union Athletic Association launched its crusade to end discrimination against black athletes by organized baseball. Inspired by Smith's interviews with major league coaches and players, the Association planned an "ending of Jim Crowism in baseball day" during the summer of 1940.[35]

The public pressure beginning to mount against organized baseball's exclusionary policies was part of the identifiable progress in interracial understanding and growing respect for nonwhite citizens in America during the end of the 1930s. There was a marked change in the attitudes of some whites towards black Americans by the close of the decade, a change that blacks often credited to the New Deal. In interracial activities, conferences were regularly being held on a variety of subjects, and though self-consciously interracial, such conferences continued to burgeon. Adults and college students met to discuss economic matters, religion, education, and, of course, civil rights. It was still a rarity; but the simple fact that a white North Carolina legislator would question a decreased allotment for a black college or a white supervisor of schools in Georgia would acknowledge the inequalities of segregated schools indicated change. The all-white Mississippi Education Association organized a committee in 1938 to suggest ways in which students might study black life, and various northern newspapers in 1940 editorially conceded the importance of Black History Week.[36]

Although the *Courier-Journal*'s campaign was affected by the liberalized racial attitudes of white Americans during the late 1930s, it took America's entrance into World War II to bring about a marked change in the newspaper's crusade to open up organized baseball to black athletes. The newspaper's efforts were stimulated by the fundamental changes that were taking place among black Americans by the time of the Pearl Harbor attack. Black Americans were part of the population called to the defense of democracy in the world; but, when they responded and tried to do their share, they were turned away. The result was a general feeling of disappointment and a lessening of the blacks' enthusiasm for the war effort, as contrasted with the rest of American society. But paradoxically, the black American's morale was both high and low. The same slogans that caused blacks to react sarcastically also served to accentuate the disparity between the tenets and the practice of democracy as far as black Americans were concerned. Because of their inferior position in society, blacks responded to the war as both Americans and blacks. Discrimination against them had given rise to a cynical attitude toward national goals but simultaneously resulted in a positive attitude toward racial aims and aspirations. Black Americans, stimulated by the democratic ideology of the war, were reexamining their position in American society and exhibiting a spirit they had never shown before. Part of the newfound spirit among blacks expressed itself in increased militancy and a readiness to protest loudly and unremittingly against grievances.[37]

The war crisis, therefore, gave the *Courier-Journal* more reason and opportunity to protest racial discrimination in the National Game than at any time during the previous eight years. The hypocrisy and absurdity involved in fighting a war for the Four Freedoms against a country that proclaimed a master race ideology, while concurrently upholding racial discrimination in organized baseball, were too obvious. The war provided the newspaper with a unique opportunity to expose the gap between America's creed and its practice. The democratic ideology and rhetoric with which the war was waged kindled hope in the *Courier-Journal*'s campaign because the newspaper could fasten its racial demands to the same ideology in its efforts to see that the National Game was finally integrated. The newspaper could utilize the present crisis to illustrate that the game of baseball was not the great leveler and was not a sport within the reach of all men. As Smith so aptly put it: "big league baseball is perpetuating the very things thousands of Americans are overseas fighting to end, namely, racial discrimination and segregation."[38]

That the *Courier-Journal*'s campaign effort was gaining momentum by the time America entered the war is evidenced by the increasing amount of attention being paid to the baseball controversy by the newspaper's sportswriters other than Smith. Cumberland Posey, Alvin Moses, and Chester Washington, in particular, were stepping up their coverage of the baseball issue by the first part of 1942, in spite of the responsibilities they had in covering other sporting events. These writers were veterans in the newspapers' crusade to reform organized baseball, but now they protested the sport's racial policies as never before and assisted Smith with their own renewed vigor. Washington, for instance, wrote a letter to Commissioner Kenesaw Mountain Landis in May 1942, telling him that major league baseball would be wise to follow the lead of the Navy and treat blacks with more dignity. "The Navy was big enough," wrote Washington, "to catch the spirit of the times and realize the trend toward democracy in all of the American institutions. So it dropped some of the bars of segregation as Secretary Knox announced a change in racial policy. Organized baseball would do well if it sensed the swing toward liberalism and allowed qualified Blacks to participate in the game."[39]

The contributions made by Washington and the other sportswriters on the *Courier-Journal*'s staff notwithstanding, it was Smith who continued to set the tone of the campaign and most vigorously opposed discrimination in the National Game. In August 1942, an apparent turning point in the campaign occurred when Smith was asked by William E. Benswanger, president of the Pittsburgh Pirates, to recommend four black players for a tryout with his National League team.[40] Benswanger, who was being pressured by the American Communist Party's *Daily Worker* to give black players an opportunity with his club, consented to hold a tryout in the early part of September, but only for those athletes picked by the *Courier-Journal*.[41] Smith combed a list of approximately two hundred black players and finally selected Josh Gibson, Willie Wells, Sam Bankhead, and Leon Day for the tryout with the Pirates. Smith was absolutely ecstatic about the proposed tryout and lavish in his praise of Benswanger, calling the Pirate president the greatest liberal in baseball history. In his willingness to give black players a tryout, Benswanger was risking "the wrath of his associates for an ideal which has been contrary to the general pattern of the exclusive sport in which he operates."[42]

Smith need not have been so complimentary about Benswanger, because the Pirate president reversed his decision and never did grant the tryout to the black players. Looking back, it is safe to say that Benswanger probably never had any intention of upholding his commitment but merely expressed a willingness to conduct the tryouts in an attempt to placate the *Daily Worker,* which had been pressuring him to sign black players. Benswanger was not cut out for the role of pioneer and, like many other white Americans, was generally opposed to any changes in racial policies.[43]

The steps taken by Smith and the *Courier-Journal* to see that blacks were included in organized baseball were frustrated by the general attitude being exhibited by a large majority of white Americans during this period. The increasingly liberalized attitude of some white Americans during the latter 1930s was still not shared by a large portion of the population in this country. In 1942, after almost ten years of agitation by the newspaper, six out of ten white Americans, according to one poll, felt that black Americans were satisfied with the way things were and received all the opportunities they deserved. A vast majority of whites in all sections of the country believed that the black Americans' restricted role in society was the result of their own inadequacies rather than anything whites had done. More than half of all whites interviewed in the western part of the country believed that there should be separate restaurants, separate schools, and separate neighborhoods for the races.[44] The sociologist Howard W. Odum wrote from the South that there was "an unmeasurable and unbridgeable distance between the White South and the reasonable expectation of the Negro."[45] White southerners were accusing outsiders from the North of attempting to undermine segregation under the claim of wartime necessity.

The white opposition to racial change added to the bitterness of black Americans and resulted in increased racial tensions in all sections of the country. Communist agitators sought to take advantage of the growing racial unrest and participated in various schemes in an attempt to widen the division between the races. The mounting racial tensions reached crisis level in 1943, with riots in Detroit, Harlem, and Beaumont, Texas. The Harlem riots were so severe that Mayor La Guardia declared that section of the city off limits to servicemen. The New York City mayor also organized a committee on unity, designed to keep racial tension in check and thwart potential violence.[46]

It was in this atmosphere that Smith continued his fight in 1943 against racial discrimination in organized baseball. Left with few available options, Smith asked that the federal government set an example for baseball's top brass by supporting integration in the game. Like most black Americans, Smith wanted a show of good intention from the federal government that changes would be made in the racial status quo.[47]

He was particularly adamant in calling upon President Roosevelt to adopt a "Fair Employment Practice Policy" in big league baseball just as he had done in war industries and governmental agencies. It was disconcerting to Smith that Roosevelt had never seen fit to issue a statement regarding the exclusion of blacks from major league baseball. The president had been conspicuously inconsistent in telling certain segments of society that they must hire without discrimination and at the same time giving "such a discriminating organization as big league baseball a nod of approval."[48] Contributing to Smith's unhappiness was Roosevelt's temerity in speaking on several occasions about the importance of maintaining the quality of organized baseball throughout the duration of the war. Smith noted that if the president were really concerned about sustaining the caliber of play in organized baseball, he should make sure that blacks were allowed in the game.

Not unexpectedly, the president failed to respond to Smith's request for governmental assistance in the *Courier-Journal*'s campaign effort. Roosevelt's refusal to intercede on behalf of the black ballplayer was part of the president's reluctance to recognize the revolutionary changes occurring among black Americans during the war years. Smith could at least take bitter solace in knowing that Roosevelt's lack of enthusiasm for reform in race relations was not restricted to baseball. For instance, Edwin R. Embree of the Julius Rosenwald Fund urged Roosevelt in February 1942 to establish a commission of experts on race relations to advise him on what steps the government should take to facilitate reform. Roosevelt's response indicated that race relations was an item low on his list of priorities during the war years. The president believed that such a commission was "premature" and that "we must start winning the war . . . before we do much general planning for the future." Roosevelt did arouse himself over outrageous racial incidents. When Roland Jones, a well-known black singer, was beaten and jailed in a small Georgia town, Roosevelt sent off a note to his attorney general: "Will you have someone go down and check up . . . and see if any law was violated. I suggest you send a Northerner."[49]

The disappointment that Smith felt over the president's inaction did not deter him from continuing the crusade on behalf of the black ballplayer. If anything, he was more obstinate and determined than ever. Thwarted in his efforts to get Roosevelt involved in the campaign, Smith spent a good portion of 1943 admonishing Clark Griffith, owner of the Washington Senators, for his blatantly racist view of black ballplayers.[50] Griffith was the one owner in major league baseball who chose to speak out against the black athlete. While most big league owners did not express their anti-integrationist views in public, Griffith was not the least bit hesitant in letting people know that he did not favor black participation in organized baseball. On one occasion, Griffith expressed his belief that blacks should devote all their time and effort to developing their own leagues.[51] Griffith emphasized that black baseball should be a separate entity, unencumbered by any relationship with white organized baseball. Smith realized, as did other black Americans, that Griffith's stance on black baseball was guided more by financial concerns than by altruistic considerations. Like other big league owners, Griffith would do whatever was necessary to perpetuate the existing black leagues because he made a good deal of money renting his ball park to the Homestead Grays.

Smith naturally abhorred Griffith's view and wrote that the philosophical position taken by the owner of the Washington Senators was in direct opposition to everything that black Americans had been fighting for. The real source of Smith's anger, however, was not Griffith's stance on black baseball but his willingness to sign players of every racial and ethnic group other than black Americans for his ball club. Smith and his fellow *Courier-Journal* sportswriters were particularly disturbed over the big league owners' outlandish hiring practices during the war years. For obvious reasons, organized baseball was in desperate need of players during World War II; but major league owners still refused to sign quality black players, who were more than willing to fill the void. Instead of soliciting the services of outstanding black athletes, big league owners would travel all over the world searching for and signing foreign-born players for their ball clubs. Griffith was the most aggressive in this endeavor. "Griffith is one of the big league owners," Smith noted, "who prefers to go outside the borders of these United States and bring in players, rather than hire American citizens of color. He has so many foreigners on his team it is necessary to have an interpreter, and if you ever hear this conglomeration of personalities talking to each other in the airport, you'd swear you were sojourning in Madrid, Lisbon, or Havana."[52]

Smith spent much of 1943 not only criticizing Griffith but also in trying to get the leaders of black baseball to make an official statement as to how they felt about the possibilities of blacks in the major leagues. He believed it was imperative that the two leagues in black baseball "go on record" with respect to black players in the big leagues. Black baseball was one group, wrote Smith, that was particularly affected by the campaign, and it seemed only natural that they should voice their opinion on the subject.[53] Much to Smith's chagrin, no official statement on the campaign was made by the leaders in black baseball until the year had almost come to a close. That the owners remained virtually silent on the issue throughout most of 1943 was interpreted by Smith to mean that they were opposed to the campaign effort. Smith had theorized for a number of years that the owners in black baseball looked upon the fight from a "selfish, ungrateful angle," and would undermine the newspaper's crusade if given the opportunity.[54] The seeming reluctance on the part of the owners to make an announcement simply reconfirmed Smith's suspicions and caused him to brand the owners as traitors.

The first person from black baseball to speak out on the campaign was J. B. Martin, president of the Black American League, who did not voice the opinion of the owners in his league until late 1943. Martin noted that the owners in his league were no different from Smith and other black Americans in wanting to see black athletes have the opportunity to participate in organized baseball. He wanted it clearly understood that his league was not opposed to any campaign that would advance black players into the major leagues. Martin went on to add, however, that black baseball could not be expected to rectify the exclusion of black players from major league baseball. The leaders in black baseball, said Martin, could not "force big league owners to admit Negro players, nor would they assume that responsibility."[55]

To Martin and other leaders in black baseball, it was simply bad business to lend their support because they understood that they had a great deal to lose and nothing to gain from the campaign effort. In fact, the owners were farsighted enough to realize that the entrance of blacks into organized baseball meant, in all likelihood, the eventual dissolution of the black leagues. The owners did not share Smith's belief that black baseball would continue to survive once the color line was broken. The magnates in organized baseball would simply entice the outstanding black players to join their clubs, which would mean the beginning of the end for black baseball. This possibility was particularly disconcerting to the owners at this time because black baseball, after years of struggling financially, was finally enjoying a period of relative stability.[56] It was only during the war years that black baseball reached its peak in player salaries, attendance, and number of scheduled games. To support the campaign during lean years would have been difficult enough for the leaders in black baseball. But now, with the league functioning on a more solid foundation, it was nearly impossible for the owners to throw their support behind the movement. Even if the owners wished to see blacks become successful in organized baseball—and some of them undoubtedly did—it was not enough to rationalize the support of a campaign that could result in the ultimate demise of a league they had worked so hard to make successful.

Frustrated in his attempts to get an official statement from the owners in black baseball, Smith's next move in the campaign effort was to contact the commissioner of organized baseball, Judge Kenesaw Mountain Landis, and ask him to meet with the Black Newspaper Publishers Association in December 1943 at the winter baseball meetings.[57] Smith desperately wanted this confrontation because it would give an influential group of black Americans a perfect opportunity to plead their case on behalf of black ballplayers in front of Landis and the major league owners. Fortunately, Landis agreed to meet with Smith and the other members of the delegation, which included seven Black newspapermen plus the famous black singer and activist Paul Robeson. This was a significant meeting, first of all, in that it was the first time that black representatives were given the opportunity to come face to face with the leaders in organized baseball and argue for the inclusion of blacks in the National Game. The meeting was also important because it gave Landis the perfect occasion to tell America that he was not responsible for the discrimination against black ballplayers. Often targeted as the man most accountable for the color line in organized baseball, Landis sought to refute those claims.

Landis began the meeting by emphasizing that he wanted it "clearly understood that there is no rule, nor to my knowledge, has there ever been, formal or informal, or any understanding, written or unwritten, subterranean or subanything, against the hiring of Negroes in the major leagues." With that behind him, Landis then introduced Robeson to the club owners. "I brought Paul here," Landis explained, "because you all know him. You all know that he is a great man in public life, a great American." Robeson, an All-American football player and Phi Beta Kappa student at Rutgers University, was the first of four delegates to address the club owners on the issue of black ballplayers. He told the owners that he came to the meeting "as an American and former athlete." He said that it was time for organized baseball to change its racial policies and "beseeched the owners to hire Negro players." After Robeson had completed his speech, Landis introduced John Sengastacke to the club owners. Sengastacke, president of the Black Newspaper Publishers Association and manager of the *Chicago Defender*, said that the ban against blacks in organized baseball was "neither wise nor practical." He stressed the "un-American, undemocratic implications which the gentlemen's agreement imposed upon the face of this country."[58]

Ira Lewis, president of the *Courier-Journal*, followed Sengastacke to the podium and proceeded to refute each argument that organized baseball was accustomed to using when defending its decision not to allow blacks in the National Game. Lewis began by stating that it was simply untrue that major league players would refuse to play against black athletes. The interviews that Wendell Smith had conducted for the *Courier-Journal* made it clear that most big league managers and players were not opposed to having black players in organized baseball. Lewis noted that, in addition to managers and players, the American public was also ready to accept blacks in the National Game. As an example,

Lewis observed that Americans, both black and white, had approved of black participation in college track and professional boxing. Concerning the playing abilities of black ballplayers, Lewis pointed to the number of victories garnered by black teams against barnstorming major leaguers. On the question of travel accommodations, Lewis told the club owners that black stage performers with white casts managed to handle the perplexing problem without any difficulty and saw no reason why black ballplayers could not do the same. Finally, on the question of holding spring training in the South, Lewis suggested that training sites be moved from that part of the country to Cuba and other areas of Latin America where excellent facilities were available.[59]

After demolishing each argument, Lewis then created considerable tension in the meeting by pointing out that Commissioner Landis's opening statement was not completely true and that there was, indeed, an unwritten law against black athletes in organized baseball. At that point, the energetic Landis, visibly upset by Lewis's remarks, jumped to his feet and angrily reiterated his opening statement. When Landis had finished, Lewis bowed diplomatically in recognition of the commissioner's position and with a sly smile on his face, said: "But Judge Landis, we believe that there is a tacit understanding, there is a gentlemen's agreement that no Negro players be hired." Lewis's comments obviously impressed the club owners. He was the one black delegate who had the courage to make such a bold statement; for the first time since the meetings began, the room was filled with total silence. Lewis continued his speech by telling the club owners that like all blacks he "felt the bitter pangs of sorrow and disappointment over the unfair and unjust attitude of organized baseball toward Americans of color." He implored the owners to do away with the gentlemen's agreement and allow the national pastime to "become a game for all the boys in America."[60]

The last member of the delegation to speak on behalf of black ballplayers was Howard H. Murphy, business manager of the *Baltimore Afro-American*. Murphy summed up the comments that had previously been made and then read four recommendations that the black publishers wanted acted upon by the club owners: that immediate steps be taken to accept black players "into the framework" of organized baseball; that the "process for promotion and elevation" in baseball be applied without prejudice; that the same system of selection of players be used; and that a "joint statement be made by the two leagues."[61]

When the publishers completed their appeals, Landis asked if any of the forty-four officials in attendance from organized baseball had any questions or comments they would like to make concerning the issue of black ballplayers. Tellingly, not one of the officials from organized baseball asked any questions of the publishers. It was not until the meetings were over and they had the chance to meet privately that the owners issued this oft-repeated statement: "Each club is entirely free to employ Negro players to any and all extent it pleases. The matter is solely for each club's decision, without restriction whatsoever."[62]

Smith and the other members of the delegation were grateful to have had the chance to air their grievances in front of baseball's highest officials and were confident they had made a good showing. They realized, however, that the official statement issued by the baseball magnates was mere rhetoric and a public relations gimmick. Landis and the owners could talk all they wanted about each team being free to employ black players, but none of the big league clubs had any intention of signing these athletes.

The statements by Landis were particularly irritating to members of the *Courier-Journal* staff who for years had pinpointed him as the man most responsible for the color line in organized baseball. Shortly after becoming commissioner in 1921, Landis prevented players form wearing major league uniforms in exhibition games against black clubs.[63] He apparently hoped that this move would keep people from finding out that barnstorming major leaguers were losing to black clubs. In 1938 the two managing editors of the *Courier-Journal*, Robert L. Vann and William G. Nunn, met with Landis to ask him about the exclusion of blacks from the National Game.[64] In customary fashion, Landis said the time was not right for blacks in baseball and that black fans could boycott major league games if they wanted. That same year Wendell Smith began to taunt Landis for his refusal to take a stand on the issue and force club owners in organized baseball to sign qualified black players.[65] On the occasion of Landis's death in the latter part of 1944, nearly a year after he had met with members of the Black Newspaper Publishers Association, Smith wrote an article in the *Courier-Journal* that summed up the feelings of most black Americans toward the late commissioner. Smith noted that Landis had always held himself up as a symbol of honesty and courage before the entire sports world. The commissioner was against anything that might reflect negatively on the National Game. But the fact remained, wrote Smith, that Landis never used the powers of his office to do anything about the discrimination against Black athletes. The question of blacks in organized baseball was an issue that he preferred to let ride. It was the one problem that Landis "never faced with the courage and exactness that he faced others" in his nearly twenty-five years as baseball's top executive.[66]

It was not until nearly a year and a half after the Black Newspaper Publishers Association had presented its case at the 1943 winter baseball meetings that there was any indication that club owners might be willing to give blacks an opportunity to play in the major leagues. In April 1945,

Joe Bostic, sportswriter of the *People's Voice*, a New York-based black newspaper, and Jimmy Smith, sportswriter of the *Courier-Journal*'s New York edition, were able to arrange a tryout for two black ballplayers with the Brooklyn Dodgers. This now well-known tryout took the Dodger officials completely by surprise. Bostic and Smith had decided the time was right to demand a tryout and simply showed up at the National League club's spring training camp at Bear Mountain, New York, on a Friday morning with Terry McDuffie, a pitcher with the Newark Eagles and Dave ("Showboat") Thomas, first baseman of the New York Cubans. Bostic, acting as a spokesman for the group, asked that the two black players be given a tryout immediately. Robert Finch, an assistant on the Dodgers' staff, told Bostic that the day's training schedule had already been planned and that the team gave tryouts only to those players invited to camp. Bostic responded to Finch by asking him if the group could speak with the Dodgers' president, Branch Rickey, about the matter. Finch consented to the request and arranged for a meeting.[67]

The meeting with Rickey proved to be a success, the Dodgers' president agreeing to give the two black players a tryout with the club the following day. Rickey was not pleased, however, with the way Bostic and Smith had handled the situation. He resented the fact that the two men had pressured him into giving the black players a tryout. Believing that he and the Brooklyn Dodgers had been put in a very embarrassing situation, Rickey reprimanded both Bostic and Smith for not writing to him ahead of time and asking for the tryout.[68]

As it turned out, Rickey did not have to make a difficult decision because it became obvious to almost everyone during the tryout that McDuffie and Thomas were simply not major league material. Both of the men were in their late thirties, and their best years in baseball were behind them. These two players were probably the only ones that Bostic and Smith could get who were willing to go along with the plans. On completion of the tryouts, Wendell Smith wrote in the *Courier-Journal* that Rickey's decision not to sign the two black players to a contract with the Dodgers was probably the right one. But he told the newspaper's readers that this would not be the last time a major league club owner would be confronted with black candidates. In the near future, Rickey and his colleagues would have to make a decision on younger black players "who will have better records and greater possibilities."[69]

Smith's prediction was a correct one. On April 16, 1945, just one day after the Bear Mountain tryout, three other black players were given a tryout by the Boston Red Sox at Fenway Park.[70] This tryout came about through the efforts of Smith and Isadore Muchnick, a white city councilman from Boston. Muchnick, who represented a largely black neighborhood, had repeatedly asked the officials from both the Red Sox and the Braves to give black players a tryout. Unable to get any response, Muchnick threatened to support the recurring movement by religious groups to ban Sunday baseball in Boston unless the two clubs consented to giving tryouts to black ballplayers. Smith, recognizing the sincerity of the threat, contacted Muchnick and told him that he could provide black players of major league quality if the Boston city councilman really wanted to exert more pressure on the two clubs. Muchnick told Smith that he did and asked the *Courier-Journal* sports editor to bring the best black players he could find to Boston.

Less than a week later, Smith arrived in Boston with three players he believed were the ideal candidates for such a tryout: Sam Jethroe, an outfielder for the Cleveland Buckeyes; Marvin Williams, an infielder for the Philadelphia Stars; and Jackie Robinson, infielder for the Kansas City Monarchs. The reception that Smith and the three players received when they got to Boston was not very cordial. Expecting to be in Boston just one day, the players were put off for nearly a week and a half before the Red Sox management finally agreed to give them a tryout on April 16.[71] The delay in the tryout did not visibly affect the players, who generally performed magnificently in the hour and a half tryout. "Nobody put on an exhibition like we did," Robinson later recalled. "Everything we did, it seemed like the good Lord was guiding us." The Red Sox manager Joe Cronin and his coach Hugh Duffy admitted that the three players had looked awfully good during the brief tryout.[72]

When the tryout ended, the three players were asked to fill out application blanks and told that the Red Sox would contact them sometime in the near future. Unfortunately, nothing happened. The three players returned to their respective ball clubs and fruitlessly waited for some response from Red Sox officials. Smith was naturally disappointed that the Red Sox did not see fit to sign any of the three players. In contrast to the black players trying out for the Dodgers at Bear Mountain, the three players in Boston, particularly Robinson, were relatively young and possessed definite big league potential. The only excuse the Red Sox management could give was that the tryout was too brief to determine the playing abilities of the black athletes. Robinson, Jethroe, and Williams would have to be tested under game conditions before any decision could be made.[73]

Contributing to Smith's sense of frustration was the fact that the Boston tryout did not get the kind of national publicity he had hoped for. Unfortunately, Smith's old nemesis, President Roosevelt, died just one day after the Boston tryout and American newspapers were filled with details of his passing rather than the results of the tryout. This lack of national exposure combined with the refusal of the Red Sox to sign any of the black players, only tended to fuel the resentment of an already angry Smith. Five black players had had tryouts with major league clubs in two days, and not one of them had been signed to a contract. It was a humiliating experience that Smith would not easily forget.[74]

On the day after the Boston tryout, Smith traveled to Brooklyn to attend the press conference Branch Rickey had called to announce plans for his newly formed United States League. The new league consisted of six black baseball teams, one of which was Rickey's own Brooklyn Brown Dodgers. Ostensibly set up to be a "legitimate and valuable alternative for Negro players," the new league was actually organized by Rickey to conceal the fact that he was scouting black players for the Brooklyn Dodgers. Under the pretext of seeking players for his new club in the United States League, Rickey could now seek out black athletes for the Brooklyn Dodgers without fear of retribution from the enemies of integrated baseball.[75]

The black writers in attendance at the press conference were livid about Rickey's refusal to respond to questions about black players in the major leagues. Not knowing of Rickey's real intentions, the black press accused the Dodgers' boss of trying to uphold segregation while at the same time exploiting black players. They could see no difference between the black leagues and Rickey's proposed United States League. Ingeniously, Rickey answered his detractors by saying that his new league would be better organized and financially more stable than the black leagues. The ultimate objective, said Rickey, was to have the newly formed league absorbed into organized baseball.

Smith tended to be just as skeptical about Rickey's new league as the other members of the black press. Considering the frustrating events of the last few days, Smith found it particularly difficult to accept the United States League as a genuine project, and he told Rickey so at the press conference. It was during this meeting, however, that Rickey pulled Smith aside and asked the *Courier-Journal* sports editor if he knew of any black athletes capable of playing in the major leagues. Recognizing the role Smith had played in the recent Boston tryout and the campaign he had been waging for a number of years, Rickey evidently believed that this was the man most knowledgeable about the talents of black ballplayers. Smith responded to the question by telling the Brooklyn Dodgers' boss: "If you aren't serious about this, Mr. Rickey, I'd rather not waste our time discussing it, but if you are serious, I do know of a player who could make it. His name is Jackie Robinson." At that point, Rickey sat back in his chair and said: "Jackie Robinson, you say. It seems to me I've heard of that fellow somewhere."[76]

The conversation between Rickey and Smith at the Brooklyn press conference was influential in that it prompted a more thorough investigation of Robinson's background and ultimately led, of course, to the signing of the former UCLA athlete. The conversation also had the immediate effect of lessening Smith's feelings of distrust towards Rickey. Disappointed initially by Rickey's refusal to discuss openly the issue of blacks in organized baseball, Smith had a change of heart after the Dodgers' general manager questioned him in private about the capabilities of black athletes. In fact, about a week after the press conference, Smith wrote a column in the *Courier-Journal* praising Rickey's open-mindedness and his apparent interest in black players. Smith said that there was no doubt in his mind that Rickey had a sincere interest in both black ballplayers and the black leagues. Regardless of whether he employed a black player for the Dodgers, Rickey deserved the highest accolades possible for both his willingness to give black players a tryout and the fact that he was the first man in the major leagues to "inject himself forcefully" into the structure of black baseball. "From this perch," wrote Smith, "it appears to me that Branch Rickey, one of the wisest and shrewdest men in baseball, looms as a valuable friend, both for organized Negro baseball and the cause of the Negro player in the majors."[77] A few months later, Smith would find his assessment to be true.

While Rickey was busy searching for black talent, there were a number of other efforts being made to integrate organized baseball—efforts that Smith and the *Courier-Journal* were apparently not always aware of. In May 1945, Rickey and Larry MacPhail, president of the New York Yankees, were designated by their respective leagues to head a four-man committee to examine the question of blacks in organized baseball.[78] At about the same time, Vito Marcantonio, congressman from New York, asked that a congressional investigation be made concerning the discrimination against black ballplayers. Marcantionio announced that A. B. ("Happy") Chandler, newly elected baseball commissioner; the two league presidents; and all the major league owners would be called to testify on the baseball issue.[79] A few months later, Mayor La Guardia of New York City appointed Branch Rickey to a committee of ten organized to examine the question of blacks in organized baseball. The committee, which was never mentioned by Smith and the *Courier-Journal*, finished its work in November 1945, and strongly recommended that major league baseball accept black athletes.[80]

The recommendation made by the committee of ten was actually a little late in coming, because just one month earlier Rickey had announced that Robinson had signed a contract with the Dodgers. The signing of Robinson, certainly the biggest sports story of the year, was the culmination of the nearly twelve-year campaign waged by Smith and the *Courier-Journal* against organized baseball's discriminatory policies.

Not unexpectedly, Smith and the newspaper's other sportswriters were ecstatic when they found out about the historic signing of Robinson.[81] They found particular satisfaction in knowing that they were partly responsible for Rickey's decision to bring a black player into organized baseball. The newspaper's plethora of editorials, feature-length articles, and interviews with major league players and managers, as well as its active role in both the Bear Mountain and Boston tryouts were instrumental in keeping the race issue squarely on the minds of organized baseball's leading officials. Of all black newspapers, the *Courier-Journal* was the most vocal and persistent in its condemnation of lily-white baseball.

Wendell Smith, of course, was the catalyst of the newspaper's campaign effort. It is difficult to say with any degree of certainty just what influence Smith had on Rickey and the rest of the magnates in organized baseball. It seems safe to say, however, that without people such as Smith it might have been years before blacks were allowed in the National Game. What Smith did as effectively as anyone else was to point out that discrimination in organized baseball symbolized the dubious status of blacks in American society. On several occasions, Smith expressed the feeling that until blacks could participate fully in the National Game, they could not lay claim to the rights of full-fledged citizenship. He made it clear that the campaign was not merely a fight to wear a baseball uniform. It was a struggle for status, a struggle to take the concept of democracy off parchment and give it life. To Smith, the discrimination against blacks in organized baseball cut deeper into his feelings than any other area of employment discrimination. If baseball was indeed the National Pastime, the great leveler in society, then it naturally followed that black athletes deserved to participate in it. Smith realized, like many other black Americans, that the inclusion of blacks in organized baseball was only a temporary expedient, at best only an indirect way of achieving participation in American life. The participation of blacks in organized baseball would clearly be no solution to the problems of the race because political and economic dominance would still remain in white hands. Yet Smith believed that the desegregation of baseball would give blacks a new sense of dignity and self-esteem, ingredients that were not only inspiring in and of themselves but also necessary for the ultimate destruction of discrimination in this country. Fortunately, the war effort provided Smith with the perfect opportunity to shame major league owners into a more civilized attitude towards the black ballplayer. Without that feeling, the owners in big league baseball might have continued their racist policies and the *Courier-Journal*'s campaign would have had to go on indefinitely—Smith most certainly would have continued to lead it until his dream of blacks in organized baseball had become a reality.

6

"The Year of Awakening"

Black Athletes, Racial Unrest, and the Civil Rights Movement of 1968

The year was pivotal and messy," wrote the staff writer Lance Morrow in a cover story for *Time* magazine. "It produced vivid theater. It reverberates still in the American mind."[1] The year Morrow referred to was 1968, a turbulent period marked by campus uprisings, racial unrest, deaths of heroes, military escalation, political turmoil, and a youth movement that challenged American moral and economic values.

The year began with North Korea's capture of the USS *Pueblo* and ended with Apollo 8's circling of the moon. Sandwiched between these two historic events were such incidents as the launching of the Tet offensive in Saigon, the assassinations of Martin Luther King and Robert Kennedy, student rebellion at Columbia University, a poor people's march in Washington, D.C., and riots at the Chicago Democratic Convention. Those who lived through 1968 carry indelible memories of Richard Nixon saying "Sock it to me," Dustin Hoffman being seduced by Anne Bancroft, and the Rolling Stones singing about the *Street-Fighting Man*. The year severed past from future, signaling the end of Lyndon Johnson's great social vision and the Civil Rights struggle while ushering in the Women's Liberation Movement and newfound interest in environmental issues. Each event during the year seemed to be a momentous occasion and played out with an unusually high degree of intensity, except perhaps for Goldie Hawn's dancing in body paint and Tiny Tim's "tiptoeing through the tulips." In all, 1968 combined both revolutionary bombast and spiritual fulfillment, ecstacy and self-destruction, success and failure.[2]

Black athletes formed one group that was highly visible in 1968 and went through alternating periods of success and failure. For example, shortly before the Green Bay Packers' Super Bowl victory over the Oak-

104

land Raiders and the Houston Cougars' renowned victory over the UCLA Bruins in college basketball, the American public learned of the racial turmoil among the St. Louis Cardinals players that threatened to tear the football team apart. The disturbance was followed at the beginning of the year by such events as Sugar Ray Robinson's election to boxing's Hall of Fame, Muhammad Ali's continued battle with the federal courts, the boycott of the New York Athletic Club's 100th anniversary track meet at the new Madison Square Garden, and the beginnings of several black athletic revolts at predominantly white universities across the country. During the middle of the year, the Atlanta Braves secured a lifetime pension for Satchel Paige by signing the legendary pitcher to a major league contract; the former football great Jimmy Brown was brought up on charges of assault with intent to murder after a young model was found lying unconscious below his second-floor apartment; Wilt Chamberlain was signed to a five-year contract by the Los Angeles Lakers; Monte Ervin became the highest-ranking black official in baseball when he was appointed a special assistant to commissioner William Eckert; and the Baltimore Bullets' Earl "the Pearl" Monroe was named Rookie of the Year in the National Basketball Association. In the last months of 1968, Arthur Ashe made history by becoming the first black to capture the U.S. Open tennis title; the St. Louis Cardinals' Bob Gibson capped an amazing baseball season by garnering the most valuable player and Cy Young Awards; O. J. Simpson beat out Purdue's two-way star Leroy Keyes and Notre Dame's quarterback Terry Hanratty for college football's Heisman Trophy; Jimmy Ellis retained the World Boxing Association title by defeating Floyd Patterson in a controversial bout in Stockholm; John Carlos and Tommie Smith shocked the world by giving their Black Power salutes at the Mexico City Olympics, and the Boston Celtics' Bill Russell was named Sportsman of the Year by *Sports Illustrated*.[3]

Of all these events perhaps none were more significant to black athletes than those that concerned their involvement in civil rights issues. During that year black athletes, both individually and collectively, vented long-held frustrations and disillusionments through active protest against racial discrimination. Although never approaching the degree of activism evident among some members of their community, and not always prepared for the rigor or consequences of racial protest, black athletes in unprecedented numbers became participants in the civil rights struggle. They tried to come to grips with their conflicting role demands as athletes and black Americans by continuing to distinguish themselves in sport while at the same time combining with others in the black community to denounce everything from the lack of black executives in professional sport to racial exploitation in college athletics.[4]

The increased activism of black athletes during the year did not happen overnight but grew out of an already well-established black power movement, student rebellions, Muhammad Ali's example of race pride, and the intermingling of other factors, such as the Vietnam War and South Africa's apartheid policies. In large part, the intensity of racial disturbances by black athletes reached a crescendo in 1968 only after several years of growing frustration and almost as quickly dissipated under the weight of new civil rights legislation and the accommodation of many Americans to the idea of integration. This fact did not lessen the importance, however, of involvement by black athletes in racial disturbances during the year. These revolts, while powerless to make sweeping changes in the country's racial policies, were significant because they made the problems of racial discrimination in sport and the larger society more visible to the American public and the international community. Even those with only a passing interest in sport were made aware of racial discrimination by virtue of the increased outspokenness of black athletes. Black athletes also set the stage for protests lodged by athletes in the white community. As in many other aspects of the cultural and civil rights revolution, white athletes took the lead from their black counterparts and spoke out against the racial inequities evident in sport. They had been forced to look in the mirror and eventually involve themselves in unprecedented criticism of an institution that had traditionally been considered free of discrimination and apolitical in nature.[5]

Perhaps nothing was more noteworthy in 1968 than Muhammad Ali's attempts to outmaneuver various courts of justice. At the beginning of the year, Ali was embroiled in intense legal battles over his conviction on draft evasion charges and the subsequent loss of his heavyweight title. In January, the United States attorney Morton L. Susman argued in a brief to the United States Court of Appeals that Ali had "used his religion as a last-ditch excuse to escape the draft after several other claims were rejected." On May 6, the United States Court of Appeals for the Fifth Circuit in New Orleans upheld Ali's conviction, announcing that the former heavyweight champion had "been fairly accorded due process of law and without discrimination." About a month later the same New Orleans court denied Ali's request for a rehearing. On July 6, Ali asked the United States Supreme Court to throw out his draft conviction, only to have the Justice Department urge denial of the request. Finally, on December 16, Ali began serving five days of a ten-day sentence for an overdue traffic violation.[6]

Ali's trouble with the law in 1968 caused a myriad of reactions from the American public. A large portion of the country's white community and a small segment of the black population were appalled by Ali's actions, believing that the former champion deserved nothing but disdain and ridicule because of his refusal to fight for his country. In the opinion of some people, no punishment was too harsh for Ali, including the possibility of a long jail sentence, denial of a passport, and restrictions on earning a livelihood. Other people in American society threw their support behind Ali, arguing that the former champion had been unjustly stripped of his title by self-righteous hypocrites who had no business questioning an individual's personal religious beliefs. Howard Cosell, Robert Lipsyte, and other well-known media personalities praised Ali for his courageous stand while criticizing his detractors for their unreasonable positions.[7]

Still others in American society viewed Ali as a genuine hero and a figure of almost legendary proportions. Many people in the black community viewed Ali in this manner, considering him a champion of the black Civil Rights movement who bravely defied the norms and conventions of the dominant culture. An indication of black America's lofty regard for Ali can be gleaned by noting the number of protests and boycotts staged on his behalf in 1968. For example, on January 14 six members of a group called the "Committee For Muhammad Ali" picketed the annual boxing writers' dinner at New York's Waldorf-Astoria Hotel in a show of support for the deposed heavyweight champion.[8] In March, a group of black militants announced their opposition to the title fight between Joe Frazier and Buster Mathis on the grounds that Ali should still be considered the heavyweight champion. The group, which included such notable black Civil Rights leaders as Floyd McKissick, Leroi Jones, and Jarvis Tyner, argued that white America could not be allowed to determine for blacks who was to be the world heavyweight champion. Jones noted that Mathis and Frazier "might tell white people that they are the heavyweight champion after this fight, [but] they will never come in the black community claiming that they are the heavyweight champion. They know that little kids would laugh them out of the streets."[9]

No one was influenced more by Ali than other black athletes. Inspired by Ali's defiance and unwillingness to compromise his beliefs, black athletes at various levels of sport became less accommodating and more willing to protest racial discrimination within sport and the larger American society. It became increasingly apparent as the year progressed that black athletes had emerged as outspoken critics of the American social order rather than models of passivity and subservience. Representative forms of rebellion by black athletes eventually evolved into acts of protest and boycotts that, in the minds of many people, seemed to threaten the future of organized sport and the basic fabric of American society.[10]

A well-known movement inspired by Ali was the proposed boycott of the Mexico City Olympic Games. Towards the latter part of 1967, Harry Edwards, an instructor of sociology at San Jose State College, brought together a number of black athletes to discuss the possibility of an Olympic boycott. Frustrated by racially discriminatory practices committed against blacks, eager to express pride in their color, and recognizing the enormous attention engendered by any attempts to disrupt the sacred institution of sport, Edwards and his band of black athletes announced at a carefully orchestrated news conference in New York City that they would boycott the Mexico City Games unless certain demands were met. The demands included the reinstatement of Ali as world heavyweight champion, the ousting of Avery Brundage as president of the International Olympic Committee, an end to the discrimination against blacks and Jews by the New York Athletic Club (NYAC), the appointment of an additional black coach to the Olympic track and field team, the selection of a black man to the United States Olympic Committee, and the barring of South Africa and Rhodesia from Olympic competition.[11]

The disgruntled black athletes, who called their venture the Olympic Project for Human Rights (OPHR), first targeted the NYAC by organizing a boycott of the club's 100th anniversary track meet scheduled for February in the new Madison Square Garden. Shortly after the meeting in New York City to announce their six demands, Edwards and members of the OPHR began making plans to keep black athletes from competing in the track meet. The purposes of the NYAC boycott were quite simple. Black athletes wanted to realize a new sense of dignity by refusing to participate in a sporting event sponsored by a club that did not allow blacks as members, and to keep the discussion of an Olympic boycott in full view of the American public.[12]

It became apparent toward the end of January that the NYAC boycott would be successful. With the help of such people as Jay Cooper, chairman of the Columbia University Black American Law Students Association; Omar Ahmad, co-chairman of the 1966 Black Power Conference; Roy Innis, Associate National Director of CORE; H. Rap Brown, chairman of the Student Non-Violent Coordinating Committee; and Marshall Brown, an AAU official, the OPHR was able to garner support from various interest groups and a large majority of athletes and teams scheduled to compete in the meet. World-class athletes such as Tommie Smith, John Carlos, Lee Evans, Bill Gaines, Martin McCrady, Kirk Clayton, and Paul Drayton chose not to compete. Entire teams from Manhattan College, New York University, St. Johns, Rutgers, Villanova, Maryland State, and Morgan State decided not to take part. The Russian national track team, which had been asked not to compete by the OPHR, chose not to participate in the meet. The boycott also received full support from the NAACP, Urban League, and Anti-Defamation League of

B'nai B'rith. In a joint statement, the three organizations praised the boycotters for bringing the discriminatory practices of the NYAC to the attention of the American public and the world community.[13]

The NYAC meet went off as scheduled, but not without distractions and a cloud of controversy hanging over Madison Square Garden. The night before the competition, Edwards, Brown, Innis, Ahmad, and a number of other supporters of the movement held a press conference to reiterate the specific aims of the boycott. On the night of the meet, picket lines gathered outside the Garden to protest against the holding of competitions. The meet itself was marked by substandard performances, and attendance was down significantly from previous years. The meet director, Ray Lumpp, tried to make the best of an impossible situation by attracting talent, but he was never able to overcome the loss of about one hundred boycotting black athletes. In all, the NYAC boycott was a significant event for Edwards and members of the OPHR. For one thing, it served as a rallying point for black athletes. In the words of Vince Matthews, a participant in both the 1968 and 1972 Olympic Games, the meet became "the first element to unify black athletes from coast to coast." Perhaps most significantly, the NYAC boycott proved to Edwards and his followers that they could successfully organize an active and nonviolent protest.[14]

On the same day as the NYAC boycott, Avery Brundage announced at a press conference in Grenoble, France, that the International Olympic Committee (IOC) had decided to let South Africa compete in the Mexico City Games. The decision of the IOC, which further angered Edwards and other members of the OPHR, inadvertently contributed to the boycott movement by placing the issue of racial discrimination in an international context. By allowing South Africa to compete in Mexico City, the IOC had not only legitimized the efforts of the OPHR but jeopardized the Olympic Games themselves by casting its vote for a country that practiced apartheid. Edwards responded by stating that the South Africa ruling would force the black man to fight. Of the IOC he said, "They've virtually said the hell with us. Now we'll have to reply let Whitey run his own Olympics."[15] Only hours after Brundage's announcement, Ethiopia and Algeria announced their withdrawals from the games, and a number of other countries soon followed. The American Committee on Africa (ACOA), an educational and action organization concerned with freedom in Africa and a sympathetic United States policy, advocated a boycott of the Mexico City Games because of the IOC's acceptance of South Africa. The ACOA (whose members included such luminaries as Senator Eugene McCarthy, Sidney Poitier, Jackie Robinson, and Martin Luther King) contended that racist policies in South Africa violated Olympic Rules against discrimination and political interference.[16]

On April 20, the IOC reversed its decision on South Africa, voting to expel that country from Olympic competition after receiving intense pressure to do so. This latest decision softened the attitude of many black athletes and resulted in symbolic protests rather than an actual boycott of the Mexico City Games. Tommie Smith and John Carlos startled the world on October 16 when they bowed their heads in defiance and raised black-gloved fists high into the air while on the Olympic victory stand after their first-and third-place finishes in the 200-meter dash. Other less dramatic but equally impressive demonstrations by black athletes soon followed when word spread that Smith and Carlos had been kicked out of the Olympic Village for their display. For example, Bob Beamon protested against the expulsion of his two teammates by standing with his black socks exposed while on the victory stand to receive a gold medal for his record-shattering performance in the long jump.[17]

While the Olympic boycott movement was playing itself out, some thirty-seven black athletic disturbances were taking place on predominantly white university campuses across the country. The year was marked by black athletic disturbances at the University of California at Berkeley, Western Michigan University, Princeton University, Michigan State University, Oklahoma City University, the University of Texas at El Paso, San Francisco State College, Marquette University, the University of Kansas, and the University of Oklahoma. These revolts sprang from the increased black student activism on university campuses throughout the year. Black students at major universities across the country made life miserable for administrators and support personnel by not only protesting against racial discrimination but also demanding such reforms as the inclusion of black studies courses in university curricula and the hiring of more black faculty members.[18]

Nearly all the black athletic disturbances during the year involved confrontations with white coaches and players. Under pressure from their fellow black students to become more actively involved in black political activities, black athletes exerted a newfound sense of independence and exhibited a willingness to challenge racially discriminatory practices. They refused to follow the dictates of their coaches and hammered away at racial injustices in sport and the larger university community in an effort to avoid being labeled "Uncle Tom" and to be considered an integral part of the black Civil Rights movement. Their increased willingness to speak out on racial matters raised the ire of white coaches who desperately needed the services of black athletes but refused to give in to certain demands for fear that their authority would be weakened and team unity disrupted. Some white athletes came to the defense of their coaches, believing that black athletes were using the situation to help alleviate the conflicting demands they faced as black men and competitive athletes in American society.[19]

Certainly one of the more notable black athletic disturbances during the year took place at the University of Texas at El Paso. Better known for its athletic accomplishments than for its academic programs, the university had received national attention for its active recruitment of black athletes. Bobby Dobbs, Wayne Vandenberg, Don Haskins, and other coaches at the university had enticed black athletes from all over the country to attend the school once known as Texas Western. Unfortunately, while black athletes would play a large part in the success of the athletic program, problems eventually emerged between them, the athletic department, and university administration. Armed with a new sense of black pride and disgusted with the racial climate on campus, black athletes at the university banded together and spoke out on such matters as interracial dating, housing, unemployment, social isolation, and quality of education.[20]

Racial unrest among black athletes at the University of Texas at El Paso was evident as early as 1963. David ("Big Daddy") Lattin, a member of the university's national championship basketball team in 1966, recalled that during his freshman year the black players on the squad called a meeting with the athletic director, George McCarty, to complain about McCarty's enunciation of the word *negro*. The players were adamant that McCarty should "get himself together" and learn how to pronounce "that word." Black athletes on campus gradually moved away from questions of semantics to racial issues of more significance. For instance, many black athletes, experiencing a sense of isolation and social exclusion on campus, denounced the pressure athletic department officials placed on them for their interracial dating practices. There were also numerous complaints from black athletes about the lack of employment opportunities in El Paso for them and their spouses or girlfriends because of discrimination in the marketplace, with local townspeople giving jobs to less qualified whites. Black athletes denounced, moreover, the inadequate housing available to them, both on and off campus; fraternities were closed to them, dormitory rooms poorly staffed, and the best apartments and houses in town reserved primarily for whites.[21]

The most intense period of racial unrest among black athletes at El Paso took place between approximately September 1967 and May 1968. Early in the autumn of 1967, black members of the football team, including the All-Americans Fred Carr and Charlie West, staged a sit-in in the lobby of the athletic dormitory to protest the treatment they had received at the hands of coach Bobby Dobbs and other members of the athletic department. Their complaints were remarkably similar to those voiced by black football players on college campuses throughout the country. The players told Dobbs, among other things, that they wanted to date whomever they pleased, refused to be the butt of jokes from white teammates, desired better-paying jobs for their spouses, requested better living arrangements, were tired of being stacked into particular playing positions, and would not tolerate those coaches who always viewed their injuries with suspicion. Unfortunately for the black players, nothing constructive resulted from their small protest. Although Dobbs promised to look into the complaints, he went about his business as usual, refusing to acknowledge the existing problems within the team. Black players became convinced, however, that after the incident recruiting practices at El Paso changed dramatically. One member of the athletic department was overheard stating that "from now on the only negroes they'd recruit would be stars like O. J. Simpson." The university was "through with the so-so negro athletes because they used up too much of the grub and they caused too much trouble."[22]

Perhaps the only consolation for the disgruntled black football players was the fact that their sit-in set the stage for bolder and more dramatic forms of protest by black members of the university's nationally ranked track-and-field team. The school's black track stars were well aware of the various protests being staged by black athletes around the country, having themselves been pressured to boycott the NYAC track meet in February. They elected to compete in the NYAC meet, initially arguing that their absence would not accomplish anything, but they later admitted that their decision was also based on a desire to visit relatives in New York. By April, the attitude of the black trackmen changed suddenly and they became much more willing to speak out on racial issues and protest discrimination on their own behalf. The reason for the change in attitude was the assassination of Martin Luther King. Black trackmen at El Paso, like black Americans everywhere, were inspired—and moved to action—by the untimely death of the great civil rights leader. Any reservations they had about actively protesting racial discrimination were wiped out by the death of King.[23]

Just a week after King's tragic death in Memphis, black trackmen at El Paso made plans to boycott the Easter weekend track meet with Brigham Young University. The athletes chose not to travel to Utah, both as a gesture of reverence to King and as a protest against Mormon ideology, which proclaimed the superiority of whites over blacks. The boycotters paid for their actions. Coach Wayne Vandenburg dismissed the nine boycotting black athletes from the team and revoked their scholarships. The university president, Joseph M. Ray, and the school's faculty athletic council refused to veto Vanderburg's actions. The black trackmen's troubles did not end with the loss of their scholarships or dismissal from the track team. Bob Beamon's wife reportedly lost her job over the affair, being told by her boss that she was no longer wanted because of her husband's altercation with the school's athletic department.[24]

The sense of racial pride and the burgeoning political awareness exhibited by black amateur athletes during 1968 was duplicated at the professional level of sport. On January 5, the *New York Times* reported that black members of the St. Louis Cardinals football team had submitted a list of grievances to their head coach, Charley Winner. The team's black athletes, who included the outstanding running back Johnny Roland and the All-Pro offensive lineman Ernie McMillan, were angered by the insensitivity and racial prejudice exhibited by teammates, coaches, and the St. Louis community. Hardly anyone in the Cardinal organization was spared the wrath of the disgruntled black athletes, but much of the criticism was laid at the feet of the assistant coach, Chuck Drulis, who was accused, among other things, of using racially inflammatory language and giving preferential treatment to white players on the team.[25]

Coach Winner responded to the black athletes' complaints by establishing, shortly before the opening of summer training camp, a committee of six players responsible for reporting any racial problems on the team. As it turned out, the committee had to work only a short time. One of the more outspoken white members of the team retired. Coach Drulis apparently became more sensitive to the needs of black players, and racial tension between team members slowly dissipated as players began airing their grievances and club management focused on racial matters as well as on-the-field activities. By their opening game in the fall of 1968, many of the problems that divided players along racial lines had been rectified and the team went on to a winning season.[26]

While problems among the St. Louis Cardinals seemed to be on the wane, another racial disturbance erupted within the Cleveland Browns that threatened to divide the football team. Before the season, black and white players on the squad became embroiled in a bitter dispute over a celebrity golf tournament—a tournament promoted by the white defensive back Ross Fichtner. The source of the dispute was Fichtner's decision not to invite the black players to the tournament. He said the players were not welcome because they had refused to socialize with whites at previous tournaments. The black players did not like being slighted by Fichtner and told him so in no uncertain terms. Before the dispute was over, longstanding friendships were broken, team spirit was threatened, and both Fichtner and the black offensive guard John Wooten were put on waivers.[27]

These racial disturbances, although varying in style and approach, were significant in that a critical mass of black athletes who exhibited a collective sense of racial pride and burgeoning political awareness came together. Reminiscent of the 1965 American Football Conference All-Star Game, in which all twenty-two black players on the two squads pressed commissioner Joe Goss to move the contest to Houston from New Orleans because of the Crescent City's racial policies, black members of the Browns and Cardinals utilized group action, refusing to accept the notion of black inferiority and speaking out against racial discrimination.[28] These black football players apparently recognized, as many other black athletes would during the decade, that the fight for equality was by necessity a collective struggle and could not be based entirely on individual accomplishments. Athletic achievements, though important and noteworthy, could never eliminate the discrimination experienced by blacks because the status of individuals in the United States depended to a great extent upon group affiliation.[29]

The racial disturbances fostered by black athletes in professional football and at other levels of American sport during 1968 invariably involved white athletes, in one way or another. The reactions of white athletes to their rebellious black counterparts defy simple categorization. Many white athletes stood solidly behind members of the sport establishment, while others chose to become active participants in the civil rights struggle. The fact that many white athletes came to the defense of those individuals under attack by black athletes does not come as much of a surprise. White athletes were no different from many others in American society in having stereotyped ideas about blacks and believing that the accusations of racial discrimination lodged against coaches, players, and others in organized sport were unfair and not grounded in fact. A large segment of the white athletic community believed black athletes confused racial discrimination with the discipline and adherence to training rules necessary for the success of any athletic team. White athletes also found it appalling that anyone would question the authority of those in charge of sport and attempt to disrupt an institution that had provided a wealth of opportunities for the country's most disadvantaged minority groups. Like many other Americans, white athletes mistakenly viewed the success of selected groups of black athletes as evidence of the egalitarianism of both sport and American society.[30]

There were a number of examples in 1968 of white athletes who came to the defense of people under attack by disgruntled black athletes. A racial disturbance that took place during the beginning of the year at the University of California, Berkeley, serves as a perfect illustration of how volatile the relationship could become between black and white athletes. In January, dissension arose in the university's basketball team when Coach Rene Hêrrerias allowed the black center Bob Presley to return to the team after being dismissed just two days earlier for disciplinary reasons. The reinstatement of Presley angered the eleven white players on the squad, who contended that the university's administration, including Vice Chancellor Earl Cheit and his black special assistant,

Don Hopkins, had pressed Coach Hêrrerias to reverse his decision because of possible repercussions in the black community. They threatened to withdraw from the team unless Hêrrerias was given back his full authority as coach by the university's administration, and until Presley and the school's other black athletes took back their claims that the athletic department discriminated against them. The white basketball players, in addition to being angered by the Presley incident, strongly objected to assertions made by the school's black athletes that the athletic department had failed, among other things, to provide suitable housing for black athletes, implement good academic counseling programs for student athletes, and foster a more supportive environment by removing racist coaches and athletic trainers. In the end, white athletes softened their position on the black athletic disturbance and agreed to play the remaining thirteen games of the season.[31]

The racial antagonisms evident at Berkeley and elsewhere were offset by a number of incidents in which white athletes, either individually or collectively, came to the defense of black athletes. Although they apparently became more vocal on issues of discrimination after 1968 and were usually on the periphery of any protests because of the eagerness of blacks to maintain control over racial conflicts, some white athletes were sufficiently moved by the clamor of black athletes during the year to join the Civil Rights movement and speak out against racial injustice. For example, Hal Connolly, the four-time Olympic hammer thrower who gained international attention for his romance with the Czechoslovakian discus champion Olga Fikotova during the 1956 games in Melbourne, was very supportive of Harry Edwards and the boycott of the Mexico City games. Connolly and Ed Burke, another white hammer thrower on the United States team, both threatened to withdraw from the games after John Carlos and Tommie Smith were suspended for their Black Power salutes.[32] Another show of support for the boycott came from five members of the Harvard Olympic crew team. At a July news conference, the five crew members, led by the senior captain Curt Canning, announced that they felt a moral obligation to support the black athletes "in their efforts to dramatize the injustices and inequities which permeated our society." The crew members said they were convinced that whites in this country could no longer afford to "ignore the voices of oppressed minorities"; in showing their support for the black athletes, their "aim was the demise of bigotry and racism and the establishment of true equality of opportunity."[33]

Rebellious black athletes received the same kind of mixed messages from members of their own community that they did from white athletes. In fact, some of the most bitter criticism of their actions came from older, more conservative, former black athletes who could not countenance any

No African American athlete was more closely associated with racial unrest in 1968 than Tommie Smith, shown here capturing the gold medal in the 200-meter dash at the Mexico City Olympics. Courtesy of the United States Olympic Committee.

attack on the institution of sport. Having experienced personal athletic success and believing that sport had helped promote the goal of interracial harmony, former black athletes were sometimes highly critical of younger black athletes for their various boycotts and allegiance to the more radical members of the black community.[34]

One of the most outspoken critics of the Olympic boycott movement was Jesse Owens, the legendary track star who gained worldwide acclaim for his gold-medal performances in the 1936 Berlin Games. While acknowledging that discrimination still existed in American society, Owens was angered by what he perceived as a lack of appreciation shown towards the sport establishment by protesting black athletes. Sport not only provided blacks with unlimited opportunities for success but also, Owens felt, had done as much as any other institution to improve race relations in American society. Owens was also quick to point out that a boycott intended to dramatize racial inequities in American society was irrational considering that vast improvements had been made in this area and blacks were not furnished with "the one all-important gift of opportunity."[35]

Owens's behavior resulted in a much-publicized tiff between him and Harry Edwards, a confrontation that was probably inevitable considering the decided philosophical differences between the two men. Apart from sharing the same skin color and experiencing the effects of racial discrimination, Owens and Edwards had little in common. Owens had been taught that success was contingent upon courteously yielding to the opinions or wishes of others and being industrious in one's calling. To him, the openly negative reactions to racial discrimination expressed by Edwards were unreasonable, excessive, and, to a large degree, "un-American." In Owens's opinion, Edwards was an angry extremist intent on exploiting young, impressionable black athletes for his own purposes. The hatred that he attempted to inculcate in black Olympians was indefensible, Owens thought, particularly when it was aimed at American sport, which had always been one institution accessible to blacks.[36]

Edwards, for his part, labeled Owens a bootlicking "Uncle Tom." He was repulsed by Owens's "ridiculously naïve belief in the sanctity of athletics" and the Olympic champion's oft-repeated statements "about the friendships and understanding brought about between blacks and whites through sport." In Edwards's opinion, Owens had played into the establishment's hands and hindered the liberation efforts of blacks by publicly announcing his opposition to a boycott and expressing the erroneous belief that sports participation helped erase misunderstandings between the races. Owens was no different from Edwards's own father and many other blacks of previous generations in that he lacked a critical understanding of American society and was unable or unwilling to get beyond the personal experiences of his life. The American dream of individual success and the moral formula needed to realize that success might have worked for Owens, but not, Edwards felt, for the majority of blacks, who were destined for poverty in a society that was economically elitist and racially discriminatory.[37]

The attention garnered by rebellious black athletes is evidenced by the extensive coverage they were given in the popular press. In fact, nowhere was it more clear how conscious Americans had become of black athletes than in the pages of the best-known United States newspapers and magazines. Continual coverage and feature-length essays on the plight of black athletes appeared during the year under such titles as "The Angry Black Athlete," "The Black Rebel Who Whitelists the Olympics," "Black Hired Hands," and "The Revolt of the Black Athletes" in *Life, Time, Newsweek, U.S. News and World Report, Sports Illustrated,* and other nationally recognized publications. Various issues were covered in these publications, but most of the writings centered around a discussion of black athletic exploitation and how the victims of this exploitation were angrily fighting back.[38]

Perhaps the year's most notable piece on black athletes was Jack Olsen's five-part series of articles in *Sport Illustrated*.[39] Olsen's articles, which formed the basis of his book *The Black Athlete: A Shameful Story, the Myth of Integration in American Sport,* described the world of black athletes largely through interviews with coaches and black athletes themselves. More than any other writer in the popular press, Olsen provided readers with a detailed look at black athletes and how they coped with prejudiced white players and coaches while striving for success in an institution that considered itself the bastion of equality. He educated the American public by telling the largely untold story of how black athletes were forced to submit to the racial slurs of prejudiced whites, unable to transcend the dominant culture's stereotyped view of black intellectual and athletic abilities, denied any kind of social life on college campuses, and incapable of altering both the quota and inadequate reward system in professional sport. In many regards, Olsen went a long way towards shattering the myth that sport was apolitical, free of racial discrimination, and the great leveler in society.[40]

The status of black athletes in American sport was further illuminated by a number of black autobiographies published in 1968. Patterned in some ways after the earlier self-portrayals by Jim Brown and Bill Russell, Bob Gibson's *From Ghetto to Glory,* Frank Robinson's *My Life in Baseball,* and Henry Aaron's *Aaron, R.F.* described many of the difficulties faced by blacks in baseball and sports generally.[41] Not content to paint an idyllic picture of life in sports, the three baseball stars offered insights into the socialization process and the role of the contemporary black athlete. Gibson, in particular, furnished a penetrating account of the struggles faced by black athletes and the discriminatory practices they encountered.

Insightful as these autobiographies were, they did not portray the real anger and disillusionment felt by many in the black community towards American sport. This was left to Eldridge Cleaver, the famous ex-inmate of Soledad, Folsom, and San Quentin prisons, whose largely autobiographical *Soul on Ice* (1968) served as one of the decade's best-known personal statements on the black Civil Rights movement. Although not necessarily representing black athletes, Cleaver's book does speak on behalf of many in the black community who viewed American sport with a great deal of skepticism. In a chapter entitled "Lazarus Come Forth," Cleaver grouped black athletes and entertainers into one category and described how they had been used by the dominant culture for its own selfish purposes. He argued that black Americans had been kept in subjugation by the "systematic emasculation" of outspoken blacks and the simultaneous support of black "celebrities from the apolitical world of sport and play." "The tradition is that whenever a crisis with racial overtones arises," said Cleaver, "an entertainer or athlete is trotted out and allowed to expound a predictable conciliatory interpretation of what's happening. The mass media rush forward with grinding cameras and extended microphones as though some great oracle were about to lay down a new covenant from God. When in reality, all that has happened is that the blacks have been sold out and cooled out again."[42]

Cleaver pointed out that by the decade of the 1960s the black athletes and entertainers of yesteryear, subservient and unconcerned with ideology, were slowly disappearing from the scene. Taking their place were more brash and outspoken black athletes and entertainers who lashed out at the American social system rather than embracing it. The man who best represented the new breed of black athlete—and other young Americans, for that matter—was Muhammad Ali. "In the context of boxing," wrote Cleaver, "Ali was a genuine revolutionary, the black Fidel Castro of boxing." White America had always demanded that its black heavyweight champion possess a "brilliant, powerful body and a dull, bestial mind—a tiger in the ring and a pussycat outside the ring." Every black heavyweight champion of the past had been a puppet, said Cleaver, "manipulated by whites in his private life to control his public image." With the coming of Ali, however, "the puppet-master was left with a handful of strings to which his dancing doll was no longer attached. For every white man, feeling himself superior to every black man, it was a serious blow to his self-image; because Muhammad Ali, by the very fact that he leads an autonomous private life, cannot fulfil the psychological needs of whites."[43]

Cleaver's analysis, significant for summing up much of the radical black community's beliefs about American sport, helped set the stage for the increased scholarly research that would be completed on black athletes during the early 1970s. It is noteworthy that as they gained greater acceptance from the American public and involved themselves less often in public protests after 1968, black athletes became the subject of serious scholarly inquiry by scholars from various disciplines. Events of 1968 helped to catapult black athletes into the white consciousness, which in turn spawned a plethora of research studies dealing with their role in American sport. By the first few years of the 1970s, books and academic journals were filled with hundreds of pages devoted to black athletes. Although no topic escaped attention, scholars concentrated on various forms of discrimination in sport, particularly the phenomenon known as "stacking," inadequate rewards and authority structures in sport, and performance differentials between black and white athletes.[44]

In all, 1968 proved a most memorable year for black athletes. They were forced to assess how far they could push for civil rights without sacrificing years of training and forgoing the opportunity to achieve lasting fame. It was an extremely difficult decision. They were, to be sure, athletes first and civil rights activists second. They had been taught early on to be humble and accommodating to authority, labored for many years to hone their athletic skills, and had been brought up to believe in the power of sport to bridge gaps between people of different ethnic and racial origins. Suddenly to turn their backs on this way of thinking and assume positions as civil rights activists was a frightening proposition for even the most courageous black athletes. On the other hand, unprecedented numbers of black athletes during 1968 were challenged by more radical elements of the black community who wanted them to lash out at racial discrimination and become more involved in the Civil Rights movement. They were constantly being told by black activists that problems of blacks were common to them as a group rather than as individuals and the best way to combat those problems was through collective action. Although personal accomplishments in sport and other areas of life were praiseworthy, the fight for equality was by necessity a collective struggle, because the rights and privileges of individuals in American society depended largely upon the status of the group to which they belonged.

This interplay between individual success in sport and the imperatives of group action on civil rights issues caused many black athletes to seek a middle ground where they could continue to seek their goal of athletic success while at the same time launching various forms of attack against discriminatory practices in sport and the larger society. Sometimes donning dashikis, sporting large Afros, and exhibiting other outward trappings of racial militancy, many black athletes in 1968 stopped just short of quitting sport by attacking the myriad forms of discrimination in American society. They stopped acquiescing to mistreatment at the hands of the dominant culture, shed their traditionally conservative approach to racial matters, and used an effective mixture of rhetoric and substantive action to blast white coaches, administrators, and anybody else they deemed enemies of equality of opportunity.

The involvement of black athletes in the 1968 civil rights movement brought a not unusual combination of reactions and controversy. Many people in the sporting establishment believed that black athletes were nothing but ungrateful scamps who foolishly heeded the advice of opportunistic black activists and unnecessarily jeopardized their futures in an institution that had always been free of racial discrimination. This view was also taken by more conservative members of the black community who could not understand how black athletes could risk their careers in sport when that institution provided so many opportunities for minority groups and had always been devoid of politics. Perhaps no group was more troubled by the turn of events in 1968 than former athletes, both black and white, who believed that black athletes naïvely followed the dictates of selfish black activists while ignoring the fact that sport participation had done as much as, or more than, any other institution to improve race relations.

All the attention paid to the racial turmoil surrounding sport was exactly what rebellious black athletes and their supporters had hoped for. They realized that the best way to draw attention to racial inequities was by disrupting, in some manner, the sacred institution of sport. Questioning the dictates of coaches, refusing to stand at attention during the playing of the national anthem, or boycotting an athletic event were sure to draw the wrath of the American public and result in the volume of publicity necessary to prick the consciousness of people who were reluctant to acknowledge racial discrimination in sport and the larger society.

The use of sport in dramatizing racial issues was so effective in 1968 that it tended to overshadow the great performances of black athletes and conceal the source of much of their motivation for dramatizing the plight of black Americans. Disturbances during the year resulted as much from efforts by black athletes to exert their sense of racial pride and manhood as anything else. In a very real sense, black athletes were having their honor attacked by the more radical members of the black community, who were emphasizing a need for the celebration of black culture, the merits of black life-styles, and the value of racial pride. Black athletes were pressured, in a variety of ways and in different circumstances, to exhibit a sense of *noblesse oblige* by boldly flaunting their racial heritage and speaking out on behalf of less fortunate blacks. In addition, black athletes themselves recognized that participation in sport traditionally implied the supremacy of everything white and the inferiority of everything black. It was apparent to an increasing number of black athletes that access to American sport was achieved only at the expense of being denied their own identity and sense of racial heritage. In their efforts to climb the ladder of success, black athletes had traditionally been forced to curry favor with the sporting establishment and jeopardize their sense of dignity by deferring to the wishes of white employers and benefactors.

The threat to their racial pride and sense of manhood was enough to assure the involvement of black athletes in the Civil Rights movement of 1968. Additional factors also seemed to play an important role, however, in their newfound activism. Black athletes were, ironically enough, awakened as never before to the fact that their physical skills placed them in an enviable bargaining position because white society stood to benefit handsomely from their performances in sport. They also came to understand that their status allowed them an opportunity to air their grievances and express their beliefs without the constant threat of retaliation.

They took advantage of their privileged positions by threatening to withhold their services from the very institution that provided them with major successes and national acclaim. In the process, black athletes in 1968 gained a degree of satisfaction, a much-needed sense of racial pride, and the realization they had captured the attention of America and the international community. The turmoil they caused during the year reverberates still in the American mind, conjuring up images of tormented white coaches, anxious college presidents, and raised black fists.

These images should be seen, however, in the context of the larger Civil Rights movement and not blind anyone to the fact that a large segment of the black community continued to believe that success in sport served as an important symbol of possibility and a much-needed example of achievement. It is significant that Harry Edwards himself, in his book *The Revolt of the Black Athlete*, devoted ten pages of one of his appendixes to a long list of black record holders in baseball, basketball, football, and track and field.[45] The man who was responsible for much of the racial turmoil in 1968 and who spent a great deal of time trying to debunk the myth surrounding sport and upward social mobility merely reflected the view of black Americans who believed that the enduring legacy of outstanding black athletes was as exemplars and models of success rather than as political activists. As in the past, much attention was given to black athletes who achieved prominence in American sports —particularly in competition against whites—because it presumably helped to destroy the stereotype of the black man's inferiority and had an uplifting effect on blacks themselves. Each triumph of a black athlete that came to public attention, such as Tommie Smith's gold-medal performance in the Olympic Games or Arthur Ashe's victory in the U.S. Open, had significance far beyond the importance of the triumph itself. All things considered, the actions taken by black athletes during 1968 mirrored the age-old vision of black Americans who recognized that the future of the race was contingent not only upon fashioning a positive self-image, but upon fashioning it in America.

7

"The Future of College Athletics Is at Stake"

Black Athletes and Racial Turmoil on Three Predominantly White University Campuses, 1968–1972

Life on America's predominantly white university campuses between 1968 and 1972 was anything but tranquil. Boards of trustees, university presidents, provosts, deans, and administrative support personnel were faced with a myriad of problems that threatened the basic structure of higher education in this country. Socially conscious faculty members became increasingly outspoken on administrative policies, involved themselves in a number of hotly debated issues and radical movements outside the basic purview of the university community, and generally took a more active role in university decision making. Students on university campuses during this period, participating in such organizations as the Students for a Democratic Society (SDS), were decidedly different from many students of previous generations in openly adopting radical life-styles symbolized by long hair, tie-dyed shirts, drugs, and rock music. Perhaps most alarming to administrators on predominantly white university campuses were the demands being placed on them by black students. Sometimes in concert with sympathetic white students and faculty members, black students at institutions all across the country were pressuring administrations to hire black faculty members, include black studies in the university curriculum, help support black student organizations on campus, and make a more serious effort to recruit minority students. The pressure exerted by black students on university administrations took many forms, including sit-ins, boycotts, and occasional violence.[1]

One group that played a significant role in the black student revolts of the late 1960s and early 1970s were black athletes. Shedding their traditional conservative approach to racial matters, black athletes spearheaded the "athletic revolution" by challenging the racial discrimination that existed in athletic departments at various universities across the country. The sport sociologist Harry Edwards estimated that in 1968 alone some thirty-seven black athletic revolts took place on predominantly white university campuses.[2] Although there was a gradual decline in the number of revolts on university campuses during the next four years, some of these black athletic disturbances were so alarming that coaches, athletic directors, and school presidents believed the future of college athletics was at stake. On some campuses the disturbances became so intense that black athletes lost their scholarships, black and white teammates became bitter antagonists, coaches either quit or were fired, athletic directors had their powers usurped, newly created organizations were established on campus expressly to look into the problems of racial discrimination, and national organizations such as the NAACP were called in to settle campus disputes.

Most of the revolts during this period emanated from confrontations that took place between black athletes and white coaches. John Underwood, in a three-part series of articles in *Sports Illustrated* entitled "The Desperate Coach," was entirely accurate in describing college coaches as "bewildered, angry and disillusioned, no longer certain of their mission, or, in some cases of their relevance."[3] Their authority was being challenged by various groups of people, most noticeably black athletes. Because they lacked consistency of status on predominantly white campuses and felt pressure to become actively involved in black political activities, black athletes were exerting both a newfound sense of independence and an apparent willingness to speak out on racial issues. To guard against being labeled "Uncle Toms" by their black student peer group, a significant number of black athletes chose not to conform to the dictates of their coaches and took a more active role in the more militant aspects of the Civil Rights movement. This path was paved with dire consequences, however. Coaches could not allow team rules to be transgressed for fear that their authority would be undermined and team discipline disrupted. As a result, black athletes who refused to follow the dictates of their coaches were sometimes dismissed from the squad and therefore ended up sacrificing both their education and years of training that might have landed them in professional sports. Coaches, on the other hand, lost the services of athletes who were, in many cases, crucial to the success of their teams and the overall quality of the school's total athletic program.[4]

Black athletic revolts took place on different kinds of campuses in various locations across the country and resulted from black athletes' complaints about everything from unfair dress codes to inadequate treatment of injuries by prejudiced athletic trainers. For example, in 1968 racial unrest among black athletes erupted at the University of Washington. The school's black athletes accused the football coach, Jim Owens, of various forms of discrimination and threatened to boycott all athletic events until a black coach or administrator was hired on a full-time basis. That same year, nine track and field stars at the University of Texas at El Paso, including the long-jump champion Bob Beamon, were kicked off the team by Coach Wayne Vandenburg for protesting the Mormon Church's treatment of blacks.[5] In January 1969, five black football players at Princeton accused the varsity coach, Dick Coleman, and the freshman coach, Walter "Pat" McCarthy, of "racist tendencies in coaching." The players complained that while being publicly praised, they were passed over for starting positions, particularly in the backfield. In October of the same year, Coach Lloyd Eaton of the University of Wyoming kicked fourteen black players off the football team for asking if they could help draw attention to the Mormon Church's racial policies by lodging some form of protest in their upcoming game against Brigham Young.[6] About a month after the Wyoming incident, Coach John Pont of Indiana University dismissed fourteen black players from the football team when they boycotted practice two days in a row. The players complained, among other things, that Pont had created an atmosphere that was "mentally depressing and morally discouraging to blacks."[7] In 1970 several black members of Buffalo State's basketball team quit the squad, charging the athletic department with discrimination. The feud resulted in a violent disturbance on campus in which bands of students smashed windows, set fire to a truck, and used two cars as battering rams against the campus police headquarters. In December 1970 black athletes at the University of Pittsburgh charged the school's athletic department with racial discrimination. The players accused the department of not actively recruiting black athletes, failing to give adequate publicity to black athletes, and denying black athletes equal opportunity for starting positions. Then, in 1972 the head baseball coach at Oregon State, Gene Tanselli, was brought to court by his one and only black player on charges of racial discrimination. Although Tanselli was found innocent of the charges, the incident eventually led to his dismissal as baseball coach.[8]

This essay explores the racial turmoil that took place at the University of California, Berkeley; Syracuse University; and Oregon State University. These confrontations were not necessarily any more significant than the disturbances that occurred on other predominantly white university campuses across the country but serve as examples of the kinds of conflicts that ensued between white coaches, administrators, and black athletes at well-known institutions with major sports programs. My primary purpose here is to outline the major grievances and issues that sparked the three revolts and analyze the institutional responses to those disturbances. On occasion, I draw parallels between the three revolts and those that occurred on other predominantly white university campuses.

Trouble in the Den of the Cal Bears

The troubles at Berkeley began on January 18, 1968, when the basketball coach, Rene Hêrrerias, dismissed the star center, Bob Presley, from the team for missing a practice. Two days later, Hêrrerias reinstated Presley, giving no details as to why he had decided to overturn his previous decision. Little did he suspect that his reinstatement of Presley would result in internal racial strife on the team and eventually lead to his resignation as basketball coach.[9]

The reinstatement of Presley immediately raised the ire of the white members of the squad. On January 22, just two days after Presley was allowed back on the team, the eleven white players announced that they would refuse to play any more games until "administrative pressure" on Hêrrerias was lifted. They contended that the University's administration, fearing repercussions because Presley was black, forced Cal's athletic director, Pete Newell, and Hêrrerias to allow Presley back on the squad after the two-day suspension. The white players claimed that Vice Chancellor Earl Cheit and his black special assistant, Don Hopkins, met with Newell and Hêrrerias and pressured them to allow Presley back on the squad. While admitting that they had discussed the Presley incident with Cheit and Hopkins, Newell and Hêrrerias steadfastly denied the accusations made by the white players. Hêrrerias claimed that the decision to reinstate Presley was his and his alone.[10]

The allegations made by the white players were tame in comparison to what took place on the Berkeley campus the following day. On the afternoon of January 23, twenty-five of the school's thirty-five black athletes, including Presley and the four other black members of the basketball team, held a press conference in which they demanded that Hêrrerias, two assistant football coaches, and the athletic department's business manager be dismissed because of their "incompetence' and "unwillingness to relate to black athletes." Dubbing their newly created organization "The Black Athletes of the University of California," the group of twenty-five, through their spokesman, the football star Bobby Smith, noted that unless the four men were fired and discrimination was eliminated in the athletic department, they not only would refuse to participate in any future athletic events but also would discourage other black athletes from attending the university. The twenty-five black athletes also used the occasion to list several grievances that had been festering in their group for some time. The athletes complained that members of the athletic department made derogatory comments about their personal appearance, that athletic trainers and student coaches unfairly regarded the injuries suffered by black athletes either as cases of "hypochondria or goldbricking," that coaches grouped black athletes at positions in which they would encounter maximum competition to make the teams, that the university reneged on its promise to find suitable housing for black athletes, that black athletes were given inferior academic advice and counseling, and, perhaps most important, that the athletic department had failed to hire black coaches.[11]

Athletic department officials and the university administration responded to the black athletes' complaints in predictable fashion. Newell, a former basketball coach himself, was taken aback by the grievances expressed by black athletes. He believed that the athletic department had made "real progress in race relations" during the last few years, noting that Berkeley had only five black athletes in 1960 but had increased the total to thirty-five in 1968 "through accelerated recruiting." Newell acknowledged that the school's stringent academic requirements, lack of "Negro coeds," and a "not-too-adequate living situation" made it difficult to recruit black athletes, but said those situations had improved markedly over the previous couple of years. The chancellor of the university, Roger W. Heyns, reacted to the black athletes' grievances by appointing a three-member fact-finding committee to investigate the entire dispute. Heyns charged Arleigh Williams, dean of students and a former California football and baseball player himself; Donald Hopkins, special assistant to the vice chancellor; and William G. Dauben, professor of chemistry and chairman of the faculty's committee on athletic policy, with investigating the dispute and making specific recommendations about the grievances lodged by the black athletes.[12]

The complaints voiced by the black athletes further infuriated the white members of the basketball team. Just hours after the black athletes' press conference on the afternoon of January 23, the eleven white players met to discuss whether they should reconsider their boycott plans. After much debate, the players elected to go ahead with the boycott, stating that they would agree to play out the season only if the truth were made known about the pressure exerted on Hêrrerias, full authority was given back to Hêrrerias to direct the team as he saw fit, and several statements made by black athletes at their press conference were retracted. As things turned out, the hard line taken by the white players would not last lang. The following morning they met with Hêrrerias and ended up deciding to attend that afternoon's practice session and play the remaining thirteen games of the season. At a hastily called press conference with Hêrrerias, the players explained why they relented on their previous decision and made it perfectly clear how they felt about the Presley incident. The players revealed, through a prepared statement read by the student manager, Pat Gilligan, that Hêrrerias had assured them that any player who violated training rules would not be allowed on the team. Unfortunately, said the white players, Bob Presley had lied at the previous day's press conference about why he was dismissed from the basketball team. He was not discriminated against and kicked off the team for the length of his hair. Those people knowledgeable "of California basketball, black or white, know that Bob Presley was dismissed because of numerous violations of basketball ethics. We support our coach 100%. We are basketball players and want to play basketball." [13]

Shortly after the white players held their press conference, the racially torn basketball team reported en masse to practice in Harmon Gymnasium as a crowd of about two hundred looked on. There was an obvious discomfort between the black and white players. The two groups had engaged in a lot of mudslinging over the previous few days, and tensions ran high. Perhaps the most bitter feelings on the team were between Presley and Russ Critchfield, a senior guard who had earned second-team All-American honors the previous season. While it is not entirely clear what caused the antagonism between the two players, it is apparent that Presley and Critchfield were very different kinds of people who were vying to become the team's star attraction. Presley, a 6'10" junior from the ghettos of Detroit, was regarded as a big, gangly villain by some basketball fans in the Pacific Eight conference and frequently encountered racial slurs during the games at other conference schools. Not one to hide his feelings or back down from controversy, Presley accused Critchfield of being selfish and refusing to play team basketball. "Everyone's trying to make Critchfield an All-American," said Presley. "We just look for him at all times to pass to. . . . The negro players want to play team ball." [14]

Critchfield was different from Presley in almost every way. He was a white 5'10" guard who became an instant hero wherever he played. He was a symbol of the little guy or underdog making good. He was also a pesky little player who could talk almost as quickly as he could shoot. When he found out that he had been referred to as a "white honkie" at the black athletes' press conference on January 23, Critchfield responded by saying, "talk like that doesn't bother me," and "I don't care what they [black athletes] think of me." Concerning Presley in particular, Critchfield implied that the disgruntled black player had not been on the Berkeley campus long enough to make a fair evaluation of the athletic department and the university administration. Critchfield noted, in a rather sarcastic fashion, that he had been at Berkeley for three years, while Presley had been around for only twelve games. [15]

Presley, Critchfield, and the rest of the team put their differences aside long enough to make it through the January 24 practice. The white players decided there was nothing more they could do to alleviate the racial turmoil on campus, while the black players were apparently content to remain on the team until Chancellor Heyns's three-member fact-finding committee came out with its report. The remainder of the season also went remarkably well for the racially torn basketball team. There were no apparent confrontations between the players, and the team surprised most of the experts by finishing the season in the upper half of the league standings. Hêrrerias proclaimed during the latter half of the season that he thought the "conflict at Cal was over. . . . Things are positive right now as far as I'm concerned." [16]

Despite Hêrrerias's apparent optimism, "things" were not all right at Berkeley. It became noticeable before long that lurking behind the facade of tranquility on the Berkeley campus was a lingering racial problem that would result in personnel changes within the athletic department and university administration. On March 12, Pete Newell dropped a bombshell on the university community when he announced that he was stepping down as the school's athletic director. About a month later, Hêrrerias resigned his position as basketball coach. Not surprisingly, both men denied that the racial disturbances within the athletic department had influenced their decisions. Newell told reporters that he had decided to resign as athletic director immediately after the football season ended on November 18 and that the current racial problems did not affect him one way or the other. He failed to mention that he had turned down lucrative job offers in the past because of his desire to upgrade Cal's athletic program. Hêrrerias also denied that the current racial problems on campus influenced his decision to resign as basketball coach, insisting that his motivation for stepping down as coach arose from a desire to seek new challenges and was not a result of confrontations with Presley and other black athletes on the team. "I feel I'm leaving the program at California on solid footing," said Hêrrerias. "Now I must look to new horizons." [17]

The university wasted little time in filling Hêrrerias's position. On April 25, it was announced that Jim Padgett, Hêrrerias's top aide the last few years, had been hired as head coach and Earl Robinson, the black coach from Laney Community College, appointed as assistant. The hiring of these two men was heartily endorsed by the black players on the team. Padgett was well liked by the black players, and Robinson was viewed as a good choice by the university community. As in the case of the resignations of Newell and Hêrrerias, no one was willing to admit that the hiring of Robinson had anything to do with the racial turmoil at Cal. Padgett emphasized that Robinson's "qualifications as a coach and as a man" were the sole criteria for the selection. "He's [Robinson] a very versatile, talented guy," said Padgett. "You just can't afford to pass up a chance to get a man like that." [18]

The racial confrontation at Berkeley came to an end, for all intents and purposes, when Chancellor Heyns's fact-finding committee finally released its report during the latter part of the school year. Although the committee found no evidence of overt racial discrimination, it made seventeen recommendations intended to improve racial conditions on campus. The committee suggested, among other things, that the school's athletic department develop an in-service training program that would enable its members to become knowledgeable about minority cultures and the problems of minority students at the university, make a determined effort to recruit minority coaches and administrative personnel, develop a recruitment program that was consistent with the university's policy of nondiscrimination, and enlist the participation of black athletes in the educational, social, and other meaningful functions of the university. Many of these recommendations, plus a number of others, were put into effect almost immediately. In addition to the hirings of Earl Robinson in basketball and another black assistant coach in football, a recruitment plan was designed to bring more blacks to the campus, and courses in black philosophy, history, and literature were included in the curriculum for the first time.[19]

Chronic Racism at Syracuse

The circumstances surrounding the black protest at Syracuse University were decidedly different from those at the University of California, Berkeley. It was not the length of hair but the desire for a black coach that caused the disturbance at Syracuse. Racial tension on the school's football team had been running high since at least 1968, after a black student had been beaten by a white football player. From all available accounts, the black student started the fight by jumping the white player with a club, but decided to file racial charges anyway against the football team with the Human Rights Commission. The university, shaken by the incident and obviously concerned about the outcome of the racial charges filed by the black student, asked the head coach, Ben Schwartzwalder, to talk to his players about racism.[20]

Schwartzwalder, a major in the 82nd Airborne during World War II who had been the recipient of several medals for heroism in combat, was ill-prepared to talk about racial matters. After much persuasion, however, he agreed to hold a meeting with his players to talk about the problems of discrimination. It proved to be a disaster. Instead of improving matters, Schwartzwalder's little speech widened the racial gap between white and black players on the team. Blacks on the squad resented Schwartzwalder's patronizing attitude towards them, while the white players were angry at what they viewed as the coaching staff's preferential treatment of their black teammates. Schwartzwalder himself acknowledged that the meeting had hurt team unity. "Before the talk the team was a unit," he noted. "After that it was two groups: one black, one white. If I had known what was going to happen, I would have refused to hold that stupid meeting."[21]

Racial antagonisms became more apparent before spring football practice in 1970, when the black players on the team asked if one of two recently vacated coaching positions could be filled with a black. According to the players' story, they had been promised a black coach, but instead had to endure the verbal blasts of Floyd Little, the former Syracuse All-American who was brought in to work with the team on a voluntary basis. Frustrated by Little's barrage of insults, nine of the ten black players on the squad walked out of spring practice after three days, charging Schwartzwalder with reneging on his promise to hire a full-time black coach. Alarmed by the turn of events, the chancellor at Syracuse, Dr. John E. Corbally, Jr., met with the boycotting black players periodically during the next week and ordered Schwartzwalder to hire a black coach by the start of fall practice. The crusty sixty-year-old head coach met the demand by hiring Carlmon Jones, a recent graduate of Florida A & M, who had been an outstanding player under the legendary Jake Gaither. Schwartzwalder, however, showed no leniency towards the boycotters, informing seven of the nine black players that they were no longer members of the Syracuse football team. An eighth player, Greg Allen, eventually elected to join the seven dismissed black athletes, stating that if the others couldn't play, then neither would he. In all, Schwartzwalder had lost the services of eight of his best football players. In addition to Allen, the suspended players were Al Newton, senior halfback; Bucky McGill, senior defensive end; Duane Walker, senior defensive halfback; John Lobon, junior linebacker; Dana Harrell, senior linebacker; John Godbolt, senior halfback; and Dick Bulls, sophomore fullback.[22]

Schwartzwalder's decision to kick the black players off the football team caused further chaos on an already turbulent college campus and in the Syracuse community. In the early part of August 1970, three of the dismissed black players, including Newton, the team's leading ground-gainer from the 1969 season, filed discrimination charges against Schwartzwalder, his coaching staff, and the university with the Onondaga County Human Rights Commission. The lack of black coaches was not the only complaint lodged by the disgruntled black athletes. There were far more serious problems on the football team and in the school's athletic department that raised the ire of the black players. Like many black athletes on other predominantly white university campuses during this period, the revolting black players complained that a "double standard in discipline" existed on the team, the team doctor gave preferential treatment to white players, there was a lack of academic advising and tutoring for black players, coaches on the football team used "racist language," black players received fewer "fringe benefits" than their white counterparts, and "discrimination existed in placing players on the first, second and third teams."[23]

Shortly after the black players filed their complaint with the commission, Chancellor Corbally decided once again to intervene in the affair. Over the bitter complaints of Schwartzwalder, Corbally worked with Norman Pinkard, executive director of the Civil Rights Commission, to draw up a plan that would have allowed the black players to return to the team. The chancellor announced that the black players could rejoin the team if they signed "a code for Syracuse athletes" that obligated them to play any position designated by the coaching staff, to give 100 percent effort in all drills, and to follow a set of procedures for airing grievances.[24]

Corbally's plan did not receive universal support. The Syracuse alumni quickly let the chancellor know that they were disappointed with his decision. Already upset with Corbally for his decision to close the campus early the preceding year and for allowing seniors to graduate without taking final exams (not clear from evidence, but perhaps because of rioting on campus), the alumni believed that the chancellor was giving in to unappreciative, troublemaking black athletes. Perhaps even more despondent over Corbally's actions were the white players on the team. The sixty-six whites on the squad, along with the one remaining black player, walked off the practice field a couple of days before fall practice in a symbolic counterboycott in response to the boycott staged earlier in the year by the dismissed black players. Paul Paolisso, a quarterback and one of the team's three captains, noted at the time that the remaining members of the squad were in "full support of Coach Ben Schwartzwalder and his staff."[25]

The black players did not sign Corbally's plan and failed to show up for the opening of fall practice on August 28. Corbally, making good on his promise to punish anyone who did not sign his plan and with an apparent eye toward the alumni, suspended the eight black players for the 1970 season. Two weeks into the season, the black players changed their minds, signed the "code for Syracuse athletes," and asked to be reinstated to the team. The remaining members of the squad, apparently under pressure from the administration, voted to allow the players back on the team. The vote turned out, however, to mean very little. The four black players who had not either dropped out of school or been declared academically ineligible ended up changing their minds once again. On September 27 they announced that they were going to continue the boycott indefinitely and reiterated that they wanted the university to conduct a full-scale investigation of its athletic department.[26]

Chancellor Corbally acceded to the players' request by forming a twelve-member trustee-faculty-student investigative group that was to look into the discrimination charges leveled against the athletic department. From the latter part of September to the end of November 1970, the committee conducted some twenty-eight hearings and questioned more than forty witnesses, including the athletic director, current and former players, university administrators, Chancellor Corbally himself, and all coaches. The committee's findings were made public on December 8, 1970, in a student-owned newspaper called the *Dialog*. In a 38-page report, the committee declared that racism in the athletic department, while largely unintentional, was chronic and that the suspension of the eight black football players was "an act of institutional racism unworthy of a great university." The committee noted, among other things, that the personnel in the athletic department were insensitive to the needs of black players and that the school's athletic director, James Decker, responded to the "year-long crisis" in a "totally unsatisfactory" manner. Corbally was asked by the committee to review the duties of the athletic director with the "purpose of strengthening the authority of the office." The committee also suggested that the suspended black players should not be punished for "focusing attention on the need for a racially diversified coaching staff" and should be granted an additional year of eligibility. It was strongly recommended, moreover, that the current administrative board of athletics be dissolved and replaced by an "Athletic Policy Board" that would have the "responsibility for overall policy and direction, control and supervision of intercollegiate and intramural athletics at Syracuse." Last, the committee recommended that a "new code of athletics" be set up at Syracuse that would guarantee athletes the same basic personal rights as all other students at Syracuse, including individual choice in such matters as personal appearance, social activities, and political expression.[27]

The university took little action on the committee's recommendations. The school's administration was politically astute enough to publicly acknowledge the hard work of the committee and state that it would take a serious look into the committee's recommendations, but the changes they eventually made in the athletic department were merely cosmetic in nature. Two days after the committee's report appeared in the *Dialog*, Chancellor Corbally announced that he saw no reason why there needed to be personnel changes in the athletic department. "I want to state firmly and unequivocally," said Corbally, "that I find no mandate or suggestion in the report or its recommendations that leads me to conclude that personnel changes are necessary to accomplish the purposes of the report." Corbally was similar to many other college administrators in his reluctance to initiate changes in athletic department personnel over the wishes of alumni and financial contributors to the institution. And at Syracuse the alumni were not prepared to make personnel changes in the athletic department just because a group of rebellious black athletes complained about not having a black coach on the football staff. The Syracuse faithful were certainly not going to permit Ben Schwartzwalder to be dismissed. A legend at Syracuse, he had led his team to several bowl games since 1949 and coached such famous players as Jim Brown, Ernie Davis, Floyd Little, and Jim Nance. Perhaps most important, Schwartzwalder did not yet have to concern himself with answering the age-old question "What have you done for me lately?" His 1970 team, remarkably enough, went 6–4 for the season and Schwartzwalder was named the East's outstanding coach in at least one poll.[28]

In all, the revolt of black athletes at Syracuse ended just about the way it had started. The administration went on with the normal course of business at the university while waiting for the whole incident to blow over. The dismissed black athletes, on the other hand, were left to find their own way in the world without much help from those who had induced them to attend the university in the first place. No one emerged a winner from the incident at Syracuse. For every person who emerged with greater sensitivity to racial matters, there were a dozen others who were left with a bitter taste in their mouths over the whole incident. Chronic racism still existed at Syracuse, but under a different cover.[29]

"Shave Off That Thing": The Great Pumpkin and Fred Milton Affair at Oregon State

The last place you might expect a black athletic revolt to take place was at Oregon State University. Located in Corvallis, the quintessential college town situated in the beautiful Willamette Valley, Oregon State was not a hotbed for social causes and radical movements. Perhaps the only serious controversy that ever occurred on campus was when the school's arch-rival, the University of Oregon, was perceived as getting preferential treatment from the local press or the Board of Regents. All the apparent tranquility on campus, however, would change suddenly in 1969. In February of that year, Dee Andros, the burly head football coach known affectionately as "The Great Pumpkin," happened to cross paths with one of his black players, Fred Milton, while taking a walk across campus. It was a chance meeting for not only Andros and Milton but the university community at large. Andros, while obviously not realizing it at the time, sparked a campus uprising by telling Milton to shave off his mustache and Vandyke beard by the following Monday or be dismissed from the team.[30]

Milton refused to honor Andros's request. When Monday rolled around, Milton was not yet clean-shaven and Andros followed through on his threat by informing the junior linebacker from Richmond, Washington, that he was no longer a member of the football team, although his scholarship would be honored through the remainder of the year. "He [Milton] did not conform to the rules set up for the team," Andros noted. "It is the policy of the team and the athletic department that no mustaches or beards will be permitted to be worn by an Oregon State athlete. It has nothing to do with discrimination but the fact we try to produce a team that the students, alumni, and ourselves can be proud of." [31] Milton went immediately to the Black Student Union (BSU) and filed complaints against Andros and the athletic department, alleging that his human rights had been violated.

The BSU was in full support of Milton and wasted no time in drawing attention to his case. On the evening of February 24, the BSU announced that its fifty-seven members, who included seventeen black athletes, would boycott all classes and athletic events at Oregon State until a satisfactory solution to the Milton affair could be found. The following morning the BSU made a more dramatic declaration of protest. Just before Dr. Linus Pauling, a two-time winner of the Nobel Peace Prize was to deliver the Centennial Lecture, approximately thirty members of the BSU and about an equal number of white sympathizers, crowded in front of the stage in Oregon State's Gill Coliseum and asked if they could explain to the several thousand people in attendance the reasons behind the proposed boycott. James Jensen, president of the University, who was already on stage with most of the other top administrators, consented to the request, giving the protesting students three minutes to explain their position. Rich Harr, a sophomore defensive back on the football team, and Mike Smith, president of the BSU, made short speeches to the crowd asking support for the boycott, which was scheduled to start the very next day. Interrupted by occasional catcalls or applause, the two black student leaders stressed the point that the Milton case was not simply a black issue but should be a concern of everyone in the community. Following the brief speeches by Harr and Smith, President Jensen mounted the podium amid much applause from the crowd and acknowledged his gratitude to the two students for speaking out, "We believe that at Oregon State University we have kept the channels open," Jensen noted. "I pledge myself and I pledge to you to do what I can to see that there is no discrimination on this campus." [32]

The BSU's disruption of the Centennial Lecture was just the beginning of a very long day at Oregon State. Five hours later the BSU held a rally in the Memorial Union Commons dining hall, where it tried to drum up additional support for the planned boycott of classes. The offi-

Fred Milton was at the center of the storm in the racial confrontation that took place between African American athletes, coaches, and administrators at Oregon State University. Courtesy of Oregon State University.[33]

cials of the BSU emphasized that the boycott should be an orderly affair and not marred by demonstrations, picketing, or violence. They also stressed that the struggle for human rights and the right of black students to "follow their culture, their beliefs, and select mode of dress and hair style" would be seriously compromised if students who opposed the boycott were prevented from attending classes.[33]

At about the same time the BSU was holding its Memorial Commons rally, Oregon State's coaches and white athletes began to express their feelings on the Milton affair. The school's coaches let their opinions be known at the noontime luncheon meeting of the Beaver Booster Club. All the coaches of the major sports except Andros, who was out of town at the time, extolled the virtues of college athletics and spoke of the importance of team discipline and refusal to give preferential treatment to individual players. Oregon State's white athletes completed the day's events by presenting President Jensen with a petition signed by some 173 athletes supporting Andros's decision to dismiss Milton from the football team. Less encumbered by restrictions governing what they could say on the Milton case than the school's coaches, white athletes at Oregon State were very outspoken in their support of Andros and the athletic department. With the notable exceptions of Dick Fosbury, gold medalist in the high jump at the 1968 Mexico City Olympics, and Bill Enyart, an All-American fullback, Oregon State's white athletes closed ranks and stood solidly behind Andros's decision. John Didion, an All-American center on the Beaver football team, became the chief spokesman for the white athletes, leading about sixty of them on a walk from Gill Coliseum to President Jensen's office to present him with the signed petitions. Jess Lewis, an All-American defensive tackle and NCAA heavyweight wrestling champion, was also a member of that group, as were such other Beaver notables as Steve Preece, Billy Main, Vic Bartolome, Bobby Mayes, Greg Marks, and Bob Beall. To these athletes the Milton case was not a racial matter at all, but merely the instance of a head coach handing out proper punishment to an athlete who failed to follow team rules. In their opinion, Fred Milton understood Andros's rules and the consequences if he failed to abide by them. He made his own bed; now he would have to sleep in it.[34]

The BSU's scheduled boycott of classes officially began on February 26. It was not, however, a smashing success. The fifty-seven black students on campus participated in the boycott, along with a handful of sympathetic white students, who were apparently motivated by the support shown by the student body president, John Frazer, and the surprise backing of the usually conservative student senate the previous evening. University officials could not determine the impact of the boycott on class attendance, but it apparently was slight. Unless they had known ahead of time, visitors to Oregon State would not have noticed anything unusual about student traffic on campus—or that a boycott of classes was even taking place.[35]

The relative peacefulness at Oregon State lasted for only a short time. On February 27 the battle lines between the school's athletic department and the BSU were clearly drawn as the two groups staged separate noontime rallies to defend their particular positions and to throw verbal barbs at each other. A crowd estimated at 5,000 crowded together on the quad outside the school's Memorial Union Ballroom to hear the coaching staff reiterate its position on the Milton affair. The central theme of the speeches was that coaches had the right to establish team rules without the consent of players and that individual sacrifices on the part of players led to a kind of discipline lacking in most areas of contemporary society. The school's coaches, like coaches everywhere, viewed competitive athletics as one of the last arenas in which to develop character, self-control, and loyalty; college athletics was one of the last bastions against long hair, drug freaks, and a world generally gone mad. Andros, the portly ex-football star at Oklahoma and Marine war hero whom sportswriter John Underwood once described as a 250-pound man in a 170-pound body, was obviously upset with having his authority challenged and very sensitive to charges of racial discrimination. He noted, in his deep, gravelly voice that inspired many imitators among members of his own football team, that "there has never been nor will there ever be racism in the athletic department." "I just ask you to believe," said Andros, "that I have never discriminated against any athletes, regardless, black or white. And I promise you that I will always try—and I know my staff will always try—to be 100 percent fair with every athlete that chooses to further his education at Oregon State University."[36]

The BSU's rally took place in the Home Economics auditorium, not more than one hundred yards from where the coaches were delivering their speeches. This meeting was very different from the one held by the coaches at the Memorial Union. Staged before a standing-room-only crowd of about 1,000, the BSU rally was more spirited, involved a more heterogeneous group of people, and included participants from outside the Oregon State community. Substantially outnumbered and with far fewer resources than their antagonists, the BSU realized the importance of expanding their power base and they did so by enticing people of high profile to address the rally. Both John Frazer, president of Oregon State's student body, and his counterpart at the University of Oregon, Dick Jones, pledged their support of the BSU, as did representatives from the SDS. Dave Roberson, a football letterman from the University of Oregon, brought the house down when he announced that black athletes at Oregon had voted unanimously not to take part in athletic contests with Oregon State until the present conflict had been resolved. The real headliner at the BSU rally was John Carlos—the same John Carlos who sent half the world into a tizzy with his Black Power salute at the Mexico City Olympics. Carlos told the audience that coaches had no right to dictate what athletes should wear or how they should look. He emphasized that a beard could be "very special and significant to a black man and to force him to remove it" was inexcusable. Like the other speakers, Carlos laid most of the blame at Andros's feet. "This cat [Andros] must be an idiot," Carlos said at one point. "Without athletes he doesn't have a game."[37]

While the BSU and the athletic department were engaging in verbal warfare, the seventeen black athletes and university administrators at Oregon State were faced with some difficult decisions. The school's black athletes found themselves between a rock and a hard place, with seemingly no effective way to maintain an allegiance to their fellow black students and at the same time continue to participate in competitive athletics, which was helping to pay for their education and serving as a training ground for a possible career in professional sports. Being members of a numerically small racial minority at a predominantly white university, Oregon State's black athletes could not easily say no to their fellow black students, because these same students were almost their only source of social contact outside of athletics. Oregon State's black athletes found that the familial relationship they had established with other black students on campus was very supportive at times but also could be stultifying and restrictive. They risked being scorned, if not ostracized, by their black peer group if they did not show at least tacit support of the BSU boycott and stand up to the school's sport establishment.[38]

The predicament for Oregon State's black athletes was that they also felt an allegiance to the school's coaches and athletic department. As competitive athletes, they had been taught since their careers began to be loyal, obedient, and respectful to those in authority. Breaking the rules and defying the authority of their coaches was incomprehensible to most of Oregon State's black athletes. On a more practical level, the school's black athletes were careful to follow the dictates of their coaches because to do otherwise might cost them their scholarships, limit their playing time, or ultimately hurt their chances of advancing to the next level of sport. Sacrificing those things was far from easy, particularly for a player who felt that the coach had not merely treated him fairly but also had served as his mentor, both on and off the field.[39]

The school's black athletes handled the pressure in various ways. Although early press reports indicated that all seventeen athletes would withdraw from the university, only two of them who figured to get any playing time in their respective sports withdrew from school. Fred Milton, the central figure in the whole affair who, by some accounts, never had any intention of playing football for the Beavers the following fall, reportedly transferred to Portland State. Rich Harr, a defensive back on the football team, transferred to the University of Washington, where he continued to be active in black student affairs. The school's four black basketball players put their careers on the line by failing to report for practice after the announcement of the proposed boycott of classes and athletic events. Coach Paul Valenti immediately dismissed the players— who included Freddie Boyd, a star freshman guard; Andrew Hill, a redshirt junior college transfer; Dave Moore, a starting guard; and Jim Edmunds, a reserve guard—from the team and threatened to have their scholarships revoked. The dismissals forced Valenti to go into the last two weeks of the season without any black player and caused Oregon State's opponents to withhold their black athletes from competition.

Some black athletes at Oregon State continued to concentrate on athletics while simultaneously espousing the BSU party line and keeping their distance from the racial problems on campus. Two athletes who seemingly fell into this category were Willie Turner, the leading sprinter on the school's track team, and Tommie Smith's younger brother, Ernie, who was Oregon State's second best sprinter.[40]

The university's administrative officials made legitimate efforts to respond to the BSU demands. President Jensen, actually seeming to relish the spotlight, attempted to negotiate in good faith on behalf of the university. Although it was not easy to give in to the BSU demands in the face of personal insults and bitter condemnations, Jensen seemingly made every effort to settle the dispute between black students and the school's athletic department. On February 28 he charged the Committee on Minority Affairs with the "responsibility of bringing the B.S.U. and the athletic department together to identify issues and needs more clearly and to define the proper boundaries of disciplinary control." Five days later, Jensen appointed another committee, called the Commission on Human Rights and Responsibilities, which was asked to settle disputes that arose when decisions by coaches or other university personnel conflicted with a student's individual human rights. Jensen stressed that the committee, which was chaired by James Oldfield, head of the Animal Science Department, and included five other faculty members and three students, would not supersede the Committee on Minority Affairs.[41]

The BSU found Jensen's proposals unacceptable. On the same day he announced the formation of the Commission on Human Rights and Responsibilities, the BSU held yet another rally at the Memorial Union Commons, at which it blasted Jensen for his actions and declared that some forty-seven black students planned to withdraw from the university. The president of the BSU, Mike Smith, branded Oregon State a "corrupt and racist institution" and said that black students would leave the "university with its plantation philosophy of operation." Smith called Jensen a "spineless figurehead" and accused him of relegating "authority to numerous other college officials in his attempt to solve the problem." At the conclusion of his brief speech, Smith led a group of about forty black students on a symbolic march across campus and off the university grounds.[42]

Oregon State's athletic department was slightly more optimistic than the BSU about Jensen's proposals, including the establishment of the Commission on Human Rights and Responsibilities. Although the department was obviously concerned about having its power usurped by the newly created commission, it publicly expressed support for Jensen's plan. The athletic department's stand on the Jensen proposals and the entire Milton affair was most fully expressed by the athletic director,

James Barratt, at an Oregon State Faculty meeting on March 6. Barratt, who had been relatively silent on the subject up to this time, did not leave a stone unturned in his address to the faculty senate, touching upon everything from Fred Milton's possible motives for breaking team rules to specific changes made by the athletic department to foster a more positive relationship with Oregon State's black students. Barratt told members of the faculty senate that the Milton affair was "not, and never has been," a case of racial prejudice. In his opinion, Oregon State's black students had confused "discipline for discrimination." Barratt stressed that the athletic department was "not for an all-white program" and that the apparent decision by the school's black students to leave the university "distresses all of us." In an obvious tone of discouragement, Barratt noted that since 1951 the department had had a terribly difficult time attracting black student-athletes to Oregon State. He cited the lack of a black community in Corvallis, high out-of-state entrance requirements, and lack of a black studies program as primary reasons for not being able to recruit more black athletes. Last, Barratt pointed out that all black student-athletes were "welcome back to the athletic department at any time under absolutely no duress."[43]

The Commission on Human Rights and Responsibilities began their work almost immediately, asking Fred Milton and Oregon State's athletic board to submit written reports detailing their side of the story. However, between the time that the committee began its investigation in March and filed its final report two months later, a number of events took place that would keep the racial problems at Oregon State in full view of the sporting public. On March 6, the Portland chapter of the NAACP endorsed the black walkout at Oregon State in protest of Andros's decision to dismiss Milton from the football team. Silent on the issue until now so that black students and the school's athletic department could iron out their own differences, the NAACP conducted an investigation that illuminated more fully the specific grievances of Oregon State's black students. Thomas R. Vickers, chairman of the NAACP's local chapter, conducted the investigation, interviewing several black students about the Milton affair. In perhaps the most accurate appraisal to date, Vickers reported that the "beard blowup" was merely a symptom of other black student grievances at Oregon State, grievances that had been festering for some time. Vickers was told by black students, for example, that Corvallis "merchants and businessmen had gone to deliberate lengths to make blacks feel uncomfortable and leave their places of business." Racism also extended to the housing facilities provided black students on campus. A majority of black students complained to Vickers that they were consistently housed in second-class dormitories so inferior to white student housing that it appeared to be "official university policy." Perhaps the most frequently mentioned complaint of Oregon State's black athletes was about the athletic department's "unwritten policy" that they date only women of their own race. Black athletes told Vickers that pressure was quickly brought to bear on them if they dated white coeds.[44]

Following closely on the heels of Vickers's investigation were two incidents involving Oregon State black athletes that also would keep the university's racial problems a hot topic of conversation. On April 8, Bryce Huddleston, a black wingback from California, showed up for spring football practice wearing a mustache. Andros, who by this time was more determined than ever to enforce team rules, kicked Huddleston off the squad, with the understanding that he could return once he was clean-shaven. Huddleston immediately appealed to the Commission on Human Rights and Responsibilities. The committee adopted, with the approval of Jensen, a rather nebulous directive, telling the Board of Intercollegiate Athletics "that pending final decision, Huddleston shall be granted an excused absence from spring football practice and not be penalized under any disobedience clause." The committee further confused the issue by declaring that all other athletes must comply with "existing rules and physical appearance until pending cases are settled."[45]

Andros's response to the committee's actions was anything but nebulous. While obviously concerned about disobeying the edict of Jensen and the committee, Andros noted, nonetheless, that he could not run a football program "by letting a kid appear when he wants to. As far as I am concerned, he [Huddleston] is off the squad." Any questions of ultimate authority in the case eventually became a moot point because Huddleston was allowed to rejoin the team after shaving his mustache and admitting the error of his ways. He had missed three days of practice, just enough time to go from first-string wingback to last on the depth chart.[46]

Perhaps more noteworthy than the Huddleston affair were the problems encountered by Willie Turner and Ernie Smith about three weeks later during a dual track meet with the University of Washington. Turner and Smith traveled to Seattle with every expectation of gaining big points for their team against the largely outmanned Huskies. Circumstances, however, would prevent them from doing so. No sooner had the two athletes stepped off the bus in Seattle than members of Washington's BSU began pressuring them not to compete in the track meet. Under the leadership of its president, Larry Gossett, and the former Oregon State football player Rich Harr, the Washington BSU was determined to keep Smith and Turner from participating because it believed the two athletes had turned their backs on black student rights by rescinding their initial commitment to leave Oregon State. Smith and Turner were traitors, plain and simple.[47]

The pressure exerted by Washington's BSU proved successful. On the advice of Coach Berny Wagner, Smith and Turner decided not to compete, returning to Corvallis on the day of the meet. The two athletes were bitter about the treatment they had received at the hands of the Washington BSU. A day after their arrival back in Corvallis, Smith and Turner issued a statement through the Oregon State Athletic Department in which they condemned the actions of the "misled black students" from the University of Washington. The two athletes saved most of the criticism for Harr. The former Oregon State athlete was accused by Smith and Turner of being, among other things, insensitive to the needs of black students at both Oregon State and the University of Washington. Harr, they said, encouraged black students to forgo their educations, knowing full well that you "can't deal with the educated without being educated yourself." Harr had run away from his problems; now he was selfishly pressuring everyone else to do the same.[48]

After two months of eager anticipation, the university's Commission on Human Rights and Responsibilities finally came out with its report. Not the most decisive document ever published, the report contained the kind of double-talk that would have done Oliver North and John Poindexter proud. The gist of the four-page document was that Fred Milton's human rights had been violated. The committee stressed, however, that the violation was not deliberate but resulted from "insufficiently sensitive discipline rules." Andros and his staff were insensitive to the changing needs of individual team members, "including the emerging social and cultural values of members of the black community." At the same time, the committee was quick to point out that it shared Andros's "sincere dedication to the principle that effective discipline is essential to successful organizational endeavor" and is a valuable and necessary instrument in constructive character formation. The committee specifically recommended that the Board of Intercollegiate Athletics request the football coaching staff to reexamine and modify its "neatness" clause; that a suitable channel of appeal open to all athletes and coaches be maintained by the Board of Intercollegiate Athletics; that a list of team regulations be presented to all of the school's athletes and to all prospective recruits before making a formal commitment to Oregon State; and that Fred Milton be given every opportunity to reenroll at the university and become a member of the 1970 football team.[49]

Neither Milton nor Andros was pleased with the commission's report. Milton believed the committee's recommendations were worthless because President Jensen had not established guidelines to ensure that they were enforced. Andros was troubled by the commission's announcement that he had violated Milton's human rights. But rather than automatically accepting the committee's recommendations, he dug in and stubbornly declared that "as long as I am head football coach at Oregon State, my staff and I will make the rules and policies of our football program."[50]

Andros's reaction to the committee's report was not surprising. While he enjoyed playing the role of the country bumpkin, Andros was not stupid. He was well aware of his status in the university community and realized that the commission had done nothing to usurp his power as football coach. It would be no exaggeration to say that other than President Jensen, Andros was the single most powerful person at Oregon State. He had led the school's football program back into national prominence, realizing the kind of success on the gridiron that had been unknown at Oregon State since the glory years of Tommy Prothro. Andros had the support of most of the alumni and the majority of the faculty at Oregon State. He had parlayed his popularity into a recently agreed upon contract with the school, utilizing a job offer from the University of Pittsburgh as leverage in the negotiations. Word had it that Andros had asked for and been promised total control of the football program by the school's administration.[51]

With such enormous support shown for his program, Andros was not about to make drastic changes in his coaching philosophy and succumb to pressure from a small minority of disgruntled students. Andros genuinely believed that the rules he set down were in the best interests of his players, the football team, and Oregon State. Like many other college coaches around the country, he saw himself as the one man on campus who was in a position to teach such neglected values as sportsmanship, self-sacrifice, and team loyalty. Furthermore, Andros was not prepared to redress the grievances of black students because he believed he had already made substantial changes in team regulations in an attempt to accommodate the special needs of his athletes. He was certainly more progressive than his predecessor, Tommy Prothro, who supposedly prohibited his players from smiling the day before a game and forced them to march two by two onto airplanes. Andros proudly noted that he had made concessions to his players by shortening practices, making changes in meals at the training table, and not forcing team members to live in an athletic dormitory. On the other hand, Andros was reluctant to be too accommodating for fear that he would be viewed as capitulating to black students. In fact, his show of force seemed to be motivated as much by concern that he would not be seen as yielding to group pressure as by his fear of the consequences of the black student revolt. Andros believed, moreover, that because the athletic department was paying for the services of black athletes, he had every right to ask them to obey team rules and regulations. Although he would never admit it publicly, Andros believed that athletes like Fred Milton showed a serious case of ingratitude by refusing to follow the dictates of those who had made it possible for them to receive a free education.[52]

Athletic department officials were terribly disappointed by the report but promised to consider seriously the commission's various recommendations. Athletic Director Barratt and Wallace E. Gibbs, chairman of the Board of Intercollegiate Athletics, noted that reforms would be made in the athletic department to reflect a changing society and proper concern for human rights. Both Barratt and Gibbs seemed serious about making changes in the athletic department. But, as was the case in many of the black athletic revolts at predominantly white universities, the changes made would be only token gestures, not anything substantive. Barratt announced, for example, a new "personal appearance code" that would allow players to wear facial hair during the off-season. One of the most talked about changes made in the athletic department was the appointment of a black coach. Gene Hilliard, a thirty-year-old teacher and coach at Highland Junior High School in Corvallis and a former Beaver football player, was hired by Andros as an assistant football coach, becoming the first black to join the Oregon State coaching staff on a full-time basis. Hilliard was expected to help recruit black players, act as a counselor to minority athletes, and coach.[53]

The Oregon State Athletic Department came out of the Milton affair relatively unscathed. Andros had his armor tarnished slightly, but not dramatically enough to lessen his enormous popularity in the community and around the state. Of the department's seventeen black athletes, eleven chose to stay at Oregon State and complete their education. Athletes the caliber of Freddie Boyd, Willie Turner, Ernie Smith, Mel Easley, and Bryce Huddleston continued to excel in their respective sports and bring recognition to the school. There were several developments in the athletic department, however, that did not bode well for the future of the program. Not surprisingly, there were no black players in Andros's 1969 recruiting class. Black high school football stars had been warned not to attend Oregon State, and they heeded the advice. Paul Valenti's popularity as basketball coach was waning, and he would be replaced within a few years by Ralph Miller, the former Wichita State and University of Iowa head coach. Perhaps most important, trouble would arise in the Beaver baseball program. In December 1970, thirteen members of the baseball team presented Jim Barratt with a petition asking that coach Gene Tanselli be dismissed as coach because of his failure to help players improve their skills. The charges were repeated the following year and underscored by player resignations and the threat of a boycott. Finally, in 1972, Tanselli was accused of racial discrimination by Verdell Adams,

a black outfielder from Portland. While exonerated of racial discrimination charges, Tanselli was fired as Oregon State's baseball coach on June
15, 1972. In a most revealing statement, Barratt explained that Tanselli
was being replaced because of his record. In effect, Tanselli was ill-
equipped to handle the various criticisms leveled against him because,
unlike Andros, he had made the mistake of losing more games than he
had won during the previous three seasons.[54]

Lessons to Be Learned: Black Student Athletes and the Dynamics of Institutional Conflict

One of the most striking features of the revolts at Berkeley, Syracuse,
and Oregon State was that black athletes did not go it alone but were
ably assisted by their respective black student organizations. In large
measure, black athletes whether working actively with the organizations
or serving as figureheads, were important in bringing about change in
their particular institutions. Although they felt an obligation to adhere
to their institutionally defined role as athletes, black athletes also belonged to a family of black students who worked through their campus
organizations to accomplish a range of functions, which included educat-
ing or confronting their institutions about the limitations of their programs for black students; sponsoring social and other special activities
for black students; raising funds for black programs; offering black cultural experiences for black students; providing educational or support
services for black students; and building coalitions through the "family
of black students."[55]

In all three revolts, black students confronted the administration at
the highest levels possible with their demands, assuming that that was
where the power was located. Chancellor Corbally of Syracuse, Chancellor Heyns of Berkeley, and President Jensen of Oregon State accepted the
challenge and attempted to negotiate in good faith with black athletes.
Corbally bent over backwards trying to bring Ben Schwartzwalder and
the boycotting black football players together to discuss their differences.
Jensen did the same at Oregon State, making every conceivable effort to
settle the bitter confrontation between black students and the school's
athletic department. Heyns tried desperately not only to mend the fences
between disgruntled black athletes and Berkeley's athletic department
but also to see that the school was more sensitive to the needs of all black
students on campus. Like most of his counterparts at other institutions
facing similar problems with black athletes, Heyns set up a committee to
determine the facts surrounding the confrontation and make policy
changes where necessary. Unlike many of the fact-finding committees at
other universities, however, the recommendations made by Berkeley's

committee were not mere window dressing but substantive changes—similar to those made around the Bay at both San Jose State and San Francisco State.[56]

Black students at the three institutions went to the bargaining table with university administrators armed with as many weapons as they could muster. Although black students were always careful to keep control of the confrontations, they used various types of groups to garner support or to exert pressure on the universities. Activist community leaders, black faculty, white faculty and students, and the NAACP all played, in varying degrees, a part in the revolts at Berkeley, Syracuse, and Oregon State. On the other hand, in their case, student leaders resented the fact that the school's president brought additional institutional representation into negotiations. Their demands were predicated on the assumption that the president was the person who had the power to make changes, not special university committees made up of faculty members who were largely ill-informed and possibly unconcerned about the needs of black students. Nowhere was this attitude more apparent than in the confrontation at Oregon State. Mike Smith, Annette Greene, and other BSU members at the school were adamantly opposed to President Jensen's creation of the Commission on Human Rights and Responsibilities, charging Jensen with "relegating his authority to numerous other college officials in his attempt to solve the problem."[57]

In efforts to gain bargaining power, black students at all three schools fostered confrontation and heightened tension in a number of different ways. "Symbolic behavior and gamesmanship" were certainly evident in the revolts at Berkeley, Syracuse, and Oregon State. Often expressing themselves with four-letter words, black students boycotted classes, seized and occupied buildings, and staged rallies in an attempt to seek legitimacy in a situation where they had virtually no autonomy or power. The central ploy of revolting black athletes was, of course, the threat or actual withholding of their services. Black athletes risked their educations and, in some cases, their chances at a professional career, to become involved in the struggle for human rights at their respective institutions. For example, Bobby Smith, spokesman for the black athletes at Berkeley, apparently lost out on a professional football contract because of his involvement in the racial turmoil on campus.[58] Other black athletes discontinued their collegiate athletic careers, transferred to other institutions, or dropped out of school entirely.

School officials generally did not know how to deal with the black athletes. Nor did school officials realize where their commitments would lead them or how much support they would receive from people within and outside the university community. As we have seen, presidents of the three universities responded to the revolts in similar ways, sometimes finding it difficult to distinguish between rhetoric and genuine bargaining ploys. White faculty members as a whole showed little interest in the revolts, although they expected to be kept informed about the negotiations. While in each case white faculty members served on the special grievance committee appointed by the president, they had a more limited role in the negotiations than many of their colleagues at other institutions. The few black faculty members and administrators at each institution seemed to play a more crucial role in negotiations, although it tended to be on an informal basis rather than in an official university capacity.[59] The head coaches involved in the revolts were certainly more decisive in their dealings with black athletes than other university personnel. It took Ben Schwartzwalder only a matter of minutes to dismiss the black athletes at Syracuse, Rene Hêrrerias slightly longer to get rid of Bob Presley at Berkeley, and Dee Andros some two days to say good-bye to Fred Milton at Oregon State. These were not decisions made without some forethought, however. Not one of these men wanted to get rid of players who could lead them to victory and ultimately determine their fate as coaches. But, in their minds, they were given no choice. They either disciplined their black athletes or risked having their authority undermined and team unity disrupted.

The decisiveness of the three coaches, however, did not prevent school officials from interceding in the confrontations or curbing the inevitable dispute that took place between white athletes and disgruntled black ones. In large measure, the schools' white athletes acted as willing spokesmen for coaches who did not always have the freedom to speak with total candor and recognized the advantages of having someone speak on their behalf. White athletes at the three institutions were almost uniformly loyal to their coaches, believing that black athletes were treated fairly and without racist intent by Herrerias, Schwartzwalder, and Andros. The coaches did not just have the right to dismiss the black athletes, but were obligated to because rules had been disobeyed and team discipline violated. White athletes did not take kindly to the fact that black students, using the charge of racial discrimination as a smoke screen, got away with breaking rules for which they themselves would have been seriously reprimanded. The majority of white athletes, moreover, were disturbed by what they perceived as an attempt by their black counterparts to disrupt the institution of sport, an institution that relied heavily on humbleness, submissiveness, and respect for authority. White athletes believed that their black counterparts mistakenly confused racial discrimination with the discipline that was necessary for the success of any athletic team.

Black athletes, however, were probably not so much confusing discrimination with discipline as attempting to use their coaches as scapegoats. They conveniently alleged discrimination as a justification for their actions, according to Harry Edwards's interpretation, in an attempt "to ameliorate and help resolve the dilemma of conflicting demands in which they found themselves." The black athletes at Berkeley, Syracuse, and Oregon State were enrolled at institutions with a relatively small number of blacks in the total school population, and their informal social contacts at these institutions were limited to this small minority. While this situation provided black athletes with an important support system, it also placed enormous pressure on them because they were unable to seek out new social contacts when their role as athletes conflicted with the political views of the majority of blacks on campus. By alleging discrimination, black athletes could simultaneously express empathy with the black protest movement—or become actively involved in it—and convince themselves that they had not violated their proper role as athletes.[60]

It became apparent that the charges of racism lodged by black athletes were partly an ideological justification when white athletes were disciplined or actually dismissed from a team for the same reasons as their black counterparts. Black athletes paid virtually no attention, let alone claimed discrimination, when a white athlete was dismissed from a team for length of hair or some other rules infraction. When the white sprinter Bob Hertan was kicked off Oregon State's track team by coach Berny Wagner for refusing to shave his mustache and sideburns, the black athletes on campus voiced no complaints about Wagner and his coaching methods. They acted as if the incident never took place. The sit-in staged in the office of Wallace E. Gibbs, University Registrar and chairman of the Board of Intercollegiate Athletics, to protest the dismissal of Hertan was composed entirely of white students.[61]

Perhaps the most glaring indication that white coaches were used as scapegoats was the fact that organized turmoil was virtually nonexistent at historically black colleges. Eddie Robinson of Grambling, Jake Gaither of Florida A & M, and coaches at other black schools adhered to similar policies, required the same discipline among their players, and meted out similar kinds of punishments to rebellious athletes as their counterparts at predominantly white institutions. They never experienced, however, charges of racial discrimination by their athletes. The reasons for this disparity are not entirely clear, but it probably stemmed, first of all, from the fact that black athletes were among the numerical majority on black campuses and could always pursue alternative social contacts to alleviate the pressure arising from their sometimes conflicting role demands as both athletes and black men in American culture. As Harry Edwards has argued, the black athletes at historically black colleges, unlike their fellow athletes at white institutions could find new social contacts when particular groups of black students made demands on them that were not consistent with their role as athletes. Second, black athletes could not be true to the essential values of the black student movement if they treated the black coach as a scapegoat and charged discrimination. Black athletes realized that the whole movement was, to a large extent, predicated on the assumption that all blacks were potential converts to their way of thinking and, attacks on black coaches were illogical as well as counterproductive. Last, attacking black coaches at predominantly black colleges was out of the question because such action was inconsistent with the Black Power movement's demand for more black coaches in organized sport.[62]

The utilization of coaches as scapegoats did not erase the fact that black student athletes experienced various forms of insensitivity and discrimination on predominantly white university campuses across the country. The small number of blacks in the total school population did play a part in the revolts at Berkeley, Syracuse, and Oregon State. In many respects, the three schools were guilty of condemning black athletes to an inadequate social life and intraracial as well as interracial discord by deliberately recruiting them to their schools but failing to attract a large number of other black students. While blacks entered these institutions of their own volition and were given an opportunity to receive a free education and participate in college athletics, they were thrust into an environment where people did not always understand black culture, racial slurs were common, and acts of discrimination were committed on a regular basis. Berkeley in particular was begging for trouble by recruiting more black athletes but failing to attract a substantial number of other black students to its institution. As athletic director, Pete Newell could brag that the department had more than tripled its number of black athletes during his eight-year tenure at the school. At the same time, however, he and his coaches were unwittingly assembling a critical mass of black athletes who were capable of exerting a great deal more pressure on athletic department policy than their counterparts at either Syracuse or Oregon State.

Playing a part in the revolts were the types of communities in which the three institutions were located. Oregon State was ripe for racial disturbances because it was located in a small, rural town with few black citizens. The athletic department at the school inadvertently put its black athletes in an almost impossible position because there was no local black community in Corvallis in which the athletes could feel at home nor, in some cases, was there any off-campus housing available to them.[63] In contrast to black students at colleges located in areas with a local black community, the black athletes at Oregon State felt uncomfortable patronizing the community facilities because they were so much in the minority. In this situation, black athletes and many of their fellow black students were left with the feeling that they had been recruited by a school that was more interested in improving its institutional prestige than in helping them as individuals. Oregon State was terribly slow in making its nearly all-white location acceptable to blacks. By the time the school got around to revising campus housing patterns, liberalizing social regulations, and offering various social and cultural programs for blacks, a number of black athletes and other black students had chosen other universities which were either located near large black population centers or were more sensitive to the needs of minorities.

In sum, the black athletes who participated in the revolts at these three predominantly white universities were forever changed by their experiences. Witnessing firsthand the inner workings of university administrations, they found their experiences at once exhilarating and enormously frightening. Because of their youth, their constrictive role as athletes, and their limited experience in the political arena, black athletes made some tactical mistakes that put them in a vulnerable position not only with coaches and university administrators, but with other black students as well. They were forced to do some real soul-searching and ultimately decide what was most important for them personally. It was not an enviable position to be in, particularly for some black students who were only a year or two out of high school. While their fellow students faced the usual problems of preparing for classes and deciding upon a major, black athletes had not only to deal with these matters but also to decide how they could maintain an allegiance to other black students and remain in the good graces of their coaches. Whatever path individual black athletes chose to follow, it was one they decided upon very carefully. It was their future at stake, not the future of college athletics.

8

Victory for Allah

Muhammad Ali, the Nation of Islam, and American Society

I envy Muhammad Ali," declared Bill Russell, the basketball great, following a well-publicized meeting between the famous boxer and several other prominent black athletes in Cleveland during the summer of 1967. "He has something I have never been able to attain and something very few people I know possess. He has an absolute and sincere faith."[1] Russell's assessment of Ali's religious belief, which came just a month before the fighter's conviction for refusing induction into America's armed forces, was entirely accurate; Ali embraced the Nation of Islam with great fervor and has shown unquestioning devotion to Muslim leadership and complete faith in Allah throughout his adult life. Even after being suspended from the movement during the late 1960s, Ali never wavered from his commitment to Allah or to the religious teachings of Elijah and Wallace Muhammad.[2] He willingly submitted to the rigid discipline of a movement designed to control the total behavior of its members.[3] In doing so, he rejected many of the essential values of American society to which other middle-class citizens adhered and set himself apart as perhaps the most influential and significant athlete in history.

Ali's conformity to the dictates of Muslim philosophy was a primary reason for his influence on the black community and the broader American society. Muslim doctrine gave him the faith and single-mindedness necessary to combat injustices in American society. Much of the black community's adulation for Ali stemmed from his refusal to seek a middle ground while he simultaneously pursued athletic success and maintained beliefs that were often antithetical to those found in sport. Ali was not universally endorsed by the black community because he rejected Christianity and talked of racial separation. But he satisfied the wishes of the Muslim leadership by being recognized as an autonomous, proud black

152

man who was not dependent on the heavyweight championship for his sense of self-worth or his livelihood. He became the movement's most important symbol of black masculinity, a man of heroic stature who came to represent the struggle for civil rights in a society torn by racial divisions and by war.

To many in the white community, Ali's membership in the Nation of Islam was both frightening and detestable. His involvement with a group that advocated separation of the races was reprehensible to whites who expected black champions to concentrate on boxing and refrain from speaking out on racial and political issues. Rather than acquiescing to the sport establishment and assuming the subservient role traditionally assigned black athletes, Ali acted "inappropriately" by showing contempt for white authority and values. Instead of acting appreciative for his many opportunities, Ali had the audacity to call America an oppressive society and insist on a separate homeland for blacks. Ali was considered a traitor for refusing induction into military service on religious grounds instead of rallying around the flag.

Ali ultimately attained an honored position among broad segments of American society and won grudging admiration from even the most conservative blacks and whites. The transformation of much of the Nation of Islam into a more orthodox Islamic religion, along with improved race relations, resulted in a growing admiration for Ali that transcended race and eventually led to his becoming one of the world's most revered persons. The aging Ali, more appreciated than ever because of his contributions to boxing and his unwillingness to sacrifice his religious principles, endeared himself to a wide audience by abandoning the idea of racial separateness and supporting integration and the democratic process. Ali's changing beliefs, while criticized by Muslims who continued to hold a racialist position, seemed to be natural for a man whose fundamental generosity and racial tolerance was never subsumed by rhetoric about black superiority and white devils. Once feared and despised because of his religious faith, Ali became a beloved figure, lionized by people of all races and backgrounds.[4]

Acceptance of Allah and the Nation of Islam

Ali became involved with the Nation of Islam long before it was known to the American public. The young Cassius Clay first heard of Elijah Muhammad and his followers during a Golden Gloves boxing tournament in Chicago in 1959. Two years later in Miami, Clay met a follower of Muhammad named Sam Saxon (now known as Abdul Rahaman) who convinced him to attend a meeting at the local Muslim temple. This meeting, as Clay would later proclaim, was a turning point in his life.

Saxon, along with two other Muslim ministers, Jeremiah Shabazz and Ishmael Sabakhan, inculcated Clay with Muslim philosophy and the teachings of Elijah Muhammad. They taught him that Allah was a black man who, in contrast to the white man's Jesus, was a "powerful prayer-answering God" genuinely concerned about the plight of the oppressed black masses. They explained to him that blacks had been brainwashed, led to believe that anything of value was always white rather than black. They told him that Elijah Muhammad was the only black leader in America with enough courage to tell the truth about the white man. And they assured him that the solution to the black man's suffering was separation of the races rather than integration.[5]

Though cautious at first about what he heard, Clay was enthralled by the Muslim doctrines and gradually embraced them with great passion. He seemingly found comfort in the elaborate rules of behavior prescribed by the Nation of Islam. As with members of more orthodox religions, there was a side to Clay that relished leaving decisions to higher authorities who dictated what to eat, how to pray, what clothes to wear, and how to spend free time. He was enamored with the Nation's work ethic. He believed strongly in the group's insistence that its members engage in hard, honest labor; practice thrift and sobriety; refrain from gambling and idleness; and adhere to principles of good nutrition and personal hygiene. Clay also believed in the Nation of Islam's more extreme teachings, which claimed that there was no heaven or hell, that Christianity was a religion organized by the enemies of the black community, and that whites were a genetically engineered race of devils.[6]

Moreover, Clay was infatuated with Elijah Muhammad, the self-professed Messenger of Allah who assumed leadership of the Nation of Islam in 1934 following the sudden disappearance of his mentor, the spiritual founder of the movement W. D. Fard.[7] In Muhammad, Clay found a surrogate father, a powerful man who would teach him the ways of the world and nurture his latent sense of social and political responsibility. Clay was awakened, most noticeably, by Muhammad's talk of black pride in the face of white domination. Inspired by Muhammad's dreams of a separate black nation and talk of a glorious African heritage, Clay could now take pride in his own negritude and align himself with other blacks to overcome the effects of white oppression that had lingered since childhood. Like many other blacks at this historical moment, he was outraged by the crimes committed against blacks by white Americans.[8]

Clay initially tried to hide his allegiance to the Nation of Islam from the American public. There was a heavyweight championship in his future, and Clay, aware that many people hated and feared the Nation, believed that knowledge of his ties to the movement would jeopardize his chances for a title fight. He spent the next couple of years quietly entering Muslim meetings through the back door and keeping talks with other believers secret.[9]

Despite his good intentions, Clay's attempts at religious privacy were destined to fail as his star rose in boxing. In the months leading up to his championship fight with Sonny Liston in Miami, newspapers reported Clay's attendance at Muslim rallies across the country and speculated about his level of involvement in the black nationalist movement. As Thomas Hauser noted, Clay's interest in the Nation of Islam first came to public notice in September 1963 when the *Philadelphia Daily News* reported his appearance at a local Muslim gathering. Some five months later, the *New York Herald Tribune* ran a front-page story describing Clay's involvement in a Muslim rally, noting rather prophetically that the young fighter's presence at meetings of the Nation of Islam lent the group immediate prestige. Two weeks after the appearance of the *Herald Tribune* column, the *Louisville Courier-Journal* published an interview in which Clay expressed his agreement with the Muslims' opposition to integration and announced his refusal "to impose myself on people who don't want me."[10]

Any remaining doubts about Clay's religious leanings were laid to rest by activities at the young fighter's training camp in Miami. He was accompanied virtually everywhere by clean-shaven, conservatively dressed Muslims with short-cropped hair—men who looked more like uniformed guards than boxing fans. One black man who stood out from the rest, conspicuous for both his light skin and reddish hair, was Malcolm X, the brilliant and controversial Muslim minister. Malcolm was in town at the request of Clay, who had invited the famous Muslim leader and his family to Miami as a sixth wedding anniversary present. The two men had established a close friendship, which extended back to 1962, when Clay and his brother, Rudolph, had journeyed to Detroit to hear a speech by Elijah Muhammad.[11]

Malcolm's stay in Miami was not a typical wedding anniversary celebration. Although attempting to enjoy the excitement surrounding the championship fight, Malcolm found himself embroiled in turmoil and controversy. Recently suspended from the Nation of Islam by Elijah Muhammad, Malcolm X was not welcomed by everyone in Miami. He and his Muslim friends cast a shadow over the whole affair. The fight's promoter, Bill MacDonald, believed that the Muslim presence had alienated the local community and caused sluggish ticket sales. Worried about financial losses, MacDonald, with the help of Harold Conrad, a boxing promoter and friend of Clay's, convinced Malcolm to leave Miami until the day of the fight.[12]

In truth, Malcolm's decision to leave Miami was as much a result of

A young Muhammad Ali (at the time Cassius Clay) in a sparring session prior to his joining the Nation of Islam. Courtesy of the Amateur Athletic Foundation of Los Angeles.

pressure from the Muslim leadership in Chicago as anything else. He showed some vestiges of respect for Elijah Muhammad by disassociating himself publicly from Clay's camp. Muhammad feared that Malcolm's presence in Miami would ultimately be an embarrassment to the Nation of Islam. Muhammad expected Clay to be defeated by the heavily favored Sonny Liston, and any association of Malcolm X or other members of the Nation of Islam with the losing fighter would reflect negatively on the movement. Perhaps the best indication of the Nation of Islam's approach to the fight was the fact that no writers from the organization's official publication, *Muhammad Speaks*, were in Miami to cover the fight.[13]

Malcolm returned to Miami in time to offer Clay encouragement just before his battle with Liston. He tried to convince Clay of the symbolic importance of the fight—that it was no ordinary heavyweight championship bout between two black gladiators but an encounter pitting the "cross and the crescent" in the prize ring for the first time. "It's a modern Crusades—a Christian and a Muslim facing each other with television to beam it off telstar for the whole world to see what happens," Malcolm wrote in his autobiography. "Do you think Allah has brought about all this intending for you to leave the ring as anything but the champion?"[14]

Armed with a belief in his own ability and the power of Allah, Clay made short work of Liston. He made the "Big Bear" look amateurish, pummeling his face and wearing him down until he refused to answer the bell for the seventh round. The real excitement, however, did not take place until the following morning at a Miami Beach press conference. Responding to a question about his rumored membership in the Nation of Islam, Clay explained that he was no longer a Christian but a believer "in Allah and in peace." "I know where I'm going," said Clay, "and I know the truth and I don't have to be what you want me to be. I'm free to be what I want."[15]

At a second press conference the following morning, Clay could not have been more direct about his religious affiliation. He told those in attendance, "Islam is a religion and there are 750 million people all over the world who believe in it, and I'm one of them. I ain't no Christian."[16] That same day, Elijah Muhammad acknowledged Clay as a member of the Nation of Islam. "I'm so glad that Cassius Clay was brave enough to say that he was a Muslim," Muhammad told a cheering crowd at the Nation of Islam's annual convention in Chicago. "I'm happy that he confessed he's a believer. Clay whipped a much tougher man and came through the bout unscarred because he has accepted Muhammad as the Messenger of Allah."[17] Several days later, Clay was again seen in the company of Malcolm X, this time in New York touring the United Nations and taking in a film of the championship fight.[18] Finally, on the night of March 6, Elijah Muhammad provided the ultimate affirmation of Clay's status in the Nation of Islam by announcing in a radio broadcast from Chicago that he was giving the fighter the name Muhammad Ali. Muhammad thereby repudiated the champion's "slave name" and bestowed upon him a name that signified his rebirth as a proud black man in racist white America.[19]

The Movement's Leading Symbol of Black Pride

The American public reacted swiftly to Ali's membership in the Nation of Islam. The initial disbelief expressed by many white Americans quickly turned to disdain. Northern liberals, veteran sportswriters, southern conservatives, and ordinary citizens expressed both fear and loathing toward Ali because he had joined a movement that advocated separation of the races, denounced Christianity, celebrated negritude, and accused America of being a racially oppressive society. The new champion provoked trepidation among white Americans because of his membership in a group that was willing to confront civil authority, rebel against social norms, and engage in militant acts of defiance. Ali was a threat because he belonged to a religious organization that challenged white supremacist ideology through a celebration of black intellect, culture, and physical beauty. Perhaps most important, Ali was denounced because he joined a group that challenged the authority associated with the dominant conceptions of the sacred in America. The champion deserved to be vilified, many believed, because he had turned his back on the Christian God and pledged faith in Allah as the source of all power, wisdom, and authority.[20]

Segments of the black community, while sometimes hesitant to speak out too loudly against the new champion for fear that criticism would be construed as racial disloyalty, were disturbed by Ali's membership in the Nation of Islam for many of the same reasons expressed by white Americans. Both Joe Louis and Floyd Patterson were troubled by Ali's rejection of the Christian religion, believing the ties between the heavyweight championship and the black separatist group would ultimately prove fatal to boxing.[21] Perhaps no member of the black community was more appalled by Ali's new religion than his own father, Cassius Marcellus Clay, Sr. The elder Clay despised the Muslims, not so much for their religious beliefs but because he believed they were exerting too much control over his son and had designs on his money. He told the sportswriter Pat Putnam before the Liston fight that the Nation of Islam had brainwashed Cassius and his younger brother, Rudolph. "They have ruined my two boys," said Clay senior; "they should run those Black Muslims out of the country before they ruin other fine people."[22]

Negative reactions to Ali's membership in the Nation of Islam were quickly countered by Elijah Muhammad. He realized the symbolic importance of a Muslim heavyweight champion and proceeded to orchestrate a public relations campaign that transformed Ali into the movement's leading example of black pride. He used the controversy surrounding Ali to his own advantage, branding criticism of the heavyweight champion as religious persecution and hatred of Muslims. With Malcolm X now defrocked and discredited within the Nation, Ali could step in as a charismatic leader who would spread the word. He could serve as an example of righteousness for blacks who had been instilled with a false sense of racial inferiority by white Christian Americans. Elijah Muhammad envisioned Ali as the Nation of Islam's model citizen, a beautiful black man who would lend credibility to the movement, embodying Muslim ideals and the Islamic way of life. In one of his first discourses on Ali in *Muhammad Speaks*, Elijah Muhammad declared that America hated the new champion because he had given up the life of a Christian, sought the "hereafter and not the world," courageously elevated himself "to the side of the true god," and "shaken off the sla-vemaster's ways." "The heavyweight champion's name," proclaimed Muhammad, "will live forever."[23]

Shortly after receiving Muhammad's blessings, Ali embarked on a trip to Africa. Arranged by Osman Karriem, a close friend of Malcolm X, the month-long tour was ostensibly intended to provide Ali with some rest and remove him from the controversy surrounding his recent religious conversion. In truth, the trip served more as a promotional tour for the Nation of Islam and as an opportunity for Ali to nurture ties with his black brethren and gain a sense of his cultural heritage. *Muhammad Speaks* covered the trip in great detail and was always careful to mention that the enthusiastic reception of Ali in the African countries indicated approval of Elijah Muhammad.[24]

Ali's trip was marked by a number of memorable moments, but none of them seemed to affect him so deeply as his chance meeting with Malcolm X in Ghana. After months of quarreling with Elijah Muham-mad over a variety of issues, including Muhammad's supposed sexual misbehavior and financial transgressions, Malcolm had embarked in early spring 1964 on a pilgrimage to Mecca. While in the lobby of Ghana's Hotel Ambassador preparing for his return to the United States, Malcolm bumped into Ali, who had just come back from a morning walk around the city. Accounts of the unexpected meeting differ, but observers agree that the encounter was awkward and strained.[25] Al-though they had once respected and genuinely admired each other, the two men were now headed in opposite directions—the split caused by their conflicting racial ideologies and religious beliefs.

Malcolm's pilgrimage to Mecca helped to solidify his already chang-ing view of the Nation of Islam by convincing him that true Muslims believed in the brotherhood of all people irrespective of color. His travels through the Muslim world gave him "a new insight into the true religion of Islam" and a better understanding of America's entire racial di-lemma.[26]

The change in Malcolm did not stop him from caring for Ali. Dis-traught at the prospect of losing Ali as a friend, Malcolm claimed he had tried to avoid the encounter at the Hotel Ambassador because it might prove embarrassing for the heavyweight champion, who had undoubt-edly been prohibited by the Nation of Islam from associating with him. After his return to the United States, Malcolm sent a telegram to Ali imploring him "to make sure he'd never let his enemies . . . exploit his reputation."[27] For Malcolm, it was obviously difficult to stop being a spiritual adviser to his former student even if that student had chosen a different path to fulfillment.

Ali, for his part, found his strong allegiance to Elijah Muhammad and the Nation of Islam cemented by his trip to Africa. His sojourns in Ghana and Egypt, in particular, heightened his sense of black separateness and his belief in the righteousness of Muhammad's cause. Unlike Malcolm, Ali did not gain faith in the brotherhood of all men. "In America," Ali explained to a Ghanese audience, "everything is white— Jesus, Moses and the angels. I'm glad to be here with my true people." [28] Osman Karriem perhaps said it best when he noted: "I'll remember that trip to Africa as long as I live, because that was where I saw Cassius Clay become Muhammad Ali." [29]

For Ali, coming face to face with Malcolm meant confronting the Nation of Islam's chief apostate. The heavyweight champion believed that Malcolm had forgotten his degraded past and that Muhammad had transformed him from a hustler and pimp into a proud and committed black man. When asked about Malcolm's telegram warning him of possible exploitation at the hands of his enemies, Ali showed his disgust by commenting to reporters about his former comrade's appearance in Africa: "Did you get a look at Malcolm? Dressed in that funny white robe and wearing a beard and walking with that cane that looked like a prophet's stick? Man he's gone. He's gone so far out he's out completely. Nobody listens to Malcolm anymore." [30]

The split between Ali and Malcolm paled in comparison to what took place several months later. On February 21, 1965, Malcolm was murdered while delivering a speech at the Audubon Ballroom in New York City.[31] Ali had no public response to the death of one of the most controversial figures in American history. He let Elijah Muhammad and Malcolm's own brothers, Philbert and Wilfred, vilify the slain black leader, whose "foolish teaching brought him to his own end." [32] At the Nation of Islam's annual Savior's Day Convention in Chicago shortly after Malcolm's death, Ali cheered on Elijah Muhammad as the leader announced: "We didn't want to kill Malcolm and didn't try to kill him. They know I didn't harm Malcolm. They know I loved him." [33]

Ali's much-publicized association with Malcolm tended to overshadow the relationship he had forged with Herbert Muhammad, the third son of Elijah Muhammad. Shortly after capturing the heavyweight title from Sonny Liston in 1964, Ali found himself in the company of Herbert Muhammad, who had been asked by his father to shield the new champion from hangers-on and other people with questionable motives. Elijah Muhammad, who always preferred to stay behind the scenes and who recognized the advantages of working through an intermediary, wanted Herbert to guide Ali so as to protect the interests of the Nation of Islam as well as the champion himself. He did not want people preying on Ali, taking money out of the pockets of the heavyweight champion, who was expected to give over a portion of his yearly earnings to the

Nation of Islam. Perhaps most important, he wanted to ensure that the public image he was trying to cultivate for Ali was going to be protected and promoted in the appropriate fashion.[34]

Herbert Muhammad, who operated both *Muhammad Speaks* and a small photography studio in Chicago, had journeyed to Africa with Ali and increasingly spent time with him on their return to America. Ali hardly made a move without first consulting Herbert, seeking his advice on everything from legal issues to religious doctrine. The two men became close friends and eventually formed a business partnership (Herbert became Ali's manager) that proved financially beneficial to both of them and, by extension, to the Nation of Islam.[35] "He [Herbert] has made it possible for me to help change the history of manager/boxer relationships," noted Ali in the acknowledgments to his autobiography, "and is forever encouraging me not only to give the best performance to the people, but to be concerned with the progress of the people and to stand for the principles of peace, justice and equality—to show that in a profession which is mainly known for brutality and blood, a man can have nobility and dignity. It is not only I who owes Herbert Muhammad a debt of gratitude, it is the entire boxing and athletic world."[36]

Testing Ali's Religious Convictions

The alliance between Ali and Herbert Muhammad coincided with the controversy over the champion's opposition to the Vietnam War and his refusal to enter military service. Of all the factors in the debate over Ali's draft status, perhaps the central issue was his membership in the Nation of Islam. In February 1966, Ali created a national furor when he requested deferment from military service due to financial hardship and on various procedural grounds.[37] Once deferment was denied, Ali appealed his 1-A reclassification and fought for exemption from the draft before various boards and courts of justice. He then decided, however, to abandon his original argument for deferment and to seek exemption from military duty based on conscientious objector status. From spring 1966 until his conviction on draft evasion charges on June 20, 1967, Ali went through a number of appeals to overturn his 1-A reclassification, with the central questions usually focusing on his membership in the Nation of Islam: Was Ali's objection to military service based on political and racial considerations rather than on religious grounds? Was the Nation of Islam a true religion?[38]

Ali spelled out his religious convictions and opposition to the war on August 23, 1966, at a special hearing before Lawrence Grauman, a retired circuit court judge, who was brought in to determine the merits of the heavyweight champion's request and to make a recommendation to the Kentucky Appeal Board. Under oath, Ali testified that he sincerely believed in the teachings of Elijah Muhammad and the Holy Quran, which forbade true Muslims from participating in wars "on the side of nonbelievers." He illustrated the depth of his faith by pointing out that he would not have risked losing large sums of endorsement monies nor sacrificed his public image unless he was genuinely committed to the Nation of Islam.[39]

Lawrence Grauman surprised most people by concluding that Ali was sincere in his religious opposition to war and should be granted conscientious objector status. Grauman's recommendation was countered by the Department of Justice, which claimed in a written communiqué to the Appeal Board that Ali's opposition to the war was based on political and racial considerations rather than religious beliefs. The appeal board ultimately sided with the Department of Justice, and Ali's claim for conscientious objector status was rejected.[40] Eight months later, Ali's 1-A classification was upheld by the National Selective Service Presidential Appeal Board. On April 28, 1967, during induction ceremonies in Houston, Ali refused to take the customary one step forward signifying entrance into the army. In a written statement, he rejected induction because he was "a minister of the religion of Islam."[41] Ten days later, Ali was indicted by a Federal Grand Jury in Houston for refusing induction.[42] Finally, on June 20, 1967, he was found guilty of draft evasion by a twelve-person jury that returned its verdict after only twenty minutes of deliberation. Mort Susman, head of the United States Attorney's Office for the Southern District of Texas, expressed the belief of many people when he declared shortly after the verdict had been returned "that he had studied the Muslim order and found it as much political as it is religious."[43]

Susman's beliefs about the Muslim order seemed to strike at the heart of Ali's problems with the United States government. Because he belonged to a movement that was not considered a legitimate religion, Ali found it difficult to convince anyone that he deserved the same status as conscientious objectors who came from the Mennonite Church and other Christian groups. Ali's claim of pacifism was contradicted by the Nation of Islam's blending of radical social and political philosophy with religious doctrine. The Muslim militancy invoked hostile responses from a society that granted legitimacy only to those religions that complied with societal norms such as accommodation and submissiveness. Ali had to convince people of the sincerity of his religious beliefs while belonging to a movement that was overtly political, one that took uncompromising positions on racial issues and insisted on a separate state for black Americans. The burden of proof ultimately rested with Ali because the government would not accord Muslims the same constitutional and legal rights enjoyed by more traditional faiths. Because the Nation of Islam merged religion and politics, Ali was unable to enjoy the benefits granted other faiths and could not avoid the hardships that typically befell members of secular protest movements.[44]

The Nation of Islam took no official position on Ali's draft status and his struggles with the United States government. But it took a keen interest in Ali's fight for conscientious objector status and used the whole affair to help legitimize its own goals, stir up an already angry black community, and point out the injustices and hypocrisy of white America. *Muhammad Speaks* ran one article after another reporting the wide-ranging support for Ali from individuals and groups around the world, including the philosopher Bertrand Russell, the civil rights activist Floyd McKissick, and Martin Luther King, Jr. It also began describing Ali's religious commitment in greater detail, referring to him more frequently as a great Muslim minister as well as the heavyweight champion of the world. Though unable to sway the courts directly, the Nation of Islam realized it was essential to portray Ali as a man who performed clerical functions if his fight for conscientious objector status was to be taken seriously. In a March 3, 1967, column titled "World Champion Moves Step Closer to Full-time Task as Muhammad's Minister," the newspaper announced that Ali "took complete charge" of the Muslim mosque in Houston because the regularly assigned minister was on a temporary leave of absence. "Reaction to the young athlete's assumption of his spiritual duties," noted the newspaper, "was not only highly favorable among the believers, but exclamations of admiration were many among leaders of the black community here [Houston]—many of whom jammed into the temple to hear Muhammad Ali expound upon the teachings given him by the Honorable Elijah Muhammad, the Messenger of Allah."[45]

Elijah Muhammad dealt with Ali's military status with uncharacteristic openness. Careful not to incriminate himself in any wrongdoing, Elijah Muhammad, who had served time in jail for draft evasion during World War II, nurtured Ali's public identification with the Nation of Islam while maintaining that the fighter's refusal to be inducted into military service was done independently of anyone else. In a rare and carefully orchestrated interview broadcast by the major networks in May 1967, Muhammad announced that Ali's refusal to be inducted into the armed forces was the champion's own decision and an indication that he had learned the truth about himself and the status of blacks in American society. When asked if Ali sought his advice on the draft, Muhammad responded by saying that "every one of my followers is free to make his own choice. I gave him no more advice than I gave the faithful ones who followed me to the penitentiary in 1942." When asked if he thought Ali should be excused from the draft because he was a Muslim minister, Muhammad noted that he himself was a minister when he went to jail and that the United States government "does not excuse you for righteousness because by nature, it is against righteousness." When questioned as to whether Ali was being mistreated at the hands of the government simply because he was a Muslim, Muhammad replied: "It can't be anything else. Muhammad Ali is harassed to keep the other mentally sleeping so-called Negroes fast asleep to the fact that Islam is a refuge for the so-called Negroes in America."[46]

Notwithstanding these comments, in the late 1960s and early 1970s Muhammad willingly stepped aside as an ever-increasing number of people began speaking out on behalf of Ali and his right to freedom of religion. Attitudes had changed. The hatred and disdain once directed at Ali gave way to genuine respect as a result of the increasing dissatisfaction with the war, a consensus on civil rights, a gradual acceptance of athletes' struggles against racism, and the Nation of Islam's diminishing antiwhite rhetoric. In addition, Ali's willingness to suffer the loss of fame and fortune for his ideals had garnered him adherents of all colors and from different strata of society. Sportswriters, entertainers, politicians, Christian leaders, business people, orthodox Muslims, and more conservative black organizations such as the Congress of Racial Equality (CORE) praised Ali's courage. Articles in such major publications as *Christian Century, Newsweek, Sports Illustrated,* and *Esquire* commended him for maintaining his sincerity and dignity in the face of persecution from America's power structure, which unfairly took his title and denied him the right to make a living.[47]

It was in this atmosphere that Ali's battles with the government finally drew to a close. In April 1971 his draft evasion case came up before the United States Supreme Court. During oral argument, Solicitor General Erwin Griswold contended that Ali was not truly a conscientious objector because he had claimed on several occasions that as a member of the Nation of Islam he would not go to war unless it was declared by Allah. Five of the eight justices agreed with Griswold and decided Ali should go to jail. The members of the majority were especially worried that a vote in Ali's favor would result in hordes of blacks joining the Nation of Islam in an effort to avoid military service.[48]

Chief Justice Warren Burger selected Justice John Harlan to write the majority view. In preparing the draft opinion, however, two of Harlan's clerks told him they were convinced that Ali's religious beliefs did qualify him for conscientious objector status. They suggested that Harlan read the *Autobiography of Malcolm X* and Elijah Muhammad's *Message to the Blackman in America* to gain a greater understanding of the Nation of Islam. Harlan took their advice and was transformed by the two books, enough to change his vote and convince him that the government had mistakenly characterized Ali as a racist and distorted the Black Muslim religion. Harlan's change in position put the vote at 4 to 4, but it still meant that Ali would go to jail.[49]

Equally divided decisions by the justices were never accompanied by an opinion—meaning that Ali would go to jail without knowing why his conscientious objector status had been denied. To resolve the stalemate, Justice Potter Stewart suggested that Ali could be set free because of a technical error made by the Justice Department. Stewart noted that the draft appeal board had never indicated the specific reasons for denying Ali conscientious objector status. It was possible, therefore, that the denial contradicted the government's previous acknowledgment before the Supreme Court that Ali's opposition to the war was sincere and based on religious training. A decision based on a technicality would ensure that the ruling in the case would not establish a precedent or expand the classification under which others could assert conscientious objector status. After much debate, the justices agreed to go along with Stewart's compromise and voted unanimously to set Ali free. The decision was announced on June 28, 1971, ending Ali's five-year struggle against the United States government.[50] "I thank Allah," Ali said after hearing about the decision in Chicago, "and I thank the Supreme Court for recognizing the sincerity of the religious teachings that I've accepted."[51]

Suffering the Wrath of Elijah Muhammad

One of the ironies of Ali's struggle against the United States government was that his status within the Nation of Islam had changed dramatically between the time he was found guilty of draft evasion in June 1967 and the point four years later when the Supreme Court finally granted his freedom. In early 1969, Howard Cosell asked Ali during an ABC television interview if he thought he would return to the ring soon. Ali responded, in effect, by telling Cosell he would return to boxing because he needed the money.[52]

Ali's comments angered Elijah Muhammad. In an April 4, 1969, column in *Muhammad Speaks*, entitled "We Tell the World We're Not with Muhammad Ali," the Messenger explained that he wanted everyone to know that Ali had "stepped down off the spiritual platform of Islam to go and see if he can make money in the sport world." In stating his intentions to return to boxing, noted Muhammad, Ali had "plainly acted the fool to the whole world," placed "his hopes and trust in the enemy of Allah (God) for survival," and showed his love for "sport and play," which the "Holy Quran teaches him against."[53]

Muhammad continued to blast Ali in the next issue of *Muhammad*

Speaks and announced that the champion was "out of the circle of the Brotherhood of the Followers of Islam for one (1) year" and would be referred to as Cassius Clay rather than recognized "under the Holy Name Muhammad Ali." Muhammad showed the extent of his indignation by publishing statements of support for his actions from two of Ali's closest associates, Herbert Muhammad and John Ali. Herbert declared to the world that he was "no longer manager of Muhammad Ali (Cassius Clay)" nor was he "at the service of anyone in the sports world." The Nation of Islam's national secretary, John Ali, in a much lengthier declaration of support for the Messenger, announced that he was "with the Honorable Elijah Muhammad in his defense of Islam against the reckless statements by Muhammad Ali." He noted that the boxer's need to fight in order to pay off debts resulted from the champion's "own ignorance and extravagance." Ali had failed to follow the teachings of Elijah Muhammad, who advised all of his disciples to be prudent in handling their money. "Neither Messenger Muhammad, the Nation of Islam nor the Muslims," stated John Ali, "have taken any money from Muhammad Ali. In fact, we have helped Muhammad Ali. Even Muhammad Ali's sparring partners made better use of their monies than Muhammad Ali who did not follow the wise counsel of Messenger Muhammad in saving himself from waste and extravagance."[54]

Ali's difficulties with the Nation of Islam obviously resulted from a number of interrelated factors. Elijah Muhammad was always suspicious of organized sport, believing it greatly harmed the black community. Like many others, he argued that white America had intentionally encouraged blacks to participate in games in order to divert their attention from the real source of their problems and to keep them from advancing as a civilized people. Sport, and the associated evils of gambling, drunkenness, and crime, was another tool used by white Christian society to keep blacks in a state of confusion and ignorance. In his book *Message to the Blackman in America*, Elijah Muhammad stated that "poor so-called negroes are the worst victims in this world of sport and play because they are trying to learn the white man's games of civilization. Sport and play (games of chance) take away the remembrance of Allah (God) and the doing of good, says the Holy Quran. Think over what I am teaching, my people, and judge according to justice and righteousness."[55]

Although Muhammad's feelings about the "white man's games of civilization" seemed genuine, it was not Ali's participation in sport or boxing per se that drew his wrath. Muhammad was troubled more by Ali's departure from the party line as interpreted by Muhammad himself and articulated by his ministers. Like Malcolm X a number of years earlier, Ali had failed to overcome his own impulses and adhere to the Nation of Islam's exclusive code of behavior. He mistakenly expressed a dependence on white society rather than having faith that Allah would provide him with the material goods and other necessities required for an abundant life. Such attitudes revealed Ali's self-absorption and his lack of complete trust in Muhammad, the Nation of Islam, and its doctrines. Ali's remark about the reason for returning to boxing angered Muhammad since it left the impression that the Nation of Islam had taken advantage of Ali by funneling the heavyweight champion's earnings into its own coffers. Muhammad was troubled by any comments, including those from Ali himself, that might confirm rumors that the Nation of Islam was not merely not looking after Ali's best interests but had actually stolen the champion's money.[56]

Muhammad's suspension of Ali, then, was his own attempt to rehabilitate the champion. He wanted to ensure a public image for Ali that fit his own needs as Messenger of Allah and those of the Nation of Islam. He was intent on guaranteeing that Ali mold himself to the requirements of the Nation of Islam and project an image of himself as an autonomous, proud black man. Muhammad ingeniously passed off Ali's success as evidence of black superiority and as a means to pay homage to Allah. At the same time he minimized the importance of the heavyweight title, which whites had once held up as a symbol of racial superiority. Muhammad believed that Ali had to be seen first as a Muslim. Otherwise, Ali would appear to be just the latest in a long line of black heavyweight champions, a mere gladiator serving entertainment-hungry white America.[57]

The severity of Ali's suspension by Elijah Muhammad became evident when he was ignored in *Muhammad Speaks,* the publication that in previous years had filled its pages with literally hundreds of photographs and stories of the champion. The newspaper did not mention anything about Ali for three years, completely ignoring his triumphant return to the ring against Jerry Quarry in 1970 and his initial bout with Joe Frazier one year later. He would not be mentioned in the newspaper again until February 4, 1972, and even then it was apparent he was not back in Elijah Muhammad's good graces. Responding to a series of questions about Ali's status in the Nation of Islam, Muhammad said in that issue that the Muslim fighter was "full of sport and he goes along with sport, too, but I think in his heart he wants to be good. As far as certain duties or posts as he used to hold as teaching the ministry," continued Muhammad, "I do not know when that will take place."[58]

Muhammad's suspension of Ali had obviously evolved into a deep dissatisfaction with the fighter that would never be completely eradicated.[59] Meanwhile, Ali seemed to gravitate toward boxing with greater urgency. He needed the money from boxing to pay off debts and stay abreast of alimony payments, but the sport also provided him with many of those things that had initially attracted him to the Nation of Islam. He was lured by the asceticism and discipline of boxing. He found sustenance in comradeship with his fellow fighters, his entourage, and the boxing world in general. He craved the attention, intense excitement, and respect that boxing brought him. As a fighter he was taken seriously, given a feeling of specialness and an unparalleled degree of adulation. He was enticed by the mystique of the ring, relishing the struggles in the sacred circle against men who were also striving for acclaim and immortality. The ring provided him with unparalleled opportunities for transcendence of self, peak experiences, and emotional "highs."[60]

Ali's status in the Nation of Islam was made most apparent by the kinds of relationships he established during the early 1970s. Although Herbert Muhammad continued to serve as his manager and confidant, Ali was no longer surrounded by Muslims who looked after his every move and protected his interests. Cassius Clay, Sr., became a more visible member of his son's entourage, which was now sprinkled with larger numbers of nonbelievers and attendants. Ali's press conference following his well-publicized return fight against Jerry Quarry was noteworthy in that he shared the podium with Mrs. Martin Luther King, Jr., and the Reverend Ralph Abernathy, "who presented him with the Dr. Martin Luther King Memorial Award for his contributions to human rights and equality."[61] Bundini Brown, whom the Muslims hated for his womanizing, heavy drinking, and other assorted vices, had returned to Ali's camp, reading poetry and clowning with the champ. Ali also chose to relocate his wife and three daughters to Philadelphia after living close to Elijah Muhammad in Chicago for a number of years.[62]

These changes never stopped Ali from openly expressing faith in the Muslim religion. Nor did they hinder the Nation of Islam from eventually breaking its silence on the champion and cashing in on the publicity generated by his success in the ring. Although his relationship with Elijah Muhammad would never be the same, Ali continued to praise the Messenger and Allah at every opportunity. He told inmates at a New York correctional facility during the latter part of 1974 that the only man who could stop blacks from wrongdoing was Elijah Muhammad. "I am a follower of the Honorable Elijah Muhammad. We are peaceful people. We don't hate nobody. We are just trying to clean up our people and unite."[63]

The Nation of Islam began publicizing Ali's accomplishments more frequently as the 1970s progressed. Elijah Muhammad's deteriorating health resulted in gradual changes in the daily operations of the Nation of Islam, and these changes in turn resulted in a resurrection of sorts for Ali. The champion seemed to resume a more prominent position in the Nation of Islam. He was revitalized as the movement's greatest symbol of black pride by virtue of his triumphs in the ring and his outspokenness on racial issues. Ali's rehabilitation was best reflected in the extended coverage that *Muhammad Speaks* devoted to his trip to Jamaica after he regained the heavyweight championship from George Foreman in 1974. Detailing Ali's every move in Jamaica, the newspaper gave him coverage reminiscent of what he had received during his tour of Africa ten years earlier. It was another promotional tour for the Nation of Islam, with Ali again the main attraction.[64]

From the Nation of Islam to the World Community of Al-Islam in the West

Ali's involvement with the Nation of Islam changed significantly following his trip to Jamaica. On February 25, 1975, Elijah Muhammad passed away, ending a forty-one-year reign as leader of the Nation of Islam. He was succeeded by his son, Wallace D. Muhammad, who took the organization in an entirely different direction through a series of policy changes and modifications in philosophy. Wallace, who had been suspended from the Nation of Islam by his father on several occasions and had considered Malcolm X one of his good friends, transformed the movement in many ways, including changing its name to the World Community of Al-Islam in the West. He reinterpreted his father's contributions to the organization, acknowledged the positive contributions made by Malcolm X, refuted the notion of black racial superiority, ceased to ask for a separate state for blacks within America, honored the American Constitution, and advocated the adoption of orthodox Islamic practices.[65] In his first official interview, Wallace Muhammad proclaimed that the World Community of Al-Islam in the West would no longer dwell on the past atrocities of white America and would accept people of all races into membership.[66]

The changes made the movement more palatable to an American public that had begun to appreciate both Muslim doctrine and the demands of the black community. For some members of the movement, however, the modifications brought about by their new leader were sacrilegious. The enormous sense of racial pride instilled in black Americans and the many other contributions made by Elijah Muhammad, including his emphasis on self-help and moral uplift, appeared to be cast aside in favor of a program that was focused more on integration than on continuing the fight for justice and freedom of opportunity. Louis Farrakhan, the former professional musician and calypso singer who became one of the Muslim's leading ministers, was so troubled by Wallace Muhammad's changes that he eventually mounted a public campaign against the new leader and rebuilt the Nation of Islam according to the early principles of Elijah Muhammad. Believing that blacks had not yet achieved liberation, Farrakhan began promulgating his beliefs through publication of the *Final Call*, taking the name of a newspaper put out by Elijah Muhammad in 1934.[67]

Ali's response to the changes made by Wallace Muhammad were the opposite of Farrakhan's. Instead of resisting, Ali almost immediately expressed his support for the new policies, which were similar to those suggested by Malcolm X some ten years earlier. Nearly everywhere he went, Ali carefully rationalized the practical utility of Elijah Muhammad's old programs while paying homage to Wallace Muhammad and declaring enthusiasm for the new changes in the movement. He now deemphasized race and exalted the deeds of humankind, stopped talking of a separate black state and praised America as the greatest country in the world, spoke of the bonds of brotherhood in the Muslim faith, and avoided any mention of white devils. A perfect illustration of Ali's changing attitudes was an interview he did on May 2, 1976, on the CBS program "Face the Nation." In the interview, which was published in its entirety in the *Congressional Record*, Ali noted that it was necessary for Elijah Muhammad to speak of white devils because during much of the first half of the twentieth century, black Americans "were being castrated, lynched, deprived of freedom, justice, equality, raped." Because of improved racial conditions in society, continued Ali, "Wallace Muhammad is on time. He's teaching us it's not the color of the physical body that makes a man a devil. God looks at our minds and our actions and our deeds."[68]

Ali had no sooner declared his support for the World Community of Al-Islam in the West than Wallace Muhammad began chiding him for his continued involvement in boxing. Like his father, Wallace was concerned about the image the fighter was projecting. He was particularly alarmed by the unsavory people and temptations associated with boxing. He was troubled by Ali's illicit associations with women because they called to mind his own father's indiscretions and could prove embarrassing to the World Community of Al-Islam in the West.[69] Wallace feared, moreover, that Ali's reputation would be tarnished by inferior performances in the ring and worried about the harm the sport was inflicting on his physical well-being. Wallace argued that boxing provided much-needed income for the participants and necessary pleasure and excitement for blacks in this country, but he hated to see Ali struggling against opponents who would have been no match for him earlier in his career.[70]

Other Muslims, as well as millions of fans of both races, would eventually join in calling for Ali's retirement from the ring. People were heartbroken by the champion's diminishing abilities and the punishment he absorbed with each successive fight. As they witnessed the erosion of Ali's physical skills, people who had identified with the champion because of his triumphs and stands against social injustice were reminded of their own frailty. To see Ali flounder in the ring was tragic for his followers because he had touched the hearts of so many. He was much more than an athlete or celebrity or entertainer. He had won respect and adulation because he combined incredible abilities as a boxer with moral courage and a social conscience. Nassar Akbar, an inmate in a Michigan prison, captured the prevailing mood when he asked: "Do you, Brother Ali, wish to bring tears to our eyes, sadness to our hearts by returning to the fight game? Or would you like to see smiles on the faces of your brothers and sisters?"[71]

Ali failed to heed the advice of his supporters and continued to fight without any apparent regard for his physical well-being. He remained addicted to the excitement of the ring, but the fights he entered only damaged him further and caused heartbreak for his fans. The long march to destruction finally ended when Ali retired from boxing following his defeat at the hands of Trevor Berbick in 1981. After more than a quarter century of lacing up the gloves and doing battle in the squared circle, Ali now faced life without boxing.[72]

Ali's retirement from the ring allowed him more time to work on behalf of Wallace Muhammad and the World Community of Al-Islam in the West.[73] He was involved throughout the 1980s in everything from helping to promote the annual Muslim-sponsored Patriotism Day parade and distributing religious literature on the streets to being a member of the Muslim Political Action Committee (MPAC) and raising funds for the Sister Clara Muhammad School Educational Fund. Interspersed with these activities was his involvement with several Muslim-related businesses, including the marketing of "Muhammad Ali Ummmee Brand Seafood Sausage."[74] Ali even found time to visit the White House and present Ronald Reagan with a copy of Wallace Muhammad's *Prayer and Al-Islam*.[75]

Further evidence of Ali's commitment to the World Community of Al-Islam in the West came when he took on Louis Farrakhan and the resurrected Nation of Islam. He was appalled by Farrakhan's continued belief in racial superiority and separatism. In 1984, for example, Ali took Farrakhan to task for his derogatory remarks about Jews and made every effort—as did Jesse Jackson, then a presidential candidate—to dissociate himself from the new leader of the Nation of Islam. At an Independence Day celebration in Washington, D.C., Ali chastised Farrakhan for his recent anti-Semitic remarks and misrepresentation of true Islam. "What he teaches is not at all what we believe in," noted Ali when asked to comment about Farrakhan's controversial remarks. "We say he represents the time of our struggle in the dark and a time of confusion in us and we don't want to be associated with that at all."[76]

Ali's dissociation from Farrakhan resulted from his involvement in a religious movement that now stressed a more democratic decision-making process and spiritual fulfillment even while it put less emphasis on controlling the total behavior of individual members. Al-Islam in the West was sympathetic to the capitalistic system, committed to the United States Government, and open to nonblack peoples.

Without the tight reins of control and almost mesmerizing influence of Elijah Muhammad, Ali now exercised more freedom of thought. He had been transformed from a black rebel into a conservative American who favored steady progress for his people within American society. The emphasis Ali once placed on racial separateness and black solidarity had been undermined by the very things they were meant to produce—namely, equal justice and more freedom of opportunity for black Americans. Ali had inspired and helped foster pride among the most deracinated African Americans by spreading the belief in white devils and in the superiority of blacks. He now discarded those notions yet maintained a strong sense of racial consciousness, adhered to the distinctive creed of Islam, and embraced a more disparate group of individuals.[77]

Commitment to Boxing and Faithfulness to the Muslim Religion

The changes in Ali's religious beliefs capped a long spiritual journey marked by steadfast devotion and commitment. Though renowned for his sexual appetite and enjoyment of worldly pleasures, Ali was unwavering in his faithfulness to the Muslim religion and his belief in Allah. He derived strength and a sense of freedom from unquestioning obedience to Muslim leadership and belief in the omnipotence of Allah. His commitment to the Nation of Islam also supported him in his own quest for a sense of identity and racial consciousness. His loyalty to the movement gave him the confidence necessary to express pride in his blackness and the merits of black culture. He shed the humility and accommodating attitude typically associated with black athletes and defiantly rebelled against the limitations imposed by American society.

The Nation of Islam benefited as much from Ali's membership as the fighter himself. Elijah Muhammad might have preached black separatism, railed against the evils of commercialized sport, and viewed boxing with disdain, but he had recognized the value of having Ali as a member of the Nation of Islam. Muhammad knew that what ultimately set Ali apart from anyone else in history was that he was both a Muslim and the heavyweight champion of the world, a combination that would attract unprecedented attention for the Nation of Islam, act as an uplifting force in America's black community, and cause impassioned responses in a society that placed unremitting faith in the power of sport to break down racial barriers. Ali could simultaneously be held up as a symbol of unlimited possibilities for black achievement and be portrayed as a proud black man who received his basic sustenance from the Muslim religion. He proved invaluable to the Nation of Islam because he encouraged believers to rebel against social oppression and helped to create unity among competing factions.

Ali's importance to the Nation of Islam can be measured to a large extent by his influence on both the black and the white communities in this country. His membership in the Nation of Islam, along with the heavyweight championship, elevated him to hero status of almost mythic proportions among many black Americans. Even those blacks who were appalled by the Nation of Islam's extremism and segregationist policies were infused with racial pride because of the champion's boldness in upholding a religion that accused America of everything from crass materialism to racial oppression. By embodying Muslim ideals, triumphing in the ring, and refusing to acquiesce to either the sport establishment or the broader American society, Ali helped invert stereotypes about blacks and inspired members of his race whose daily lives were often filled with drudgery and belittlement. Black Americans of every age group, economic class, political affiliation, and religious denomination were inspired by Ali's refusal to sacrifice his principles when the clash came between individual success in sport and the imperatives of group action.

Although he garnered respect from white Americans for his great boxing skills and for the courage of his convictions, large segments of the dominant culture were appalled by Ali's membership in a movement that talked of "white devils," scorned Christianity, refused to fight for their country, and believed in black racial superiority. To many whites, Ali was a traitor, pure and simple—an ingrate who had turned his back on America and joined forces with hate-filled blacks who worshiped an unfamiliar god and refused to abide by the guiding principles of this country. They believed that Ali was a misguided soul who had been taken in by manipulative charlatans interested merely in self-aggrandizement rather than true religion. It was inconceivable to many whites that Ali could criticize a country that had provided him with limitless opportunities and the chance to secure wealth beyond that of ordinary citizens.

The transformation of the Nation of Islam after the death of Elijah Muhammad—along with the winding down of the war in Vietnam, the lessening of racial tensions, and other societal changes—would eventually contribute to greater admiration of Ali by members of all races. Refusing to join forces with Louis Farrakhan and other blacks who remained loyal to Nation of Islam policy, Ali adhered to the orthodox Islamic religion adopted by Wallace Muhammad and the World Community of Al-Islam in the West. In so doing, Ali assumed an honored place in the public consciousness. Like the World Community of Al-Islam in the West, Ali seemingly evolved from a revolutionary who was intent on promulgating social upheaval to a conservative American more concerned with spiritual salvation than racial confrontation.

The discipline, self-help, and strict moral code Ali was expected to observe as a member of the Nation of Islam would be forcefully transmitted into his new religion. Finding himself in an atmosphere more favorable to African Americans, and armed with a transformed religiosity, Ali shed his racism to speak of the brotherhood of man and the power of God. His new religious beliefs did not sit well with blacks who continued to worship at the shrine of Elijah Muhammad, but it was a relatively smooth transition for the heavyweight champion, who realized that the promise of freedom in American society served to diminish the belief in racial separatism. Ali had helped to liberate African Americans psychologically. He now involved himself in the uplifting of all people through the promotion of Islam. For Ali, separatism had given way to integration, devils and saints were now members of both races, and Christians were no longer responsible for all the evils in the world.

Part Three

Race Relations and the Ideology of Sport

9

"Great Speed but Little Stamina"

The Historical Debate over Black Athletic Superiority

Environmental factors have a great deal to do with excellence in sport," wrote Martin Kane, a senior editor for *Sports Illustrated*, in a 1971 article entitled "An Assessment of Black is Best," and continued, "but so do physical differences and there is an increasing body of scientific opinion which suggests that physical differences in the races might well have enhanced the athletic potential of the Negro in certain sports." The assertion by Kane that black athletic superiority in sport was perhaps due to innate racial characteristics caused a furor among many people not only because it lacked scientific proof but also because it came out during a period of intense interest in black Americans and appeared in one of this country's most popular and widely circulated magazines. Kane's comments resulted in a flurry of responses that ranged from outright rejection of the claim that black athletes were innately superior athletically to a grudging acceptance that blacks were much better than their white counterparts in some sports and decidedly inferior in others.[1]

Martin Kane was hardly the first person to raise the question of black athletic superiority. Since at least the latter part of the nineteenth century, professionals in many fields—coaches, athletes, trainers, cultural anthropologists, psychologists, sociologists, physical educators, biologists, medical doctors, and sportscasters—have put forth their own theories regarding racial differences and their possible effects on sport performance. Although certain trends were evident in their comments, and the issue of black athletic superiority had different ramifications for whites and blacks, the weight of the evidence indicates that the differences between participation patterns of black and white athletes are primarily a consequence of different historical experiences that individuals and their particular racial group underwent. Elite championship athletes are blessed with a certain genetic makeup that contributes to

177

their success in sport, but these inherited attributes transcend any racial groupings.

Early Scientific Principles and the Black Athlete

Edwin B. Henderson, the noted physical educator and early historian of the black athlete, claimed that the question of black athletic superiority was first advanced when John B. Taylor, the great track star from the University of Pennsylvania, was capturing collegiate championships in the quarter mile during the first decade of this century. Henderson wrote that some people of the era attributed Taylor's outstanding track performances to the fact that he was built more like a white runner, possessing larger gastrocnemius and soleus muscles then are found in the "African Negro."[2]

While Henderson was correct in acknowledging the debate over Taylor's prominence in track and field, there is little question that discussion of black athletes' special talents occurred long before the University of Pennsylvania track star came on the scene. In the latter half of the nineteenth century, the fact that a number of outstanding black athletes distinguished themselves in predominantly white organized sport did not escape the attention of contemporary white academicians and social commentators who were already busily involved in studying racial differences. Investigators on both sides of the Atlantic were intent on determining the hierarchy of races and distinguishing one from another by examining such things as skull sizes, facial angles, skin color, structure of human hair, and the different varieties of body lice. The upshot of the various investigations—even when the results did not withstand the testing methods of science—were that blacks were physically different from whites and possessed an accompanying character and temperament that was unique to their species.[3]

One of the first black athletes who was talked about in terms of the scientific principles of the day was Peter Jackson, the great Australian boxer, probably best known as the man John L. Sullivan refused to fight. Many people in boxing tried to explain Jackson's dominance over his opponents by depicting him as a natural-born fighter who was more skilled at physical combat than most white pugilists. Jackson was reminiscent of the primitive man whose essential attribute was physical power. He was, in the words of one contemporary newspaper, a "human fighting animal," a phrase suggesting the time before civilization when African men had to survive on strength alone.[4] However, in keeping with the scientific theories of the period, Jackson also possessed certain weaknesses that were indigenous to other black fighters. The common opinion in boxing circles was that Jackson could be beaten if forced to go the distance because he lacked stamina. In addition, Jackson could be taken out by a blow to the stomach, an inherent weak spot of all black fighters. The secret to beating Jackson was to "pummel his ribs" and he would soon lose his willingness to fight.[5]

The use of racial theories to explain athletic performance spilled over into the twentieth century. In 1901, Marshall "Major" Taylor, the famous bicycle racer from Indianapolis, was examined by a group of physicians at the Academy of Sciences in Bordeaux, France, in an attempt to test the racial stereotypes of the period. The doctors examined his heart, took anthropometric measurements, x-rayed him, and concluded by stating that Taylor "could be said to be absolutely perfect were it not for the fact that because of his bicycle racing, which has exaggerated the size of certain of his leg muscles, his thighs were a little over developed."[6]

The discussion of Taylor's special talents was followed by additional comments over the next few years about the abilities of the runner John B. Taylor, the heavyweight boxing champion Jack Johnson, and occasionally other outstanding black athletes. Over the first and second decades of this century, however, there was a noticeable decline in the amount of attention given to the question of black athletic superiority. The reason for the decline is easy to understand. By this time the majority of black athletes had been successfully shunted behind segregated walls and eliminated from white organized sport. With the occasional exception of some outstanding performances turned in by black athletes in Olympic competition, on predominantly white university campuses, and in professional boxing, the largest number of black athletes were left to compete among themselves on their own amateur and professional teams.[7]

Jesse Owens and Other "Black Auxiliaries" Intensify Debate

The discussion of black athletic superiority resurfaced following the 1932 Olympic Games in Los Angeles and then accelerated after Jesse Owens's record-breaking performances at the Big Ten Track Championships in 1935. The exploits of Owens and other black track stars such as Eddie Tolan, Ralph Metcalfe, Ed Gordon, Eulace Peacock, and Ben Johnson resulted in a number of comments from various people ascribing the success of these athletes in the sprints and jumping events to either longer heel bones or stronger Achilles tendons than those of their white competitors or implying that in some way it was due to racial characteristics. In 1936, for example, Frederick Lewis Allen, in *Harper's Monthly Magazine*, noted that one of the most intriguing "athletic phenomena of our time is the emergence of American negroes as the best sprinters and jumpers in the world." Allen speculated that the rise to athletic supremacy by black Americans was primarily a sociological phenomena. He added, however, that blacks were perhaps particularly "well fitted emotionally for the sort of brief, terrific effort which sprints and jumps required." The Yale track coach, Albert McGall, suggested that in some cases black sprinters perhaps got better leverage—and a little advantage over white sprinters—because of the projecting heel bone that was frequently found among blacks. Dean Cromwell, the well-known University of Southern California and Olympic track coach, believed that blacks excelled as sprinters and jumpers because they were closer to the primitive than white men. "It was not long ago," said Cromwell, "that his [the black's] ability to sprint and jump was a life-and-death matter to him in the jungle. His muscles are pliable, and his easy-going disposition is a valuable aid to the mental and physical relaxation that a runner and a jumper must have."[8]

These kinds of speculations caught the interest of W. Montague Cobb, the well-known black physical anthropologist from Howard University. Cobb, who had long been interested in the physical constitutions of American blacks, refuted the claims that athletic success was based on racial characteristics. In a 1936 article in the *Journal of Health and Physical Education* entitled "Race and Runners," Cobb argued that no particular racial group has ever exercised a monopoly or supremacy in a particular kind of event in track and field. Although acknowledging that athletes with ceratin physical (and mental) characteristics tended to find specific events more appropriate for them than other events, he noted that "split-second differences" in the performances of the great black and white sprinters were insignificant from an anthropological standpoint. The physiques of champion black and white sprinters in general, and Jesse Owens in particular, revealed no indications that "Negroid physical characters are anatomically concerned with the present dominance of Negro athletes in national competition in the short dashes and the broad jump."[9]

Cobb also questioned, as have many cultural anthropologists, whether there was even such a thing as a racial group, considering the enormous lack of racial homogeneity within both the black and white cultures. He noted that Howard Drew, the former sprinter from the University of Southern California, was "usually taken for a white man by those not in the know." Ed Gourdin, the great sprinter and long jumper from Harvard, had dark straight hair, no distinctly black features, and a light brown complexion. Cobb pointed out that Jesse Owens did not even possess what was generally, but erroneously, considered the "Negroid type of calf, foot and heel bone." The measurement of Owens's gastrocnemius, in fact, was more in line with that of a "caucasoid type rather than the negroid." Cobb suggested that proper training and incen-

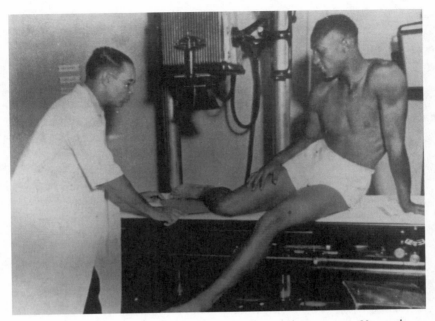

W. Montague Cobb, the well-known professor of anatomy at Howard University, was so intrigued by the debate over black athletic success in track and field that he took anthropometric measurements of Jesse Owens to determine if racially linked physical characteristics accounted for differences in sport performance. Cobb, shown here taking measurements of Owens, ultimately concluded that proper training and motivation to succeed were the most important factors in determining athletic success. Courtesy of the Chicago Defender.

tive were the key factors in the making of a champion and implied that black athletes, like their white counterparts, were stimulated by a "desire to emulate their predecessors."[10] In essence, Cobb was similar to other prominent intellectuals of the decade in that he espoused the theory that environment, not race, determined the individual capabilities of man. This was certainly the underlying thesis, or the message, of E. Franklin Frazier's book *The Negro Family*, Richard Wright's novel *Native Son*, and Ann Petry's novel *The Street*.

Cobb was not the only scientist during the 1930s to examine the physical differences between the races and determine the possible effects they had on athletic performance. Eleanor Metheny, the noted physical educator from the State University of Iowa, was intrigued by the debate being waged over the reasons for the prominence of black athletes in track and field. In 1939, Metheny conducted a study in which she attempted to determine if there were some differences between blacks and whites in proportions of the body that gave blacks an advantage in certain types of athletic performances. She took anthropometric measurements of 51 black and 51 white male students at the State University of Iowa and analyzed the differences between the two groups. Metheny found statistically significant differences in bodily proportions between the two groups of students.[11]

On the basis of her anthropometric measurements of the black and white students, Methany determined that her findings were similar to those of other investigators. She also presented several kinesiological implications for athletic performance. While careful to point out that her findings were only tentative and that such things as reaction time, muscle viscosity, and various psychological factors played an important role in determining success in particular activities, Metheny postulated the possible effects different body types could have on sport participation. She suggested, for example, that blacks could be at an advantage in throwing and jumping events because of their longer forearms and hands. In jumping, the longer, heavier arm is able to develop greater momentum, and this momentum, when transmitted to the body as a whole, would assist blacks in jumping. She also noted that the longer legs and narrower hips of blacks would aid them in running because they permitted longer strides and less angular reaction to the forward stride. On the other hand, the chest construction and markedly lower breathing capacity of blacks would handicap them in distance running and other events of longer duration.[12]

The clinical psychiatrist Laynard Holloman presented several theories about black athletic superiority in his 1943 essay "On the Supremacy of the Negro Athlete in White Athletic Competition." He implied that hatred and a desire for revenge against whites was one reason for the supremacy of black athletes in certain American sports. Black fighters dominated boxing, for instance, because it was an ideal way for them to express their hatred for the white man and get revenge. Unable to discharge their hatred toward the white man directly, black boxers fought against white opponents with a kind of savageness they did not exhibit when fighting members of their own race. In the squared ring, a black boxer expressed his pent-up emotions, discharged latent energies, satisfied his restless ego, and healed his wounded narcissism. Holloman also hypothesized that blacks strove for excellence in sport because it was a means to compensate for their feelings of inferiority. Black athletes, said Holloman, sought "victory with a drive that is much more forceful and insistent than that for a medal or the plaudits of the crowd." What they fought for on the playing fields was a "quieting of the strife that goes on in the mind that thinks itself inferior, to quiet the yelling of a group that claims itself superior."[13]

Black Dominance in the Manly Art

Much of the discussion about black athletic superiority during the 1950s centered on boxing. Especially during the early part of the decade, there was a good deal of speculation about why blacks ruled boxing and whether their overrepresentation in the sport would lead to its demise. The black-owned journal, *Our World*, asserted in 1951 that blacks ruled boxing because it was a way to make big money, fast. The large majority of black boxers were "underprivileged kids" who discovered they could capture their "pot of gold" by using their fists. The former heavyweight champion Jack Dempsey offered his own explanations as to why blacks dominated the fight game. An unlikely candidate to discuss black domi-nance since he had supposedly ducked the great black boxer, Harry Wills, Dempsey argued that factors other than financial ones accounted for the preponderance of black boxing champions. He noted, in terms not typically applied to blacks, that one reason black boxers dominated the sport was their penchant for hard work. Black fighters were willing to pay the price necessary to become champions. As a group, they trained more diligently and more conscientiously than whites. Mike Jacobs, the famous boxing promoter, echoed Dempsey's comments, arguing that black boxers worked harder than their white counterparts. Generally coming from underprivileged backgrounds, black boxers learned early in life that they had to fight hard to survive and to succeed.[14]

The comments of Dempsey and Jacobs seem important for two rea-sons. First of all, both men used terms to describe black boxers that were antithetical to white America's stereotype of blacks. While other whites often characterized blacks as docile, lazy, irresponsible, and childlike, Dempsey and Jacobs utilized such terms as "hard working" and "pro-gressive" to depict black fighters of the period. This choice of words seems significant because the implication in any discussion of black ath-letic superiority was that blacks achieved success in sport by virtue of their naturally endowed physical skills and not through hard work, sacri-fice, self-discipline, and other admirable character traits. Perhaps no-where was the stereotypical image of the black athlete more fully expressed than by the Harlem Globetrotters, the famous all-black basket-ball team founded by Abe Saperstein in 1927. The Globetrotters perpetu-ated the black Sambo stereotype with all its negative connotations, coming across as frivolous, somewhat dishonest children who were lazy and given to wild bursts of laughter. Running about the court emitting shrill jungle sounds and shouting in thick southern accents, the Globetrotters employed a style of play that reflected all the prejudices that this country's dominant culture had built up about blacks. The Globetrotters had innate physical skills and exhibited "natural rhythm," but were in need of "mature white handling." The sportswriter Jack Olsen noted that "the white man's encapsulated view of the whole negro race [was] set to the rhythm of 'Sweet Georgia Brown.'" [15]

Mike Jacobs's comments were noteworthy in that they were followed closely by a lengthy debate about boxing's future and whether the overrepresentation of blacks in the sport would cause its ultimate demise. Certainly underlying the discussion of black athletic superiority was the fear that the preponderance of blacks in any sport would diminish fan interest, cut gate receipts, and seriously jeopardize the future of individual sport franchises. Club owners were no doubt aware of the potential problems involved in asking white spectators to identify with a racial minority they had historically rejected. [16]

Olympic Competition and Resurgence of the Debate

The discussion of racial differences and sport performance waned somewhat during the latter 1950s but resurfaced again the following decade. In fact, during the 1960s the debate seemed to rise and fall in every Olympic year. The outstanding performances of black athletes in Olympic competition and their increased involvement in professional sport refueled the debate over black athletic superiority. The British physician James M. Tanner garnered some attention at the beginning of the period with his book *The Physique of the Olympic Athlete*. He admitted that "economic and social circumstances" probably accounted for the large number of blacks in competitive sport but noted that in the case of track-and-field performers the differences between the body types of the blacks and those of the other athletes were perhaps responsible for their tremendous success in certain events. From the anthropometric measurements of 137 athletes at the Rome Olympics in 1960 and earlier at the British Empire and Commonwealth Games, Tanner and his associates concluded that there were large and significant racial differences among track-and-field performers that might well have enhanced the athletic potential of blacks in particular events like the sprints, high jump, and long jump, while inhibiting their performance in events such as the marathon. [17]

Each time the performance of black athletes contradicted Tanner's theory of physical differences, he offered either an alternative explanation or said that more research needed to be done on the topic. He noted, for example, that the body type of blacks should make them particularly well-suited for the pole vault. But blacks did not distinguish themselves in the event, said Tanner, "perhaps only for reasons of tradition." [18]

Tanner, like Metheny and a host of other academicians, never illustrated exactly how physiological differences translate into outstanding athletic performances. He presented no evidence that success in sprinting is influenced by slimmer calves per se or that the ability to achieve great heights in the pole vault is directly related to arm length.

In 1964 the writer Marshall Smith published an article in *Life* entitled "Giving the Olympics an Anthropological Once-Over," in which he summarized the various opinions given on the question of racial differences and athletic performance. Smith relied to a great extent on the expertise of Carleton S. Coon, a former Harvard and University of Pennsylvania anthropologist, and Edward E. Hunt, Jr., an anthropologist from Harvard, both of whom believed that inherited physical adaptations seemed to play a part in the abilities of certain members of particular races to excel in different sports. They admitted that social factors and/or motivation played a part in the success of black athletes but contended that the particular body type of blacks made them more suitable for certain sports. Coon, for example, described the feet of black men, with their longer heel bone and thicker fat pads, as a "marvelous organ for mobility, leaping, jumping and landing with a minimum of shock." In addition, the black man, whose slender calves had tendons proportionately longer than those of whites, had an overall appearance of loose-jointedness that was characteristic, said Coon, of "living things (cheetahs, for instance) known for their speed and leaping ability."[19]

One of the more thorough examinations of the topic was undertaken by the sportswriter Charles Maher in a five-part series on the black athlete written in 1968 for the *Los Angeles Times*.[20] In two seperate articles, entitled "Blacks Physically Superior? Some Say They're Hungrier," and "Do Blacks Have a Physical Advantage? Scientists Differ," Maher presented the various arguments concerning racial differences and athletic performance. Besides citing the work of Montague Cobb, Carlton S. Coon, and other experts mentioned above, he also contributed additional insights by quoting opinions of well-known sport scientists, coaches, and athletes. By and large, the people Maher quoted attributed the success of black athletes to factors other than physical superiority. Thomas K. Cureton, professor of physical education at the University of Illinois, who spent a lifetime studying the physical characteristics of champion athletes, said that performance differentials were not the result of race. "Because of years of training, yes," noted Cureton. "Because of motivation, yes. Because of social goals, yes. Those make a difference. But not race." John Wooden, the legendary basketball coach at UCLA, said he doubted that the athletic success of blacks had anything to do with physical superiority. "I think he [the black athlete] has just a little more ambition to excel in sports," noted Wooden, "because there aren't enough other avenues open to him." Tommy Hawkins, a black basket-ball player for the Los Angeles Lakers, probably came close to the truth when he noted that the black athlete's preoccupation with sports in this country was a self-perpetuating condition. "From an early age" said Hawkins, "you identify with people who have been successful. From a Negro standpoint, those people would be in sports and entertainment."[21]

Serious Dialogue Between Kane and Edwards

Three years after Maher's series of articles appeared, Martin Kane pub-lished his essay in *Sports Illustrated* that was mentioned earlier, detailing the numerous arguments given about possible black athletic superiority. Kane attempted to present evidence supporting the notion that outstand-ing athletic performances in particular sports were based on racial char-acteristics indigenous to the black population. Utilizing the expertise of coaches, black athletes, athletic researchers, and physicians, Kane sug-gested that racially linked physical, psychological, and historical factors have given rise to black dominance in sport.[22] There were a number of interesting speculations made by various people in Kane's article, but perhaps the strongest comments on the subject came from James Coun-cilman, the Indiana University and former United States Olympic swim-ming coach. Councilman argued that black athletes were markedly superior to white athletes in those sports that required speed and power because they had more white muscle fibers. Commenting that exercise physiologists were afraid to admit this fact publicly, Councilman pointed out that the white muscle fibers so prominent in black athletes were adapted for speed and power, while red muscle fibers, which white ath-letes had in abundance, were adapted for endurance. At the same time, Councilman asserted that the lack of great black swimmers resulted pri-marily from socioeconomic reasons. Blacks did not have the opportunity to be good swimmers because they generally lacked the money to have access to the facilities that were necessary to achieve excellence in the sport.[23]

Kane's article drew an angry response from Harry Edwards, who refuted all of the sportswriter's theories.[24] Edwards noted that Kane's attempt to establish a connection between racially linked physical char-acteristics and black athletic superiority suffered from serious method-ological problems and debatable assumptions about the differences between the races of men. Edwards pointed out, like Montague Cobb and other scholars earlier, that there exist "more differences between individual members of any one racial group than between any two groups as a whole." This fact precluded any assertion by Kane that particular racial groups were predisposed to certain physical activities. Edwards also disputed Kane's assertion that blacks had a peculiar psychological disposition that contributed to their overwhelming success in sport. Specifically, the notion that black athletes are better able to relax under pressure than white athletes not only lacked scientific foundation but was "ludicrous as even a common sense assumption." Lastly, Edwards refuted Kane's suggestion that slavery had weeded out the "hereditarily and congenitally weak" among the black population and created a physically superior group of people. He maintained that the major implication of Kane's assertion about the effects of slavery was that "it opens the door for at least an informal acceptance of the idea that whites are intellectually superior to blacks." The white population lost nothing by supporting the idea of black physical superiority. If anything, they reinforced the old stereotype that blacks were "little removed from the apes in their evolutionary development."[25]

Edwards concluded by asserting that a variety of societal conditions were responsible for the high value black youths placed on sport and the resultant channeling of a disproportionate number of talented blacks into sport participation. While whites had more visible and prestigious role models and greater job alternatives, black Americans were restricted to a very narrow range of occupational choices. Sport, and to a lesser extent entertainment, appeared to be the most achievable goals for blacks, and as long as that remained the same, black athletic superiority would go unchallenged. This circumstance was most unfortunate, said Edwards, because it encouraged blacks to strive for success in a highly competitive profession that left only so much room for athletes of any color. The vast majority of black aspirants ended up back in the ghetto, either because they lacked the talent to become a superstar or because they were unwilling to accommodate themselves to the oppressive tendencies of the American sport establishment. The dream of athletic success became a reality for only a small number of black youths. The large majority were left with unfulfilled fantasies of stardom, glamour, and wealth.[26]

Coinciding with the debate over black athletic superiority during this period was an equally controversial discussion taking place in academic circles regarding differences between black and white intellectual ability. Just two years before the appearance of Kane's article, Arthur R. Jensen, a psychologist from the University of California at Berkeley, rekindled the age-old debate over black and white intelligence differences with the publication of a 123-page study in the *Harvard Educational Review* entitled, "How much can we boost IQ and Scholastic Achievement?" Jensen, who apparently was influenced by William B. Shockley, a well-known professor at Stanford and a Nobel laureate in physics, caused an uproar by arguing that "it is not an unreasonable hypothesis that genetic factors are strongly implicated in the average, negro-white intelligence difference." Jensen pointed out that heritability measures indicated that about 80 percent of the determinance of intelligence was due to genes and some 20 percent to environment. Jensen noted that after having several discussions with well-known geneticists he could safely conclude that "any groups which have been geographically or socially isolated from one another for many generations are practically certain to differ in their gene pools, and consequently are likely to show differences in any phenotypic characteristics having a high heritability." In addition, said Jensen, "genetic differences are manifested in virtually every anatomical, physiological, and biochemical comparison one can make between representative samples of identifiable racial groups. There is no reason why the brain should be exempt from this generalization."[27]

Jensen's ideas caused such an uproar that the *Harvard Educational Review* reprinted his entire article in its very next issue, along with critiques by theorists of education, psychologists, and a population geneticist.[28] The issue was in turn followed by a number of articles on the subject in various academic journals, a book in 1975 edited by Ashley Montagu devoted specifically to Jensen's ideas, and a myriad of essays since that time on the topic that is sometimes referred to as "Creeping Jensenism."[29] The rebuttals took many forms, but the most general criticism came from scholars who viewed Jensen's work with skepticism because of illogical claims in his presentation and his rather naïve conception of the interplay between genetic and environmental factors in behavior. Steven Jay Gould argued, for example, that Jensen had no new data on the subject of intelligence testing and "what he did present was flawed beyond repair by inconsistencies in the data itself and by inconsistent claims in his presentation."[30]

The Jensen affair was similar in many ways to the debate over black athletic superiority. Both debates were centered around some controversial research studies, were concerned with trying to distinguish environmental factors from genetic ones and the possible effects the latter had on performance, and were marked by volatile responses from many members of both the white and black communities who feared that the discussion led to a perpetuation of long-standing stereotypes rather than an enlightened perspective on racial issues. In essence, the debates were nearly one and the same. Jensen and his cohorts could not fail to discuss physiological differences between the races when speaking of intelligence, and individuals involved in the debate over black athletic superiority could not avoid the implication that blacks were somehow inferior to whites intellectually.

Impact of the Debate in America's Black Community

The increasing number of blacks participating in sport, combined with the burgeoning interest in blacks in general throughout the 1970s, caused much speculation about the special skills of black athletes. Much of the discussion was taken up by people from within this country's black community. Black Americans were obviously interested in a debate that concerned them most. In 1972 the black Harvard psychiatrist Alvin F. Poussaint argued that black men, stripped of their social power, focused their energies on other symbols of masculinity, particularly physical power. Writing in an *Ebony* article attractively titled "Sex and the Black Male," Poussaint noted that the need of many black men to display physical power has produced impressive athletic achievements. He pointed out that whites like to be entertained by athletically gifted black men, "as long as it doesn't take the form of having sexual intercourse with white women. Whites want black men to be virile on the work gang and on the playing field, but impotent everywhere else." Unfortunately for whites, argued Poussaint, the success of blacks in athletic competition has enhanced their sexual image. Black men want to "outclass whites on the ballfield, on the dance floor, and in the boxing ring. Black men have an image to maintain and a great psychological victory to win." One of the regrettable consequences of the need to be physically superior, noted Poussaint, "has been the contempt in which many young blacks hold their peers who have opted for success in more sedate activities."[31]

In 1974, Jesse Owens, a man whose own performances contributed to the debate over black athletic superiority, told members of the American Medical Association that physical differences had no bearing on the overrepresentation of blacks in American sport. Citing the anthropometric measurements that Montague Cobb had taken of him some forty years earlier, Owens argued that desire rather than physiological differences accounted for the large number of blacks in competitive sport.[32]

In the same year that Owens addressed the American Medical Association, the sportswriter Bill Rhoden wrote an extended article in *Ebony* entitled "Are Black Athletes Naturally Superior?" Rhoden added nothing new to the debate but reiterated the various theories espoused by Cobb, Edwards, Metheny, Poussaint, and others. In 1977, *Time* ran an article titled "Black Dominance" in which the opinions of well-known black athletes, among other well-known people, were given concerning the question of black athletic superiority. Almost to a man, the black athletes who were quoted argued that physical differences accounted for the superior performances of blacks in sport. O. J. Simpson, the great running back of the Buffalo Bills, said that blacks were physically geared to speed, an important attribute considering that most sports were geared to speed. "We are built a little differently," noted Simpson, "built for speed—skinny calves, long legs, high asses are all characteristics of blacks." Echoing similar feelings was Joe Morgan, the outstanding second baseman of the Cincinnati Reds. "I think blacks, for physiological reasons, have better speed, quickness, and ability," said Morgan. "Baseball, football, and basketball put a premium on those skills."[33]

In 1980, Legrand Clegg published an essay in *Sepia* magazine entitled, "Why Black Athletes Run Faster," in which he reported the research studies on the question of black athletic superiority being conducted by several black scientists on the West Coast. Clegg explained that Malachi Andrews, an associate professor in physical education at California State University, Hayward—along with several black scholars in the School of Ethnic Studies at San Francisco State—were convinced that the abundance of melanin in blacks was responsible for their outstanding athletic performances. The researchers believed that melanin, rather than being a fairly inert pigment important only for its ability to protect the skin from harmful effects of the sun, was capable of absorbing a great deal of energy, which blacks utilized to achieve superior speed in running events.[34]

Comments like those of Simpson and Morgan quoted above no doubt arose from a feeling of racial pride and a recognition of the symbolic importance of athletic success. Decidedly image conscious, members of America's black community had often expressed the belief that the success of individual black athletes could possibly hasten the advancement of the whole race. Blacks saw accomplishment as ammunition in the barrage against unreasonable barriers. A great deal of attention was always directed at those blacks who achieved prominence in American life—particularly in those fields in which they excelled in competition with whites—because their achievements presumably helped break down the prevailing opinions of the black man's inferiority and had an uplifting effect on blacks themselves. Every act of a black man that came to public attention, such as a rushing title by Simpson or Most Valuable Player award for Morgan, had expressive connotations far beyond the importance of the act itself.[35]

The same people who were proudly pointing out the success of black athletes in American sport were also emphasizing that blacks should strive for success in other fields of endeavor. One of the important facts about the escalating debate over black athletic superiority during the 1970s was that the more blacks were recognized for their special athletic abilities, the more America's black intelligentsia stressed how essential it was that younger blacks develop their "brains" as well as their "brawn." Like Harry Edwards, the more learned members of this country's black community were forever trying to reverse the stereotype that blacks were intellectually inferior to whites and feared that the channeling of an disproportionate number of blacks into sport and other forms of entertainment might perpetuate that stereotype. Well-informed members of the black community also realized that the chances of a black athlete (or a white athlete, for that matter) ever playing professional sport were very small; rather than slavishly aspiring to a career in professional sport, blacks would be better served by honing those skills necessary to achieve success in other professional fields.

America's black intelligentsia recognized, moreover, that success in sport would never completely eradicate the problems of the race. However psychologically satisfying, or however materially advantageous to a few, success in athletics was not a satisfactory solution to the problem of discrimination because whites continued to control political and economic matters. In large measure, then, America's learned blacks were rather ambivalent toward sport. While they believed sport was a worthy activity, viewed athletic success as a legitimate goal, and proudly pointed to the achievements of individual black athletes, America's black intelligentsia continually cautioned against an overemphasis on sport and stressed the importance of preparing for life after basketball.[36]

Examples of this ambivalent attitude toward sport are numerous. Earl Graves, publisher of *Black Enterprise* magazine, said he understood why black children would be attracted to sport. Dreams of fame and the chance to make large sums of money had a seductive effect on black children in the ghetto. Graves pointed out, however, that at best only one out of every four thousand black children ever participates in professional sport. Considering these sobering statistics, black children are foolish to throw their "heart and soul into the pursuit of an athletic career."[37] Perhaps no one expressed more eloquently the black community's ambivalent attitude towards sport than Arthur Ashe, the black tennis star from Richmond, Virginia. In a frequently cited open letter to black parents in the *New York Times* entitled "Send Your Children to the Libraries," Ashe argued that "black culture expends too much time, energy and effort raising, praising, and teasing our black children as to the dubious glories of professional sport." He pointed out that blacks have been on the sports and entertainment road for too long. "We need to pull over," says Ashe, "fill up at the library and speed away to congress and the supreme court, the unions and the business world."[38] More recently, Alan Page, former defensive lineman of the Minnesota Vikings and Chicago Bears, used the occasion of his induction into the Pro Football Hall of Fame to express his belief about the overemphasis on sport and the importance of education in America's black community.[39]

Sport Sociologists Examine the Overrepresentation of Black Athletes

The question of black athletic superiority caught the interest of not only Edwards and other black Americans but also sport sociologists, who were busily studying various aspects of the black athlete's involvement in American sport. Virtually every textbook and anthology in sport sociology that came out during the 1970s and early 1980s included a discussion of the topic. While many of these books merely summarized the oft-repeated arguments of Kane and Edwards, some of them offered additional insights into the controversy. For example, Stanley Eitzen and George Sage suggested in *Sociology of Sport* (1978) that two of the more likely reasons for black dominance in sport were occupational discrimination and what the sociologist John Phillips has termed the sports opportunity social structure. The authors pointed out that black athletes perhaps were more determined and better motivated to succeed in sport because their opportunities for vertical mobility were limited in American society. Blacks perceived athletics as one of the areas in which they could realize a measure of success in American culture.[40]

Eitzen and Sage also noted that black athletes tended to participate —and be successful—in those sports in which they had access to coaching, facilities, and competition, while being underrepresented in those activities in which those advantages were unavailable to them. This accounted for the success of black athletes in such sports as basketball because the skills necessary to achieve a level of proficiency in those activities could be learned in school and community recreation programs. This also accounted for the dearth, of black athletes in golf, tennis, and other sports typically taught in private clubs, which have historically denied membership to certain minority groups for economic and social reasons.[41]

In *Sport in Society: Issues and Controversies*, Jay Coakley furnished some possible insights into the question of black athletic superiority by discussing the notion of racial differences and their effect on sport performance. Coakley argued in this widely cited book that racial differences in sport were not the result of genetic factors but instead were caused by a combination of the different characteristics of particular kinds of sport activities, the patterns of discrimination, and the motivation of individual athletes. Coakley pointed out, for example, that the black athletes' selection of sports was predicated on how they defined their chances for success. Like anyone else, black youngsters were likely to adopt highly successful athletes as their role models. The youngsters' choice of particular role models, in turn, would play a part in their career goals and future aspirations in sport. Because the vast majority of these role models participated in only certain sports, the chances were good that younger black athletes would elect to take part in the same sports.[42]

Coakley also suggested that the level of involvement of black athletes in sport was contingent on both the needs of those individuals who controlled sport and "the amount of off-the-field social contact" that was prevalent in a particular sport. He argued that the lure of big profits has caused owners in professional sport to become less concerned about the race of particular athletes and more interested in their skills. Black athletes with requisite skills can gain access to particular sports if they are viewed as potentially big winners, and gate attractions who will generate big profits. Lastly, Coakley pointed out that blacks were most often found in those sports where social distance was increased (boxing, track, baseball, football, and basketball) and underrepresented in those sports that were closely associated with "informal, personal, and often sexually mixed relationships" (golf, bowling, tennis, and swimming).[43]

Among the more thought-provoking discussions of black athletic superiority was a 1982 essay by the sociologist James LeFlore entitled "Athleticism Among American Blacks." LeFlore acknowledged that genetic, environmental, and economic factors certainly played a part in the athletic success of black athletes but believed that a more comprehensive explanation for black dominance in sport was grounded in what he termed "subcultural and informational poolings." He argued that the disproportionate number of black athletes in certain sports was at least partly a result of both the cultural setting in which black athletes found themselves and the information available to them and their subculture group. Generally speaking, black athletes arranged their world according to available information, interpreted the feedback data, and eventually made decisions that they hoped would result in social rewards.[44]

LeFlore pointed out that members of the black subculture interpreted their social system through what he termed a generalized and specific pool of information. Sports that fostered disapproval from the larger social system were typically avoided by black athletes, while those sports in which blacks were expected to take part attracted a disproportionate number of participants. At the same time, argued LeFlore, the black athletes' decision to participate in some sports but not others was, to a great extent, determined by the subculture's perception of those sports. Blacks who choose to participate in fencing or golf, for example, have to confront the perceived status of these sports within their subculture. If perception of those sports is negative, either because they are viewed as unmanly or deemed unworthy—or simply because the group views the activities as elitist and snobbish—then the black athlete must deal with this negativism. Continued participation in these sports may have a decidedly detrimental effect on the relationship between black athletes and other members of the subculture.[45]

The Jimmy the Greek Incident

LeFlore's 1982 article did not signal the end of the debate over black athletic superiority. The last few years have been marked by a continuing discussion about black athletes' special talents and overrepresentation of black athletes in particular sports. Perhaps the best example of the current status of the debate over black athletic superiority comes from the incident involving Jimmy "The Greek" Snyder, a twelve-year veteran on the CBS show *The NFL Today*, who received national attention on January 15, 1988, when he told a local television interviewer in Washington, D.C., that blacks were better athletes than whites because they were "bred to be that way since the days of slavery" and that if more blacks became coaches "there's not going to be anything left for the white people."[46] Responding to a question by Ed Hotaling about the progress of blacks in sports, Snyder argued that the beginnings of black athletic superiority were during the Civil War period, when "the slave owner would breed his big black with his big woman so that he could have a big black kid." Black athletes can "jump higher and run faster," said Snyder, because of their "thigh size and big size." White athletes will never be able to overcome those physical advantages, continued Snyder, because they are lazy and less motivated than their black counterparts.[47]

Snyder's comments caused a great deal of controversy and drew heated responses. The editors of *Sports Illustrated* said that "Snyder's ramblings betrayed an ignorance of both U.S. history and sport" and that the sports prognosticator "was also guilty of the sort of sweeping generalizations on which racial stereotypes and prejudices are built." Harry Edwards called Snyder "obviously incompetent and abysmally ignorant." "I'm not sure that his [Snyder's] views in this regard necessarily disqualify him for choosing a betting line," said Edwards later, "but I think a more overriding concern is that he is a disgrace to the network." John Jacob, president and chief executive officer of the Urban League, said that "one would expect a man like Jimmy the Greek or anyone who has this kind of exposure on the national media involving athletics not to deal with myths but empirical data. Its dumb for Jimmy the Greek to make such a ludicrous comment." Susan Kerr, spokesperson for CBS, issued a statement just an hour after Snyder's interview was aired locally in Washington, D.C., stating that CBS Sports deeply regretted the remarks made by Snyder and emphasizing that his remarks did not reflect the views of the network.[48] One day after Kerr issued her statement, CBS made it perfectly clear how they felt about Snyder's comments by firing him.[49]

During his interview Snyder made several mistakes for which he would later apologize and seek forgiveness. As noted by his critics, Snyder's remarks displayed an ignorance of both sport and American society. He left himself open for criticism by insisting that the preponderance of blacks in certain sports resulted from physical differences between the races and not acknowledging that other factors perhaps contributed to the outstanding performances of black athletes. His views that blacks had bigger thighs than their white counterparts would certainly not hold up under scrutiny by physical anthropologists. Although blacks suffered cruel indignities during slavery, Snyder's notion of selective reproduction was certainly not one of them. Snyder also did not endear himself to anyone when he complained that blacks would soon take control of sport.

Perhaps more than anything else, however, Snyder was criticized not so much for what he said but for what he didn't say. Dorothy Gilliam, a writer for the *Washington Post,* poignantly noted that many people reacted to the "implications and unstated assumptions that lie behind the Greek's statements." Gilliam made it clear that for many people, including individuals like Harry Edwards, the flip side of any discussion about black athletic superiority was the implication that blacks were intellectually inferior. In large part, Snyder's comments were interpreted more as an indictment of black intellectual ability than acknowledgment of black athletic superiority.[50]

Genetic Freaks or Well-Trained Gladiators?
Continuing Questions in an Unending Debate

The "Snyder-bashing," as one writer called it, was followed by yet another series of comments about possible racial differences and their effects on sport performance. For example, Arthur Ashe in the spring of 1988 noted that he would like to see more research completed on the subject, mentioning as he did on a number of other occasions, that he thought blacks were especially gifted at such activities as running.[51] Brooks Johnson, the black track coach at Stanford, was quoted that summer in the *New York Times* as saying that the domination of black sprinters reflected "racism in society in general"; he connected the instant gratification of sprint races with the sense of urgency felt by many blacks because of their lowly economic conditions. Calvin Hill, the former star football player with the Dallas Cowboys and one of the most frequently quoted athletes on the subject of black athletic superiority, speculated in the *Journal of Sport History* that the outstanding performances of black athletes resulted from the large number of positive black role models in particular sports, the emphasis on instant gratification in America's black community, and the fact that black athletes were descendants of the physically gifted slaves who survived the harsh "Middle Passage" to this country.[52] In April 1989, Tom Brokaw hosted an NBC special devoted to the question of black athletic superiority that included guests such as Harry Edwards, Arthur Ashe, the anthropologist Robert Malina, and Richard Lapchick, director of the Center for the Study of Sport and Society at Northeastern University. The NBC special received front-page headlines in American newspapers and caused widespread reactions, ranging from outright disgust that the program was even aired to acknowledgment that the subject must be broached if stereotypes were to be eliminated.[53]

The comments mentioned above indicate not only that the subject of black athletic superiority has continued to fascinate people of various backgrounds but also that one of the most conspicuous features of the debate in this country down through the years has been the diversity of opinions and theories expressed—among groups of blacks and groups of whites as well as between the black and white communities. This is accounted for by the fact that a person's race was seemingly less influential than educational background or any number of other variables in determining their particular philosophy of black athletic superiority. Harry Edwards's position on the subject was, for example, aligned more with Jay Coakley's than it was with either Arthur Ashe's or Calvin Hill's. As academically trained sociologists, Edwards and Coakley could be expected to have views different from those of the two black athletic stars—possessing perhaps a more critical understanding of American society and better able to understand the reasons for the abject powerlessness of many blacks in this country.

Although race seemed to be less influential than other factors in determining an individual's view of black athletic superiority, there seems little question that there were certain trends evident in the comments emanating from within this country's black and white communities, and that the topic had differing ramifications for the two groups. For many in the black community, the overrepresentation of blacks in competitive sport was a source of both pride and concern. On the one hand, black Americans took great satisfaction in the fact that black athletes dominated certain sports because these performances served as sources of inspiration and much-needed examples of achievement. Great black athletes served as role models and could become symbols of what was possible. At the same time, the black intelligentsia recognized that success in sport would never completely eradicate the problems of the race. Moreover, the preponderance of blacks in competitive sport possibly served to reinfoce the stereotypical notion that blacks could excel in physical pursuits, but not in the life of the mind.

White Americans perhaps had even more at stake in the discussion of black athletic superiority. They were both fascinated and troubled by the dominance of black athletes in particular sports. By and large, whites in this country leaned towards a physiological explanation for black athletic superiority and were reluctant to acknowledge possible sociological reasons for the phenomenon. By acknowledging a physiological basis for athletic superiority, whites could more easily maintain their belief in the inferior character traits and mental abilities of black Americans. Believing that physical differences accounted for the overrepresentation of black athletes in certain sports seemed quite natural, considering that the dominant culture traditionally and stereotypically viewed blacks' behavior as being diametrically opposed to the Protestant ethic. The notions of hard work, dedication, and sacrifice were rarely used by white commentators to describe the efforts of such athletes as John B. Taylor, Eddie Tolan, Ralph Metcalfe, Jesse Owens, and Isiah Thomas.

Perhaps the best indication of the dominant culture's attitude about black dominance in sport can be gleaned by noting the comparatively little attention paid to the overrepresentation of white ethnic groups in particular sports throughout American history. Unlike the numerous studies completed on the black athlete, very little time has been devoted to questioning the possible physiological basis for such matters as the dominance of Irish boxers in the nineteenth century, the high proportion of Jewish basketball players in the early part of the twentieth century, or the disproportionate number of Slavic football players in line positions during the 1930s and 1940s. There might be occasional comments about the physical strength, speed, or stamina of these athletes, but more often than not their success was accounted for by such factors as low economic background, pride in performance, work habits, intelligence, and the commitment and discipline they brought to each contest. Commentators certainly had stereotypical notions about these athletes, but spoke of them in more complimentary terms than they did of black athletes—terms imbued with a spirit reflecting the deeply ingrained American virtues held most dear by the dominant culture.[54]

The argument that black athletic superiority was the result of innate physical differences was promulgated not only by some white Americans but by many blacks as well. Some people in this country's black community expressed the belief that inherent physical differences accounted for the overrepresentation of blacks in certain sports. Although racial pride, educational background, social class, and any number of other factors contributed to this reasoning, the fact remains that some blacks tried to explain black athletic superiority along racial lines. Many blacks unthinkingly accepted the ethnic and racial stereotypes created by the dominant culture and thus helped perpetuate the idea that black athletic superiority was largely the result of physical differences between the races. The notion of race undoubtedly had different connotations for blacks than for whites, but it was still a convenient way for them to explain the complex phenomenon of black athletic superiority. This fact perhaps tells us nothing more than that portions of the black community were similar to their white counterparts in sometimes being guilty of prejudicial assumptions and having a penchant for using a simple explanation to account for a phenomenon that was not easily explainable.

For all that, the question still remains: Why are black athletes dominant in certain sports and underrepresented in others? One thing that can be said with a degree of assurance is that there is no scientific evidence of genetic association or linkage between genes for individual and group athletic achievement among black Americans. We know as little about the contribution of genes to athletic ability as we do about the genetics of intelligence. Athletic ability is clearly a function of many genes in interaction with a number of other variables such as economic background, motivation, facilities, and coaching. How many genes may be involved in athletic ability is difficult, if not impossible, to determine because there is no way to separate out the contributions made by the aforementioned variables to sport performance.

Drawing links between genetic makeup and athletic ability is inadvisable, moreover, because as Cobb, Edwards, and other academicians have made plain through the years, it is highly questionable whether there is such a thing as a racial group, considering the enormous lack of racial homogeneity within this country's black and white communities. The anthropometric differences found between racial groups are usually nothing more than central tendencies and, in addition, do not take into account wide variations within these groups or the overlap among members of different races. This fact not only negates any reliable physiological comparisons of athletes along racial lines but makes the whole notion of racially distinctive physiological abilities a moot point.

The weight of the evidence indicates that the differences between participation patterns of black and white athletes is primarily due to differences in the history of experiences that individuals and their particular racial group have undergone. Blacks in this country have traditionally not enjoyed equal cultural and socioeconomic opportunities, having been oppressed, discriminated against, impoverished, and generally excluded from the good things in life. The result is that blacks and whites have shown different preferences and inclinations in their choice of sports. The lack of other job opportunities is partly to blame for the considerable importance attached to sport by many black Americans. The lower-class black community's religious fervor for sport is directly proportional to the disillusionment it feels over inadequate employment opportunities. If blacks place a premium on physical virtuosity through sport, as many people have claimed, they do so more because of their particular station in life than because of any hereditary factors.

Lacking money and access to certain equipment and facilities has guaranteed that black athletes will focus their attention on certain sports and disregard others. It takes very little in the way of equipment and facilities to participate in basketball and track and field, while such activities as golf and tennis demand resources that are out of reach for most blacks. The participation patterns of black athletes has also remained remarkably similar through the years, largely because of the stereotyping of black athletes by the dominant culture and the fact that younger blacks tend to emulate and follow in the footsteps of their athletic forebears. There is no reason to believe this situation will change in the near future. The economic plight of black Americans has not changed dramatically enough nor has the basic structure of organized sport evolved to the point where black athletes would suddenly find themselves overrepresented in golf and excluded from basketball.

The continued overrepresentation of black athletes in particular sports will certainly continue to draw attention from academicians and various other people in society. Let us trust that these people will not treat black athletes as though a stereotype were sufficient and as though the individual could be ignored. Such an attitude would only contribute to a continued escape from the consideration of the effect of social and economic inequities upon black sport participation and a continued insistence on attributing the outstanding performances of black athletes to inherent racial differences. The spirit of science necessitates, however, that academicians continue their research to determine whether the success of black athletes is somehow the consequence of racially distinctive chromosomes. The worst thing to happen would be for researchers to refrain from examining the possible physical differences between black and white athletes for fear that they would be transgressing an established political line or be labeled racist. Like all areas of research, the topic of black athletic superiority needs to be examined from a broad perspective, not from a preconceived and narrowly focused one. If the truth is to be known about outstanding black athletic performances, scholars need to investigate the topic from a biosocial perspective while at the same time recognizing the inequities in our pluralistic society and acknowledging that the overrepresentation of black athletes in certain sports had its counterpart among white athletes who excelled in their own activities without fear of being branded genetic freaks.

10

The Notion of Double-Consciousness and the Involvement of Black Athletes in American Sport

W. E. B. Du Bois wrote in his classic book *The Souls of Black Folk* that blacks in this country have always felt a sense of being "an American, a Negro; two souls, two thoughts, two unreconciled strivings, two warring ideals in one dark body whose dogged strength alone keeps it from being torn asunder. . . . The history of the American Negro is the history of this strife."[1] This double-consciousness of being both black and American, which DuBois pointed out in 1903, has been evident in the careers of the most successful black athletes involved in American sport since the latter half of the nineteenth century.

Outstanding black athletes in this country, like other members of their race, were compelled to live split existences because of American discriminatory practices. On the one hand, black athletes were proud of their race for its forbearance and ability to survive and fought against the negative images of black inferiority. On the other hand, black athletes' aspirations to success in American sport necessitated that they adhere to values upheld in the dominant society. This duality was intertwined with a number of other important considerations, including economic issues, questions of gender, and the fact that black athletes strove for success in an institution not only controlled by whites but whose basic structure was defined by white standards.

The likelihood of maintaining a black identity, let alone gaining admission into sport, was made difficult for black athletes because the white Americans' stereotype of blacks inverted their own Protestant ethic. Blacks were categorized variously as docile or savage, faithful or tricky, childish or oversexed. These wide-ranging and sometimes contra-

200

dictory characterizations deserved no respect and did not accommodate the ideal image of athletes who achieved success through dedication and hard work. In addition, black athletes were involved in an institution that fancied itself the great leveler in society but in actuality was one of the most conservative, tradition-laden institutions in America. To achieve success, it is necessary for black athletes, even more than for their white counterparts, to submit to the dictates of coaches and other support personnel, display evidence of moral rectitude, and exhibit high levels of conformity and respectability as well as physical skills. In contrast to a black cultural form such as jazz, there was less room in American sport to deviate from accepted white standards of performance and forge any notion of racial consciousness.

Black athletes devised an assortment of responses to their uncertain position in American sport, responses that served as both a palliative and a source of liberation. Like athletes of other minority groups, they dealt with their institutional constraints with a high degree of fluidity, periodically speaking out against racial injustice and other forms of discrimination while knowing full well that reticence and conformity were the usual set of behaviors necessary to survive in sport. Although not politically conscious as a group and sometimes even choosing to disassociate from lower-class blacks they believed were largely responsible for the stigmatized condition of all blacks, many outstanding black athletes felt an obligation to reach out to less fortunate members of their race while at the same time striving for individual success in sport. This balancing of individual ambition and more collective action, which obviously varied in degree from one athlete to another, was tied to the black athlete's quest to realize a sense of identity amid the constraints of organized sport. In a very real sense, then, black athletes moved in and out of their respective roles as blacks, athletes, and Americans with a high degree of regularity in an attempt to foster a positive self-image and realize success in one of this country's most prominent institutions.

In the years immediately following Reconstruction, a number of black athletes made their mark in predominantly white organized sport and became household names for sports fans of both races. Though they were involved in almost every sport in America during the second half of the nineteenth century, it was in horse racing and boxing that black athletes became most prominent and had the largest representations.[2] Black athletes gained greater success in these two sports partly because the sport establishment believed they were suitable to the black man's abilities and partly because of the stigma attached to the sports themselves. The prominent role played by black jockeys during this period, for example, was primarily due to the horse racing establishment's approach to blacks and the jockey profession in general. The profession was closely identified with life on southern plantations where slaves had been exploited as jockeys by their masters. Owners of thoroughbreds believed success on the track depended on the bloodlines of their horses rather than who rode them and that the jockey profession was ideally suited for intellectually inferior but physically gifted blacks. In other words, riding horses for a living was, for a time, nothing more than "nigger work," and white riders generally did not challenge the black jockeys' preeminence because of the stigma attached to working at the same job as a black.[3]

Regardless of these circumstances, successful black athletes in the latter half of the nineteenth century sometimes realized the numerous benefits typically reserved for whites. Each one of them received their share of plaudits and adulation from America's sporting public, earned large sums of money from their athletic exploits, and attained a standard of living unknown to most blacks. Success in sport allowed them not only an opportunity to support themselves and their families but also a chance to bolster their self-esteem. They enjoyed a degree of self-respect and sense of accomplishment generally denied blacks during the late nineteenth century. As a group, successful black athletes of the period worked extremely hard at their particular sports and parlayed physical skills and connections with white employers into better lives.[4]

One of the most visible signs of their better lives was property ownership. Several well-known black athletes in the latter half of nineteenth-century America held some type of real estate. Besides furnishing income and adding a degree of comfort, property ownership had enormous symbolic importance to black athletes as it did to other black Americans. Whites might downplay their athletic skills, but land, houses, and other material evidence were impossible to disregard. These possessions furnished tangible evidence of the black athletes' capabilities while at the same time countering the white stereotype of the lazy and incompetent black. Isaac Murphy, the celebrated black jockey who captured the Kentucky Derby three times, used his wealth to purchase real estate in his home town of Lexington and as far away as Chicago. Moses "Fleetwood" Walker, the first black to play major league baseball, owned a hotel and several motion picture theaters in Steubenville, Ohio, and an opera house in nearby Cadiz.[5]

Although successful black athletes in the latter half of the nineteenth century worked hard to achieve their privileged positions, they never fully escaped the dictates of the American sport establishment. Regardless of the success they enjoyed and the possessions they accumulated, black athletes of the period were unable to realize the degree of independence granted white athletes of comparable abilities. In efforts to climb the ladder of success, black athletes curried favor with the sport establishment, but such an approach frequently increased their dependence on whites. Even though physical skills were a necessary prerequisite for athletic achievements, black athletes of the period often depended on alliances with white employers and customers for their ultimate success. Accordingly, the close ties that frequently developed with white benefactors sometimes strengthened the black athletes' concern for white opinion and increased the distance they felt between themselves and the majority of blacks in American society. This certainly seemed to be the case for Isaac Murphy, who was compelled to establish a close relationship with Mrs. Hunt Reynolds, Ed Corrigan, and other members of horse racing's upper crust in order to realize success in the sport.[6]

Establishing ties with white employers did not necessarily mean that black athletes lost a sense of their separateness. The success of these athletes can be explained partly by their deftness at concealing their drive for success so thoroughly and by their ability to express their individuality at the appropriate times. Fluidity, in other words, was one of the greatest gifts of black athletes involved in American sport. Depending on the situation, they could be either cleverly docile, verbally persuasive, or very forceful. They were prepared to be passive if they knew they were in a vulnerable position or if they felt passivity assisted them in maintaining status. They could also become combative when encountering discrimination, even though such a stance might temporarily negate the reticence on which they most commonly relied. They realized early on that their physical skills placed them in an enviable position because white society often stood to benefit handsomely from their performances and that their status allowed them an opportunity to air grievances and express their opinions without the constant fear of reprisals. Early in his career, Peter Jackson, the celebrated black heavyweight from Australia, chided Jack Burke, a popular boxer known as the Irish Lad, for repeatedly refusing to cross the color line and fight him. He attacked Burke in a manner that belied his generally quiet nature. For instance, immediately following one of Burke's exhibition matches, Jackson stepped to the side of the ring and angrily challenged Burke: "He [Burke] says he draws the color-line. Well John L. Sullivan, who also draws the color-line, says he has no objection to meeting a colored fighter in private. If Mr. Burke is of the same way of thinking, I will gladly meet him tonight, tomorrow or any day he might select in a cellar, barn or any private room he chooses to name and will wager him 1,000 pounds on the result."[7]

The success of black athletes in nineteenth-century American sport never freed them from their sense of being exemplars. Although they consciously strove to gain acceptance as great American athletes, they never completely escaped from being defined by race. Each triumph showcased their individual talents and was a symbolic nail in the coffin of racial inferiority, while each loss was considered an individual tragedy and evidence of racial limitations. Marshall "Major" Taylor certainly became a representative figure in his races against white riders. His biographer, Andrew Ritchie, noted that "crowds wanted action and drama and a strong whiff of danger and the struggle between Taylor and his white rivals was basic and easily understandable, like a young David taking on several Goliaths at once—full of an unstated but obvious racial symbolism."[8]

Late nineteenth-century black athletes were often disturbed by their inability to be classified by anything other than race. They recognized the symbolic importance of their triumphs to the black community but wanted to be acknowledged as outstanding athletes rather than simply outstanding black athletes. To do otherwise only served to demean their accomplishments and denied them full recognition as Americans who had achieved success in one of this country's most visible and cherished institutions. Their views were similar to those expressed by other well-known blacks of accomplishment. For instance, E. Franklin Frazier, the prominent sociologist known for his work on the black family, remarked shortly after a trip to Brazil in 1941 that in the United States an "Afro-American scholar was regarded first as black, secondarily as a scholar." "When his work is recognized," stated Frazier, "it is usually pointed to as the work of a negro. He is a competent negro sociologist, an able negro economist, an outstanding negro historian. Such recognition is as much the product of the racist mentality as the negro rest rooms in the Montgomery airport are."[9]

Although they desired full recognition as people who had achieved success by means of the American virtues of individualism and self-reliance, their shared color and experiences of discrimination ultimately led some black athletes to be group conscious and collective.[10] In the most extreme cases, it meant loyalty to only race and family. Moses Fleetwood Walker, for example, struggled for some seven years to establish himself in organized baseball. Lured by the chance to gain prestige and status, he wanted to participate in America's national pastime with color being irrelevant to his success. Walker would also become, however, a leader in the back-to-Africa movement that was popular among some blacks around the turn of the century. In his 1908 book, *Our Home Colony*, Walker advocated separation of the races, arguing that blacks would never become equal participants in American life. "There can be given no sound reason against separation," wrote Walker. "All experience, and every deduction from the known laws and principles of human nature and human conduct are against the attempt to harmonize two alien races under the same government. When the races are so differentiated in mental and physical characteristics, as the Negro and Anglo-

Saxon, the government that undertakes the experiment rests at all times on a volcano." [11]

The American dream of unlimited possibilities was ultimately shattered for black athletes. By 1900 most of them had been excluded from American sport and were forced to establish their own separate sporting organizations. The most famous of these were the black baseball leagues, a loose aggregate of teams that did not achieve much organizational structure until Rube Foster founded the Negro National League (NNL) in 1920. Like other black cultural institutions of the period, black baseball offered a viable alternative for black athletes excluded from the major leagues. Hidden from the view of most white Americans, black baseball was considered by many in the black community to be a temporary institution that would cease to exist once integration in organized baseball was realized. Although black Americans were concerned about the survival of their own leagues, they did not consider these leagues preferable to having black players in the major leagues. Not unexpectedly, those with a vested interest in black baseball took a different view of baseball integration than the majority of black Americans, realizing the entry of blacks into the major leagues would jeopardize their business or, worse yet, put them out of business. They did not, however, actively oppose the campaign for integration in baseball that was waged throughout the first half of the twentieth century because to do so would have been considered, in the words of the historian Janet Bruce, "racial treachery in the black community." [12]

It was also unrealistic to expect talented black athletes to forego their chance of success in organized baseball in order to sustain the black leagues. Black players were no different from their white counterparts in that they had always dreamed of one day participating in major league baseball. Organized baseball would not only give them a chance to gain money and prestige but would furnish them an opportunity to compete against the best players in the world and showcase their abilities before a larger audience. Even though black players enjoyed their own leagues and occasionally competed against white major leaguers in exhibition games, they yearned to be a part of organized baseball because it would help them define themselves and verify their talents. Participation in the National Game would give black players a chance to measure their achievements against white players, who had always been used as the standard for success. [13]

The leaders in black baseball realized that regardless of what happened in organized baseball, black Americans should make an effort to maintain their leagues for a time so as to promote their own interest in the sport and supply employment for the largest number of black players. More specifically, the leaders in black baseball were determined to make their leagues successful institutions because they served as an example of black enterprise and, concomitantly, helped prove that black players belonged in America's national game. Because of the enormous gap between ideal and practice in organized baseball, most blacks, while desiring access to the major leagues, at the same time felt obliged to support their separate leagues that operated with very little white interference.[14]

Perhaps no one expressed these sentiments more clearly than the architect of black baseball himself, Rube Foster. For example, Ed Bolden, the black owner of the Hillsdale, Pennsylvania, baseball club, withdrew from the NNL in 1992 because of travel difficulties and the following year organized the rival Eastern Colored League (ECL). Foster opposed formation of the new league for obvious business reasons, but he was also troubled by the fact that the majority of owners in the ECL were white. Although he realized the races could work together for mutual benefit—as was indicated by the amicable working relationship he established with the owner of the Kansas City Monarchs, J. Leslie Wilkinson —Foster was fearful of the intentions of white owners in the new league and the possibly deleterious effect they might have on black baseball. "There can be no such thing," said Foster, "as [a black baseball league] with four or five of the directors white any more than you can call a street car a steamship. There would be a league all right, but the name would have to be changed."[15]

In large measure then, black baseball was at once an institution remarkably similar in organizational structure to the major leagues and a distinctive entity that in many ways reflected black culture. Like the major leagues, black baseball was divided into two leagues, played an all-star game composed of the best players from the two leagues, and at season's end held a championship series between the winners of the two leagues. Many of the black teams used major league ball parks and copied everything from uniform styles to special-order baseball hats. For example, when Bill Robinson, the famous dancer known affectionately as Mr. Bojangles, purchased the New York Black Yankees, one of his first acts was to buy year-old Yankee uniforms.[16]

In actual play, black players were generally more daring, unpredictable, and prone to improvise than their white counterparts. They emphasized speed and played "tricky baseball" or "unwritten baseball." Black players viewed their sport more as a form of entertainment in which each player could express his individuality and at the same time contribute to his team's overall effort. Perhaps the primary reason why the annual East-West All-Star game was the premier event in black baseball and overshadowed the leagues' World Series, was the fact that it was a perfect opportunity for black players to display their unique performance styles. The most noteworthy individual style was that of Leroy "Satchel" Paige,

Andrew "Rube" Foster, the architect of black baseball, was concerned about the effects white owners would have on his league. Courtesy of the National Baseball Library, Cooperstown, New York.

one of the black leagues' legendary players. Always the master showman, Paige captured newspaper headlines and the imagination of baseball fans with his unique windups and pitching delivery. He threw, in his own words, "bloopers, loopers, and droopers . . . [a] jump ball, bee ball, screw ball, woobly ball, whipsy-dipsy do, a hurry-up ball, a nothin' ball, and a bat dodger." [17]

Notwithstanding these apparent differences, black leaguers were still subject to the same rules, regulations, and codes of ethics as those players in major league baseball. They also undisputedly had home run hitters in the league and could play the power game that dominated organized baseball by the 1920s. In addition, the men in black baseball sometimes emulated and frequently identified with players from both leagues. Having played against Dizzy Dean, Bob Feller, and other barnstorming major leaguers in exhibition games, black leaguers came to admire their more famous white counterparts and sometimes patterned their play after them. Perhaps most important, many leaders in black baseball exhorted their players to "be like major leaguers." Individual performance styles were recognized and appreciated in the black leagues, but many people in black baseball disapproved of the more flagrant clowning and funny stunts used to heighten the entertainment value of games because they believed this approach to the sport merely perpetuated the negative stereotypes whites had of blacks. One sportswriter who covered the black leagues on a regular basis castigated the Indianapolis Clowns for capitalizing on "slap-stick comedy and the kind of nonsense which many white people like to believe is typical and characteristic of all Negroes."[18]

While blacks were fashioning their own separate world of black baseball, several individual black athletes successfully participated in predominantly white organized sport. The most notable of these were Jack Johnson, America's first black heavyweight boxing champion; Joe Louis, the second black boxer to capture the heavyweight crown; and Jesse Owens, the famous track star from Ohio State who won four gold medals in the 1936 Olympic Games in Berlin. Of the three, Johnson was certainly the most controversial. Perhaps no black athlete incurred the wrath of such a broad segment of the white population—and simultaneously offended part of the black population—as Johnson. To whites, he possessed many of those personal qualities found so reprehensible in blacks. He was ill-mannered, defiant, and absolutely incorrigible. He had also ignited their worst fears by not only marrying three white women but also capturing the heavyweight championship, which had come to symbolize the Anglo-Saxon belief in racial superiority. By the same token, many blacks, including the likes of Booker T. Washington and to a lesser extent Du Bois, were appalled by Johnson's actions and believed he hindered the progress of the race. Though a hero to many in the black community, others considered him an embarrassment and the worst possible representative of black Americans because he refused to assume the subservient role assigned to him by whites.[19]

Much of what Johnson did, however, was merely an expression of the American way of life. His entire career was a quest for freedom to choose his own distinctive style while gaining access to the material things of this world.[20] Like other black boxers, he adopted a defensive style of fighting, relying to a great extent on feints, cross-counters, and deceptive maneuvers. As Randy Roberts noted, this style reflected black culture, which has always found it necessary to place a high value on the ability to retort and defend.[21] Perhaps even more significant was that Johnson resembled other black performers in consciously adopting a style that was undisputably his own. It was extremely important to him that he fashion an individual performance style that was personally developed and publicly acknowledged. He wanted clear and unquestioned claim to the image he had cultivated.

Johnson's life outside the ring was much more complex. He adopted no apparent political stance and would not hesitate to shift his allegiance when he found himself in a vulnerable or dangerous situation. Nonetheless, Johnson never stopped identifying with other blacks and receiving his basic sustenance from America's black community. His resentment of outstanding black boxers such as Sam Langford, Harry Wills, and Joe Louis indicated more his longing to be recognized as black America's only true champion than any need to divorce himself from other blacks. His numerous relationships with white women were one way he could exert a sense of power and control, but not necessarily an indication of a lack of interest in his race or a yearning to be a part of the white world. Johnson's apparent lack of political consciousness should not be construed as a disregard for other members of his race. He protested discrimination by proving himself as a black man and an American. His triumphs in the ring and his refusal to accept any limitations were Johnson's statement on behalf of racial justice and civil rights. Lawrence Levine, in his well-known *Black Culture and Black Consciousness*, wrote that Johnson "was not prone to see himself as a representative of any larger cause" but "was inevitably affected by the clamor" made over him by the black community. By the time Johnson fought Jim Jeffries, said Levine, he realized that not just the championship was at stake but also his "own honor, and in a degree the honor" of his own race.[22]

Johnson's career was more controversial and tumultuous than those of Joe Louis and Jesse Owens. While the latter two famous athletes had things in common with Johnson, they generally lived their lives much differently and with more restraint than America's first black heavyweight champion. White Americans continually expressed the belief that other blacks would do well to emulate Louis and Owens, who always acted like gentlemen and were cognizant of their proper place in society. In public, they usually adopted an ingratiating and compliant manner with members of the dominant culture. Their manner and gestures were deliberate and almost always understated. Perhaps most important was the fact that Louis and Owens regularly spoke about how much they loved their country and how much they owed America. Louis, for instance, donated his share of two title defenses to the army and navy relief funds during World War II. When criticized by some blacks for giving away his prize money while being fully aware of the racially discriminatory policies maintained by the navy, Louis responded by saying: "I'm not fighting for nothing, I'm fighting for my country."[23]

The irony of it all was that Louis and Owens were not necessarily submissive. It took ambitious and determined men to make it as far in American sport as they had. They were merely experts at concealing their drive for recognition. Owens and Louis adhered to traditional athletic expectations by being highly disciplined, obedient, and respectful of authority. As black athletes, they were also aware that they were allowed far less room to deviate from expected modes of behavior than their white counterparts. Both of them genuinely believed, moreover, in the American dream of individual success and the moral formula needed to realize that success. Owens and Louis were no different from most other American-bred youths in being taught that the path to success was contingent upon displaying proper decorum, courteously yielding to the opinions or wishes of others, showing deference to the good tastes and sensibility of others, and being industrious in one's calling. Bad manners and uncontrolled emotions were inappropriate, particularly in black culture, where the ability to control oneself and exercise restraint was highly valued. Louis's mother told him that "a good name" was "better than money" and encouraged him to work hard and become somebody. His managers, John Roxborough and Julien Black, urged him to be clean living and sportsmanlike and to practice restraint.[24]

No degree of decorum, however, could stop Louis and Owens from identifying with the black race. It was not always evident, but neither one of them abandoned the larger black population. While family, friends, and individual success were of paramount importance to Louis and Owens, the two athletes eventually recognized their significance to black society and strove to set positive examples for the whole race by maintaining a public image that was attractive—and not threatening— to all segments of society. They also reached out to other blacks, even though often very cautiously and only after being persuaded to do so by other blacks. Louis and Owens were aware that openly negative reactions to racial discrimination were often seen by whites as unreasonable, hypersensitive, and even "un-American." They often couched their complaints of racial discrimination in words acceptable to whites. Both men went to great lengths to avoid any interpretation by whites that their complaints of racial inequities were an expression of their merely being black or, perhaps stated more explicitly, "acting like a Nigger."[25]

At the same time, the help Louis and Owens gave other blacks seemed to border on the type of paternalism practiced by many whites. For this reason, as well as because of generational differences, Owens and, to a much lesser extent, Louis were sometimes viewed with suspicion, if not overt hostility, by younger blacks in this country. Taking a more conservative approach to racial issues and having isolated themselves somewhat from the black masses, the two athletes during the latter stages of their lives never completely won the confidence of more forceful and politically conscious blacks. Vince Matthews, who was involved in the proposed boycott of the 1968 Olympic Games in Mexico City, recalled the cold reception he and his fellow black athletes gave Owens when the former track star met with them the day after Tommie Smith and John Carlos gave their much publicized Black Power salutes. "When Jesse walked into the room," noted Matthews, "most of us tried to show him respect because of his age and his athletic accomplishments. But when he got up at the meeting and said he wanted the white athletes in the room to leave because 'these are my brothers' and I want to talk to them, you could see the snickers on some of the faces."[26]

All things considered, Louis and Owens were like other black Americans in that they responded in various ways to racial discrimination in order to rid themselves from an imposed sense of inferiority and transcend their stigmatized condition in American society. Significantly, these efforts often proved futile for Louis and Owens because American society typically relegated blacks to a single, racially inferior category. The stereotypical notion of black inferiority seemed so strong in America that regardless of how great their individual prestige, Louis and Owens could never be fully disassociated from less privileged members of their race or completely extricated from the "black image in the white mind." Although white Americans would refrain from identifying them by the color of their skin and trumpet their victories as symbolic triumphs of "America over Nazi Germany" or "America over Fascist Italy," the two athletes would always be linked with character traits supposedly innate to their racial group. It is precisely for these reasons that Owens tried to rise above his color and insist that he be seen as a "human being first and last, if not always," and questioned if there was not "something deeper, richer, better in this world than the color of one's skin."[27]

America's black community never forgot that Louis and Owens were black and that they were, to some extent, being exploited by this country's sports establishment. The success of two black athletes in international competition could not erase the fact that Jim Crow America continued to prohibit black athletes from participating in all sports. The sport that best illustrated the precarious status of black athletes and the injustices of American society was professional baseball. The "Gentlemen's Agreement" by major league owners prohibited any black players, regardless of ability, from entering white organized baseball. This form of discrimination was terribly frustrating to black Americans who believed that until blacks could participate fully in the National Game, they could not lay claim to the full rights of citizenship.[28]

Fortunately, America's entrance into World War II gave blacks more reason—and more opportunity—to protest discrimination in the National Game than at any other time in history. The hypocrisy involved in fighting a war for the Four Freedoms—against aggression by a country proclaiming a master race ideology—while concurrently upholding racial discrimination in organized baseball and society at large provided blacks with a perfect opportunity to expose the gap between America's creed and its practice. The democratic ideology for which the war was fought kindled hope in black Americans because they could fasten their racial demands to the same ideology in their attempts to integrate the national game. Blacks used the war to illustrate that the game of baseball was not the great leveler in society and a sport within the reach of all Americans.[29]

It was in this kind of atmosphere that Branch Rickey took the bold step of signing Jackie Robinson to a contract with the Brooklyn Dodgers. The signing of Robinson was received with unabated enthusiasm by America's black community. Robinson immediately became a hero in black America, surpassed in popularity perhaps only by Joe Louis. Some black Americans questioned, however, whether Robinson's sometimes volatile personality would prevent him from achieving success in organized baseball. He was an intensely proud black man who was quick to defend his rights and seldom, if ever, backed down from racial confrontations. He had spoken out against discriminatory practices while at UCLA and during his brief stint in the military. If Robinson was to survive in organized baseball, he would have to do his best to avoid racial conflicts with prejudiced white players.[30]

Serious altercations between Robinson and white opponents, however, never materialized. As things turned out, Rickey chose the ideal player to integrate the game. Although Robinson had a tendency to be high-spirited, he also knew his responsibilities as organized baseball's first black player and was careful to avoid any skirmishes that might jeopardize his chances for success. Robinson wanted a long-lasting career in organized baseball. Like other young men in America, he had dreamed of one day participating in major league baseball and frequently spoke of ultimate integration in the sport. For him the segregated black leagues signified second-class citizenship. He supported the black leagues in principle but never grew accustomed to their loose scheduling and erratic play.[31]

Robinson also grudgingly ignored racial slurs thrown at him by white players and fans—partly because Rickey wanted him to, partly out of fear of retribution at the hands of the dominant culture, and partly out of a genuine concern for his race. He realized that the hopes of many black Americans rested on his shoulders and, rather than take the more forceful approach he had adopted in previous interracial contacts, he acquiesced and let his athletic performance do the talking. As modern day baseball's first black player, Robinson was suddenly catapulted into the public eye and, as a result, almost immediately realized a sense of serving as an example. If he handled himself properly, he could point the way for other black ballplayers and perhaps make it possible for them to participate someday in the National Game. As a role model, he could become a symbol of possibility and a much-needed example of black success. In many ways, Robinson was similar to great black athletes who preceded him in that he was inevitably defined by the color of his skin. In his autobiography Robinson commented on his role as a representative of black Americans: "Many [blacks] who came to the ball park had not been baseball fans before I began to play in the big leagues. Suppressed and repressed for so many years, they needed a victorious black man as a symbol. It would help them believe in themselves." [32]

Following Robinson's breakthrough with the Dodgers, a number of blacks gained entry into organized sport at both the college and professional levels. These athletes shared many of the same attitudes toward racial issues and the American sports establishment. Although occasionally speaking out against discriminatory practices, they tended to deemphasize black consciousness and redefine themselves in accordance with the policies established by the leaders in organized sport. The gradual desegregation of sport, combined with the post-World War II propaganda about the brotherhood of man, caused them, like other black Americans, to think less about blackness as a cultural identity and more about their loyalty to this country and its ideals. Black athletes were concerned about their rights as human beings but were reluctant to protest for fear that their actions would be construed as un-American and possibly jeopardize their careers in sport. Althea Gibson, the first black player to participate in the United States Tennis Championships at Forest Hills, wrote in her autobiography that she did not consider herself a racially conscious person or a crusader. "Someone once wrote," noted Gibson, "that the difference between me and Jackie Robinson is that he thrived on his role as a Negro battling for equality whereas I shy away from it. That man read me correctly." [33]

The patriotism exhibited by black athletes during the 1950s was not wasted on the youthful Cassius Clay. From the time he captured a gold medal in the 1960 Olympics to his defeat of Sonny Liston for the heavyweight championship some four years later, Clay was universally hailed as a great athlete whom all Americans could admire. During this period, Clay was variously described as loyal, patriotic, witty, charming, articulate, and clean-living. He seemingly had no interest in civil rights issues and mounting tensions between blacks and whites. Many of his public statements were reminiscent of those made by Joe Louis nearly twenty years earlier. When asked by a Soviet reporter in 1960 about racial discrimination in America, Clay responded by saying, "Tell your leaders we got qualified people working on that, and I'm not worried about the outcome. To me, the U.S.A is still the best country in the world, counting yours." [34]

Althea Gibson, the great tennis star who broke several racial barriers in the sport, did not see herself as a champion of civil rights. Courtesy of the Library of Congress.

Shortly after his title fight with Liston in 1964, Clay stunned the sports world by announcing he had changed his name to Muhammad Ali and joined the Black Muslims. Ali's conversion to a black separatist group like the Muslims, his sudden willingness to speak out against racial inequities, and his eventual refusal to join the military resulted in a myriad of reactions from the American public. He became a hero in the black community and was admired by many liberal-minded Americans but was looked upon with disdain and branded a traitor by those who supported the war and followed traditional societal values. Gene Tunney and Jack Dempsey both castigated Ali, telling him that he was undeserving of the heavyweight title and that his actions were un-American. Similar comments were made by sportswriters, governors, U.S. senators and representatives, and such organizations as the American Legion and Veterans of Foreign Wars.[35]

Ali's refusal to be inducted into the military was just one reason members of the establishment found him disruptive. He was also not the type of athlete the conservative white sporting world appreciated. While the sports establishment expected their heroes—particularly black ones —to be humble and accommodating, Ali was always flamboyant, immodest, and defiantly confident. Perhaps most troubling to whites was that Ali never sacrificed his cultural distinctiveness, the merits of a black lifestyle, and the value of his negritude. To the white majority, Ali's celebration of black culture challenged the existing social order because it helped eliminate the negative self-image prevalent among some blacks and encouraged black consciousness, a necessary foundation for the promotion of black political and economic power. Members of the establishment were, moreover, infuriated by Ali because he exposed, for all the world to see, an America that was unwilling to honor its own precepts. With no need to nourish this country's dreams and myths, Ali continually made clear that freedom, equality, and fair representation were not available to all Americans.[36]

The willingness to express pride in his blackness was not an indication that Ali wished to sever himself from American society. In fact, one of the truths of Ali's career was that, even while he was preaching a separatist position, his very actions indicated he was a man who believed that the American dream of unlimited possibilities, though imperfect and perhaps even fanciful, was worth striving for. Ali wanted to participate in American life and realize the numerous benefits that derived from being successful in sport, but not if it implied the supremacy of everything white and the inferiority of everything black. America would have to compromise and accept him on his own terms or not at all.[37] A composite of several types of heroes in black folk culture, Ali was nonetheless always his own man, someone who clung tenaciously to his racial past while simultaneously seeking immortality in the boxing ring and resisting the standards of behavior imposed by white society.[38]

Ali's refusal to succumb to the dictates of the dominant culture was particularly significant because it helped spawn a black athletic revolution. Inspired by the champion's racial consciousness, a number of black athletes followed Ali's lead and began to speak out against racial discrimination and other inequities in American society. Perhaps the most noteworthy phase of this revolution was the proposed boycott of the 1968 Olympic Games in Mexico City. The planned boycott, which was spearheaded by Harry Edwards, an instructor of sociology at San Jose State, was aimed at exposing the racism prevalent in the United States and around the world. Although civil rights legislation was sometimes responsible for the increased participation of blacks in American society, the implications of this type of participation were greater than Edwards and a growing number of black athletes were prepared to accept. It was apparent to them that participation in American society was possible for blacks, but only at the expense of being denied their own identity and their African heritage. In brief, black athletes involved in the proposed boycott were similar to other black Americans in that they were interested in disclosing this country's racial inequities while at the same time expressing the distinctiveness of black culture, the quality of black life, and the value of black pride. Tommie Smith, the great sprinter from San Jose State, explained shortly after the announcement of the boycott in December 1967 that he would give up not only participation in the Mexico City Games but his life as well if it meant the elimination of injustice and oppression in American society.[39]

Smith did not give up his life or participate in any boycott. Other than the Black Power salute given by him and John Carlos, the games went on without interruptions. The overriding reason for the failure of the boycott was that Edwards never succeeded in unifying the black athletes. While black Olympians supported the boycott in principle, the vast majority ultimately concluded that the price to pay for nonparticipation was simply too high. First of all, South Africa, because of its discriminatory practices against blacks, was eventually kicked out of the games by the International Olympic Committee. This fact softened the militant stance of many black athletes who had originally agreed upon a boycott because of their desire to expose the racial inequities existing in South Africa and ultimately to see that the country was barred from Olympic competition. Edwards was also wrong to think black athletes would follow through on something as radical as a boycott. Almost everything Edwards asked of the black Olympians was in direct opposition to what they had always been taught was the proper behavior of a competitive athlete. While black athletes—and white athletes, for that matter—were expected to be humble, tolerant, and respectful of power, Edwards encouraged them to be outspoken, defiant, and disrespectful of authority. In essence, Edwards urged black athletes to be something they were not. Participation in Olympic competition was also the highlight in the careers of most black athletes and perhaps their ticket to a brighter future and more rewarding way of life. Public adulation awaited those black athletes who came home from Mexico City victorious. Few athletes, regardless of color, were willing to squander that type of attention and forego a chance to compete against the best athletes in the world. Black athletes eventually concluded, with varying degrees of conviction, that achievement in sport was an ideal starting point for wiping out inequities due to race.[40]

The boycott was hurt, moreover, by Edwards's reluctance to take advantage of all the resources available to him. Conspicuous by their absence from the movement were black female athletes. Such outstanding performers as Wyomia Tyus and Jarvis Scott were not consulted by the men, privy to the inner workings of the Olympic Project for Human Rights (OPHR), or invited to the various strategy sessions and meetings organized by Edwards and his cohorts. This was particularly disconcerting to the black female athletes because they realized, like other black women, that they needed to work alongside men for the ultimate liberation of black Americans. It was absolutely essential to black female athletes that the struggle for civil rights be in concert with black males, since the root cause of their problems was not sexism but racial oppression in American society.[41]

The unwillingness to involve black female athletes in the boycott stemmed largely from what the historian Paula Giddings called the "male-conscious motif" that dominated American society in the 1960s.[42] The boycott masterminded by Edwards was as much a "male revolt" as it was a "black athletic revolt." Confronted by racial discrimination, challenged by a caste system that left little room for display of their masculinity, and having their honor attacked by more radical members of the black community who were emphasizing the need for the celebration of black life-styles, Edwards and his followers consciously exerted both their sense of racial pride and manhood to the exclusion of black female athletes. There simply was no room for women in a movement where black men were trying to rid themselves of their imposed status as "Negroes" through the raising of black gloved fists, threats of nonparticipation in the world's greatest athletic festival, and other exhibitions of "black power." Like the men in many black civil rights organizations, the boycotting black athletes' desperate need for male affirmation necessitated that their female counterparts be pushed into the background and not permitted to take an active role in the rebellion. Their unstated fear was that they would be robbed of their manhood if women such as Wyomia Tyus and Jarvis Scott were allowed to share in decision making and strategic planning. "We were most disappointed that our feelings were not brought out," noted Scott about the boycott movement. "While the men issued statements and held conferences, finding out what we felt was only a last minute thing."[43]

All things considered, then, the most telling aspect of the boycott was the interplay not only between Edwards and the black athletes but among the black athletes themselves. The situation required them to make a sophisticated assessment of individual and group costs to determine which line of action—that is, resisting or yielding to group pressure —would produce more benefits. There certainly was no question in Edwards's mind as to what the black athletes should do. Notwithstanding the exclusion of women from the movement, Edwards tried to convince black athletes that the problems of blacks were common to them as a group rather than as individuals. He continually emphasized that the fight for equality was by necessity a collective struggle and could not be based solely on individual achievements. Personal accomplishments were praiseworthy, but they could never completely eliminate the discrimination experienced by blacks, because the rights and freedoms of individuals in American society depended to a great extent upon the status of the group to which they belonged. In essence, Edwards urged the kind of race consciousness that marked the larger black protest movement of the 1960s. In the end, however, black Olympians took an approach that seemed to be, at least on the surface, less race conscious and collective. They ultimately answered in the negative to questions posed by the well-known long jumper Ralph Boston before the games: "Will a boycott advance the cause of freedom? If it doesn't is it fair to ask the athletes to make the sacrifice needlessly?"[44]

The revolts staged by black athletes would decrease dramatically after the early 1970s. The women's movement, lessening racial tensions in American society, and problems associated with inflation and unemployment would converge with a host of other factors to take some steam out of the black athletic revolt just as it had done with the larger Black Power movement. The decline in the number of protests did not mean, however, that black athletes no longer occupied the attention of the American public. If anything, they began receiving unprecedented attention. Evidence of this fascination with black athletes can be gleaned from the outpouring of popular articles and research studies published over the last two decades dealing with such topics as inadequate reward structures in sport and racial differences in sport performance.[45]

Of such topics, perhaps none has been more reflective of black athletes' continued stigmatization and their sense of being both black and American than the discussion concerning racial differences in sport performance. Although such a debate had been waged in American society since at least the beginning of this century, during the last two decades there has been a particularly heated discussion revolving around the outstanding performances of a disportionate number of black athletes in sport. As the historians Randy Roberts and James Olson have contended, whites have increasingly come to see black athletes as a more diverse group of individuals; nonetheless, people of all races and backgrounds have continued to explain away the overrepresentation of blacks in sport by arguing that they are endowed with innate physical skills that lead to superior athletic performances.[46] The implication is that blacks have come by their great athletic performances naturally and not through hard work, dedication, and other character traits so admired in American society.

Black athletes, while not always verbalizing their anger, have been disturbed about being characterized differently merely because of skin color and stereotyped as athletes who realized success through no effort of their own. They are like other athletes in American sport in wanting to be acknowledged for the hard work and dedication that go into their performances. To do otherwise demeans their accomplishments and serves only to perpetuate longstanding beliefs about the black race's lack of intelligence and faulty character.[47] One black athlete who publicly expressed his resentment over the divergent characterizations of black and white athletes was Isiah Thomas, the outstanding guard of the Detroit Pistons. Shortly after the Pistons lost the seventh and final game to the Boston Celtics in the 1987 Eastern Conference championship, Thomas told reporters he agreed with the earlier comments of his Piston teammate, Dennis Rodman, that Larry Bird was a very good basketball player, but if he were black, "he'd be just another guy." In an attempt to explain what he meant by this comment, Thomas later told reporters that he was not referring to Bird so much as he was "the perpetuation of stereotypes about blacks." "When Bird makes a great play, it's due to his thinking and his work habits," noted Thomas. "It's all planned out by him. It's not the case for blacks. All we do is run and jump. We never practice or give a thought to how we play. It's like I came dribbling out of my mother's womb."[48]

The frustrations expressed by Thomas have been heard less frequently from black athletes recently. Although they continue to be sensitive to discriminatory practices, cognizant of the stigmatized condition of blacks in American society, and burdened by the pressures of the white world, black athletes in contemporary sport are generally refraining from speaking out on racial matters and larger issues of the day. This is partly a result not only of black sportsmen's adherence to the traditionally conservative athletic role but also of the fact that more blatant forms of racial discrimination have largely disappeared from highly organized sport. It is also a result, however, of the marginalized position of black athletes in the African-American community and the larger American society. Having garnered millions of dollars and realized a heightened sense of accomplishment and prestige as a result of their performances in sport, black athletes feel a distance between themselves and the masses of black people that has weakened their notion of group consciousness and led them to approach racial protests with caution.

The burden for black athletes of today, regardless of the distance they feel between themselves and other blacks, is that they continue to be defined by race and expected to serve as symbols of possibility and role models for members of the black community. Although more thoughtful and sensitive blacks have constantly lamented the fact that the entry of a disproportionate number of blacks into sport delimits the conditions of black identity within American society, they also believe black athletes are obligated to lead lives that are above reproach.[49] Michael Jordan and Charles Barkley are just two of the great performers who are not only expected to fulfill their role as athletes but counted upon to serve as positive examples for members of their race. Insisting that black athletes such as Jordan and Barkley serve as role models is, perhaps more than anything else, a reflection of the lack of leadership in a black community sensitive to white America's continued questioning of their character and competence. The late Arthur Ashe was troubled by the obsession with role models in the black community, particularly when they were drawn from the sport and entertainment industries. In his last book, *Days of Grace: A Memoir*, Ashe wrote: "The very fact that we [the black community] speak of 'Leaders' and 'Role models,' as much as we do tells of our lack of power and organization. . . . We even think of athletes and entertainers in this way; we see basketball players and pop singers as possible role models, when nothing could be further, in most cases, from their capabilities."[50]

In sum, to maintain an ethnic identity while actively participating in organized sport and the larger American society was not an easy task for black athletes. Burdened by the desire to sustain group loyalties, and at the same time striving to uphold the American virtue of individualism, blacks were moved to demonstrate their racial pride in different ways depending on particular circumstances. Although some black athletes were more adept at this approach than others, the vast majority proved to be remarkably flexible and honored the basic tenets of their own culture while simultaneously accommodating themselves to adverse situations. Outstanding black athletes were able to compete with other Americans for status and social equality because they realized early on that success in this country was ultimately linked with the process of adaptation and differentiation and the need to assume multiple roles. It was a complex situation that clearly indicated that the careers of black and white athletes, though quite different in many respects, were always intertwined and mutually dependent. From the moment they were first allowed into organized sport, black athletes were involved in a continually changing and sometimes ambivalent relationship with white athletes and American society that contributed to their sense of identity as black people and Americans. The achievements of black athletes perhaps have done little to change racial attitudes in the dominant culture, but their successes have served, ironically enough, as symbols of possibility for members of the black community who strive for recognition with the same earnestness as their white counterparts and who attempt to forge their own identities in an America that hold fast to racial stereotypes and often refuses to honor its own precepts.

11

Edwin Bancroft Henderson, African American Athletes, and the Writing of Sport History

Charles Drew, who attended the prestigious Dunbar High School in Washington, D.C., later starred in several sports at Amherst College, and eventually became a famous surgeon and blood bank pioneer, noted in a 1940 letter that he was very grateful to Edwin Bancroft Henderson. "I owe you and a few other men like you," Drew noted, "for setting most of the standards that I have felt were worthwhile, the things I have lived by and for and whenever possible have attempted to pass on." [1] Drew's comments, which came nearly ten years before his death in a tragic automobile accident, stemmed from an obviously deep admiration for Henderson, who had been both his teacher and mentor during his days as a student in Washington's segregated school system. [2]

The Edwin Bancroft Henderson that Charles Drew so much admired was born on November 24, 1883, in Washington, D.C., to William and Louisa Henderson. He graduated in 1902 from the famous M Street School, attended Dudley Allen Sargent's celebrated Harvard Summer School of Physical Education (HSSPE), and headed the Department of Physical Education in Washington's segregated school system from 1925 until his appointment some twenty-six years later as Director of Physical Education, Safety, and Athletics. Henderson's career was marked by extraordinary accomplishments and many successes, both within and outside the physical education profession. He introduced basketball to black children in Washington, D.C., and organized the district's Public School Athletic League. He co-founded the Washington, D.C. Pigskin Club and helped establish such important organizations as the Inter-Scholastic Athletic Association of Middle Atlantic States; the Eastern Board of Officials; the Washington, D.C., chapter of the American Alliance for Health, Physical Education, Recreation, and Dance

221

(AAPHERD); the Colored Citizens Protection League of Falls Church, Virginia; and the Falls Church, Virginia, branch of the National Association for the Advancement of Colored People (NAACP). Through his numerous organizational initiatives, Henderson fought against various forms of racial discrimination. He waged war against Jim Crow transportation facilities in Virginia, led campaigns to eliminate segregated recreational and organized sports programs on both the local and regional levels, and fought to prohibit southern states from excluding blacks from membership in local AAHPERD chapters.[3]

Henderson was, moreover, a prolific writer. He penned literally hundreds of "Letters to the Editor" to newspapers across the country, wrote numerous unpublished documents as part of his civil rights struggles, contributed important articles to professional journals, and wrote the first books on the history of African Americans in sport. Henderson's achievements did not go unrecognized. He was given the YMCA Distinguished Service Award, selected as a Howard University Alumnus of the Year, appointed Honorary President of the North American Society for Sport History, and elected as a charter member of the Black Athletes Hall of Fame.[4]

Of all these accomplishments and honors, it is Henderson's writings on African American athletes that have proved most far-reaching and had the greatest influence on subsequent generations. Popular writers, academicians from various disciplines, and scholars of both races and different philosophies have all depended on Henderson's work for source material, analysis, and clues in the designing of their own publications dealing with African American athletes. If the number of citations is any indication of the importance of one's scholarship, Henderson's work merits great respect and he rightfully deserves to be called the "Father of Black Sport History."[5] Nearly every article, book chapter, and survey text written over the last half-century that includes information on the history of African American athletes has seemingly been influenced by Henderson's work in one way or another. Andrew S. "Doc" Young, in the acknowledgments to his *Negro Firsts In Sports* (1963), was absolutely correct when he noted: "Mr. Henderson was the first person of any race to dig deeply into the total history of Negroes in American sports. A great deal of knowledge which is now shared in common by sports authorities was originally ferreted out, with painstaking effort and no little difficulty, by Mr. Henderson."[6]

Henderson's writings were intended to foster pride among African Americans and alter white racial beliefs. With the commitment and deep emotional involvement that characterized some of the earliest scholarly work of black academicians, Henderson's writings were instrumental in proving that African Americans were just as capable as whites on the playing field and, by extension, in other areas of American life. Possessing boundless optimism in the power of sport to break down racial prejudice and contribute to a more integrated society, Henderson focused much of his attention on the individual accomplishments of black athletes in an effort to provide much-needed evidence of African American progress. Even when faced with unremitting racial discrimination, Henderson's writings reflected an undying faith in the integration functions of sport. In large measure, Henderson was, to utilize the terminology of the historian Patrick B. Miller, a "muscular assimilationist" in that he viewed society as an established system of interrelated parts in which sport transmitted shared values and norms and contributed to communal feelings between whites and African Americans.[7]

Henderson's first significant publication occurred in 1910 when he began editing, along with William A. Joiner, an instructor from Wilberforce University and a longtime promoter of sport, the first of a series of four books entitled *Official Handbook: Inter-Scholastic Athletic Association of Middle Atlantic States.* Published as part of the Spalding Athletic Library collection, the books provide a wealth of information, many photographs, rules, and records concerning the involvement of African American athletes at various levels of amateur sport in the Middle Atlantic States. The series is especially significant because it reflects both the immense pride that African Americans took in their own sporting organizations during the early decades of the twentieth century and their simultaneous concern that these organizations be as pristine as possible, devoid of much of the corruption that characterized white amateur sport during this period. No one can read Ernest Marshall's "The Negro Athlete" in the 1910 edition or George William Lattimore's "Some Facts Concerning Athletic Clubs in Brooklyn and New Jersey" and Conrad V. Norman's "Athletics in New York City" in the 1911 edition without realizing that African American organizations were crucial because they served as examples of black enterprise and symbols of possibility in racially torn America. At the same time, no one can read the series without recognizing its emphasis on such issues as appropriate athletic behavior, eligibility requirements, protests and sanctions, and definitions of amateurism. The emphasis on these issues in the *Official Handbook* was part of the broader national discussion among African American educators and social reformers about the proper management of their segregated sporting organizations. In short, educators and social reformers realized that these organizations had to be above reproach if they were not to subvert the cultural achievements and other accomplishments of blacks living in a society that had always allowed them far less room than whites to deviate from standard modes of behavior.[8]

Henderson's co-editorship of the *Official Handbook* set the stage for a number of articles he would publish on African American athletes in prestigious black publications over the next three decades. His first article, "The Colored College Athlete," was published in the *Crisis* (July 1911: 115–18), the NAACP's new monthly journal edited by the great intellectual and civil rights activist W. E. B. Du Bois. The article, which followed closely on the heels of some other noteworthy essays on black athletes in such black periodicals as *The Voice of the Negro* (1904– 1907) and *The Colored American Magazine* (1900–1909),[9] primarily recounts the success of African Americans in intercollegiate sport at predominantly white institutions in the North. Adopting an approach that would become a trademark of his many writings, Henderson attempted to chart both the progress and prove the equality of African American athletes by pointing out the exploits of such former and current college stars as Dartmouth's Matthew Bullock, Amherst's and Harvard's William H. Lewis, William's Ernest Marshall, Western Reserve's Edward Williams, Michigan's Leonard Lapsley, Oberlin's Merton Robinson, Pennsylvania's John B. Taylor, Harvard's Ted Cable, and Amherst's John Pinkett, Ed Gray, and William Tecumseh Sherman Jackson.

While "The Colored College Athlete" undoubtedly brought him some notoriety and national attention from blacks, Henderson secured his reputation as the foremost authority on African American athletes with a series of articles in the *Messenger* between March 1925 and January 1928. Henderson's articles in the *Messenger*, the more militant journal edited by A. Philip Randolph and Chandler Owen, are particularly interesting from a journalistic point of view because they were written during the last three years of the magazine's existence and at a time when it had shifted from an emphasis on black workers to the Talented Tenth and the Black Bourgeoisie.[10] Henderson's articles, appearing most often in a column usually titled simply "Sports," were published alongside others devoted to society news, literary accomplishments, successful entrepreneurs and businessmen, and issues related to women and children. He clearly understood that his articles on sports would be attractive to many readers, a fact certainly not lost on the editors of a magazine that had always struggled to remain financially solvent. "Sport writings are proving a tonic to dead print matter," Henderson wrote in the June 1925 issue of the magazine. "Many men and boys to whom our newspapers were unknown now read the sport sheets, and take interest in various local, national and international affairs. The athletic page is a good advertising method for news of more serious import" (p. 234).

True to the new orientation of the magazine, Henderson focused primarily on elite African American athletes and college sport. Although he wrote frequently of the proposed boxing match between Harry Wills and Jack Dempsey and occasionally the performances of other black professional athletes and teams, Henderson spent most of his time chart-ing the progress of black college athletes in celebratory terms, stressing the value of amateur sport, and emphasizing the importance of organiza-tional structure and administrative oversight in intercollegiate sport at historically black colleges.

This latter topic was obviously of great importance to Henderson, just as it was to W. E. B. Du Bois, George Streator, and a host of other African American intellectuals during the early part of the twentieth century.[11] As in his writings in the *Official Handbook: Inter-Scholastic Athletic Association of Middle Atlantic States*, Henderson devoted much space in the *Messenger* to a discussion about the need for improved management of black college sport because of inappropriate recruiting practices, lack of eligibility requirements, and a number of other rules violations. Always the reformer and forever conscious of what was tak-ing place at all levels of sport, Henderson pointed out some of the prob-lems, publicized new policies being implemented, and made his own recommendations to eliminate the corruption that characterized athletic programs in black colleges. Henderson considered the most serious prob-lems plaguing sport in black colleges to be the limited opportunities, lack of respect, and inequitable pay afforded African American officials. Henderson, who had the distinction in 1906 of becoming the first African American to officiate in the Howard and Lincoln (Pa.) Thanksgiving Day Football Classic and in 1915 established the all-black Eastern Board of Officials, was especially disturbed by the fact that members of his own racial group frequently chose white rather than black officials because of their perceived competence, trustworthiness, and ability to handle the stressful situations in athletic contests.[12] "How it happens that our pigmy-minded victory-at-any-cost-blinded race people imagine the work of white officials superior to that done by Savoy, Gibson, Westmoreland, Washington, Abbott, Robinson, Pinderhughes, Wright, Morrison, Trigg, Coppage and Douglass and many others is a puzzle to me," wrote Hen-derson in the January 1927 issue of the journal. "The only advantage arriving from the use of white officials is from the fact of the peculiar psychology that presents itself when white officials work which causes the poor driven cattle to become blinded to the same errors of commis-sion and omission that would not have escaped had the officials been of the colored race" (p. 20).

In addition to his discussion about black college sport, Henderson devoted much time in the *Messenger* to outlining forms of racial discrimi-nation and attempting to burst racial stereotypes associated with black athletes and organized sport. Very attuned to white fears of black bodies and the various forms of racial discrimination in this country, Henderson was especially fond of pointing out how these factors influenced the sport participation patterns of African American athletes and how this participation was perceived by members of both races. He was cognizant of the complex racial ideology that was used to rationalize the performances of African American athletes based on skin color, intelligence, moral character, and physical skills. In the June 1925 issue Henderson encouraged African Americans to compete in track and field because "any man who can clip a second from a race consistently or leap an inch farther or higher is sought out by the coach whether he be Negro, Chinaman, or Indian Chief." It was much more difficult, however, for African Americans to transcend racial barriers in those sports that either required close personal contact between the participants or were identified with white America's upper crust. "In the team games," Henderson noted, "especially the personal contact games like football or basketball it takes a very good Negro athlete to make prejudiced frats and college directors see him. For baseball, crew, tennis, golf and a host of minor sports traditions are in most places yet against him" (p. 234). In the April 1927 issue, Henderson continued this theme by arguing that African Americans found limited opportunities in wrestling because of the close contact the sport required. "Colored boys got their biggest opportunities in non-contact sports, where time and distance records are to be overcome," wrote Henderson. "Wrestling affords the closest contact. Like forms of social contact, it stirs much racial prejudice. Seldom do colored boys get a full chance in such games" (p. 112).

In the May 1927 issue, Henderson refuted the popularly held belief that blacks did not excel in distance running because they lacked discipline and other positive character traits possessed by white Americans. He hypothesized that the small number of African American distance runners resulted from the unwillingness of coaches to spend the requisite time with them in training to ensure their success. "A colored boy who could start with a bunch from a century dash scratch," Henderson said, "and lead them to the tape, at once got the eye of the coach, but not so the purveyor of distance wares. The coach has to try him out with time and patience. This is one reason why many of our boys have not been distance champions" (p. 148). Finally, in both the March 1926 issue (p. 91) and the June 1927 one (p. 189), Henderson took exception to those sportswriters who claimed that John B. Taylor, the great black quarter-miler from the University of Pennsylvania, was actually a member of the white race. Henderson was incensed by their refusal to accept the fact that the great performances of Taylor could have been executed by a black man. In the March 1926 issue, he wrote: "Years back when John Taylor of the U. of Pa. was the 440 yards champion, some enterprising Nordic claimed the swarthy son of America for the Nordic race on account of his bulging calves. Our galaxy of champions in sprint events, distance runs, field events, all-around athletic competition, and athletic games have made way with the fallacy. They said the wide-nostrilled, deep-chested colored man of African extraction was physically unsuited to Northern climes, but Matthew Henson, who was a member of Robert Perry's 1909 expedition that erected the American Flag at the North Pole, stepped out on to the North Pole and is yet with us. When the bars are more generally down, it will be found that colored athletes with centuries of dormant potential energies will more than match many inbreeding white race opponents."

Henderson's pieces in *The Messenger* were also important because they were among the plethora of articles that were published on African American athletes in both black specialty magazines and more comprehensive and nationally recognized journals between the two world wars. The development of separate black sporting organizations at both the amateur and professional levels of competition, increased involvement of African Americans in sport at predominantly white institutions and in the Olympic Games, and the renewed sense of racial pride in the black community as well as the parallel emergence of what Theodore Kornweibel termed the "new journalism" for the "new crowd Negro," all combined to produce a number of important articles on the black athletic experience.[13] For instance, Binga Dismond, the former track star from the University of Chicago, edited a special section on sports titled, "In the Sun," in a short-lived journal, the *Champion Magazine: A Monthly Survey of Negro Achievement*, just before America's entrance into World War I.[14] The *Crusader*, the radical magazine edited and published in New York City between 1918 and 1922 by Cyril Valentine Briggs, ran several pieces on basketball during its four-year existence. Briggs, who loved basketball and apparently was good friends with Robert L. Douglas, the founder and manager of the famous Renaissance Five basketball team, wrote a number of pieces on the sport.[15] Romeo L. Dougherty, well-known sporting editor of the *New York News* and later the *New York Amsterdam News*, was a contributor to the magazine, including an insightful article in the January 1921 issue, entitled "Behind the Scenes in Basketball" (3: 13–14). Providing even more expanded coverage of African American athletes was the *Competitor*, a sports periodical published by Robert L. Vann, the longtime editor of the *Pittsburgh Courier-Journal*. Although in existence only from January 1920 to June 1921, the magazine published articles on everything from the importance of black referees and the future of black basketball to sport in historically black colleges and the founding of the National Negro Baseball League.[16] The *Southern Workman*, initiated and first edited by Samuel Armstrong of Hampton Institute, included coverage of sport, such as Elizabeth Dunham's 1924 essay on "Physical Education of Women at Hampton Institute" and Charles H. Williams's articles on the formative years of the Colored Intercollegiate Athletic Association and black participation in both the 1932 and 1936 Olympic Games.[17] The *Crisis*, with a number of talented and well-known contributors, such as Rollo Wilson, George Streator, Roy Wilkins, William A. Brower and Dan Burley, published a number of cogent and nicely written articles on black participation in sport.[18] Finally, the National Urban League's official journal, *Opportunity: A Journal of Negro Life*, published several outstanding articles on the black athlete. With insightful and intelligent analysis, the articles described both the accomplishments of African American athletes and the forms of racial discrimination evident in sport.[19]

Among the writings in *Opportunity* was Henderson's 1936 article "The Negro Athlete and Race Prejudice," one of his most important and enduring works.[20] He provided an important analysis of the status of African American athletes in contemporary sport, his fullest argument yet for sports power to break down racial prejudice and serve as the optimal agent for assimilation, and made public the increasing debate over alleged black athletic superiority. Henderson explained, with astuteness and a sociologist's eye for human behavior and social relations, that black college athletes had to be athletically superior to their white counterparts to find success in team sports. They were forced to "make adjustments" when dealing with racial teammates, had to "learn to take plenty from opponents," and suffered the humiliations of "separate lodgement when on tour" and being denied the opportunity to participate in games against the "service schools or the gentlemen of the south." The black "professional or money-seeking athletes in the profit making game," Henderson noted, encountered different problems and situations (p. 77). While denied the opportunity to take part in major league baseball and many other white organized sport programs, black professional athletes were sometimes allowed to participate in integrated sport by white promoters and entrepreneurs who were willing to suspend their own racist beliefs if it was financially profitable to do so. Henderson explained, without elaborating, that a multitude of factors other than financial ones helped determine the process of desegregation in sport: that "barnstorming 'big leaguers' do not disdain playing against good colored—pros when the gate pays," that "Professional All-Colored basketball teams also find it possible, with an occasional paying venture playing white teams as far south as Washington, D.C.," and that "football professionals are finding expression and compensation by playing on or with white Pro-teams" (p. 78).

In addition to discussing the status of African American athletes at both the amateur and professional levels of sport, Henderson provided the interesting and detailed argument that these same athletes had done as much as any group to spread tolerance and improve race relations in American society. Although black intellectuals, noted Henderson, had "risen to high planes of social relationships with individuals of other races that transcend the physical," it was African American athletes who made the greatest contribution to racial understanding and sensitivity. The reasons were clear to Henderson. It was African American athletes, rather than black musicians, and artists, and writers, who were able to instill pride among members of their own community and bring the race greater respect because "the main springs of action are still located in the glands" and the "keenest pleasures and most poignant pains" for human beings "are born of feelings rather than of intellect" (p. 79). To Henderson, then, white supremacist ideology, which was carefully maintained by convincing blacks that they had ugly bodies, were intellectually inferior, and were culturally less civilized, was best confronted by African American athletes, whose great sport performances were unparalleled in producing the visceral responses necessary to alter racial stereotypes and attitudes. The transformational power of sport helped explain why Joe Louis "captivated the fancy of millions"; why Jesse Owens, Ralph Metcalf, Eddie Tolan, and a host of others have likewise provided a feeling of pride and joyful relationship for many: why African American athletes "are emulated by thousands of growing youth of all races"; and why "above all they gain for themselves and the Negro the respect of millions whose superiority feelings have sprung solely from identity with the white race." It is also the reason, Henderson claimed, why every educational institution and agency involved in racial uplift should place more emphasis on the "social use of athletics" (p. 79).

His last major issue was the debate over alleged black athletic superiority. He noted that during the preceding year people from all walks of life had advanced various theories as to why such a seemingly large number of African Americans had put together so many outstanding track-and-field performances. These theories, "many of them honest," Henderson was quick to point out, were intended to prove that African American athletes "were endowed with some peculiar anatomical structure of foot, leg or thigh that enables them to run or jump better than white athletes" (p. 78).

To combat these theories of innate racial characteristics and sport performances, Henderson cited the work of W. Montague Cobb, a well-known professor of anatomy at Howard University, future president of the NAACP, and one of Henderson's former students from the segregated public schools of Washington, D.C., who had taken extensive anthropological measurements of Jesse Owens to help determine the physical dimensions of white and black track athletes.[21] Utilizing the data that had appeared just two months earlier in Cobb's article "Race and Runners" in the *Journal of Health and Physical Education*,[22] Henderson noted that Cobb, through "painstaking research, tests, and x-rays of the body of Jesse Owens," had "scientifically disproved the one and twenty theories that Negro athletes have peculiar anatomical structures" (p. 78). Henderson, never one to avoid debate and always willing to provide an opinion on controversial matters, then entered the fray by stating: "When one recalls that it is estimated that only one negro slave in five was able to live through the rigors of the 'Middle Passage,' and that the horrible conditions of slavery took toll of many slaves who could not make biological adjustments in a hostile environment, one finds the Darwinism theory of the survival of the fit operating among negroes as rigorously as any selective process ever operated among human beings. There is just a likelihood that some very vital elements persist in the histological tissues of the glands or muscles of negro athletes" (p. 79).

Taken as a whole, Henderson's article is not only thought-provoking but also full of more than just a bit of irony. Although he made cogent observations on the status of African Americans in sport, he helped contribute at the same time to the mythologizing of black athletic performance and to the erroneous belief that sport serves as the great leveler in American society. There is no evidence to support his contention that African American athletes have helped foster greater respect for their race or contributed "to the spread of tolerance and improved race relations." If anything, the passage of time has shown that the entry of a disproportionate number of African American athletes into certain sports has served to limit the range of black possibilities in a society still divided by race and characterized by unequal distribution of power and economic resources. Perhaps most important, Henderson's suggestion that the outstanding performances of African Americans in sport resulted from the elimination of physically weaker slaves during the "Middle Passage," a suggestion he would continue to proffer throughout his life, lent credence to the belief in innate physiological gifts of black athletes espoused by the very same people he had previously condemned. By offering this theory, Henderson inadvertently provided corroboration for the racialists whose arguments for innate physiological differences have served to maintain the stereotypical notion that African Americans could not excel in the life of the mind and that their outstanding sport performances came naturally and not through hard work, dedication, and other character traits so admired in American society.[23]

In 1939, Henderson published *The Negro in Sports,* the work he is most closely identified with and the one that perhaps has had more influence than any other on subsequent research dealing with the history of the black athlete in American sport.[24] Appearing one decade after the publication of John A. Krout's groundbreaking study *Annals of Ameri-*

can Sport (1929) and in the same year as Robert B. Weaver's *Amusements and Sports in American Life* (1939), Henderson's book, the first survey ever completed on African American involvement in sport, was commissioned by Carter G. Woodson, the Harvard-trained Ph.D. known as the "Father of Negro History."[25] Henderson's book, which includes seventeen chapters, a rather lengthy appendix, and many photographs, fits nicely into the Woodson genre in that it chronicles the individual success of African American athletes to inspire others and serve as examples of black achievement in a hostile environment. Although the exact number of copies sold is not known, Henderson claimed that "it was the best seller of his [Woodson] publications for a while" and was "distributed to libraries all over the world. State departments of education, schools and colleges demanded it."[26]

Like his other works, Henderson's book is very readable and intended for a popular audience rather than specially trained academicians. Because he insisted that the writing be free of undue complexity and easily accessible to as wide an audience as possible, he had confrontations with Woodson over grammar and writing style. "We had many arguments as to style," noted Henderson. "He wanted to use only precise English in describing a football game or a boxing event. I insisted this would prove dull reading to those who loved or knew sports."[27]

The Negro in Sports is based partly on experiential knowledge. Henderson's own involvement in the sporting life of the black community was so extensive that his data often emanated from organizations he had been involved with and his subjects were frequently people he knew personally, either athletes he had coached or students he had mentored or individuals who had befriended him. Henderson also depended on published sources for his information. Although he never cited his sources, Henderson obviously depended a great deal on black sportswriters for much of his information and analysis. He recognized early on that black sportswriters such as Wendell Smith of the *Pittsburgh Courier-Journal*, Romeo Dougherty of the New York *News*, Rollo Wilson of the *Pittsburgh Courier-Journal*, "Fay" Young of the *Chicago Defender*, St. Clair Bourne of the New York *Amsterdam News*, and Sam Lacy and Art Carter of the Baltimore and Washington, D.C., *Afro-American*, were a great source of information on both African American and predominantly white organized sport. He realized, perhaps better than anyone before or since, that black sportswriters often had direct access to African American athletes, were intimately involved in campaigns to break down the racial barriers in sport, and sometimes established close working relationships with black as well as white entrepreneurs of sport.[28]

Henderson put his sources to good use. He charted the contributions of African American athletes behind segregated walls and in the larger society at both the amateur and professional levels of sport. His most compelling topics were African American women athletes and what he terms "The Meaning of Athletics." While holding on to stereotypical notions concerning the emotional and physiological differences between the sexes, Henderson provided the first extended analysis of African American women and their involvement in sport and physical activity. He wrote about such outstanding organizations as the Philadelphia Tribune Basketball team and New York Mercury track club as well as great black women athletes like Ora Washington, Lucy Slowe, Isadore Channels, and Lula Ballard. Henderson's expanded coverage of African American women athletes perhaps stemmed from their relatively greater involvement in sport, his commitment to providing as many examples of black achievement as possible, and the fact that the black community was seemingly more receptive and encouraging to women athletes. As academicians have recently suggested, women athletes in the African American community were in a more favorable environment than their white counterparts. Not considered "real" women by the dominant white culture and never encumbered by the Victorian definition of the innately fragile woman, African American female athletes participated in more "masculine" sports like basketball and track and field without experiencing the social stigma and role conflict so prevalent among white female athletes.[29]

In the concluding chapter of *The Negro in Sports*, "The Meaning of Athletics" (pp. 287–316), Henderson summed up much of his philosophy concerning sport and its purpose. He began with a brief yet telling discussion of "play in antiquity." Sounding much like a combination of Charles Darwin, and Herbert Spencer, Henderson wrote that "primitive man learned early that fleetness of foot or strength of limb and body were means by which to escape from danger or to live in health. As civilized man found substitutes for labor in slaves—human, chemical or physical—he found in games a method to insure growth and normal physiological functioning of the body. More recently organized play serves to combat the individual and social deteriorating forces of urban life."[30] After discussing "play in antiquity," he describes the role of games and sport in ancient Greek and Roman societies. As is the case in many of his publications, Henderson wrote admiringly of Greek athletics, contrasting the differing roles of sport in ancient Greece and Rome, and drawing parallels between sport in those two cultures with sport in modern American society. Henderson glorified ancient Greek culture, particularly Athens, for its devotion to competitive sport, emphasis on the harmonious development of mind and body, and belief that physical education should be an integral part of the educational process. Henderson then turned to a familiar theme: the role that sport plays in developing character, fostering sportsmanship, and contributing to individual and national health in the increasingly urbanized environment of modern society. Utilizing such phrases as "health engineers," "physical machine," and "animal bodies," all terms suggesting both evolutionary theory and the objectified, reified view of reality so prevalent in the physical education profession, Henderson wrote of the decline in delinquency, development of emotional balance, and other educational outcomes resulting from participation in sport. Henderson then finally discussed sport and African American athletes. After suggesting that the performances of Jesse Owens and other outstanding African American athletes obliterated the belief in Aryan racial superiority, he reviewed the debate over alleged black athletic superiority and reiterated the importance of physical activity for the development of optimal health among African Americans.[31]

Henderson's decision to draw a link between Ancient Greek society and African American athletes helps explain his attitudes toward race, civil rights issues, and the use of sport as an assimilatory tool. Henderson faced a dilemma experienced by other African Americans: He always felt a need to promote a sense of racial pride and solidarity through a celebration of individual black achievements, but at the same time he was reluctant to express any notion of racial separateness or distinctiveness for fear it would jeopardize his integrationist goals.[32] In "The Meaning of Athletics," he dealt with these two seemingly incongruent objectives by chronicling the exploits of African American athletes within the context of Western civilization. This approach allowed Henderson an opportunity, in what was the last chapter of the book, to illuminate the parallels between ancient and modern sport as well as to hold up African American athletes as symbols of black possibility while continuing to promote sport for its ability to "develop a real Christian brotherhood among men of the minority and majority groups in our cosmopolitan American life, and in the greater field of international relationships" (p. 310). At the same time, Henderson celebrated the outstanding accomplishments of African American athletes while emphasizing white racism and avoiding any mention that these accomplishments somehow reflected a distinctive black culture. Unlike early black scholars such as George Washington Williams, William T. Alexander, and Lelia Amos Pendelton, Henderson avoided tracing any connection between the achievements of African American athletes and a distinct black culture in order to prevent imposing yet another barrier to African American assimilation into American society.

Most of Henderson's writings in the following decade were in the form of "Letters to the Editor," position statements, and committee reports dealing with his civil rights struggles against Uline Arena, the

Edwin B. Henderson, pictured here in his office, was a tireless worker who fought his entire life on behalf of African Americans in their struggle for racial justice and equal opportunity. Courtesy of the Moorland-Spingarn Research Center, Howard University.

local AAU, and other segregated institutions in and around Washington, D.C. In 1949, however, Henderson came out with a revised edition of *The Negro in Sports*, which included an expanded appendix and two new chapters reflecting the changes that had taken place in American sport since 1939. The revised edition of the book brought Henderson special satisfaction, allowing him to recount the recent elimination of the color line in several sports, a change that reaffirmed his belief in the conciliatory power of sport and its ability to bring the African American greater respect. The level of optimism in the book, not apparent in the previous edition, was an obvious result of Henderson's conviction that the desegregation of sport, particularly the reintegration of professional football and baseball, was clear evidence that America was close to fulfilling its principles of fair play and equal opportunity. He wrote in the preface that "we doubt that the future will necessitate another edition since integration and the growth of true democracy seem nearer."[33]

Henderson proved to be right about another edition, but perhaps overly confident about this country being closer to true integration and democracy.

The optimism Henderson displayed in his revised book was also evident in the December 1951 issue of the *Negro History Bulletin* *(NHB)*, a special issue on "The Negro in Sports," which he had edited. This special issue seemed perfectly suited for the *NHB*, the journal founded by Carter Woodson in 1937 and intended, unlike his *Journal of Negro History*, for an audience consisting primarily of public school teachers and their clientele.[34] It had, in addition to a photograph of Jackie Robinson gracing the cover, a foreword by Henderson and a concluding essay on "Democracy Through Sports" written by Albert N. D. Brooks. The issue included ten articles, three by Henderson,[35] written on everything from African American involvement in the Olympic Games and intercollegiate football to the part they played in tennis and golf. All the authors, many of them close friends of Henderson's, either worked or lived in the Washington, D.C., and Baltimore area. For instance, Brooks was Woodson's former junior high school principal in Washington, D.C.; Arthur Carter, who wrote "New Day in Intercollegiate Football," was a sportswriter and future managing editor of the Washington *Afro-American;* and David Brown, author of "The Negro in Baseball," was a coach at Washington's Phelps Vocational Senior High School.[36] The issue is also noteworthy in that all the authors depended a great deal on Henderson's revised edition of *The Negro in Sports* (1949) for much of their information and analysis. In fact, the similarities in organization, writing style, and content are so great between the two publications, it seems that Henderson should probably be credited with writing more than a forward and three essays.[37]

The special issue of the *NHB*, which came out just three years before his retirement as Director of Health, Physical Education, and Safety in the segregated public schools of Washington, D.C., was Henderson's last major publishing effort until the latter part of the 1960s. The increased involvement of black athletes at all levels of sport, the Civil Rights movement, and growing fascination in the life and history of African Americans by scholars of both races all combined during this period to create a renewed interest in Henderson's work.[38] The result was that Henderson published four major works on the African American athlete between 1968 and 1976. These publications, while intended for different audiences and varying in historical significance, were very similar in that they all included much of the same material from Henderson's previous work intermixed with the latest information on African American athletes and their various accomplishments. It was customary, even formulaic in some ways, for Henderson to blend new information with recycled material.

Writing, as he almost always did, in a topical rather than chronological fashion, Henderson raised once again the question of alleged black athletic superiority, traced the accomplishments of African American athletes, and chronicled key events and individuals involved in the struggle to eliminate racial discrimination in sport.

In 1968, Henderson published *The Black Athlete: Emergence and Arrival*, written with the assistance of the editors of *Sport* magazine, which had always shown a keen interest in African American athletes. Written at the request of Charles H. Wesley, the successor to Carter Woodson as president of the Association for the Study of Afro-American Life and History, the book is one of Henderson's most frequently cited works. One reason the book has garnered so much attention is that Henderson provided a voluminous amount of details about African American athletes from the early nineteenth century through the 1960s. Up to that time, no scholar (and few since) had been so expansive in covering the topic, particularly in regard to an analysis of the outstanding African American athletes who integrated various other sports after Jackie Robinson's debut with the Brooklyn Dodgers. Equally significant is the book's extensive bibliography. Henderson furnished an invaluable list of secondary and primary materials subdivided under the topical headings of general sources; baseball; football; basketball; tennis; boxing; track and field; Olympics; other sports; integration in sports; and education, recreation, and school sports.[39]

In 1970, Henderson published "The Negro As Athlete" in *Crisis*, his last article in the journal. Recapitulating much of his earlier work, Henderson did briefly mention such new topics as television and sport and the great performances of women track-and-field stars from Tennessee State. Two years later he published "Physical Education and Athletics Among Negroes" in *The History of Physical Education and Sport*, edited by Bruce L. Bennett. Originally given as a presentation at the Big Ten Symposium on the History of Physical Education and Sport, the chapter is included alongside others written by such well-known sport historians as John R. Betts, Guy Lewis, Ellen Gerber, and Clarence Forbes. Finally, in 1976, Henderson published "The Black American in Sports," a chapter in Mabel M. Smythe's *The Black American Reference Book*. The chapter, which was Henderson's last publication, had the distinction of appearing in a book sponsored by the Phelps-Stokes Fund, always one of the major financial supporters of scholarship dealing with African American life and history.[40]

In all four of these publications, Henderson continued to laud sport for the way it brought people together and created the unity and integration necessary to maintain order in American society. It is easy to understand why he did so. Since his early years in Washington, D.C., when segregation was the norm and blatant racial discrimination the rule, Henderson had witnessed the desegregation of sport and enormous success experienced by individual African American athletes at various levels of competition. He now found himself, however, living in a society where various individuals and groups, including academicians, social commentators, and some athletes, were criticizing sport as a capitalistic tool in which athletes became alienated from their bodies, those in power maintained their privilege through coercion and control, and harmful feelings of nationalistic pride and militarism were encouraged.[41] Even more significant, at least for Henderson, was that some African Americans of the period were highly critical of white organized sport, arguing that it was characterized by various forms of discrimination, perpetuated racial stereotypes and inequities, and helped divert attention from the real source of the problems inflicting the race. From the time Henderson wrote *The Black Athlete: Emergence and Arrival* in 1968 to the 1976 publication of his essay, "The Black American in Sports," America had witnessed the Harry Edwards-led protests of the Mexico City Olympic Games, a plethora of black athletic disturbances on predominantly white university campuses, and numerous racial uprisings in professional sport.[42]

Henderson's attitude toward the black athletic revolt is difficult to discern because he provided such limited information and even less analysis of the topic in his professional publications. He mentioned nothing about the various protests lodged by African American athletes in either his 1970 article in *Crisis* or his chapter "Physical Education and Athletics Among Negroes" in Bruce Bennett's 1972 symposium proceedings. No information was provided on Tommie Smith, John Carlos, Vince Matthews, or any number of other African American athletes who staged protests, lodged complaints against their white coaches, and disrupted sport at all levels of competition and by almost any means possible. In both *The Black Athlete: Emergence and Arrival* and his chapter in Mabel M. Smythe's *The Black American Reference Book*, Henderson mentioned the protests staged by African American athletes without condemning their actions,[43] despite his exaggerated belief about the positive effects of sport and philosophical opposition to the Black Power movement. Why he chose not to pass judgment on protesting black athletes is open to speculation. Perhaps it was the result of restrictions placed on Henderson by publishers insisting on a more encyclopedic approach with limited personal assessments in their reference works.

It is more likely, however, that Henderson chose not to write anything that would diminish the accomplishments or reflect negatively on African American athletes, not just because it might somehow affect their continued involvement in sport, but out of respect for them personally and in recognition of their efforts, however misplaced and illogical, on behalf of other members of their race. While disapproving of the tactics employed by Black Power advocates, Henderson was always a gentleman and showed the same tolerance toward protesting African American athletes that he had toward other people who made sacrifices and fought for racial justice and freedom of opportunity. Perhaps he also recognized that however different his methods were from those of militant African American athletes, they both used sport as a tool to help eliminate racial inequities and discrimination. Whereas protesting African American athletes used sport to call attention to economic exploitation and oppression, Henderson promoted sport for its power to bring diverse people together and create the unity and integration necessary to maintain order in American society. "We read and hear much irrationality in the oratory and philosophy of black power," wrote Henderson in the *Birmingham News* of April 2, 1967, "but to this writer the courage, stamina and sportsmanship of our Negro athletes evidences real power. Sociologists might well heed the news found on the sport pages. Is it not possible that in the playing together of white and colored boys on the courts and fields more of understanding and good will is thereby developed than in most other social settings?"

In the final analysis, Henderson's writings have proven to be enormously significant and influential. His numerous publications on the African American athletes' past, particularly *The Negro in Sports* (1939, 1949), and *The Black Athlete: Emergence and Arrival* (1968), served as the framework and historical foundation for the works of other writers and academicians who have examined the topic. Journalists, sport studies specialists, historians, and other scholars from both races have employed Henderson's basic typology, utilized his source material, and researched topics he had originally broached.

Evidence of Henderson's influence can perhaps best be gleaned from the monographs completed on African American athletes by black authors. Although limited in number and often falling into the category of popular rather than scholarly treatises, there are a number of important works of this genre that rely heavily on Henderson's pioneering research efforts and writings. Henderson's influence is evident in Andrew S. "Doc" Young's frequently cited *Negro Firsts in Sports*. Young used much of the information originally mined by Henderson in his nicely written and more interpretive analysis of black participation in sport.[44] Wally Jones and Jim Washington, former professional basketball players turned authors, utilized Henderson's works for *Black Champions Challenge American Sports*.[45] Arthur Ashe, in his well-known three-volume work *A Hard Road to Glory: A History of the African-American Athlete*, relied heavily on Henderson for information, source material, and organizational structure. Ashe, who referred in his introduction to Henderson's *The Negro in Sports* as the "first definitive historical review of black sports," patterned his own book along the same lines as some of Henderson's major works, taking a narrative approach to his subjects, focusing on the triumphs of African American athletes in both segregated and white organized sports, and including an extensive "reference section" that lists the awards and various other accomplishments garnered by blacks in sports.[46]

Just as indebted to Henderson was Harry Edwards, the well-known sport sociologist from the University of California-Berkeley, who led the proposed boycott of the 1968 Olympic Games in Mexico City and for years has warned African Americans of the dangers of focusing exclusively on sport as the way to realize full equality in America. Edwards, who helped establish the framework for much of the work completed on the black athlete in the sport sociology literature, utilizes Henderson's writings for both *The Revolt of the Black Athlete* and *Sociology of Sport*.[47] In the former book, which is a recounting of the various black athletic disturbances on predominantly white university campuses and events surrounding the proposed boycott of the 1968 Olympic Games, Edwards employs data originally mined by Henderson to discuss the emergence of both black boxers and college athletes in American society. Perhaps most important, Edwards patterned his work after Henderson's books by including a ten-page appendix devoted to "black record-holders."[48] Although troubled by the overemphasis on sport in the black community and skeptical of sports power to bring the races closer together, Edwards was seemingly no different from Henderson in recognizing the symbolic importance of black athletic triumphs for both the African American community and society at large. To Edwards and many other blacks as well, Henderson's emphasis on the individual success of African American athletes to help foster racial pride always struck a responsive chord and was considered one of the important factors in the struggle for equal rights and opportunity.

In sum, Edwin Henderson's writings were indeed an instrument, a tool that even someone as critical of sport as Harry Edwards could not easily ignore because African American athletes had always served as much-needed examples of possibility for the black community. As chronicler of these athletes, Henderson became an exemplar himself, someone who helped preserve the collective memory of his race and prove that African Americans were capable of great performances both on and off the playing field. The central theme of all his publications was that sport was an enormously influential institution capable of bringing people of diverse backgrounds together in ways that created feelings of unity and togetherness. He never lost faith, even during the most racially oppressive periods in American history, in the power of sport to strengthen social relationships and contribute to the integration of African Americans into the larger society. He continued to believe throughout his life that sport served as a source of inspiration and benefited all members of society, regardless of skin color, religious affiliation, and personal value scheme. He simply refused to acknowledge, unlike many contemporary thinkers, that sport often serves to maintain the interests of the power elite and can be an alienating rather than integrative force in American society.

Notes
Bibliographical Essay
Index

Notes

Introduction

1. David K. Wiggins, "Sport and Popular Pastimes in the Plantation Community: The Slave Experience," (Ph.D. diss., University of Maryland, 1979).

2. See Jeffrey T. Sammons, " 'Race' and Sport: A Critical, Historical Examination," *Journal of Sport History* 21 (Fall 1994): 255.

3. Bernard Mergen, *Play and Playthings: A Reference Guide* (Westport, Conn.: Greenwood, 1982); Wilma King, *Stolen Childhood: Slave Youth in Nineteenth-Century America* (Bloomington: Indiana Univ. Press, 1995).

4. John Rickards Betts, *America's Sporting Heritage: 1850–1950* (Reading, Mass.: Addison-Wesley, 1974).

5. Edward Hotaling, a television writer and producer, provides some very interesting information on Murphy and other black jockeys in his book *They're Off!: Horse Racing at Saratoga* (Syracuse: Syracuse University Press, 1995).

6. Andrew Ritchie, *Major Taylor: The Extraordinary Career of a Champion Bicycle Racer* (San Francisco, Calif.: Bicycle Books, 1988); David W. Zang, *Fleet Walker's Divided Heart: The Life of Baseball's First Black Major Leaguer* (Lincoln: Univ. of Nebraska Press, 1995). It is important to note that Ritchie and Zang were aided by the personal writings of both Taylor and Walker. See Marshall W. "Major" Taylor, *The Fastest Bicycle Rider in the World* (1928; reprint, Brattleboro, Vt.: Green-Stephen, 1972); M. F. Walker, *Our Home Colony: A Treatise on the Past, Present and Future of the Negro Race in America* (Steubenville, Ohio: Herald, 1908).

7. Schutte's private collection is essential to anyone who is working on nineteenth-century boxing. Another private collection that is very strong on early twentieth-century boxing is owned by Gary Phillips of Yuba City, California. Randy Roberts found Phillips's collection indispensable for his biography, *Papa Jack: Jack Johnson and the Era of White Hopes* (New York: Free Press, 1983).

8. The other research writing award was given for my essay, "From Plantation to Playing Field: Historical Writings on the Black Athlete in American Sport," *Research Quarterly for Exercise and Sport* 57 (June 1986): 101–116.

9. Jules Tygiel, *Baseball's Great Experiment: Jackie Robinson and His Legacy* (New York: Oxford Univ. Press, 1983).

10. See Susan Cahn, *Coming on Strong: Gender and Sexuality in Twentieth-Century Women's Sport* (New York: Free Press, 1994); Cindy Himes Gissendanner, "African-American Women and Competitive Sport, 1920–1960," in Susan Birrell and Cheryl Code, eds. *Women, Sport and Culture* (Champaign, Ill.: Human Kinetics, 1994), 81–92, and "African

American Women Olympians: The Impact of Race, Gender, and Class Ideologies, 1932–1968," *Research Quarterly for Exercise and Sport* 67 (June 1996): 172–182; Martha Verbrugge, "The Institutional Politics of Women's Sports in American Colleges," paper presented at the Twenty-Fourth Annual Convention of the North American Society for Sport History, Auburn, Alabama, May 24–27, 1996.

11. The special issue also included David Zang's interview with Calvin Hill and the following articles: William H. Wiggins, "Boxing's Sambo Twins: Racial Stereotypes in Jack Johnson and Joe Louis Newspaper Cartoons, 1908–1938; Thomas G. Smith, "Outside the Pale: The Exclusion of Blacks From Organized Football, 1934–1946; Donald Spivey, "End Jim Crow in Sports: The Protest at New York University, 1940–1941."

12. Elliott J. Gorn, *Muhammad Ali: The People's Champ* (Urbana: Univ. of Illinois Press, 1996).

13. Jeffrey T. Sammons, " 'Race' and Sport: A Critical, Historical Examination," 205.

14. An excellent analysis of this topic is Laurel R. Davis, "The Articulation of Difference: White Preoccupation with the Question of Racially Genetic Differences Among Athletes," *Sociology of Sport Journal* 7 (1990): 179–87.

15. George Eisen and David K. Wiggins, eds., *Ethnicity and Sport in North American History and Culture* (Westport, Conn.: Greenwood, 1994).

1. The Play of Slave Children in the Plantation Communities of the Old South, 1820–1860

1. See for example: Stanley M. Elkins, *Slavery: A Problem in American Institutional and Intellectual Life* (Chicago: Univ. of Chicago Press, 1959); Chase C. Mooney, *Slavery in Tennessee* (Westport, N.Y.: Negro Universities Press, 1971); Ulrich B. Phillips, *American Negro Slavery* (New York: Appleton & Co., 1918); James B. Sellers, *Slavery in Alabama* (Birmingham: Univ. of Alabama Press, 1964); Kenneth M. Stampp, *The Peculiar Institution: Slavery in the Antebellum South* (New York: Vintage, 1956); Charles S. Sydnor, *Slavery in Mississippi* (New York: Appleton-Century, 1933).

2. See, for example: John W. Blassingame, *The Slave Community: Plantation Life in the Antebellum South* (New York: Oxford Univ. Press, 1972); Eugene D. Genovese, *Roll, Jordan, Roll: The World the Slaves Made* (New York: Vintage, 1976); Herbert G. Gutman, *The Black Family in Slavery and Freedom, 1750–1925* (New York: Random House, 1976); Leslie H. Owens, *This Species of Property: Slave Life and Culture in the Old South* (New York: Oxford Univ. Press, 1977); Thomas L. Webber, *Deep Like the Rivers: Education in the Slave Quarter Community* (New York: Norton, 1978).

3. Webber, *Deep Like the Rivers*, 63.

4. George P. Rawick, ed., *The American Slave: A Composite Autobiography*, 19 vols., (Westport, Conn.: Greenwood, 1972).

5. Webber, *Deep Like the Rivers*, 15–17.

6. Rawick, ed., *American Slave*, vol. 18, *Florida Narratives*, 328.

7. Rawick, ed., *American Slave*, vol. 5., no. 4, *Texas Narratives*, 226.

8. If the younger children did not have older siblings mature enough to take care of them, they were looked after either by older cousins, one or two slaves too old to work in the fields, or some younger woman who was appointed the job. See, for example: Joseph Holt Ingraham, *The South-West by A Yankee*, 2 Vols. (London: Fisher & Co., 1842), 2: 28; Nancy B. DeSaussure, *Old Plantation Days: Being Recollections of Southern Life Before the Civil War* (New York: Duffield & Co., 1909), 38–39; Louis B. Hughes, *Thirty Years a Slave: From Bondage to Freedom, The Institution of Slavery as Seen on the Plantation and in the Home of the Planter* (Milwaukee, Wis.: M. F. Maferkorn, 1897), 44; Basil Hall, *Travels in North America in the Years 1827 and 1828*, 3 vols. (Edinburgh: Cadell &

Co., 1829), 3: 179; Frederick Law Olmsted, *A Journey in the Seaboard Slave States* (New York: G. P. Putnam's Sons, 1856), 424; John Houston Bills Diary, July 30, 1853 Southern Historical Collection, University of North Carolina; Ralph J. Jones and Tom Landess, eds., "Portraits of Georgia Slaves," *Georgia Review* 22:1 (1968), 126; Plantation Book of 1857–58 in the James H. Hammond Papers, Library of Congress, William H. Russell, *My Diary North and South* (Boston: Burnham, 1983), pp. 274–75.

    9. Rawick, ed., *American Slave*, vol. 12, no. 2, *Georgia Narratives*, 34.

    10. Rawick, ed., *American Slave*, vol. 4, no. 2, *Texas Narratives*, 120.

    11. Rawick, ed., *American Slave*, vol. 9, no. 4, *Arkansas Narratives*, 64.

    12. Webber, *Deep Like the Rivers*, 169–70.

    13. Rawick, ed., *American Slave*, vol. 14, no. 1, *North Carolina Narratives*, 245.

    14. Webber, *Deep Like the Rivers*, 180.

    15. Rawick, ed., *American Slave*, vol. 7, no. 1, *Texas Narratives*, 239.

    16. Fisk Collection, *Unwritten History of Slavery: Autobiographical Accounts of Negro Ex-Slaves* (Nashville: Social Science Institute, Fisk University, 1945), 15.

    17. Rawick, ed., *American Slave*, vol. 7, no. 2, *Mississippi Narratives*, 36.

    18. Rawick, ed., *American Slave*, vol. 15, no. 2, *North Carolina Narratives*, 58.

    19. The narratives are replete with examples of slave children engaging in "ring" dances. See for example, Rawick, ed., *American Slave*, vol. 4, no. 2, *Texas Narratives*, 120; vol. 14, no. 1, *North Carolina Narratives*, 95; vol. 10, no. 5, *Arkansas Narratives*, 162, vol. 4, no. 2, *Georgia Narratives*, 136; vol. 7, no. 1, *Oklahoma Narratives*, 98–99; vol. 3, no. 4, *South Carolina Narratives*, 168; Charles I. Perdue, Jr., Thomas F. Barden, and Robert K. Phillips, eds., *Weevils in the Wheat: Interviews with Virginia Ex-Slaves* (Charlottesville: University Press of Virginia, 1976), 203.

    20. Lyle Saxon, Edward Dreyer, and Robert Tallant, *Gumbo Ya Ya: A Collection of Louisiana Folk Tales* (Boston: Houghton Mifflin, 1945), 447.

    21. Rawick, ed., *American Slave*, vol. 7, no. 1, *Oklahoma Narratives*, 65.

    22. Rawick, ed., *American Slave*, vol. 19, no. 2, *Arkansas Narratives*, 267.

    23. Rawick, ed., *American Slave*, vol. 13, no. 3, *Georgia Narratives*, 155.

    24. Webber, *Deep Like The Rivers*, 186.

    25. Rawick, ed., *American Slave*, vol. 12, no. 1, *Georgia Narratives*, 289–90.

    26. Rawick, ed., *American Slave*, vol. 10, no. 5, *Arkansas Narratives*, 320–21.

    27. Rawick, ed., *American Slave*, vol. 5, no. 3, *Texas Narratives*, 24.

    28. Rawick, ed., *American Slave*, vol. 4, no. 1, *Texas Narratives*, 97.

    29. Rawick, ed., *American Slave*, vol. 9, no. 3, *Arkansas Narratives*, 181.

    30. Webber, *Deep Like the Rivers*, 184.

    31. Caillois uses the term *ilinx* to describe these types of games. Interestingly, he suggests that as civilizations mature, these games, "lose their traditional dominance, are pushed to the periphery of public life, reduced to roles that become more and more modern and intermittent, if not clandestine and guilty, or are regulated to the limited and regulated domain of games." See Roger Caillois, *Man, Play, and Games* (New York: Free Press, 1961), 97.

    32. Rawick, ed., *American Slave*, vol. 2, no. 2, *South Carolina Narratives*, 146.

    33. Rawick, ed., *American Slave*, vol. 3, no. 3, *South Carolina Narratives*, 62.

    34. Rawick, ed., *American Slave*, vol. 16, no. 5, *Kentucky Narratives*, 29.

    35. For an excellent discussion and analysis of the evolution of baseball, see Robert K. Henderson, *Ball, Bat, and Bishop: The Origin of Ballgames* (New York: Rockport Press, 1947), 132–95.

    36. Rawick, ed., *American Slave*, vol. 7, no. 1, *Tennessee Narratives*, 308.

    37. Rawick, ed., *American Slave*, vol. 16, no. 3, *Maryland Narratives*, 2.

    38. Perdue, Barden, and Phillips, eds., *Weevils in the Wheat*, 84.

    39. Rawick, ed., *American Slave*, vol 14, no. 2, *North Carolina Narratives*, 322.

40. Rawick, ed., *American Slave*, vol. 2, no. 1, *South Carolina Narratives*, 28.

41. Rawick, ed., *American Slave*, vol. 15, no. 2, *North Carolina Narratives*, 273.

42. See, for example: Rawick, ed., *American Slave*, vol. 4, no. 2, *Texas Narratives*, 120; vol. 6, no. 1, *Alabama Narratives*, 211.

43. See for example: Rawick, ed., *American Slave*, vol. 15, no. 2, *North Carolina Narratives*, 68; vol. 3, no. 4, *South Carolina Narratives*, 168; vol. 8, no. 2, *Arkansas Narratives*, 248.

44. See, for example: Rawick, ed., *American Slave*, vol. 5, no. 4, *Texas Narratives*, 147; vol. 4, no. 2, *Texas Narratives*, 223; vol. 8, no. 1, *Arkansas Narratives*, 11.

45. Rawick, ed., *American Slave*, vol. 4, no. 2, *Georgia Narratives*, 136.

46. Rawick, ed., *American Slave*, vol. 2, no. 1, *South Carolina Narratives*, 55.

47. See, for example: Perdue, Barden, and Phillips, eds., *Weevils in the Wheat*, 84; John W. Blassingame, ed., *Slave Testimony: Two Centuries of Letters, Speeches, Interviews, and Autobiographies* (Baton Rouge: Louisiana State Univ. Press, 1977), 641; Genovese, *Roll, Jordan, Roll*, 506.

48. See, for example: Israel Campbell, *Bond and Free: Or Yearnings for Freedom, From My Green Briar House, Being the Story of My Life in Bondage and My Life In Freedom* (Philadelphia: By the Author, 1981), 38; James Williams, *Narrative of James Williams, An American Slave Who Was for Several Years a Driver on a Cotton Plantation in Alabama* (Boston: American Anti-Slavery Society, 1838), 66; Orland Kay Armstrong, *Old Massa's People: The Old Slaves Tell Their Story* (Indianapolis: Bobbs-Merrill, 1983), 160—63.

49. John Brown, *Slave Life in Georgia: A Narrative of the Life; Sufferings and Escape of John Brown, A Fugitive Slave Now in England* (London W. M. Watts, 1855), 83.

50. Rawick, ed., *American Slave*, vol. 9, *Missouri Narratives*, 284.

51. See, for example: Henry Box Brown, *Narrative of Henry Box Brown* (Boston: Brown & Stearns, 1849), 15; Benjamin Drew, ed., *A North Side View of Slavery, The Refugee: Or the Narratives of Fugitive Slaves in Canada* (Boston: John P. Jewett, 1856), 30; Charles Ball, *Slavery in the United States: A Narrative of the Life and Adventures of Charles Ball* (Lewiston, Pa: 1836), 15—22; Lester B. Shippee, ed., *Bishop Whipple's Southern Diary: 1843—1844* (New York: Da Capo Press, 1968), 69, 88—89; Elkanah Watson, *Men and Times of the Revolution* (New York: Charles Scribner's, 1857), 69.

52. Rawick, ed., *American Slave*, vol. 9, no. 1, *Alabama Narratives*, 120.

53. Rawick, ed., *American Slave*, vol. 9, no. 3, *Arkansas Narratives*, 167.

54. Rawick, ed., *American Slaves*, vol. 7, no. I, *Mississippi Narratives*, 57.

55. Rawick, ed., *American Slave*, vol. 2, no. 7, *Missouri Narratives*, 313; Webber, *Deep Like the Rivers*, 182.

56. Webber, *Deep Like the Rivers*, 19.

57. Rawick, ed., *American Slave*, vol. 7, no. 2, *Georgia Narratives*, 85.

58. Rawick, ed., *American Slave*, vol. 12, no. 2, *Georgia Narratives*, 187.

59. Rawick, ed., *American Slave*, vol. 6, no. 1, *Alabama Narratives*, 103; vol. 7, no. 2, *Mississippi Narratives*, 26; Richard Parkinson, *A Tour in America in 1798, 1799, and 1800*, 2 vols. (London: J. Hardin, 1805), 1: 436; Genovese, *Roll, Jordan, Roll*, 515.

60. Catherine C. Hopley, *Life in the South: From the Commencement of the War By a Blockaded British Subject*, 2 vols. (London: Chapman & Hall, 1863), 1: 54.

61. H. H. Farmer, *Virginia Before and During the War* (Henderson, Ky.: By the Author, 1892), 63.

62. Rawick, ed., *American Slave*, vol. 4, no. 1, *Texas Narratives*, 212.

63. Rawick, ed., *American Slave*, vol. 6, no. 6, *Alabama Narratives*, 103.

64. Perdue, Barden, and Phillips, eds., *Weevils in the Wheat*, 109.

65. Amelia Thompson Watts, "A Summer on a Louisiana Cotton Plantation in

1832," in Louise Taylor Pharr Book, Southern Historical Collection, University of North Carolina.

66. Soloman Northup. *Twelve Years a Slave, Narrative of Soloman Northup, A Citizen of New York, Kidnapped in Washington City in 1841 and Rescued in January 1853 From a Cotton Plantation Near Red River in Louisiana* (Buffalo: Derby, Orton, & Mulligan, 1857), 261.

67. Frederick Law Olmsted, *A Journey Through Texas Or a Saddle Trip on the Southwestern Frontier With a Statistical Appendix* (New York: Dix, Edwards, & Co., 1857), 116–17.

68. Fisk Collection, *Unwritten History of Slavery*, 21–22.

69. Rawick, ed., *American Slave*, vol. 4, no. 2, *Texas Narratives*, 134.

70. Rawick, ed., *American Slave*, vol. 2, no. 1, *South Carolina Narratives*, 22.

71. Rawick, ed., *American Slave*, vol. 16, no. 5, *Kentucky Narratives*, 29.

72. Rawick, ed., *American Slave*, vol. 7, no. 2, *Mississippi Narratives*, 101.

73. Letita M. Burwell [Page Thacker], *Plantation Reminiscences* (Kentucky, 1878), 4.

74. Lancelot Minor Blackford Diary, Southern Historical Collection, University of North Carolina, Chapel Hill.

75. Ibid.

76. Ibid.

77. John M. Roberts, Malcolm J. Arth, and Robert B. Bush, "Games in Culture," *American Anthropologist* 61 (1959), 597–605; Stephen N. Miller, "The Playful, the Crazy, and the Nature of Pretense," in Edward Norbeck, ed., *The Anthropological Study of Human Play, Rice University Studies* 60, no. 4 (Summer 1974): 36; Roger Caillois, *Man, Play, and Games*, 27.

78. For examples consult any volume of Rawick, ed., *American Slave*.

79. See, for example: Letita M. Burwell, *Plantation Reminiscences*, 2; James B. Avirett, *The Old Plantation: How We Lived in Great House and Cabin Before the War* (New York: F. Tennyson), 91; Nancy B. DeSaussure, *Old Plantation Days: Bring Recollections of Southern Life Before the Civil War* (New York: Duffield & Co., 1909), 38–39; Edward A. Pollard, *Black Diamonds Gathered in the Darkey Homes of the South* (New York: Pudney & Russell, 1859), 50; John J. Wise, *The End of an Era* (New York: Houghton, Mifflin & Co., 1902), 153–54.

80. See Webber, *Deep Like the Rivers*, 91–101.

81. Genovese, *Roll, Jordan, Roll*, 516.

82. Webber, *Deep Like the Rivers*, 63–70.

83. Dickson D. Bruce, Jr., "Play, Work, and Ethics in the Old South," *Southern Folklore Quarterly* 41 (1977), 33–51.

84. Ibid.

2. Isaac Murphy: Black Hero in Nineteenth-Century American Sport, 1861–1896

1. See for example Dale A. Somers, *The Rise of Sports in New Orleans, 1850–1900* (Baton Rouge: Louisiana State Univ. Press, 1972), 286; John A. Lucas and Ronald A. Smith, *Saga of American Sport* (Philadelphia: Lea and Febiger, 1978), 269–79.

2. Frank Talmadge Phelps, "The Nearest Perfect Jockey," *Thoroughbred Record*, May 13, 1967, 1245.

3. *Louisville Courier Journal*, Feb. 13, 1896.

4. Peter Chew, *The Kentucky Derby: The First 100 Years* (Boston: Houghton Mifflin, 1974), 38; Edwin B. Henderson, *The Black Athlete: Emergence and Arrival* (New York:

Publishers Company, 1968), 50; Peggy Keilus, "The Great Isaac Murphy," *Turf and Sports Digest* 41 (Mar. 1964): 10; Phelps, "The Nearest Perfect Jockey," 1245; L. P. Tarelton, "A Memorial," *Thoroughbred Record,* Mar. 21, 1896, 136.

5. Chew, *Kentucky Derby,* 38; Keilus, "The Great Isaac Murphy," 10; Phelps, "The Nearest Perfect Jockey," 1245; Tarelton, "A Memorial," 136.

6. Chew, *Kentucky Derby,* 38; Keilus, "The Great Isaac Murphy," 10; Phelps, "The Nearest Perfect Jockey," 1245; Tarelton, "A Memorial," 136; *Kentucky Leader,* Mar. 20, 1889.

7. Phelps, "The Nearest Perfect Jockey," 1245; Tarelton, "A Memorial," 136; *Kentucky Leader,* Mar. 20, 1889.

8. Chew, *Kentucky Derby,* 38; Keilus, "The Great Isaac Murphy," 10; Phelps, "The Nearest Perfect Jockey," 1245; Tarelton, "A Memorial," 136; *Kentucky Leader,* July 29, 1891.

9. Phelps, "The Nearest Perfect Jockey," 1248; *Thoroughbred Record,* Feb. 24, 1888; *Spirit of the Times,* Aug. 29 and Oct. 17, 1885, July 17, 1886; *Louisville Courier-Journal,* July 27, 1885, May 15, 1890, May 14, 1891.

10. Phelps, "The Nearest Perfect Jockey," 1248; *Louisville Courier-Journal,* May 15, 1890; May 14, 1891; Feb 13, 1896. *Kentucky Leader,* Jan. 19, 1892; *Thoroughbred Record,* Mar. 14, 1896.

11. Phelps, "The Nearest Perfect Jockey," 1248.

12. *Kentucky Leader,* Jan. 24, 31, 1893.

13. Nate Cantrell, interview by Pamela Douglas, Mar. 15, 1976, Keeneland Library, Lexington, Kentucky.

14. Tarelton, "A Memorial," 136.

15. *Spirit of the Times,* July 11, 1891.

16. Walter Vosburgh, *Famous American Jockeys* (New York: R. A. Saalfield, 1884), 43.

17. Tarelton, "A Memorial," 136; *Louisville Courier-Journal,* Feb. 13, 1896; *Spirit of the Times,* Oct. 15, 1881.

18. *New York Tribune,* Nov. 10, 1889.

19. Tarelton, "A Memorial," 136.

20. Keilus, "The Great Isaac Murphy," 136.

21. John R. Betts, *America's Sporting Heritage: 1850–1950* (Reading Mass.: Addison-Wesley, 1974), 142–49; Dale A. Somers, *The Rise of Sports in New Orleans, 1850–1900* (Baton Rouge: Louisiana State Univ. Press, 1972), 106–14; *New York Times,* Aug. 3, 1885, Aug. 12, 1887, June 19, 21, 22, 23, 1891, Mar. 26, 1892, Dec. 26, 27, 1892.

22. *New York Times,* Aug. 12, 1887.

23. *New York Times,* Dec. 26, 1892.

24. Somers, *Rise of Sports in New Orleans,* 113.

25. Tarelton, "A Memorial," 136; Vosburgh, *Famous American Jockeys,* 42; *Kentucky Leader,* Aug. 17, 1891; *Lexington Morning Herald,* Feb. 12, 1896; *Louisville Courier-Journal,* May 15 and Dec. 29, 1890, May 14, 1891; *New York Age,* July 5, 1890; *New York Sportsman,* June 7, 1884, July 18, 1885, June 28, 1890; *Thoroughbred Record,* Feb. 15, 1896; *Spirit of the Times,* Aug. 20, 1881, Mar. 24, 1883, Sept. 1, 1883, June 5 and July 17, 1886, Aug. 27, 1887, Mar. 29 and Dec. 27, 1890, Apr. 25, 1891, June 2, 1894, Feb. 22, 1896.

26. Tarelton, "A Memorial," 136.

27. *Louisville Courier-Journal,* May 15, 1890.

28. *Spirit of the Times,* Sept. 1, 1883.

29. *Thoroughbred Record,* Feb. 15, 1896.

30. Many of the contemporary sporting journalists frequently commented that the

most honest jockeys were of the "colored persuasion." Isaac was obviously not the only black jockey who made extra efforts to abide by the rules. See, for example, *Spirit of the Times*, May 9, 1891.

31. Keilus, "The Great Isaac Murphy," 30; Phelps, "The Nearest Perfect Jockey," 1248; Tarelton, "A Memorial," 136.

32. John P. Davis, *The American Negro Reference Book* (Englewood Cliffs, N.J.: Prentice Hall, 1966), 791; Keilus, "The Great Isaac Murphy," 30; Bernard Livingston, *Their Turf* (New York: Arber House, 1973); Tarelton, "A Memorial," 136; Vosburgh, *Famous American Jockeys*, 43; *Spirit of the Times*, July 26, 1879; *Thoroughbred Record*, Feb. 15, 1896.

33. Tarelton, "A Memorial," p. 136.

34. Davis, *American Negro Reference Book*, 791; Phelps, "The Nearest Perfect Jockey," 1248; Vosburgh, *Famous American Jockeys*, 43.

35. Phelps, "The Nearest Perfect Jockey," 1248; Tarelton, "A Memorial," 136; *Kentucky Leader*, Mar. 20, 1889; *Louisville Courier-Journal*, July 12, 1885; *New York Sportsman*, Aug. 22, 1885; *Spirit of the Times*, Dec. 15, 1883, Jan. 23, 1886; *Thoroughbred Record*, Feb. 15, 1896.

36. *Louisville Courier-Journal*, June 29, 1884; *New York Sportsman*, July 5, 1884; *Spirit of the Times*, July 5, 1884.

37. *Louisville Courier-Journal*, May 11, 16, 17, 1884; *New York Sportsman*, May 24, 1884; *Spirit of the Times*, May 24, 1884.

38. *Louisville Courier-Journal*, Aug. 11, 19, 21, Sept. 15, 1885; *New York Sportsman*, Aug. 15, 22, 29, Sept. 19, 1885; *New York Tribune*, Aug. 11, 19, 21, Sept. 15, 1885; *Spirit of the Times*, Aug. 15, 22, 29, Sept. 19, 1885.

39. *Louisville Courier-Journal*, Aug. 11, 19, 21, Sept. 15, 1885; *New York Sportsman*, Aug. 15, 22, 29, Sept. 19, 1885; *New York Tribune*, Aug. 11, 19, 21, Sept. 15, 1885; *Spirit of the Times*, Aug. 15, 22, 29, Sept. 19, 1885.

40. *Louisville Courier-Journal*, June 28, 1885; *New York Sportsman*, July 4, 1885; *Spirit of the Times*, July 4, 11, 1885.

41. Tarelton, "A Memorial," 136.

42. *Louisville Courier-Journal*, June 25, 26, 28, 1890; *New York Times*, June 26, 1890; *New York Tribune*, June 26, Aug. 29, 1890; *New York Sportsman*, June 28, 1890; *Spirit of the Times*, June 28, June 12, Aug. 16, 1890.

43. Charles H. Johnson, "Murphy and Salvator," *Turf and Sports Digest*, Jan. 1957, 29.

44. *Kentucky Leader*, May 16, 1890; *Louisville Courier-Journal*, May 15, 1890; *New York Times*, May 15, 1890; *New York Tribune*, May 15, 1890, *New York Sportsman*, May 17, 1890; *Spirit of the Times*, May 17, 24, 1890.

45. *Louisville Courier-Journal*, May 14, 1891; *New York Times*, May 14, 1891; *New York Sportsman*, May 16, 1881; *Spirit of the Times*, May 23, 1891.

46. *Spirit of the Times*, Feb. 15, 1896.

47. *New York Sportsman*, July 18, 1885; Aug. 29, Oct. 17, 1885; *Spirit of the Times*, Nov. 5, 1887; Nov. 24, 1888; Mar. 30, 1890; *Louisville Courier-Journal*, May 14, 1888; May 17, 1894.

48. *Spirit of the Times*, Aug. 29, 1885.

49. *Louisville Courier-Journal*, May 4, 1891.

50. *New York Sportsman*, Jan. 8, 1887.

51. There was no uniform scale of weights until the Jockey Club assumed its leadership role in American horse racing in 1900.

52. Horse racing did not adopt an extended winter racing season until the last decade of the nineteenth century. In fact, winter racing went through a number of transformations

before it became an established institution. It was 1893, for instance, before New Orleans expanded its winter season to over one hundred days. See Somers, *Rise of Sports in New Orleans*, 106–114.

53. *Spirit of the Times,* Mar. 30, 1889.

54. *Spirit of the Times,* Nov. 5, 1887.

55. *New York Sportsman,* Aug. 27, 1887; *Spirit of the Times,* Feb. 15, 22, 1896; June 2, 1894.

56. *Kentucky Leader,* Aug. 27, 29, 1890; *Louisville Courier-Journal,* Aug. 27, 29, 1890; *New York Times,* Aug. 27, 1890; *New York Tribune,* Aug. 27, 1890; *New York Sportsman,* Aug. 30, Nov. 8, 15, 22, 29, Dec. 13, 20, 1890; *Spirit of the Times,* Aug. 30, Sept. 8, Nov. 29, 1890; Chew, *Kentucky Derby,* 40.

57. *New York Times,* Aug. 27, 1890.

58. *New York Sportsman,* Nov. 15, 22, 1890; *Kentucky Leader,* Aug. 29, 1890; *Spirit of the Times,* Dec. 27, 1890; Chew, *Kentucky Derby,* 40.

59. *Kentucky Leader,* Aug. 27, 29, 1890; *Louisville Courier-Journal,* Aug. 27, 29, 1890; *New York Times,* Aug. 27, 1890; *New York Tribune,* Aug. 27, 1890; *New York Sportsman,* Aug. 30, Nov. 8, 15, 22, 29, Dec. 13, 20, 1890; *Spirit of the Times,* Aug. 30, Sept. 6, 1890.

60. *Louisville Courier-Journal,* Dec. 29, 1890; *Kentucky Leader,* Jan. 25, 1891; *New York Sportsman,* Nov. 8, 15, 29, Dec. 13, 1890; *Spirit of the Times,* Sept. 6, Nov. 29, Dec. 27, 1890; May 23, 1891; *New York Age,* Jan. 10, 1891.

61. *Spirit of the Times,* Nov. 29, 1890.

62. *Spirit of the Times,* Nov. 19, 1892; Nov. 5, 1887.

63. *Spirit of the Times,* Sept. 15, 1891.

64. *Spirit of the Times,* Feb. 15, 1896.

65. Somers, *Rise of Sports in New Orleans,* 287.

66. *New Orleans Daily Picayune,* Aug. 16, 1892; Somers, *Rise of Sports in New Orleans,* 286.

67. James J. Corbett, *The Roar of the Crowd: The True Tale of the Rise and Fall of a Champion* (New York: G. P. Putnam's Sons, 1925), 165.

68. *Salt Lake Tribune,* Sept. 9, 1892.

69. Somers, *Rise of Sports in New Orleans,* 286.

70. W. P. Dabney, *Cincinnati's Colored Citizens* (Cincinnati, Ohio, 1908), 179; *New York Tribune,* July 29, 1900; Charles B. Palmer, *For Gold and Glory: The Story of Thoroughbred Racing in America* (New York: Karrick and Evans, 1939), 150.

71. *Livestock Record,* Aug. 6, 1892; *Kentucky Leader,* Aug. 1, 1892; *Spirit of the Times,* July 30, Aug. 6, Oct. 29, Nov. 19, 1892.

72. *Spirit of the Times,* Feb. 22, 1896.

73. *Spirit of the Times,* Dec. 1, 1894.

74. *Louisville Courier-Journal,* May 29, 1894; *Livestock Record,* June 2, 1894; *Spirit of the Times,* June 2, 1894. Murphy, in addition to his suspensions at Monmouth Park in 1890 and Latonia in 1894, was charged with striking a jockey during a race at Cincinnati in 1878. He was ultimately reinstated after the other jockey admitted his own guilt. See Tarelton, "A Memorial," 136; *Kentucky Leader,* Mar. 20, 1889.

75. *Spirit of the Times,* Feb. 22, 1896.

76. Ibid.

77. Ibid.

78. *Lexington Morning Herald,* Feb. 12, 1896; *Louisville Courier-Journal,* Feb. 13, 1896; *New York Tribune,* Feb. 13, 1896; *Thoroughbred Record,* Feb. 15, 1896; *Turf, Field, and Farm,* Feb. 14, 1896.

79. *Kentucky Leader,* Mar. 20, 1889.

3. Peter Jackson and the Elusive Heavyweight Championship: A Black Athlete's Struggle Against the Late Nineteenth-Century Color Line

1. A number of scholars have examined the racial discrimination faced by black athletes during the latter half of the nineteenth century. See, for example: David K. Wiggins, "Isaac Murphy: Black Hero in Nineteenth Century American Sport 1861—1896," *Canadian Journal of History of Sport and Physical Education* 10 (May 1979): 15—32; Jack W. Berryman, "Early Black Leadership in Collegiate Football: Massachusetts as a Pioneer," *Historical Journal of Massachusetts* 9 (June 1981): 17—28; G. B. McKinney, "Negro Professional Baseball Players in the Upper South in the Gilded Age," *Journal of Sport History* 3 (winter 1976): 273—80.

2. Jackson's early childhood is chronicled in Tom Langley, *The Life of Peter Jackson: Champion of Australia* (Leicester, Eng.: Vance Harvey, 1974); A. G. Hales, *Black Prince Peter: The Romantic Career of Peter Jackson* (London: Wright & Brown, 1931); Nathaniel S. Fleischer, *Black Dynamite: The Story of the Negro in the Prize Ring from 1782—1938*, 3 vols., (New York: The Ring Book Shop, 1938): 123—30.

3. For details on Foley's career, see: Alec Chisholm, ed., *The Australian Encyclopedia*, 10 vols. (East Lansing: Michigan State Univ. Press, 1971), 2: 81—84; 4: 127—128; 6: 86—87; Frank Gerald, *Millionaire in Memories* (London: George Routledge & Sons, 1936), 193—213. Foley's saloon was frequented not only by boxers but also by many of Australia's most famous track men, scullers, horsemen, footballers, and cricketers (Gerald, *Millionaire in Memories*, 193—213).

4. W. J. Doherty, *In the Days of the Giants; Memories of a Champion of the Prize Ring* (London: George G. Harrap & Co., 1931), 49.

5. Chisholm, ed., *The Australian Encyclopedia*, 2: 81—84, 4: 127—128, 6: 86—87; Gerald, *Millionaire in Memories*, 193—213.

6. See *San Francisco Daily Examiner*, Mar. 3, 1889; *National Police Gazette*, June 9, 1888; Langley, *Life of Peter Jackson*, 16—17; Fleischer, *Black Dynamite*, 131—36; *Sydney Morning Herald*, September 22, 25, 27, 30, Oct. 4, 1886.

7. W. W. Naughton, *Kings of the Queensberry Realm* (Chicago: Continental Publishing Co., 1902), 187—88; Fleischer, *Black Dynamite*, 138. To gain insight into the racial realities of Australian culture, see F. S. Stevens, ed., *Racism: The Australian Experience*, 2 vols. (Sydney: Australian and New Zealand Book Co., 1971); Humphrey McQueen, *Aborigines, Race and Racism* (Victoria: Dominion Press, 1974); Janine Roberts, *From Massacres to Mining: The Colonization of Aboriginal Australia* (London: War and Want, 1978); C. D. Rowley, *The Destruction of Aboriginal Society* (Harmonsworth, Eng.: Penguin, 1970); David Davies, *The Last of the Tasmanians* (New York: Harper & Row, 1974).

8. Naughton, *Kings of the Queensberry Realm*, 157—58.

9. *San Francisco Daily Examiner*, May 13, 1888; *San Francisco Call*, May 13, 1988; *National Police Gazette*, June 9, 1888.

10. For information on the California Athletic Club, see DeWitt C. Van Court, *The Making of Champions in California* (Los Angeles: Premier Printing Co., 1926), 11; Naughton, *Kings of the Queensberry Realm*, 55—59. See also Nathaniel S. Fleischer, *The Heavyweight Championship: An Informal History of Heavyweight Boxing from 1719 to the Present Day* (New York: G. P. Putnam's Sons, 1949), 119.

11. *San Francisco Daily Examiner*, June 4, 5, 1888; *National Police Gazette*, July 14, 1888.

12. *San Francisco Daily Examiner*, June 11, 12, July 2, Sept. 10, 1888. For information on the plight of black Americans during the latter part of the nineteenth century, see

George M. Frederickson, *The Black Image in the White Mind: The Debate on Afro-American Character and Destiny, 1817–1914* (New York: Harper & Row, 1971); August Meier and Elliott M. Rudwick, *From Plantation to Ghetto* (New York: Hill & Wang, 1963); C. Vann Woodward, *The Strange Career of Jim Crow* (New York: Oxford Univ. Press, 1966); Rayford W. Logan, *The Betrayal of the Negro from Rutherford B. Hayes to Woodrow Wilson* (New York: Collier, 1965).

13. *San Francisco Daily Examiner,* July 9, 30, Aug. 6, 1888; *National Police Gazette,* July 21, 23, 28, Aug. 4, 18, 1888; *Cleveland Gazette,* Aug. 4, 1888.

14. See Bill Edwards, *Gladiators of the Prize Ring or Pugilists of America, and Their Contemporaries from Tom Hyer to James J. Corbett* (Chicago: Athletic Publishing Co., 1895); *San Francisco Daily Examiner,* July 2, 1888; William A. Brady, *The Fighting Man* (Indianapolis: Bobbs-Merrill, 1916), 61; Donald Barr Chidsey, *John the Great: The Times and Life of a Remarkable American John L. Sullivan* (New York: Doubleday, Doran, 1942), 108–109.

15. *San Francisco Daily Examiner,* Aug. 25, 1888. See also, *San Francisco Daily Examiner,* Aug. 26, 27, 1888; *National Police Gazette,* Sept. 8, 22, 1888.

16. *San Francisco Daily Examiner,* Aug. 26, Sept. 10, 11, 1888. James Corbett would secure a championship fight with Sullivan partly on the basis of his performance in the ring against Jackson in 1891. Jim Jeffries would fight Bob Fitzsimmons for the crown in 1899, just one year after defeating Jackson in a three-round fight in San Francisco.

17. *San Francisco Daily Examiner,* Dec. 29–31, 1888; *National Police Gazette,* Jan. 12, 1889; *Cleveland Gazette,* Jan. 5, 1889.

18. *San Francisco Daily Examiner,* Dec. 29–31, Jan. 5, Apr. 21, 1889; *National Police Gazette,* Feb. 2, 1889; *Cleveland Gazette,* Jan. 12, 1889. Randy Roberts has noted that black boxers, including Jackson, normally assumed a defensive style in their fighting. "Black Fighters," says Roberts, "viewed both the ring and the object differently. The ring, like the world, was assumed to be the white man's territory, and the black fighter's objective was to yield it without suffering physical punishment, allowing his opponent to defeat himself." See Roberts, *Papa Jack: Jack Johnson and the Era of White Hopes* (New York: Free Press, 1983), 26.

19. *San Francisco Daily Examiner,* Dec. 29–31, 1888.

20. Almost everyone who wrote about Jackson mentioned his gentlemanly qualities, unassuming nature, and positive character traits. See, for example: *Sydney Morning Herald,* Oct. 4, 1886; *San Francisco Daily Examiner,* June 25, 1888; *Indianapolis Freeman,* May 17, 1890; *National Police Gazette,* Sept. 30, 1896; Alexander Johnston, *Ten and Out! The Complete Story of the Prize Ring in America* (New York: Washburn, 1945), 90; Fred Dartnell, *"Seconds Out!" Chats About Boxers, Their Trainers and Patrons* (London: T. Wener Caurie, n.d.), 170); James Butler, *Kings of the Ring* (London: Stanley Paul & Co., 1936), 139.

21. Jackson always seemed to live from day to day, with no real faith in the future. His reckless squandering of money could apparently give him a temporary illusion of plenty.

22. *San Francisco Daily Examiner,* Apr. 27, 1889; *Milwaukee Evening Wisconsin,* Apr. 27, 1889; *Cleveland Gazette,* May 4, 11, 1889; *St. Paul Western Appeal,* May 4, 1889.

23. Davies was born in Ireland in 1853. He eventually traveled to America and settled in Chicago, where he became a manager of wrestlers; star attraction was the Japanese grappler Matsada Sorokichi. Because he wore a black beard and high collars at the time, he was frequently mistaken for a preacher; thus his nickname. See *National Police Gazette,* Nov. 11, 1882; *London Evening News and Post,* Aug. 31, 1889.

24. See *St. Paul Western Appeal,* June 9, 1888, *Cleveland Gazette,* June 2, 1888, Jan. 19, 1889; *National Police Gazette,* Jan. 26, Feb. 2, 1889.

25. The Pelican Club was essentially the informal club of England's sporting aristoc-

racy during its brief five-year history. Information about the club can be gleaned from the histories written about another famous sporting organization, The National Sporting Club. See Guy Deghy, *Noble and Manly: The History of the National Sporting Club* (London: Hutchinson, 1956); A. F. Bettinson and W. Outram Tristram, *The National Sporting Club: Past and Present* (London: Sands & Co., 1901).

26. *Boston Herald,* Nov. 10, 1889; *Referee,* Jan. 15, 1890. For descriptions of the Jackson and Smith fight, see also *Cleveland Gazette,* Jan. 19, 1889; *San Francisco Chronicle,* Nov. 11, 1889; *San Francisco Daily Examiner,* Nov. 11, 12, 1889; *National Police Gazette,* Nov. 23, 1889.

27. Examples of the various offers can be found in the *Milwaukee Evening Wisconsin,* Dec. 4, 5, 10, 1889; *Referee,* Mar. 19, 1890; *San Francisco Daily Examiner,* Nov. 23, 24, 30, Dec. 9, 14, 16, 1889; Apr. 21, 22, 24, 1890; *National Police Gazette,* May 17, 1890; *Cleveland Gazette,* Nov. 30, 1889.

28. Letter from William Muldoon to Nat S. Fleischer, Apr 11, 1931. Collection of Bill Schutte, Whitewater, Wis.

29. *Cleveland Gazette,* May 31, 1890; *New York Age,* Dec. 20, Jan. 4, 1890; *Indianapolis Freeman,* Feb. 15, Apr. 5, 26, May 10, 17, July 19, Sept. 13, Dec. 6, 1890; *St. Paul Western Appeal,* May 24, 1890.

30. *Cleveland Gazette,* Mar. 15, 1890; *New York Age,* Feb. 8, May 3, 1890; *Indianapolis Freeman,* July 19, 1890; *St. Paul Western Appeal,* Apr. 26, 1890.

31. *San Francisco Daily Examiner,* Mar. 6, 8, May 20, 1890; *National Police Gazette,* Mar. 22, June 7, Dec. 6, 13, 20, 1890; *Cleveland Gazette,* Mar. 15, May 31, 1890; *Referee,* Apr. 23, 1890; *Indianapolis Freeman,* Dec. 6, 1890.

32. Before the fight there was a great deal of discussion about the relative merits of Jackson and Corbett. See *San Francisco Daily Examiner,* May 21, 1891; *Milwaukee Evening Wisconsin,* May 21, 1891; *Referee,* May 27, 1891; *Cleveland Gazette,* Apr. 4, May 16, 1891; *New York Age,* Mar. 21, Apr. 18, 1891.

33. *Referee,* June 24, 1891. For various descriptions of the fight, see *San Francisco Daily Examiner,* May 22, 23, 1891; *Referee,* May 27, June 24, 1891; *Milwaukee Evening Wisconsin,* May 22, 1891; *New York Clipper,* May 30, 1891; *Cleveland Gazette,* May 30, June 6, 1891; *Indianapolis Freeman,* May 23, 1891; Richard Kyle Fox, *Life and Battles of James J. Corbett, The Champion Pugilist of the World* (New York: R. K. Fox, 1891); James J. Corbett, *The Roar of the Crowd: The True Tale of the Rise and Fall of a Champion* (New York: G. P. Putnam's Sons, 1925).

34. See *San Francisco Daily Examiner,* June 14, 1891; *Boston Herald,* May 22, 1891; *New York Clipper,* June 6, 1891; *Referee,* June 24, 1891.

35. *San Francisco Daily Examiner,* June 14, 1891; *Referee,* June 24, 1891; *Boston Herald,* May 22, 1891.

36. *San Francisco Daily Examiner,* May 21, 1891.

37. *San Francisco Daily Examiner,* June 14, 1891; *Referee,* June 24, 1891.

38. See *Referee,* June 24, Aug. 12, 1891; *Cleveland Gazette,* June 6, 1891.

39. The relationship between Jackson, Slavin, and Leon is most fully described in Hales, *Black Prince Peter,* pp. 134—48.

40. The National Sporting Club was organized in the spring of 1891 by John Fleming and A. F. Bettinson. Originally founded as a middle-class substitute for the aristocratic and bohemian Pelican Club, it would eventually become one of the world's great centers of boxing. The club went public in 1928 and the next year was forced to close. See Deghy, *Noble and Manly;* Bettinson and Tristram, *National Sporting Club;* John Arlott, ed., *The Oxford Companion to World Sports and Games* (New York: Oxford Univ. Press, 1975), 710.

41. See, for example: Butler, *Kings of the Ring,* 140—45; Gene Corri, *Fifty Years in the Ring* (London: Hutchinson & Co., 1933); 68—74; Jeffrey Farnol, *Epics of the Fancy*

(London: Sampson Low, Marston & Co., n.d.), 213–20; John Gilbert Bohun Lynch, *Knuckles and Gloves* (New York: Henry Holt & Co., 1923), 121–26; Henry Sayers, *Fights Forgotten: A History of Some of the Chief English and American Prize Fights Since the Year 1788* (London: T. Werner Laurie, 1909), 199–205; Trevor C. Wignall, *The Story of Boxing* (New York: Brentano's, 1924), 253–56.

42. *San Francisco Examiner*, May 31, June 1, 1892; *Milwaukee Evening Wisconsin*, May 31, 1892; *New York Times*, June 1, 1892; *Cleveland Gazette*, June 4, 11, 1892; *Referee*, June 1, 8, 1892.

43. For information on Lonsdale, see L. G. Wickham Legg and E. T. Williams, eds., *Dictionary of National Biography, 1941–1950* (New York: Oxford Univ. Press, 1959), 529–30.

44. Douglas A. Lorimar, *Color, Class, and the Victorians: English Attitudes to the Negro in the Mid-Nineteenth Century* (New York: Holmes and Meier, 1978), 52–53. See also Edward Scobie, *Black Britannia: A History of Blacks in Britain* (Chicago: Johnson Publishing Co., 1972); Kenneth Little, *Negroes in Britain: A Study of Racial Relations in English Society* (London: Routledge & Kegan Paul, 1972); James Walvin, *The Black Presence: A Documentary History of the Negro in England, 1555–1860* (New York: Schocken, 1972).

45. The Corbett and Sullivan fight was certainly one of the most famous bouts in boxing history. For a discussion of the fight, see the *New York Times*, Sept. 8, 1892; *New Orleans Daily Picayune*, Sept. 8, 1892; *Chicago Tribune*, Sept. 8, 1892; *National Police Gazette*, Oct. 1, 1892.

46. *San Francisco Daily Examiner*, Feb. 12, 14, 16, 1893.

47. *Cleveland Gazette*, Feb. 18, 1893; *San Francisco Daily Examiner*, Feb. 12–14, 16, 1893.

48. *San Francisco Daily Examiner*, Feb. 21, Mar. 15, 19, 1893; *National Police Gazette*, Mar. 4, 1893; *Indianapolis Freeman*, Feb. 24, 1893.

49. *San Francisco Daily Examiner*, Apr. 10, 1894; see also *Milwaukee Evening Wisconsin*, May 1, 2, 18, 1894; *National Police Gazette*, Apr. 28, 1894; *Referee*, May 23, 1894.

50. See, for example, the *San Francisco Daily Examiner*, May 26, June 1, July 19, 28, Aug. 4, 6, 1894; *Milwaukee Evening Wisconsin*, June 1, 7, 1894; *National Police Gazette*, May 12, 19, June 9, 16, 23, dJuly 21, 1894; *Referee*, June 27, Aug. 8, 1894; *Cleveland Gazette*, Mar. 24, 1894; *Indianapolis Freeman*, Apr. 21, 28, June 9, 1894.

51. See *San Francisco Daily Examiner*, July 19, 28, Aug. 4, 6, 14, 1894; *Milwaukee Evening Wisconsin*, Aug. 14, 1894; *National Police Gazette*, Aug. 25, Sept. 1, 1894; *Cleveland Gazette*, Sept. 1, 1894. The real intentions of Jackson and Corbett in this affair will never be known. It is quite possible, however, that Corbett would have found another excuse not to fight if Jackson had agreed to the bout at the Duval Athletic Club. If that were the case, why did Jackson not call Corbett's bluff and say yes to the proposition? Perhaps Jackson believed he no longer stood a chance with Corbett and that he would be courting disaster if he accepted the champion's offer. Jackson was, after all, thirty-three years old, and he had been drinking quite heavily since his bout with Slavin. Corbett, on the other hand, had gained some twenty pounds since his fight with Jackson in 1891 and was still in reasonably good condition.

52. *Referee*, June 27, Aug. 8, 1894.

53. Roberts, *Papa Jack*, 18. See also *Referee*, June 27, Aug. 8, Aug. 22, 1894; Dale A. Somers, *The Rise of Sports in New Orleans 1850–1900* (Baton Rouge: Louisiana State University Press, 1972), 181–83.

54. *San Francisco Chronicle*, Mar. 1, 2, 1897; *Philadelphia Record*, Apr. 25, March 1, 6, 28, 1897; *Referee*, Oct. 3, 1894; Jan. 30, Feb. 20, Sept. 18, 1895; Apr. 1, 1896 (quotations); May 12, 1897; *Cleveland Gazette*, Dec. 1, 1894; Feb. 9, 1895.

55. *Referee,* Dec. 29, 1897; *San Francisco Call,* Sept. 28, 29, 1897; *Cleveland Gazette,* Oct. 16, 1897.

56. *San Francisco Call,* Sept. 28, 1897, Mar. 23, 24, 1898; *Referee,* Apr. 27, May 4, 1898; *Cleveland Gazette,* Apr. 2, 1898.

57. *Referee,* Aug. 9, Sept. 27, 29, 1899; *National Police Gazette,* Sept. 16, 1899; *Indianapolis Freeman,* Nov. 4, 18, Dec. 30, 1899.

58. W. F. Mandle; "Cricket and Australian Nationalism in the Nineteenth Century," *Journal of the Royal Australian Historical Society* 59 (Dec. 1973): 225—46.

59. *Sacramento Union,* Mar. 22, 1900; *San Francisco Call,* Apr. 17, 1901; *Referee,* Mar. 14, Apr. 11, 18, May 16, 23, June 13, 20, July 25, Aug. 1, Sept. 12, Oct. 17, Nov. 28, Dec. 12, 26, 1900; *Indianapolis Freeman,* Mar. 30, 31, Apr. 14, Aug. 4, 1900.

60. *Sydney Morning Herald,* July 15, 1901; *Referee,* July 31, Sept. 18, Oct. 9, 1901; *Cleveland Gazette,* Aug. 24, 1901.

4. The 1936 Olympic Games in Berlin: The Response of America's Black Press

1. See, for example: Richard Mandell, *The Nazi Olympics* (New York: MacMillan, 1972); Arnd Kruger, "Fair Play for American Athletes: A Study in Anti-Semitism," *Canadian Journal of History of Sport and Physical Education* 9, no. 1 (May 1978): 42—57; D. A. Kass, "The Issue of Racism at the 1936 Olympics," *Journal of Sport History* 3, no. 3 (winter 1976): 222—35; Judith Holmes, *Olympiad 1936: Blaze of Glory of Hitler's Reich* (New York: Ballantine, 1971); Moshe Gottlieb, "The American Controversy Over the Olympic Games," *American Jewish Historical Quarterly* 61, no. 3 (Mar. 1972), 181—213.

2. Many articles and books have been written about the black press. See, for example: James Z. Bayton and Ernestine Bell, "An Exploratory Study of the Role of the Negro Press," *Journal of Negro Education* 20, no. 1 (winter 1951): 8—15; Richard L. Beard and Cyril E. Zoerner, "Associated Negro Press: Its Founding, Ascendancy, and Demise," *Journalism Quarterly* 46, no. 1 (spring 1969): 47—52; Elizabeth M. Moss, "Black Newspapers Cover News Other Media Ignore," *Journalism Educator* 24, no. 3 (1969): 6—11; Armistead S. Pride, "Negro Newspapers: Yesterday, Today and Tomorrow," *Journalism Quarterly* 28, no. 2 (spring 1951), 179—88; Maxwell R. Brooks, *The Negro Press Re-Examined* (Boston: Christopher, 1959); Martin E. Dann, ed., *The Black Press, 1827—1890* (New York: Putnam, 1971); Frederick G. Detweiler, *The Negro Press in the United States* (Chicago: Univ. of Chicago Press, 1922); Roland E. Wolseley, *The Black Press, U.S.A.* (Ames, Iowa: Iowa State Univ. Press, 1974).

3. N. W. Ayer and Sons, *Directory of Newspapers and Periodicals* (Philadelphia: N. W. Ayer and Sons), 1933—1936.

4. Ibid.

5. *Chicago Defender,* Apr. 29, 1933; *Cleveland Gazette,* Apr. 22, 1933; *Indianapolis Recorder,* Dec. 29, 1934; *New York Amsterdam News,* Apr. 26, 1933; *Pittsburgh Courier-Journal,* July 15, 1933. See also the numerous articles in the *New York Times* of May 31, June 8, Aug. 27, Nov. 24, and December 18, 1933.

6. These issues have been discussed quite extensively in the secondary literature. See, for example: Mandell, *The Nazi Olympics,* 60—65; Kruger, "Fair Play for American Athletes," 42—46; Kass, "The Issue of Racism at the 1936 Olympics," 223—25; Gottlieb, "American Controversy Over the Olympic Games," 181—90.

7. *Chicago Defender,* Nov. 25, 1933; *Indianapolis Recorder,* Dec. 29, 1933; *Pittsburgh Courier-Journal,* Nov. 21, 1933. See also the *New York Times,* Nov. 21, 1933.

8. *Chicago Defender,* Oct. 6, 1934; *Indianapolis Recorder,* Oct. 6, 1934; *New York Age,* Oct. 13, 1934.

9. *Chicago Defender,* Nov. 25, 1933.

10. *Chicago Defender,* June 17, 1933; *Indianapolis Recorder,* Oct. 6, 1934; *New York Amsterdam News,* July 5, 1933; *Pittsburgh Courier-Journal,* July 15, 1933.

11. *Baltimore Afro-American,* Oct. 21, 1933; *Cleveland Gazette,* July 15, 1933; *Pittsburgh Courier-Journal,* July 15, 1933.

12. *Pittsburgh Courier-Journal,* July 15, 1933.

13. See Kass, "The Issue of Racism at the 1936 Olympics," 225; Gottlieb, "American Controversy Over the Olympic Games," 181–90.

14. *Chicago Defender,* Sept. 22, 1934; *Indianapolis Recorder,* Aug. 11, 1934.

15. *Baltimore Alfro-American,* Sept. 17, 1934. See also *Indianapolis Recorder,* Oct. 6, 1934.

16. Arnd Kruger, "The 1936 Olympic Games—Berlin," in *The Modern Olympics,* ed. Peter J. Graham and Horst Ueberhorst (West Point, N.Y.: Leisure Press, 1976), 173; *Baltimore Afro-American,* Dec. 21, 1935; *Chicago Defender,* Nov. 16, 1935; *Cleveland Gazette,* Aug. 24, 1935; *New York Amsterdam News,* Dec. 7, 1935; *Philadelphia Tribune,* Oct. 17, 1935; *Pittsburgh-Courier Journal,* Aug. 21, 1935; *St. Louis Argus,* Nov. 22, 1935.

17. See, for example: *New York Times,* Aug. 23, Dec. 4, 6, 1935; *New York Tribune,* Aug. 23, Dec. 5, 1935; *Los Angeles Times,* Aug. 23, Dec. 5, 1935.

18. *New York Times,* Aug. 23, 1935; Dec. 4, 7, 1935.

19. *New York Amsterdam News,* Aug. 31, 1935.

20. *Chicago Defender,* Nov. 16, 1935.

21. *Pittsburgh Courier-Journal,* Jan. 11, 1935.

22. *Chicago Defender,* Nov. 9, 1935; *New York Amsterdam News,* Sept. 7, 1935.

23. *Baltimore Afro-American,* Nov. 2, 1935; *Crisis,* Sept. 1935; *New York Amsterdam News,* Sept. 7, 1935.

24. *New York Amsterdam News,* Aug. 24, 1935.

25. *Cleveland Gazette,* Dec. 7, 1935.

26. For information on blacks during the Depression years, see such secondary works as Raymond Wolters, *Negroes and the Great Depression* (Westport, Conn.: Greenwood, 1970); Bernard Sternsher, ed., *The Negro in Depression and War* (Chicago: Quadrangle Books, 1969); Louis Cantor, *A Prologue to the Protest Movement* (Durham, N.C.: Duke Univ. Press, 1969); Dan T. Carter, *Scottsboro: A Tragedy of the American South* (Baton Rouge: Louisiana State Univ. Press, 1969); George B. Tindall, *The Emergence of the New South* (Baton Rouge: Louisiana State Univ. Press, 1967).

27. *Baltimore Afro-American,* Dec. 24, 1935; *New York Age,* Oct. 26, 1935; *Philadelphia Tribune,* Dec. 19, 1935; *Pittsburgh Courier-Journal,* Aug. 31, 1935.

28. *Baltimore Afro-American,* Dec. 28, 1935. See also *New York Age,* Oct. 26, 1935; *Philadelphia Tribune,* Dec. 19, 1935; *Pittsburgh Courier-Journal,* Aug. 31, 1935.

29. Secondary works dealing with the history of black athletes in American sport include Arna Bontemps, *Famous Negro Athletes,* (New York: Dodd & Mead, 1964); Ocania Chalk, *Black College Sport* (New York: Dodd & Mead, 1976); Edwin B. Henderson, *The Black Athlete: Emergence and Arrival* (New York: Publishers Co., 1968); John P. Davis, *The American Negro Reference Book* (Englewood Cliffs, N.J.: Prentice-Hall, 1966).

30. There have been a number of books written that discuss the nature of black protest in the twentieth century. Some of the more prominent ones are August Meir, Elliott Rudwick, and Francis L. Broderick, *Black Protest Thought in the Twentieth Century* (Indianapolis: Bobbs-Merrill, 1971); S. P. Fullinwider, *The Mind and Mood of Black America: 20th Century Thought* (Homewood, Ill.: Dorsey Press, 1969); Joanne Grant, *Black Protest: History, Documents and Analysis, 1619 to the Present* (New York: Fawcett, 1968); Herbert Garfinkel, *When Negroes March (Glencoe, Ill.: Free Press, 1949); Harold Cruse, The Crisis of the Negro Intellectual* (New York: William Morrow, 1967).

31. See, for example, *New York Amsterdam News,* Apr. 26, July 5, 1933; August 24, 31, Sept. 7, December 17, 1935.

32. The *Courier-Journal* and the *Chicago Defender* were probably the two most radical and outspoken black newspapers in the country. The editor of the *Defender,* Robert S. Abbott, was greatly responsible for persuading blacks to come north after World War I.

33. The black press ran a vigorous campaign between 1936 and 1945 in an effort to have blacks included in organized baseball. The person most influential in persuading Rickey to sign Robinson to a contract was Wendall Smith, the sports editor of the *Courier-Journal.*

34. *Chicago Defender,* Nov. 25, 1933; *New York Amsterdam News,* Dec. 14, 1935; *Philadelphia Tribune,* Dec. 19, 1935.

35. *Philadelphia Tribune,* Dec. 19, 1935.

36. *New York Age,* Dec. 14, 1935; *New York Amsterdam News,* Dec. 14, 1935; *Philadelphia Tribune,* Dec. 19, 1935.

37. This was just the first of several confrontations between Owens and the AAU. Shortly after the Berlin Games came to a close, Owens was reprimanded by the AAU for not participating in a series of scheduled exhibition meets in Europe. By the fall of 1936, Owens had again been charged with professionalism and had been denied his amateur status.

38. *New York Amsterdam News,* Oct. 26, 1935; *Chicago Defender,* Dec. 7, 1935; *Baltimore Afro-American,* Feb. 15, 1936.

39. *Chicago Defender,* Dec. 7, 1935.

40. The black athlete who was most vocal in his condemnation of the attitude and behavior of the *New York Amsterdam News* was Ben Johnson of Columbia University. See, for example, the exclusive interview he conducted with the newspaper, published Oct. 26, 1935.

41. See Donald S. Strong, *Organized Anti-Semitism in America* (Washington, D.C.: American Council on Public Affairs, 1941); and Carey McWilliams, *A Mark for Privilege. Anti-Semitism in America* (Boston: Little Brown, 1948).

42. See, for example: *Baltimore Afro-American,* Feb. 15, 1936; *Chicago Defender,* Dec. 7, 1935; *Pittsburgh Courier-Journal,* Dec. 7, 1935.

43. *Chicago Defender,* Dec. 14, 1935; *Indianapolis Recorder,* Dec. 14, 1935; *New York Amsterdam News,* Dec. 7, 1935; *Philadelphia Tribune,* Dec. 26, 1935; *Pittsburgh Courier-Journal,* Dec. 28, 1935.

44. *Philadelphia Tribune,* Oct. 17, 1935; *St. Louis Argus,* Nov. 22, 1935.

45. *New York Amsterdam News,* Dec. 7, 1935.

46. The most frequently mentioned athlete in the black press was unquestionably Joe Louis. If there was one athlete that the black community looked up to and viewed as a race hero, it was the "Brown Bomber."

47. *Cleveland Gazette,* July 18, 1936; *Indianapolis Recorder,* June 20, 1935; *New York Age,* July 4, 1936; *New York Amsterdam News,* July 18, 1936; *Pittsburgh Courier-Journal,* July 25, 1936.

48. *St. Louis Argus,* Aug. 14, 1936.

49. Avery Brundage was the Olympic official most often criticized for alleged racist attitudes. His inconsistency and apparent lack of concern for all minority groups was abhorred by the black press.

50. *Chicago Defender,* July 25, 1936; *Cleveland Gazette,* July 18, 1936; *Indianapolis Recorder,* July 18, 1936; *New York Age,* July 18, 1936; *Phiadelphia Tribune,* July 16, 1936; *Pittsburgh Courier-Journal,* July 25, 1936.

51. *Baltimore Afro-American,* June 13, 1936; *Chicago Defender,* June 13, 1936; *Cleveland Gazette,* June 6, 1936; *New York Age,* June 13, 1936; *New York Amsterdam News,* June 6, 1936; *Philadelphia Tribune,* June 4, 1936.

52. *New York Amsterdam News,* June 6, 1936.

53. *Baltimore Afro-American*, June 13, 1936; *Chicago Defender*, June 13, 1936; *Cleveland Gazette*, June 6, 1936; *New York Age*, June 13, 1936; *New York Amsterdam News*, June 6, 1936; *Philadelphia Tribune*, June 4, 1936.

54. *Pittsburgh Courier-Journal*, Aug. 8, 1936; *Baltimore Afro-American*, Aug. 8, 1936.

55. *Baltimore Afro-American*, Aug. 8, 1936; *Chicago Defender*, Aug. 8, 1936; *Cleveland Gazette*, Aug. 8, 1936; *Indianapolis Recorder*, Aug. 8, 1936; *Philadelphia Tribune*, Aug. 13, 1936; *Pittsburgh Courier-Journal*, Aug. 15, 1936; *New York Times*, Aug. 3–10, 1936; Bill Henry, *An Approved History of the Olympic Games* (New York: Putnam, 1948), 174–94; Mandell, *The Nazi Olympics*, 209–30; "The Black Olympian," *Black Sports* 2 (May-June 1972): 58–62.

56. Ibid.

57. *Chicago Defender*, Aug. 8, 1936; *Baltimore Afro-American*, Aug. 8, 1936; *Indianapolis Recorder*, Aug. 8, 1936; *Pittsburgh-Courier Journal*, Aug. 8, 1936.

58. *Chicago Defender*, Aug. 18, 1936; *Indianapolis Recorder*, Aug. 8, 1936; *New York Age*, Aug. 15, 1936; *New York Amsterdam News*, Aug. 15, 1936; *Pittsburgh Courier-Journal*, Aug. 22, 1936.

59. Arnd Kruger, "The 1936 Olympic Games—Berlin," 173–86.

60. Ibid.

61. *Pittsburgh Courier-Journal*, Aug. 22, 1936.

62. *Crisis*, Sept. 1936; *Pittsburgh Courier-Journal*, Sept. 5, 1936.

63. Ibid.

64. *Pittsburgh Courier-Journal*, Aug. 1, 1936.

65. *Chicago Defender*, Aug. 29, 1936; *New York Age*, Aug. 29, 1936; *New York Amsterdam News*, Sept. 5, 1936; *Indianapolis Recorder*, Sept. 12, 1936.

66. *New York Amsterdam News*, Sept. 5, 1936.

67. *Chicago Defender*, Aug. 29, 1936.

68. *St. Louis Argus*, May 8, 1936; *New York Amsterdam News*, May 9, 1936; *Chicago Defender*, May 9, 1936; *Baltimore Afro-American*, July 25, 1936; *New York Age*, Aug. 1, 1936.

69. *Pittsburgh Courier-Journal*, July 25, 1936; *New York Amsterdam News*, Aug. 8, 1936; *Philadelphia Tribune*, Aug. 13, 1936; *Indianapolis Recorder*, Aug. 22, 1936; *St. Louis Argus*, Aug. 28, 1936.

70. *Baltimore Afro-American*, June 15, 1933; *Chicago Defender*, April 29, 1933; *New York Age*, Aug. 15, 1936.

71. *Baltimore Afro-American*, June 17, 1933.

72. See, for example: *New York Times*, July 14, Aug. 3, 4, 5, 15, 1936; *Los Angeles Times*, July 5, Aug. 4, 5, 1936.

73. The modern Olympic Games have traditionally been utilized as a platform for espousing particular political and cultural beliefs. After the 1936 Olympics, the most noteworthy Games in this respect were the 1968 Games in Mexico City, the 1972 Games in Munich, and the 1980 Games in Moscow.

74. *New York Age*, Aug. 15, 1936; *Philadelphia Tribune*, Aug. 13, 1936; *Pittsburgh Courier-Journal*, Aug. 22, 1936.

75. *Philadelphia Tribune*, Aug. 13, 1936; *New York Amsterdam News*, Sept. 5, 1936; *Pittsburgh Courier-Journal*, Sept. 19, 1936.

76. *Philadelphia Tribune*, Aug. 13, 1936; *New York Amsterdam News*, Sept. 5, 1936; *Pittsburgh Courier-Journal*, Sept. 5, 1936.

77. *Pittsburgh Courier-Journal*, Sept. 5, 1936.

5. Wendell Smith, the *Pittsburgh Courier-Journal*, and the Campaign to Include Blacks in Organized Baseball, 1933–1945

1. Jackie Robinson and Alfred Duckett, *I Never Had It Made* (New York: Putnam, 1972), 41. Smith assisted Robinson in the writing of his first book, *Jackie Robinson: My Own Story* (New York: Greenberg, 1948).

2. This was the meeting in which Rickey announced the formation of his newly formed United States League.

3. The *Courier-Journal* probably gave more extensive coverage to various sporting events than any other black newspaper. Anyone interested in the career of Joe Louis, the 1936 Olympic Games, or black baseball would find the paper a valuable source of information.

4. See for example, Harvey Frommer, *Rickey and Robinson: The Men Who Broke Baseball's Color Barrier* (New York: Macmillan, 1982); Arthur Mann, *The Jackie Robinson Story* (New York: Grosset & Dunlop, 1951); Bill Roeder, *Jackie Robinson* (New York: A. S. Barnes, 1950); Robert W. Peterson, *Only the Ball Was White* (New York: Prentice-Hall, 1970).

5. Such influential black newspapers as the *Chicago Defender, New York Age, New York Amsterdam News,* and *Baltimore Afro-American* vigorously crusaded against organized baseball's racial policies. The *Afro-American,* behind its well-known sports editor Sam Lacy, achieved particular notoriety for the feature-length articles and biting editorials it wrote on the subject.

6. N. W. Ayer and Sons, *Directory of Newspapers and Periodicals* (Philadelphia: N. W. Ayer and Sons, 1933–45).

7. Pegler's attack is mentioned often in the secondary literature. See, for example: David W. Voigt, *America Through Baseball* (Chicago: Nelson-Hall, 1976), 114; Peterson, *Only the Ball Was White,* 175; Richard C. Crepeau *Baseball: America's Diamond Mind, 1919–1941* (Orlando: University Presses of Florida, 1980), 168–69.

8. Quoted in Crepeau, *Baseball: America's Diamond Mind,* 169.

9. *Pittsburgh Courier-Journal,* Feb. 11, 18, 25, 1933; New York *Daily News,* Feb. 8, 1933; Peterson, *Only The Ball Was White,* 175; Crepeau, *Baseball: America's Diamond Mind,* 169.

10. *Pittsburgh Courier-Journal,* Feb. 25, Mar. 4, 11, 25, Apr. 15, 1933.

11. *Pittsburgh Courier-Journal,* Feb. 25, 1933.

12. *Pittsburgh Courier-Journal,* Mar. 4, 1933.

13. The person who probably best expressed this sense of ethnic dualism was W. E. B. Du Bois, the famous black intellectual and protestor of the early twentieth century. See his book *The Souls of Black Folk* (Chicago: A. C. McClurg and Co., 1953).

14. *Pittsburgh Courier-Journal,* Oct. 16, 1937.

15. See Peterson, *Only the Ball Was White,* 100–101; John Holway, *Voices from the Great Black Baseball Leagues* (New York: Dodd, Mead, 1975), 9–10; A. S. "Doc" Young, *Negro Firsts in Sports* (Chicago: Johnson Publishing Co., 1963), 63.

16. See, for example, *Pittsburgh Courier-Journal,* Aug. 12, 1933; Sept. 8, 1934; Aug. 14, 1937; Aug. 23, 1941; Aug. 15, 1942.

17. These games were undoubtedly a source of embarrassment to the officials in organized baseball. It was difficult to reconcile the victories of black clubs against the supposedly superior abilities of white major leaguers.

18. *Pittsburgh Courier-Journal,* Oct. 20, 27, 1934.

19. *Pittsburgh Courier-Journal,* Oct. 19, 1935.

20. After his tenure with the *Courier-Journal,* Smith became a sportswiter for the *Chicago American* from 1947 through 1963. Thereafter, he was a sports columnist for the

Chicago Sun-Times and a commentator for two Chicago television stations. Smith and Robinson died within three months of each other in 1972.

21. *Pittsburgh Courier-Journal,* May 14, 1938.

22. This doctrine of self-help and racial unity has most often been expressed during times of greatest frustration and discouragement. See August Meier et al., *Black Protest Thought in the Twentieth Century* (Indianapolis: Bobbs-Merrill, 1976).

23. *Pittsburgh Courier-Journal,* Jan. 14, 1939.

24. This tactic was not unique to Smith and the *Courier-Journal* but was also employed by other black newspapers. See for example, *Chicago Defender,* Sept. 7, 25, 1940; *Baltimore Afro-American,* Feb. 17, 1940; *Norfolk Journal and Guide,* Apr. 19, 1941.

25. *Pittsburgh Courier-Journal,* Feb. 18, 1939.

26. *Pittsburgh Courier-Journal,* Feb. 25, 1939.

27. *Pittsburgh Courier-Journal,* July 15, 22, 29, Aug. 4, 12, 19, 26, Sept. 2, 1939.

28. *Pittsburgh Courier-Journal,* Aug. 5, 1939.

29. The baseball situation is a good example of the black citizen's incessant yearning to be both a black and an American, a constant dilemma for blacks throughout American history.

30. *Pittsburgh Courier-Journal,* Sept. 9, 1939.

31. *Pittsburgh Courier-Journal,* May 14, 1938.

32. *Pittsburgh Courier-Journal,* Aug. 5, 1939.

33. *Pittsburgh Courier-Journal,* Aug. 5, 1939.

34. *Pittsburgh Courier-Journal,* Mar. 19, 1940.

35. *Pittsburgh Courier-Journal,* Mar. 16, 1940.

36. For examples of the apparent progress in interracial understanding during the late 1930s, see August Meier and Elliott Rudwick, *From Plantation to Ghetto* (New York: Hill & Wang, 1976); Bernard Sternsher, ed. *The Negro in Depression and War* (Chicago: Quadrangle Books, 1969); Raymond Wolters, *Negroes and the Great Depression* (Westport, Conn.: Greenwood, 1970).

37. See, for example, Cornelius L. Golightly, "Negro Higher Education and Democratic Negro Morale," *Journal of Negro Education* 11, no. 3 (July 1942): 322–28; Horace R. Clayton, "Negro Morale," *Opportunity* 19, no. 1 (Dec. 1941): 371–75; Louis Wirth, "Morale and Minority Groups," *American Journal of Sociology* 47, no. 3 (Nov. 1941): 415–33.

38. *Pittsburgh Courier-Journal,* July 25, 1942.

39. *Pittsburgh Courier-Journal,* May 30, 1942.

40. *Pittsburgh Courier-Journal,* Aug. 1, 8, 15, 29, 1942.

41. The *Daily Worker* had also been waging a lengthy campaign against organized baseball's racial policies. The Communist Party, of course, relished the opportunity to point out the discrimination and other inadequacies that often characterized American life. See Ronald A. Smith, "The Paul Robeson-Jackie Robinson Saga and a Political Collision," *Journal of Sport History* 6, no. 2 (summer 1979): 5–27.

42. *Pittsburgh Courier-Journal,* Aug. 29, 1942. It was about this time that Bill Veeck planned to purchase the Philadelphia Phillies and fill the roster with black players. See Frommer, *Rickey and Robinson,* 98.

43. Benswanger never did formally announce his decision not to give the players a tryout. He simply ignored the issue and let it run its course.

44. Hazel Gaudet Erskin, "The Polls: Race Relations," *Public Opinion Quarterly,* 26, no. 1 (spring 1962): 137–48.

45. Howard W. Odum, *Race and Rumors of Race: Challenge to American Crisis* (Chapel Hill: Univ. of North Carolina Press, 1943), 7.

46. See Joseph Boskin, ed., *Urban Racial Violence in the Twentieth Century* (Beverly

Hills: Glencoe, 1969); Alfred McClung Lee and Norman D. Humphrey, *Race Riot* (New York: Knopf, 1943).

47. This was the demand voiced by most black leaders during this period. While its racial policy had been acquiescence in segregation since the end of reconstruction, the government was now asked by blacks to set the example for the rest of the country by supporting integration.

48. *Pittsburgh Courier-Journal,* Apr. 24, May 8, 1943.

49. Quoted in Sternsher, ed., *The Negro in Depression and War,* 310. For discussions of Roosevelt's conservative attitude towards black Americans, see Arthur M. Schlesinger, Jr., *The Age of Roosevelt: The Politics of Upheaval* (Boston: Houghton Mifflin, 1957); and Frank Freidel, *F.D.R. and the South* (Baton Rouge: Louisiana State Univ. Press, 1965).

50. *Pittsburgh Courier-Journal,* Feb. 27, Apr. 24, May 8, 1943.

51. *Pittsburgh Courier-Journal,* Feb. 27, 1943.

52. Ibid.

53. *Pittsburgh Courier-Journal,* Jan. 23, 30, 1943.

54. *Pittsburgh Courier-Journal,* Jan. 23, 1943.

55. *Pittsburgh Courier-Journal,* Dec. 25, 1943.

56. See Peterson, *Only the Ball Was White,* 98; and Holway, *Voices from the Great Black Baseball Leagues,* pp. 11–16.

57. *Pittsburgh Courier-Journal,* Dec. 11, 1943. See also the *Chicago Defender,* Dec. 11, 1943; *New York Times,* Dec. 4, 1943.

58. *Pittsburgh Courier-Journal,* Dec. 11, 1943.

59. Ibid.

60. Ibid.

61. Ibid.

62. Ibid.

63. Frommer, *Rickey and Robinson,* 98.

64. *Pittsburgh Courier-Journal,* May 14, 1938.

65. *Pittsburgh Courier-Journal,* Dec. 10, 1938.

66. *Pittsburgh Courier-Journal,* Dec. 2, 1944.

67. *Pittsburgh Courier-Journal,* Apr. 14, 28, 1945. See also Peterson, *Only the Ball Was White,* 183–184; Frommer, *Rickey and Robinson,* 99–101; and Carl T. Rowan, *Wait Till Next Year* (New York: Random House, 1960), 103–104.

68. Ibid.

69. *Pittsburgh Courier-Journal,* Apr. 14, 1945.

70. *Pittsburgh Courier-Journal,* Mar. 24, Apr. 21, 28, 1945. See also the *New York Times,* Mar. 10, 24, Apr. 17, 21, 1945; Peterson, *Only the Ball Was White,* 183–84; Rowan, *Wait Till Next Year,* 96–101; Arthur Mann, *The Jackie Robinson Story* (New York: Grosset and Dunlop, 1951), 12–13.

71. In typical fashion, the officials of both the Red Sox and the Braves kept putting the tryout off in hopes that the problem would go away. See the *Pittsburgh Courier-Journal,* Apr. 21, 1945.

72. Frommer, *Rickey and Robinson,* 102.

73. *Pittsburgh Courier-Journal,* Apr. 28, 1945.

74. See Rowan, *Wait Till Next year,* 100.

75. Peterson, *Only the Ball Was White,* 187; Frommer, *Rickey and Robinson,* 103; Robinson, *I Never Had It Made,* 41–47; Rowan, *Wait Till Next Year,* 104–106.

76. Roeder, *Jackie Robinson,* 17–18. Smith realized that Robinson, though not the most talented black player, possessed the kind of temperament and intelligence essential for the person who would eventually break the color barrier.

77. *Pittsburgh Courier-Journal,* Apr. 28, 1945.

78. *Pittsburgh Courier-Journal,* May 12, 1945.

79. *Pittsburgh Courier-Journal,* Apr. 28, May 5, 1945.

80. *New York Times,* Aug. 12, 1945.

81. *Pittsburgh Courier-Journal,* Nov. 3, 1945.

6. "The Year of Awakening": Black Athletes, Racial Unrest, and the Civil Rights Movement of 1968

1. Lance Morrow, "1968," *Time,* Jan. 11, 1988, 16–27.

2. Ibid.; David Caute, *The Year of the Barricades: A Journey Through 1968* (New York: Harper & Row, 1988).

3. See, for example, *Los Angeles Sentinel,* July 11, Aug. 15, 29, 1968; *Baltimore Afro-American,* April 6, July 13, Aug. 24, 1968; *Pittsburgh Courier-Journal,* Aug. 24, 31, 1968; *New York Times,* Jan. 3, July 12, Aug. 22, Sept. 10, Nov. 27, Dec. 6, 22, 1968; Dave Sendler, "The Black Athlete-1968," in Patricia W. Romero, ed., *In Black America, 1968: The Year of Awakening* (New York: International Publishers, 1969), 325–38.

4. Harry Edwards, *The Revolt of the Black Athlete* (New York: Free Press, 1969); Jack Scott, *The Athletic Revolution* (New York: Free Press, 1971); Dick Schaap, "The Revolt of the Black Athlete," *Look,* Aug. 6, 1968, 72–77; "The Angry Black Athlete," *Newsweek,* July 15, 1968, 56–60.

5. Edwards, *Revolt of the Black Athlete;* Scott, *Athletic Revolution.*

6. See *New York Times,* Jan. 19, May 7, June 11, July 7, Aug. 7, Dec. 17, 1968; *Baltimore Afro-American,* Jan. 20, 1968.

7. *New York Times,* Jan. 15, March 1, 1968. See also Jeffrey T. Sammons, *Beyond the Ring: The Role of Boxing in American Society* (Urbana, Ill.: Univ. of Illinois Press, 1988), 203–11.

8. *New York Times,* Jan. 15, 1968.

9. *New York Times,* March 1, 1968.

10. See, for example, Edwards, *Revolt of the Black Athlete;* Scott, *Athletic Revolution;* "Revolt in Sports: Negro Athletes Demand Better Treatment, Jobs," *Wall Street Journal,* June 19, 1968, 1, 14; Ron Briley, "It Was 20 Years Ago Today: Baseball Responds to the Unrest of 1968," in Peter Levine, ed., *Baseball History: An Annual of Original Baseball Research* (Westport, Conn.: Meckler, 1989), 81–94.

11. Information on the proposed boycott of the 1968 Olympic Games can be gleaned from Edwards, *Revolt of the Black Athlete;* William O. Johnson, *All That Glitters Is Not Gold: The Olympic Games* (New York: Putnam, 1972); Donald Spivey, "Black Consciousness and Olympic Protest Movement, 1964–1980," in Donald Spivey, ed., *Sport in America: New Historical Perspectives* (Westport, Conn.: Greenwood, 1985), 239–59.

12. Vincent Matthews, with Neal Amdur, *My Race Be Won* (New York: Charterhouse, 1974), 162–65; Pete Axthelm, "Boycott Now—Boycott Later," *Sports Illustrated* [hereafter abbreviated *SI,*] Feb. 26, 1968, 24–25; "Hobbling the Winged Foot," *Newsweek,* Feb. 19, 1968, 85; "Boycott Runners," *Newsweek,* Feb. 26, 1968, 82–83; *Pittsburgh Courier-Journal,* Feb. 17, 1968; *Chicago Defender,* Jan. 31, 1968, [London] *Times,* Feb. 16, 1968.

13. Axthelm, "Boycott Now—Boycott Later," 25; "Hobbling the Winged Foot," 85; "Boycott Runners," 82–83.

14. Matthews, *My Race Be Won,* 162–65.

15. Axthelm, "Boycott Now—Boycott Later," 25.

16. *New York Times,* April 12, 1968.

17. See *New York Times,* Oct. 18, 19, 20, 28, 1968; *Los Angeles Times,* Oct. 19, 23, 1968; *Chicago Defender,* Oct. 21, 22, 24, 1968; *Pittsburgh Courier-Journal,* Oct. 26, 1968; [London] *Times,* Oct. 18, 1968; *Los Angeles Sentinel,* Oct. 24, 1968.

18. See, for example, Edwards, *Revolt of the Black Athlete,* 88; John Underwood, "The Desperate Coach," *SI,* Aug. 25, 1969, 66–68; "Shave Off That Thing," *SI,* Sept. 1, 1969, 20–27; and "Concessions—And Lies," *SI,* Sept. 8, 1969, 29–32; John Robert Lee, "Toward Black Consciousness and Acceptance: A Study of Relevant Attitudes and Practices in Big Eight Football" (Ph.D., diss., University of Kansas, 1973); David K. Wiggins, "The Future of College Athletics is at Stake: Black Athletes and Racial Turmoil on Three Predominantly White University Campuses, 1968–1972," *Journal of Sport History* 15 (winter 1988): 304–33.

19. Wiggins, "The Future of College Athletics Is At Stake," 304–33; Harry Edwards, *Sociology of Sport* (Homewood, Ill.: Dorsey Priss, 1973), 141–52.

20. Edwards, *Revolt of the Black Athlete,* 84–6; Jack Olsen, "In An Alien World," *SI,* July 15, 1968, 28–43.

21. Edwards, *Revolt of the Black Athlete,* 84–86; Olsen, "In An Alien World," 28–43.

22. Olsen, "In An Alien World," 36.

23. Ibid., 28–41.

24. Ibid.

25. *New York Times,* Jan. 5, 1968; Jack Olsen, "The Anguish of a Team Divided," *SI,* July 29, 1968, 20–35.

26. *New York Times,* Aug. 1, 1968; Olsen, "Anguish of a Team Divided," 20–35; see also Dave Meggysey, *Out of Their League* (New York: Ramparts, 1971).

27. Dave Sendler, "The Black Athlete, 1968," in Romero, ed., *In Black America, 1968,* 325–38; *Pittsburgh Courier-Journal,* Aug. 3, 10, 1968; *Los Angeles Sentinel,* Aug. 22, 1968.

28. For information on the turmoil surrounding the 1965 American Football Conference All-Star game, see Ron Mix, "Was This Their Freedom Ride?", *SI,* Jan. 18, 1965, 24–25; William J. Baker, *Sports in the Western World* (Totowa, N.J.: Rowman & Littlefield, 1982), 290.

29. See Harry Edwards, *The Struggle that Must Be: An Autobiography* (New York: Macmillam: 1980), and, *Revolt of the Black Athlete.*

30. Ibid.

31. See *Los Angeles Times,* Jan. 24, 25, 26, 30, Feb. 1, March 1, 13, April 12, 1968; *San Francisco Chronicle,* March 13, April 25, 1968; *Chicago Defender,* Jan. 25, Feb. 1, March 12, April 2, 1968; Edwards, *Revolt of the Black Athlete,* 80–82.

32. Edwards, *Revolt of the Black Athlete,* 104; *New York Times,* Oct. 19, 1968.

33. *Chicago Defender,* July 25, 1968.

34. See Edwards, *Revolt of the Black Athlete,* 62–63.

35. Jesse Owens, with Paul Neimark, *Blackthink: My Life as Black Man and White Man* (New York: William Morrow, 1970), 44.

36. Ibid., 57–84.

37. Edwards, *Revolt of the Black Athlete.*

38. See, for example, "The Angry Black Athlete," pp. 56–60; Schaap, "Revolt of the Black Athlete," 72–77; Arnold Hano, "The Black Rebel Who Whitelists the Olympics," *New York Times Magazine,* May 12, 1968, 20–29; "Black Hired Hands," *The Nation,* Aug. 5, 1968, 68.

39. Jack Olsen, "The Black Athlete—A Shameful Story," *SI,* July 1, 1968, 15–27; "Pride and Prejudice," *SI,* July 8, 1968, 18–31; "In An Alien World," *SI,* July 15, 1968, 28–43; "In the Back of the Bus," *SI,* July 22, 1968, 28–41; and "Anguish of a Team Divided."

40. Jack Olsen, *The Black Athlete: A Shameful Story* (New York: Time-Life Books, 1968).

41. Bob Gibson, *From Ghetto to Glory* (Englewood Cliffs, N.J.: Prentice-Hall,

1968); Frank Robinson, *My Life in Baseball* (New York: Doubleday, 1968); Henry Aaron, *Aaron, R. F.* (New York, 1968).

42. Eldridge Cleaver, *Soul on Ice* (New York: McGraw-Hill, 1968), 89.

43. Ibid., 92–93.

44. Examples of these types of studies can be found in the various sport sociology textbooks. See, particularly, Jay S. Coakley, *Sport in Society: Issues and Controversies*, 4th ed. (St. Louis: Mosby, 1990); Eldon E. Snyder and Elmer A. Spreitzer, *Social Aspects of Sport*, 2d ed. (Englewood Cliffs, N.J.: Prentice-Hall, 1989); Timothy S. Curry and Robert M. Jiobu, *Sports: A Social Perspective* (Englewood Cliffs, N.J.: Prentice-Hall, 1984); Stephen K. Figler and Gail Whitaker, *Sport and Play in American Life*, 2d edition (Dubuque, Iowa: Wm. C. Brown, 1991).

45. Edwards, *Revolt of the Black Athlete*, 167–77.

7. "The Future of College Athletics Is at Stake": Black Athletes and Racial Turmoil on Three Predominantly White University Campuses, 1968–1972

1. For general information on the role of black students in predominantly white universities, see Marvin W. Peterson et al., *Black Students on White Campuses: The Impacts of Increased Black Enrollments* (Ann Arbor, Mich.: Institute for Social Research, 1978); Charles V. Willie and Arline Sakuma McCord, *Black Students at White Universities* (New York: Praeger, 1972); Harry Edwards, *Black Students* (New York: Free Press, 1970); James Charles Jones, "A Study of Black Students in Integrated Universities Compared with their Counterparts in Black Universities" (Ph.D. diss., Michigan State University, 1971).

2. See Harry Edwards, *The Revolt of the Black Athlete* (New York: Free Press, 1969), 88.

3. John Underwood, "The Desperate Coach," *Sports Illustrated* (hereafter abbreviated *SI*): "The Desperate Coach," 31 Aug. 25, 1969, 66; see also "Shave Off That Thing," Sept. 1, 1969, 20–27; and "Concessions—And Lies," Sept. 8, 1969, 29–32.

4. For an interesting analysis of the relationship between black athletes and white coaches, see Harry Edwards, *The Sociology of Sport* (Homewood, Ill.: Dorsey, 1973), 142–152. See also John Robert Lee, "Toward Black Consciousness and Acceptance: A Study of Relevant Attitudes and Practices in Big Eight Football" (Ph.D. diss., University of Kansas, 1973).

5. Edwards, *Revolt of the Black Athlete*, 84–86; Jack Olsen, "In An Alien World," *SI*, 29 July 15, 1968; 28–43.

6. *New York Times*, Jan. 5, 19, Nov. 1, 15, 16, 23, 1969, Jan. 9, 1970; Pat Putnam, "No Defeats, Loads of Trouble," *SI*, Nov. 3, 1969, 26–27.

7. *New York Times*, Nov. 6, 16, 1969.

8. *New York Times*, Feb. 27, 1970, May 25, 1973; *Pittsburgh Courier-Journal*, Dec. 26, 1970; *Oregonian*, June 16, 25, 1972, May 25, 1973; *Corvallis Gazette-Times*, Apr. 18, 19, 27, June 2, 12, 13, 16, 23, May 24, 1973.

9. *Los Angeles Times*, Jan. 24, 25, 26, 1968.

10. *Los Angeles Times*, Jan. 24, 25, 1968.

11. *Los Angeles Times*, Jan. 24, 1968. Harry Edwards noted that his organization, The Olympic Project for Human Rights, lent support to the revolting black athletes at Berkeley. See his *Revolt of the Black Athlete*, 80–82.

12. *Los Angeles Times*, Jan. 24, 25, 26, Feb. 1 (quotation), 1968.

13. *Los Angeles Times*, Jan. 24, 25, 26, 30 (quotation), 1968.

14. *Los Angeles Times*, Jan. 30, 1968.

15. Ibid.

16. *Los Angeles Times*, Mar. 1, 1968.

17. *Los Angeles Times*, Mar. 13, Apr. 12 (quotation), 1968; *San Francisco Chronicle*, Mar. 13, 1968.

18. *San Francisco Chronicle*, Apr. 25, 1968.

19. See Edwards, *Revolt of the Black Athlete*, 81.

20. Pat Putnam, "End of a Season at Syracuse," *SI*, Sept. 28, 1970, 22–23.

21. Ibid., 23.

22. Ibid. See also *New York Times*, Aug. 25, 29, 1970.

23. *New York Times*, Sept. 28, 1970.

24. Putnam, "End of a Season at Syracuse," 22; *New York Times*, Aug. 25, 26, 1970.

25. Putnam, "End of a Season at Syracuse," 22; *New York Times*, Aug. 28, 1970 (quotation). See also *New York Times*, Sept. 24, 1970.

26. *New York Times*, Sept. 27, 28, 30, 1970.

27. *New York Times*, Dec. 9, 1970; *Pittsburgh Courier-Journal*, Dec. 19, 1970.

28. *New York Times*, Dec. 11 (quotation), 9, 1970.

29. *New York Times*, Dec. 9, 11, 1970.

30. Underwood, "Shave Off That Thing," 22; *Corvallis Gazette-Times*, Feb. 25, 26, 1969.

31. *Corvallis Gazette-Times*, Feb. 25, 1969.

32. *Oregonian*, Feb. 26, 1969; *Corvallis Gazette-Times*, Feb. 25, 1969.

33. *Oregonian*, Feb. 26, 1969.

34. *Corvallis Gazette-Times*, Feb. 25, 26, 1969.

35. *The Oregonian*, Feb. 27, 1969; *Corvallis Gazette-Times*, Feb. 27, 1969.

36. *Corvallis Gazette-Times*, Feb. 28, 1969. See also *Corvallis Gazette-Times*, Feb. 27, 1969; *Oregonian*, Feb. 28, 1969.

37. *Corvallis Gazette-Times*, Feb. 28, 1969. See also *Oregonian*, Feb. 28, 1969.

38. *Oregonian*, Feb. 26, 27, Mar. 1, 1969; *Corvallis Gazette-Times*, Feb. 27, 1969. See also Willie and McCord, *Black Students at White Universities*, 22–23.

39. See Edwards, *Sociology of Sport*, 142–52.

40. See *Oregonian*, Feb. 26, 27, Mar. 1, 1969; *Corvallis Gazette-Times*, Feb. 27, 1969.

41. *Oregonian*, Mar. 1, 6, 7, 8, 1969; *Corvallis Gazette-Times*, Mar. 1, 5, 6, 1969.

42. *Oregonian*, Mar. 6, 1969 (see also issues of Mar. 7, 9, 1969); *Corvallis Gazette-Times*, Mar. 7, 1969.

43. *Corvallis Gazette-Times*, Mar. 7, 1969. See also *Oregonian*, Mar. 7, 1969.

44. *Oregonian*, Mar. 7, 1969.

45. *Oregonian*, Apr. 10, 11, 12, 1969; *Corvallis Gazette-Times*, Apr. 9, 10, 1969. Another well-publicized incident occurred between a sportswriter, Jerry Uhrhammer of the *Eugene Register-Guard*, and Oregon State's coaching staff. Uhrhammer criticized Andros for his handling of the Milton incident and was thereafter temporarily barred from the Oregon State locker room. See the *Eugene Register-Guard*, Mar. 13, 1969; *Corvallis Gazette-Times*, Mar. 13, Apr. 4, 1969; *Oregonian*, Apr. 4, 1969.

46. *Oregonian*, Apr. 10 (quotation), 12, 1969; *Corvallis Gazette-Times*, Apr. 11, 1969.

47. *Corvallis Gazette-Times*, Apr. 28, 1969. See also *Oregonian*, Apr. 28, 1969; *Corvallis Gazette-Times*, Apr. 29, 1969.

48. *Oregonian*, Apr. 28, 1969.

49. *Corvallis Gazette-Times*, May 8, 10, 1969.

50. *Corvallis Gazette-Times*, May 8 (quotation), 9, 1969.

51. Underwood, "Shave Off That Thing," 23; *Corvallis Gazette-Times*, Mar. 8, 1969.

52. See *Corvallis Gazette-Times*, May 9, 24, 1969.

53. *Corvallis Gazette-Times*, May 8, 27, 1969. See also *Corvallis Gazette-Times*, May 9, 13, 24, 1969.

54. See *Oregonian*, June 16, 25, 1972, May 25, 1973; *Corvallis Gazette-Times*, Apr. 18, 19, 27, May 24, June 2, 12, 13, 16, 23, 1973; *New York Times*, May 25, 1973.

55. Willie and McCord, *Black Students at White Universities*, 115.

56. The black athletic revolts at San Jose State and San Francisco State were two of the best known and most publicized confrontations. See Edwards, *Revolt of the Black Athlete*, 153–58; James Brann, "San Jose: The Bullhorn Message," *Nation*, Nov. 6, 1967, 665–67; *Chicago Defender*, Oct. 5, 1967; *New York Times*, May 12, 1968. For strategy employed by black students, see Marvin W. Peterson, "Conflict Dynamics of Institutional Response," in *Black Students on White Campuses: The Impacts of Increased Black Enrollments*, ed. Marvin W. Peterson et al. (Ann Arbor, Mich.: Institute for Social Research, 1978), 156–58.

57. *Oregonian*, Mar. 3, 1969. See also Peterson, "Conflict Dynamics of Institutional Responses," 159.

58. Edwards, *Revolt of the Black Athlete*, 81–82.

59. Willie and McCord, *Black Students at White Universities*, 115.

60. Edwards, *Sociology of Sport*, 146–51, 148 (quotation).

61. See the *Corvallis Gazette-Times*, May 16, 17, 1969; *Oregonian*, May 17, 1969.

62. Edwards, *Sociology of Sport*, 148–51.

63. Marvin W. Peterson, "Environmental Forces: The Crucial Context," in *Black Students on White Campuses*, 111.

8. Victory for Allah: Muhammad Ali, the Nation of Islam, and American Society

1. Bill Russell, with Tex Maule, "I'm Not Worried about Ali," *Sports Illustrated* (hereafter abbreviated *SI*), June 1, 1967, 19–21. See also *Muhammad Speaks*, June 16, 1967; Muhammad Ali, with Richard Durham, *The Greatest: My Own Story* (New York: Ballantine, 1975), 208–9.

2. For secondary accounts that touch upon Ali's relationship to the movement, see Jeffrey T. Sammons, *Beyond the Ring: The Role of Boxing in American Society* (Urbana: Univ. of Illinois Press, 1988); Don Atyeo and Felix Dennis, *The Holy Warrior: Muhammad Ali* (London: Bunch Books, 1975); Budd Schulberg, *Loser and Still Champion: Muhammad Ali* (Garden City, N.Y.: Doubleday, 1972); Frederic Cople Jaher, "White America Views Jack Johnson, Joe Louis and Muhammad Ali," in *Sport in America: New Historical Perspectives*, ed. Donald Spivey (Westport, Conn: Greenwood, 1985), 145–92; Thomas Hauser, *Muhammad Ali: His Life and Times* (New York: Simon & Schuster, 1991).

3. Still one of the best analyses of Muslim philosophy is C. Eric Lincoln, *The Black Muslims in America* (Boston: Beacon, 1973).

4. Jaher, "White America Views Jack Johnson, Joe Louis, and Muhammad Ali," 145–92; Randy Roberts and James Olson, *Winning Is the Only Thing: Sports in America since 1945* (Baltimore: Johns Hopkins Univ. Press, 1989), 163–88; Sammons, *Beyond the Ring*, 184–223.

5. Hauser, *Muhammad Ali*, 92–93.

6. Ibid., 84–89.

7. *Muhammad Speaks*, May 22, 1964.

8. Ali, *The Greatest*, 35.

9. Hauser, *Muhammad Ali*, 97.

10. Ibid., 83.

11. Ibid., 97–98. Information about Malcolm X's stay in Miami and his involvement

with Ali prior to the fight can also be gleaned from Malcolm X and Alex Haley, *The Autobiography of Malcolm X* (New York: Ballantine, 1990), 305–8, 407–11; George Plimpton, "Miami Notebook: Cassius Clay and Malcolm X," *Harper's Magazine,* June 1964, 54–61; Robert Lipsyte, "Cassius Clay, Cassius X, Muhammad Ali," *New York Times Magazine,* Oct. 25, 1964, 29, 135, 140–42; Bruce Perry, *Malcolm: The Life of a Man Who Changed Black America* (New York: Station Hill Press, 1991), 245–50.

12. Hauser, *Muhammad Ali,* 66–67.

13. See Malcolm X and Haley, *Autobiography of Malcolm X,* 306.

14. Ibid., 306–7. The FBI busily charted the meetings between Malcolm X and Clay while the two men were in Miami. See Claybourne Carson, *Malcolm X: The FBI File* (New York: Carroll & Graf, 1991), 71, 248–50, 255.

15. *New York Times,* Feb. 27, 1964.

16. New York Times, Feb. 28, 1964. See also U.S. Congress, Senate, "Civil Rights and Cassius Clay," 88th Congress, 2d Session, *Congressional Record,* Feb. 28, 1964, 4006–10; *Louisville Courier-Journal,* Feb. 27, 1964; *Raleigh News and Courier,* Feb. 28, 1964.

17. *Muhammad Speaks,* Mar. 13, 1964.

18. "Cassius X," *Time,* Mar. 13, 1964, 78; "Cassius X," *Newsweek,* Mar. 16, 1964, 74.

19. *New York Times,* Mar. 7, 1964. One of the ironies is that Ali's "slave name," Cassius Clay, was taken from a famous Kentucky abolitionist who served as Abraham Lincoln's bodyguard for a time and later as his ambassador to Russia. See U.S. Congress, Senate, "Civil Rights and Cassius Clay," 4006–10.

20. Atyeo and Dennis, *Holy Warrior,* 57; John Cottrell, *Man of Destiny: The Story of Muhammad Ali, Formerly Cassius Clay* (London: Frederick Muller, 1967), 154, 180–86.

21. Martin Kane, "The Greatest Meets the Grimmest," *SI,* Nov. 15, 1965, 36–41; *New York Times,* Mar. 8, 1964; *Muhammad Speaks,* Dec. 3, 1965.

22. *Kansas City Call,* Feb. 14, 1964. See also *Baltimore Afro-American,* Feb. 15, 1964; *Miami Herald,* Feb. 7, 1964.

23. *Muhammad Speaks,* Apr. 24, 1964.

24. *Muhammad Speaks,* May 8, June 5, 10, 19, July 17, 1964. See also "Muhammad Ali in Africa," *SI,* June 1, 1964, 20–25.

25. For details of the chance meeting, see Malcolm X and Haley, *Autobiography of Malcolm X,* 359; Bruce Perry, *Malcolm,* 270; Peter Goldman, *The Death and Life of Malcolm X* (Urbana: Univ. of Illinois Press, 1979), 178.

26. Malcolm X and Haley, *Autobiography of Malcolm X,* 339–40.

27. Perry, *Malcolm,* 271.

28. "Muhammad Ali in Africa," *SI,* June 1, 1964, 20.

29. Hauser, *Muhammad Ali,* 112.

30. Quoted in Perry, *Malcolm,* 271. See *New York Times,* May 18, 1964.

31. Malcolm X and Haley, *Autobiography of Malcolm X,* 434–39.

32. Ibid., 450.

33. Ibid.

34. Hauser, *Muhammad Ali,* 119.

35. Ibid., 150–52.

36. Ali, *The Greatest,* 8.

37. Hauser, *Muhammad Ali,* 144.

38. Ibid., 144–70. See also *Muhammad Speaks,* Mar. 25, 1966; May 5, 19, June 23, 30, 1967.

39. Hauser, *Muhammad Ali,* 154–55.

40. Ibid., 155.

41. Ibid., 169.

42. Ibid., 173.

43. Ibid., 179.

44. See Oliver Jones, Jr., "The Black Muslim Movement and the American Constitutional System," *Journal of Black Studies* 13 (June 1983): 417–37.

45. *Muhammad Speaks,* Mar. 3, 1967. See also *Muhammad Speaks,* Apr. 14, 28, Oct. 20, Nov. 10, 1967.

46. *Muhammad Speaks,* May 12, 1967.

47. See Jaher, "White America Views Jack Johnson, Joe Louis, and Muhammad Ali," 175.

48. Bob Woodward and Scott Armstrong, *The Brethren: Inside the Supreme Court* (New York: Simon & Schuster, 1979), 136–39.

49. Ibid.

50. Ibid.

51. See Sammons, *Beyond the Ring,* 216.

52. See Peter Wood, "Return of Muhammad Ali, a/k/a Cassius Marcellus Clay Jr.," *New York Times Magazine,* Nov. 30, 1969, 32–33, 116, 123, 133–32; Robert Lipsyte, "I Don't Have to Be What You Want Me to Be, Says Muhammad Ali," *New York Times Magazine,* Mar. 7, 1971, 24–25, 54–59, 62, 67.

53. *Muhammad Speaks,* Apr. 4, 1969.

54. *Muhammad Speaks,* Apr. 11, 1969; see also Apr. 25, 1969.

55. Elijah Muhammad, *Message to the Blackman in America* (Chicago: Muhammad Mosque of Islam No. 2, 1965),246–47.

56. See Hauser, *Muhammad Ali,* 81–112.

57. *Muhammad Speaks,* Apr. 4, 11, 1969.

58. *Muhammad Speaks,* Feb. 4, 1972.

59. Hauser, *Muhammad Ali,* 193.

60. Those closest to Ali frequently discussed the fighter's devotion to boxing. For comments from his trainer, Angelo Dundee, see Hauser, *Muhammad Ali,* 460–61.

61. Lipsyte, "I Don't Have to Be What You Want Me to Be," 67.

62. Ibid.

63. *Muhammad Speaks,* Jan. 3, 1975.

64. See, for example, *Muhammad Speaks,* Jan. 17, 24, 1975.

65. For information on changes in the movement, see the *Washington Post,* July 5, 1977; Lawrence H. Mamiya, "From Black Muslim to Bilalian: The Evolution of a Movement," *Journal for the Scientific Study of Religion* 21 (1982): 138–52; Zafar Ishaq Ansari, "W. D. Muhammad: The Making of a 'Black Muslim' Leader (1933–1961)," *American Journal of Islamic Social Sciences* 2 (1985): 245–62; Clifton E. Marsh, *From Black Muslims to Muslims: The Transition from Separatism to Islam, 1930–1980* (Metuchen, N.J.: Scarecrow, 1984).

66. *Muhammad Speaks,* Mar. 21, 1975.

67. Mamiya, "From Black Muslim to Bilalian," 138–52; Askia Muhammad, "Civil War in Islamic America," *Nation,* June 11, 1977, 721–24; David Gates, "The Black Muslims: A Divided Flock," *Newsweek,* Apr. 9, 1984): 15,17a; "The Farrakhan Formula," *National Review,* Nov. 1, 1985, 19–20; *Washington Post,* July 5, 1984.

68. U.S. Congress, Senate, "Muhammad Ali Faces the Nation," 94th Congress, 2d Session, *Congressional Record,* May 4, 1976, 122: 12372–75.

69. *Bilalian News,* June 1, 1979.

70. See *Bilalian News,* Oct. 15, 1976; June 1, 1979.

71. *Bilalian News,* Apr. 11, 1980.

72. See Hauser, *Muhammad Ali,* 430.

73. Ibid., 500.

74. *Muslim Journal*, Dec. 4, 1987.

75. *Muslim Journal*, Nov. 18, 1988.

76. *Washington Post*, July 5, 1984.

77. See Jaher, "White America Views Jack Johnson, Joe Louis, and Muhammad Ali," 145–92; Roberts and Olson, *Winning Is the Only Thing*, 163–88; Sammons, *Beyond the Ring*, 184–233.

9. "Great Speed but Little Stamina": The Historical Debate over Black Athletic Superiority

1. Martin Kane, "An Assessment of Black Is Best," *Sports Illustrated*, Jan. 18, 1971, 72–83.

2. Edwin B. Henderson, "Physical Education and Athletics Among Negroes," in Bruce L. Bennett, ed. *The History of Physical Education and Sport*, (Chicago: Athletic Institute, 1972), 82–83.

3. See Thomas P. Gossett, *Race: The History of an Idea* (Dallas: Southern Methodist Univ. Press, 1963); George M. Frederickson, *The Black Image in the White Mind* (New York: Harper & Row, 1971); John S. Haller, *Outcasts from Evolution* (Urbana: Univ. of Illinois Press, 1971).

4. *San Francisco Examiner*, May 31, 1892.

5. See David K. Wiggins, "Peter Jackson and the Elusive Heavyweight Championship: A Black Athlete's Struggle Against the Late Nineteenth Century Color Line," *Journal of Sport History* 12 (Summer 1985): 143–68. Randy Roberts discusses the stereotype of black boxers in his biography of Jack Johnson, *Papa Jack: Jack Johnson and the Era of White Hopes* (New York: Free Press, 1983), 61–63.

6. Andrew Ritchie, *Marshall "Major" Taylor* (San Francisco: Bicycle Books, 1988), 174.

7. See, for example, Edwin B. Henderson, *The Negro in Sports* (Washington, D.C.: Associated Publishers, 1939); A. S. "Doc" Young, *Negro Firsts in Sports* (Chicago: Johnson Publishing Co., 1963); Jack Orr, *The Black Athlete: His Story in American History* (New York: Lion Books, 1969).

8. Fredrick Lewis Allen, "Breaking World Records," *Harper's Monthly Magazine* 173 (Aug. 1936): 302–10; Marshall Smith, "Giving the Olympics an Anthropological Once-over," *Life*, Oct. 23, 1964, 81–84; Dean B. Cromwell and Al Wesson, *Championship Techniques in Track and Field* (New York: Whittlesey House, 1941), 6.

9. W. Montague Cobb, "Race and Runners," *Journal of Health and Physical Education* 7 (Jan. 1936): 3–7, 52–56.

10. Ibid. Cobb published an extensive review of literature dealing with studies concerned with the anthropometric measurements of blacks. See W. Montague Cobb, "The Physical Constitution of the American Negro," *The Journal of Negro Education* 3 (1934): 340–88. A later article on the topic is James H. Jordan's "Physiological and Anthropometrical Comparisons of Negroes and Whites," *Journal of Health, Physical Education, and Recreation* 40 (Nov.-Dec. 1969): 93–99.

11. Eleanor Metheny, "Some Differences in Bodily Proportions Between American Negro and White Male College Students as Related to Athletic Performance," *Research Quarterly* 10 (Dec. 1939): 41–53.

12. Ibid., 50–52.

13. Laynard L. Holloman, "On the Supremacy of the Negro Athlete in White Athletic Competition," *Psychoanalytic Review* 30 (Apr. 1943): 157–62.

14. "Why Negroes Rule Boxing," *Our World* 6 (Nov. 1951); Jack Dempsey, "Why Negroes Rule Boxing," *Ebony* 7 (May 1950): 29–32; Mike Jacobs, "Have Negroes Killed Boxing?" *Ebony* 7 (May 1950): 29–32.

15. See Ben Lombardo, "The Harlem Globetrotters and the Perpetuation of the Black Stereotype," *Physical Educator* 35 (May 1978): 60–63.

16. See Frank T. Bannister, Jr., "Search for 'White Hopes' Threatens Black Athletes," *Ebony* 35 (Feb. 1980): 130–34; Frank DeFord, "The Big Game is Over: This Way to the Exit, Bwana," *Ovi* (spring 1973): 51, 132, 134; Harry Edwards, *Sociology of Sport* (Homewood, Ill: Dorsey Press, 1973), 214.

17. James M. Tanner, *The Physique of the Olympic Athlete: A Study of 137 Track and Field Athletes at the XIV Olympic Games, Rome, 1960*, (London: G. Allen & Unwin, 1964). For another British perspective on black athletic superiority, see Adolphe Abrahams, "Race and Athletics," *Eugenics Review* 44 (July 1952): 143–45.

18. Tanner, *The Physique of the Olympic Athlete*, 107. Olympic athletes have been the source of much attention down through the years by sport scientists interested in anthropometric measurements. See for example, Alfonso L. de Garay et al., *Genetic and Anthropological Studies of Olympic Athletes* (New York: Harcourt Brace, 1974); T. K. Cureton, *Physical Fitness of Champion Athletes* (Urbana, Ill.: Univ. of Illinois Press, 1951); Ernst Jokl, "Essay on Medical Sociology of Sports," in Ernst Jokl, *Medical Sociology and Cultural Anthropology of Sport and Physical Education* (Springfield, Ill.: Charles L. Thomas, 1964), 65–71.

19. Smith, "Giving the Olympics an Anthropological Once-over," 81–84 (quotations, 83).

20. See *Los Angeles Times*, Mar. 24, 29, 1968.

21. *Los Angeles Times*, Mar. 25, 1968.

22. Kane, "An Assessment of Black Is Best," 72–83. Anyone interested in the question of black athletic superiority would be well served by looking at some of the work of Robert Malina, the well-known physical anthropologist from the University of Texas: for example, "Anthropometric Correlates of Strength and Motor Performance," *Exercise and Sport Science Reviews* 3 (1975): 249–74; *Growth and Development: The First Twenty Years in Man* (Minneapolis: Burgess, 1975); "Secular Changes in Growth Maturation and Physical Performance," *Exercise and Sport Sciences Reviews* 6 (1979): 203–55.

23. Kane, "An Assessment of Black Is Best," 72–73. It is a common perception in this country's dominant culture that blacks make terrible swimmers because of their "unique" anthropological makeup. For a discussion of blacks in swimming, see John A. Faulkner, "Physiology of Swimming," *Swimming Technique* 6 (Apr. 1970): 14–20; Malachi Cunningham, Jr., "Blacks in Competitive Swimming," *Swimming Technique* 9 (1973): 107–108.

24. See, particularly, Edwards's articles, "The Sources of the Black Athlete's Superiority," *Black Scholar* 3 (Nov. 1971): 32–41; "The Myth of the Racially Superior Athlete," *Intellectual Digest* 2 (Mar. 1972): 58–60; "20th Century Gladiators For White America," *Psychology Today* 7 (Nov. 1973): 43–52.

25 Edwards, "The Sources of the Black Athlete's Superiority," 35, 37, 38–39.

26. Ibid, 39–41.

27. Arthur R. Jensen, "How Much Can We Boost I.Q. and Scholastic Achievement?" *Harvard Educational Review* 39 (winter 1969): 1–123.

28. See *Harvard Educational Review* 39 (spring 1969).

29. See, for example, Ashley Montague, ed., *Race and IQ* (New York: Oxford Univ. Press, 1975); C. L. Brace and F. B. Livingstone, "On Creeping Jensenism," *Race and Intelligence;* ed. C. L. Brace, G. R. Gamble, and J. T. Bonds (Washington, D.C.: American Anthropological Association, 1971).

30. See Stephen Jay Gould, "Racist Arguments and I.Q.," in Montague, *Race and IQ,* 145–150.

31. Alvin F. Poussaint, "Sex and the Black Male," *Ebony* 27 (Aug. 1972): 114–20 (quotations, 115–16).

32. *New York Times,* Dec. 2, 1974.

33. Bill Rhoden, "Are Black Athletes Naturally Superior?" *Ebony* 30 (Dec. 2, 1974): 136–38; "Black Dominance," *Time*, May 9, 1977, 57–60.

34. Legrand H. Clegg II, "Why Black Athletes Run Faster," *Sepia* 29 (July 1980): 18–22. See also "Is Black Fastest?" *Black Sports* 4 (May 1975): 18–24.

35. David K. Wiggins, "The Quest for Identity: The Dialectic of Black Consciousness and the Involvement of Black Athletes in American Sport," paper given at the annual meeting of the North American Society for Sport History, Columbus, Ohio, May 27, 1987. Almost everyone has offered an opinion on the subject of black athletic superiority, including well-known writers who have written popular works on various aspects of sport. See, for example, David Halberstam, *The Breaks of the Game* (New York: Knopf, 1981), 29–31; and James A. Michner, *Sports in America* (New York: Random House, 1976), 163–167.

36. This attitude has been prevalent in the black community for a long time. Black newspapers in the latter half of the nineteenth century, expressed the importance of developing both "Brain" and "Brawn." See, for example, *Indianapolis Freeman*, Sept. 18, 1890; *New York Age*, Dec. 20, 1890.

37. "The Right Kind of Excellence," *Black Enterprise* 10 (Nov. 1979): 9.

38. *New York Times*, Feb. 6, 1977. See also May 1, 1977, issue.

39. *New York Times*, July 31, 1988. See also Anthony Leroy Fisher, "The Best Way Out of the Ghetto," *Phi Delta*.

40. D. Stanley Eitzen and George Sage, *Sociology of Sport*, 2d ed. (Dubuque, Iowa: Wm. C. Brown, 1978), 300. See John C. Phillips, "Toward an Explanation of Racial Variations in Top-Level Sports Participation," *International Review of Sport Sociology* 3 (1976): 39–55.

41. Eitzen and Sage, *Sociology of Sport*, 301.

42. Jay Coakley, *Sport in Society: Issues and Controversies*, 3d ed. (St. Louis: Times/ Mosby, 1986), 146–50.

43. Ibid. For other discussions about black athletes from a sociological perspective, see Wilbert Marcellus Leonard II, *A Sociological Perspective of Sport*, 3d ed. (New York: MacMillan, 1988), 214–55; George H. Sage, *Sport and American Society: Selected Readings*, 3d ed. (Reading, Mass: Addison-Wesley 1980), 313–47; D. Stanley Eitzen, ed. *Sport in Contemporary Society: An Anthology* (New York: St. Martin's, 1979), 356–408; Barry D. McPherson, "The Black Athlete: An Overview and Analysis," in *Social Problems in Athletics*, ed. Daniel M. Landers, (Urbana: Univ. of Illinois Press, 1976), 122–50; Morgan Worthy and Allan Markle, "Racial Differences in Reactive Versus Self-Paced Sports Activities," *Journal of Personality and Social Psychology* 16 (1970): 439–43; James M. Jones and Adrian Ruth Hochner, "Racial Differences in Sports Activities: A Look at the Self-Paced Versus Reactive Hypothesis," *Journal of Personality and Social Psychology* 27 (1973): 86–95.

44. James LeFlore, "Athleticism Among American Blacks," in Robert M. Pankin, ed., *Social Approaches to Sport* (Toronto: Associated University Presses, 1982), 104–21. Two other articles that furnish an insightful look at the black experience in sport are Larry E. Jordan, "Black Markets and Future Superstars: An Instrumental Approach to Opportunity in Sport Forms" *Journal of Black Studies* 11 (Mar. 1981): 289–306; Hal A. Lawson, "Physical Education and Sport in the Black Community: The Hidden Perspective," *Journal of Negro Education* 48 (spring 1979): 187–95.

45. LeFlore, "Athleticism Among American Blacks," 104–21.

46. See, for example, *New York Times*, Jan. 16, 17, 1988; Jonathan Rowe, "The Greek Chorus: Jimmy the Greek Got It Wrong But So Did His Critics," *Washington Monthly* 20 (Apr. 1988): 31–34; "Of Mandingo and Jimmy 'the Greek,'" *Time*, Feb. 1, 1988, 70; "Of Fingerprints and Other Clues," *Fortune*, Feb. 15, 1988, 123–24; "What We Say, What We Think," *U.S. News & World Report*, Feb. 1, 1988, 27–28.

47. *New York Times*, Jan. 16, 17, 1988.

48. "An Oddsmaker's Odd Views," *Sports Illustrated* 68 (Jan. 25, 1988) 7; *New York Times*, Jan. 16, 1988.

49. *New York Times*, Jan. 17, 1988; see also Jan. 19, 21, 24, 1988.

50. *Washington Post*, Jan. 21, 1988.

51. John Underwood, "On the Playground: Troubling Thoughts about Top Athletes —and Too Much Success," *Life* 11 (spring, 1988). Ashe also comments on the question of black athletic superiority in his book, *A Hard Road to Glory: A History of the Afro-American Athlete*, 3 vols. (New York: Warner Books, 1989).

52. *New York Times*, July 17, 1988; David W. Zang, "Calvin Hill Interview," *Journal of Sport History* 15 (winter 1988): 334–55.

53. See *New York Times*, Apr. 26, 1989; *Los Angeles Times*, Apr. 26, 27, 1989; *Washington Post*, Apr. 26, 1989; *U.S.A. Today*, Apr. 26, 1989.

54. See, for example, William M. Kramer and Norton B. Stern, "San Francisco's Fighting Jew," *California Historical Quarterly* 53 (winter 1974): 333–46; Dennis P. Ryan, *Beyond the Ballot Box: A Social History of the Boston Irish, 1845–1917* (Rutherford, N.J.: Fairleigh Dickinson Univ. Press, 1983); Harold U. Ribalow, *The Jew in American Sports* (New York: Bloch, 1948); Ralph C. Wilcox, "In or Out of the Melting Pot? Sport and the Immigrant in Nineteenth-Century America," in Norbert Muller and Joachim K. Ruhl, eds., *Olympic Scientific Congress, 1984 Official Report: Sport History* (Niedernhausen: Schors-Verlag, 1985) 354–72; Kirson S. Weinberg and Henry Arond, "The Occupational Culture of the Boxer," *American Journal of Sociology* 57 (winter, 1952): 460–69.

10. The Notion of Double-Consciousness and the Involvement of Black Athletes in American Sport

1. W. E. B. Du Bois, *The Souls of Black Folk* (New York: Fawcett, 1961), 17.

2. See, for example, Edwin B. Henderson, *The Negro in Sports* (Washington, D.C.: Associated Publishers, 1939); A. S. "Doc" Young, *Negro Firsts in Sports* (Chicago: Johnson Publishing, 1963); Peter Chew, *The Kentucky Derby: The First 100 Years* (Boston: Houghton Mifflin, 1974).

3. Dale A. Somers, *The Rise of Sports in New Orleans* (Baton Rouge: Louisiana State Univ. Press, 1972); Charles Stewart, "My Life as a Slave," *Harpers New Monthly Magazine* 69 (1884): 730–38; David K. Wiggins, "Isaac Murphy: Black Hero in Nineteenth Century American Sport, 1861–1896," *Canadian Journal of History of Sport and Physical Education* 10 (May 1978): 15–32.

4. Marshall "Major" Taylor, *The Fastest Bicycle Rider in the World* (1928; reprint, Brattleboro, Vt.: Stephen Green Press, 1972); Moses Fleetwood Walker, *Our Home Colony: A Treatise on the Past, Present, and Future of the Negro Race in America* (Steubenville, Ohio: Herald Printing, 1908); David K. Wiggins, "Isaac Murphy"; idem, "Peter Jackson and the Elusive Heavyweight Championship: A Black Athlete's Struggle Against the Late Nineteenth Century Color-Line," *Journal of Sport History* 12 (summer 1985): 143–68.

5. D. K. Wiggins, "Isaac Murphy"; Walker, *Our Home Colony.*

6. D. K. Wiggins, "Isaac Murphy."

7. D. K. Wiggins, "Peter Jackson," 148.

8. Andrew Ritchie, *Major Taylor: The Extraordinary Career of a Champion Bicycle Racer* (San Francisco: Bicycle Books, 1988), 73.

9. Anthony M. Platt, *E. Franklin Frazier Reconsidered* (New Brunswick: Rutgers Univ. Press, 1990), 67.

10. David K. Wiggins, "Isaac Murphy;" Sidem, "Peter Jackson."

11. Walker, *Our Home Colony*, 46.

12. Janet Bruce, *The Kansas City Monarchs: Champions of Black Baseball* (Lawrence: Univ. of Kansas Press, 1985), 112.

13. John Holway, *Voices from the Great Black Baseball League* (New York: Dodd, Mead, 1975), 78—100; Donn Rogosin, *Invisible Men: Life in Baseball's Negro Leagues* (New York: Atheneum, 1983), 67—91.

14. Rogosin, *Invisible Men: Life in Baseball's Negro Leagues*, 32—36.

15. Bruce, *Kansas City Monarchs*, 32.

16. Rogosin, *Invisible Men*, 71.

17. Leroy Paige, *Pitchin' Man*, ed. Hal Lebovitz (N.p.: By the editor, 1948), 67. See also Jules Tygiel, *Baseball's Great Experiment: Jackie Robinson and His Legacy* (New York: Oxford Univ. Press, 1983), 21.

18. Rogosin, *Invisible Men*, 148.

19. See Al-Tony Gilmore, *Bad Nigger! The National Impact of Jack Johnson* (Port Washington, N.Y.: Kennikat Press, 1975), esp. 95—116; Randy Roberts, *Papa Jack: Jack Johnson and the Era of White Hopes* (New York: Free Press, 1983), esp. 97—98, 113—114; William H. Wiggins, "Jack Johnson as Bad Nigger: The Folklore of His Life," *Black Scholar* 2 (1971): 4—19.

20. W. H. Wiggins, "Jack Johnson As Bad Nigger."

21. Roberts, *Papa Jack*, 26.

22. Lawrence W. Levine, *Black Culture and Black Consciousness: Afro-American Folk Thought from Slavery to Freedom* (New York: Oxford Univ. Press, 1977), 431.

23. Roi Ottley, *Inside Black America* (London: Eyre & Spottiswoode, 1948), 157.

24. Dominic J. Capeci, Jr., and Martha Wilkerson, "Multifarious Hero: Joe Louis, American Society and Race Relations during World Crisis, 1935—1945," *Journal of Sport History* 10 (winter 1983): 6.

25. Frederic Cople Jaher, "White America Views Jack Johnson, Joe Louis, and Muhammad Ali," in *Sport in America: New Historical Perspectives* (Westport, Conn.: Greenwood, 1985), ed. Donald Spivey, 145—92; Jesse Owens with Paul G. Neimark, *Blackthink: My Life as Black Man and White Man* (New York: William Morrow, 1972), 107—22.

26. Vince Matthews with Neil Amdur, *My Race Be Won* (New York: Charterhouse, 1974), 194.

27. Owens, *Blackthink*, 182.

28. David K. Wiggins, "Wendell Smith, the Pittsburgh Courier-Journal and the Campaign To Include Blacks in Organized Baseball, 1933—1945," *Journal of Sport History* 10 (summer 1983): 5—29.

29. Horace R. Clayton, "Negro Morale," *Opportunity* 19 (Dec. 1941): 371—75; Cornelius C. Golightly, "Negro Higher Education and Democratic Negro Morale," *Journal of Negro Education* 1(July 1942): 322—28.

30. See, for example, Harvey Frommer, *Rickey and Robinson: The Men Who Broke Baseball's Color Barrier* (New York: MacMillan, 1982), 32—54; Tygiel, *Baseball's Great Experiment*, esp. 180—208.

31. Jackie Robinson as told to Alfred Duckett, *I Never Had It Made* (New York: Putnam, 1972), 36.

32. Ibid., 11.

33. Althea Gibson, *I Always Wanted To Be Somebody* (New York: Harper, 1958), 124.

34. Quoted in Benjamin Rader, *American Sports: From the Age of Folk Games to the Age of Spectators* (Englewood Cliffs, N.J.: Prentice-Hall, 1983), 330.

35. Jaher, "White America Views Jack Johnson, Joe Louis and Muhammad Ali," 145—92.

36. Muhammad Ali with Richard Durham, *The Greatest: My Own Story* (New York: Random House, 1978), 202—13, 319—31.

37. Ibid., 319–31.

38. See Eldridge Cleaver, *Soul on Ice* (New York: McGraw-Hill, 1968), 90–96.

39. "The Angry Black Athlete," *Newsweek*, July 15, 1968, 59.

40. See Harry Edwards, *The Revolt of the Black Athlete* (New York: Free Press, 1969), 91–114; "The Olympic Project for Human Rights: An Assessment Ten Years Later," *Black Scholar* 10 (Mar.-Apr. 1979): 2–8; and *The Struggle That Must Be: An Autobiography* (New York: Macmillan, 1980). I discuss some of this material in my article " 'The Year of Awakening:' Black Athletes, Racial Unrest and the Civil Rights Movement of 1968," *International Journal of the History of Sport* 9 (Aug. 1992): 188–208.

41. Donald Spivey, "Black Consciousness and Olympic Protest Movement, 1964–1980," in Spivey, ed., *Sport in America*, 248–49.

42. Paula Giddings, *When and Where I Enter: The Impact of Black Women on Race and Sex in America* (New York: Bantam, 1988), 314–24.

43. Spivey, "Black Consciousness," 248–49.

44. *Chicago Tribune*, July 4, 1968.

45. See, for example, John W. Loy, Jr. and Joseph F. McElvogue, "Racial Segregation in American Sport," *International Review of Sport Sociology* 5 (1970): 5–23; Sandra C. Castine and Glyn C. Roberts, "Modeling in the Socialization Process of the Black Athlete," *International Review of Sport Sociology* 9 (1974): 63–69.

46. Randy Roberts and James Olson, *Winning Is the Only Thing: Sports in America since 1945* (Baltimore: John Hopkins Univ. Press, 1989), 178.

47. See David K. Wiggins, " 'Great Speed but Little Stamina': The Historical Debate over Black Athletic Superiority," *Journal of Sport History* 16 (summer 1989): 158–85 [chap 9 of this book].

48. *New York Times*, June 2, 1987; see also issues of June 5 and 9, 1987.

49. See Earl Graves, "The Right Kind of Excellence," *Black Enterprise* 10 (Nov. 1979): 9; Anthony Leroy Fisher, "The Best Way out of the Ghetto," *Phi Delta Kappan* (Nov. 1978): 240.

50. Arthur Ashe and Arnold Rampersand, *Days of Grace: A Memoir* (New York: Knopf, 1993), 153.

11. Edwin Bancroft Henderson, African American Athletes, and the Writing of Sport History

1. Charles Drew to Edwin B. Henderson, May 31, 1940, Edwin B. Henderson Papers, Moorland-Spingarn Research Center (hereafter referred to as EBH Papers, MSRC). This letter is also quoted in Charles E. Wynes, *Charles Richard Drew: The Man and the Myth*, (Urbana: Univ. of Illinois Press, 1988), 56; and Spencie Love, *One Blood: The Death and Resurrection of Charles R. Drew* (Chapel Hill: Univ. of North Carolina Press, 1996), 125.

2. The esteem in which Henderson was held by his students is evidenced by the letters of appreciation they sent to him over the years. See, for example, the letter from Montague Cobb Mar. 9, 1971, and from James O. Williams, Nov. 1, 1965, EBH Papers, MSRC.

3. For further details about Henderson's life, see James H. M. Henderson and Betty F. Henderson, *Molder of Men: Portrait of a "Grand Old Man"—Edwin Bancroft Henderson* (Washington, D.C.: Vantage, 1985); "Biography—Edwin Bancroft Henderson," Sept. 1971; EBH Papers, MSRC; Edwin Bancroft Henderson, "Looking Back On: Fifty Years," *Washington Afro-American*, July 24, 31, Aug. 7, 10, 28, 31, Sept. 11, 1954; Greg Stuart, "The Beginning of Tomorrow," *Black Sports* (Feb. 1972): 62–67.

4. See Stuart, "Beginning of Tomorrow," 67; J. H. M. Henderson and B. Henderson, *Molder of Men*, 29–30; "Honors or Awards," *Journal of Health, Physical Education, and Recreation* 25 (Oct. 1954): 34–35; Marvin H. Eyler to Edwin B. Henderson, May 2, 1973, Bruce L. Bennett Papers (hereafter BLB Papers), AAHPERD Archives. Program, The First

Annual Black Athletes Hall of Fame Banquet, Mar. 14, 1974, EBH Papers, MSRC; Florence S. Savoy, "News Release," Mar. 15, 1954, EBH Papers, MSRC.

5. This is my own choice of title for Henderson, not someone else's designation.

6. Andrew S. "Doc" Young, *Negro Firsts In Sports*, (Chicago: Johnson Publishing, 1963), p. xi.

7. See Patrick B. Miller, "To 'Bring the Race Along Rapidly: Sport, Student Culture, and Educational Mission at Historically Black Colleges During the Interwar Years," *History of Education Quarterly* 35 (summer, 1995): 111–33. For insights into the style, strategy, and method of the earliest writings in African American history, see August Meier and Elliott Rudwick, *Black History and the Historical Profession, 1915–1980* (Urbana: Univ. of Illinois Press, 1986); and Dickson D. Bruce, Jr., "Ancient Africa and the Early Black American Historians, 1883–1915," *American Quarterly* 36 (winter, 1984): 684–99.

8. Henderson and Joiner, eds., *Official Handbook: Inter-Scholastic Athletic Association of Middle Atlantic States*, 4 vols., Spalding Athletic Library (New York: American Sports Publishing, 1910–1913).

9. Among such essays in the *Colored American Magazine* were the following: G. Grant Williams, "Marshall Walter Taylor [Major Taylor] The World-Famous Bicycle Rider," vol. 5 (Sept. 1902): 336–445; William Clarence Matthews, "Negro Foot-ball Players on New England Teams," vol. 9 (Mar. 1905): 130–32; Phil Waters, "Football: Its Defenders and Champions," vol. 10 (Apr. 1906): 231–35; Thomas J. Clement, "Athletics in the American Army," vol. 8 (January 1905): 21–29; Old Sport, "Zenith of Negro Sport," vol. 16 (May 1909): 295–300. For information on the magazine, see August Meier, "Booker T. Washington and the Negro Press: With Special Reference to *The Colored American Magazine*," *Journal of Negro History* 38 (Jan. 1953): 67–90.

10. See Theodore Kornweibel, Jr., *No Crystal Stair: Black Life and the "Messenger,"* *1917–1928*, (Westport, Conn.: Greenwood, 1975), especially chap. 2.

11. See Patrick B. Miller, "To 'Bring the Race Along Rapidly:' Sport, Student Culture, and Educational Mission at Historically Black Colleges During the Interwar Years," *History of Education Quarterly* 35 (Summer 1985): 111–33.

12. Edwin B. Henderson, "Athletics," *Messenger*, Apr. 1925, 170; Oct., Nov., 1925, 365; Jan. 1926, 15; Jan. 1927, 20.

13. Kornweibel, *No Crystal Stair*, 42.

14. See the *Champion Magazine: A Monthly Survey of Negro Achievement* 1: Oct. 1916, 47–48; Jan. 1917, 275–76; Feb. 1917, 316–17.

15. "Basketball," *Crusader* 1 (Jan. 1919): 17; "Basketball," *Crusader* 1 (Mar. 1919): 12; "Valentine's All-Negro All-Star Five," *Crusader* 1 (Apr. 1919): 14; C.V.B. "The Sporting Periscope," *Crusader* 2 (Dec. 1919): 17. For information about Briggs and the magazine, see Robert V. Briggs, "*The Crusader* Magazine, and the African Blood Brotherhood, 1918–1922," in Robert A. Hill, ed., *The Crusader*, 6 vols. (N.Y.: Garland, 1987), 1: v-lxvi.

16. See the following articles in the designated volume of the *Competitor*. Ira F. Lewis, "Our Colleges and Athletics," 2 (Dec. 1920): 290–92; "Who'll Be the Next?" 2 (Oct.-Nov. 1920): 221–224; and "National Baseball League Formed," 1 (Mar. 1920): 66–67; Will Anthony Madden, "The Future of Basketball," 1 (Jan. 1920): 67–68; George M. Bell, "Tennis Stars in the East," 2 (Aug.-Sept. 1920): 158–60; Dave Wyatt, "National League of Colored Clubs Prepare for Season's Opening," 1 (Apr. 1920): 73–74; C. I. Taylor, "The Future of Colored Baseball," 1 (Feb. 1920): 76–79; "Colored Athletes in the Famous Penn Relays," 1 (June 1920): 73–75; "The Colored Basketball Referee Finally Arrives," 1 (Mar. 1920): 69–70.

17. Among the essays on sport in the *Southern Workman* were Elizabeth D. Dunham, "Physical Education of Women at Hampton Institute," 53 (Apr. 1924): 161–68; and Charles H. Williams, "Twenty Years' Work of the C.I.A.A.," 61 (Feb. 1932): 65–76;

"Negro Athletes in the Tenth Olympiad," 61 (Nov. 1932): 330–34; and "Negro Athletes in the Eleventh Olympiad," 66 (Feb. 1937): 55–60.

18. The essays in *Crisis* included George Streator, "Football in Negro Colleges," 41 (Apr. 1932): 129–30, 139, 141; W. Rollo Wilson, "They Could Make the Big Leagues," 41 (Oct. 1934): 305–6; Roy Wilkins, "Negro Athletes at the Olympic Games," 39 (Aug. 1932): 252–53; and "Negro Stars on Big Grid Teams," 43 (Dec. 1936): 362–64; William A. Brower, "Our Stars: In Track and Field," 48 (Oct. 1941): 320–21, 324; Dan Burley, "What's Ahead for Robinson?" 52 (Dec. 1945): 346–47; 364.

19. See these articles in *Opportunity:* Elmer A. Carter, "Prelude to the Olympics," 10 (Aug. 1932): 246–42; and "The Negro in College Athletics," 11 (July 1933): 208–10, 219; James D. Parks, "Negro Athletes in the 1936 Olympiad," 14 (May 1936): 144–46; Edward Lawson, "Who Will Be All-American?" 16 (Oct. 1938): 300–301; Ed Nace, "Negro Grid Stars, Past and Present," 17 (Sept. 1941): 272–73; William A. Brower, "Prejudice In Sports," 19 (Sept. 1941): 260–63, and "Time for Baseball to Erase the Blackball," 20 (June 1942): 164–67.

20. Edwin B. Henderson, "The Negro Athlete and Race Prejudice," *Opportunity*, 14: 77–79. Hereafter cited by page number in text.

21. Cobb was also an outstanding track-and-field performer at Amherst College and a close follower of sport throughout his life. See Harold Wade., Jr., *Black Men of Amherst* (Amherst, Mass.: Amherst College Press, 1976), 41–77.

22. See Montague W. Cobb, "Race and Runners," *Journal of Health and Physical Education* 7 (Jan. 1936): 3–6. Cobb wrote yet another article on the subject several years later, "Does Science Favor Negro Athletes?", *Negro Digest* 5 (May 1947): 74–77.

23. For details on the debate over racial differences and sport performance, see Laurel R. Davis, "The Articulation of Difference: White Preoccupation with the Question of Racially Linked Genetic Differences Among Athletes," *Sociology of Sport Journal* 7 (June 1990): 179–87; David K. Wiggins, " 'Great Speed but Little Stamina': The Historical Debate over Black Athletic Superiority," *Journal of Sport History* 16 (summer 1989): 158–85. A critique of my article, much information on the writings dealing with race and sport, and an overall assessment of the historical literature on African American athletes are included in Jeffrey T. Sammons's important review essay, " 'Race' and Sport: A Critical, Historical Examination," *Journal of Sport History* 21 (fall 1994): 203–78.

24. Edwin B. Henderson, *The Negro in Sports* (Washington, D.C.: Associated Publishers, 1939). Hereafter cited by page number in text.

25. Information on Woodson can be found in Meier and Rudwick, *Black History and the Historical Profession;* esp. 1–71; Jacqueline Anne Goggin, "Carter G. Woodson and the Movement to Promote Black History" (Ph.D. diss., Univ. of Rochester, 1983); Patricia W. Romero, "Carter G. Woodson: A Biography" (Ph.D. diss., Ohio State University, 1971).

26. Edwin Bancroft Henderson, "Looking Back On: Fifty Years," *Washington Afro-American*, Aug. 28, 1954.

27. Ibid.

28. Scholars need to examine more closely the role of black sportswriters in the integration of sport at all levels of competition. For studies that provide information on black sportswriters, see David K. Wiggins, "Wendell Smith, the *Pittsburgh Courier-Journal* and the Campaign to Include Blacks in Organized Baseball, 1933–1945; and "The 1936 Olympic Games in Berlin: The Response of America's Black Press," *Research Quarterly For Exercise and Sport* 54 (Sept. 1983): 278–92; Thomas G. Smith, "Outside the Pale: The Exclusion of Blacks From the National Football League, 1934–1946;" William Simons, "Jackie Robinson and the American Mind: Journalistic Perceptions of the Reintegration of Baseball," *Journal of Sport History* 12 (spring 1985): 39–64; Jack E. Davis, "Baseball's Reluctant Challenge: Desegregating Major League Spring Training Sites, 1961–1964," *Journal of Sport History* 19 (summer 1992): 144–62.

29. See Susan Cahn, *Coming on Strong: Gender and Sexuality in Twentieth-Century Sport* (New York: Free Press, 1994); Linda D. Williams, "An Analysis of American Sportswomen in Two Negro Newspapers" (Ph.D. diss., Ohio State University, 1988).

30. Edwin B. Henderson, *The Negro in Sports*, 297.

31. Ibid., 298–316.

32. For the basis of this interpretation, see Bruce, "Ancient Africa and the Early Black American Historians."

33. Edwin B. Henderson, *The Negro in Sports*, rev. ed. (Washington, D.C.: Associated Publishers, 1949), p. x.

34. For information on the *Negro History Bulletin*, see August Meier and Elliott Rudwick, *Black History and the Historical Profession, 1915–1980*, 61, 189, 280.

35. "The Negro in Sports," *Negro History Bulletin* 15 (Dec. 1951): 42–56.

36. For information on Brooks, see Meier and Rudwick, *Black History and the Historical Profession*, 189; on Carter, see the Arthur Carter Papers, MSRC.

37. The same thing may be true for the *Official Handbook: Inter-Scholastic Athletic Association of Middle Atlantic States*.

38. The amount of literature on various aspects of African American life increased dramatically during the latter half of the 1960s and the early part of the 1970s. For some of the literature dealing specifically with sport and the African American athlete, see Jeffrey T. Sammons, " 'Race' and Sport," 203–78; David K. Wiggins, "From Plantation to Playing Field: Historical Writings on the Black Athlete in American Sport," *Research Quarterly for Exercise and Sport* 57 (June 1986), 101–16.

39. Edwin B. Henderson, with the editors of *Sport* Magazine, *The Black Athlete: Emergence and Arrival* (Cornwall Heights, Pa.: Pennsylvania Publishers, 1968).

40. Edwin B. Henderson, "The Negro As Athlete," *Crisis* 77 (Feb. 1970): 51–56; "Physical Education and Athletics Among Negroes," in Bruce L. Bennett, ed., *Proceedings of the Big Ten Symposium on the History of Physical Education and Sport* (Chicago: Athletic Institute, 1972), 67–83. "The Black American in Sports," in Mabel M. Smythe, ed., *The Black American Reference Book* (Englewood Cliffs, N.J.: Prentice-Hall, 1976): 927–63;

41. There is a voluminous amount of literature in the discipline of sport sociology that is highly critical of contemporary sport. See, for example: George Sage, *Power and Ideology in American Sport: A Critical Perspective* (Champaign, Ill.: Human Kinetics, 1990); Richard Gruneau, *Class, Sports, and Social Development* (Amherst, Mass.: Univ. of Massachusetts Press, 1983).

42. See Harry Edwards, *The Revolt of the Black Athlete* (New York: Free Press, 1969); David K. Wiggins, "The Year of Awakening: Black Athletes, Racial Unrest and the Civil Rights Movement of 1968," *International Journal of the History of Sport* 9 (Aug. 1992): 188–208 [chap. 6 of this book], and "The Future of College Athletics Is at State: Black Athletes and Racial Turmoil on Three Predominantly White University Campuses, 1968–1972," *Journal of Sport History* 15 (winter, 1988): 304–33 [chap. 7 of this book].

43. With editors of *Sport* magazine, *Black Athlete: Emergence and Arrival*, 260; "The Black American in Sports," in Smythe, ed., *Black American Reference Book*, 953–54.

44. Andrew S. "Doc" Young, *Negro Firsts in Sports* (Chicago: Johnson Publishing, 1963).

45. Wally Jones and Jim Washington, *Black Champions Challenge American Sports* (New York: David McKay, 1972).

46. Arthur R. Ashe, Jr. *A Hard Road To Glory: A History of the African-American Athlete*, 3 vols. (New York: Warner Books, 1988).

47. Harry Edwards, *Sociology of Sport* (Homewood, Ill.: Dorsey, 1973).

48. Harry Edwards, *Revolt of the Black Athlete*, 167–77. I also discuss Edwards' book in my article "The Year of Awakening" [chap. 6 of this book].

Bibliographical Essay

A number of important works, some of which are also mentioned in the introduction or included among the references, have been influential in my development as a sport historian and in my thinking about sport, race, and American culture. Perhaps no works have influenced my scholarship more than those that have touched upon African American cultural patterns, examined broad racial themes, and dealt with the complexities of skin color and racist stereotypes. Included among these works are: Lawrence W. Levine, *Black Culture and Black Consciousness: Afro-American Folk Thought from Slavery to Freedom* (New York: Oxford Univ. Press, 1977); David R. Roediger, *The Wages of Whiteness: Race and the Making of the American Working Class* (New York: Verso, 1991); Winthrop D. Jordan, *White over Black: American Attitudes toward the Negro, 1550–1812* (Chapel Hill: Univ. of North Carolina Press, 1968); George M. Fredrickson, *The Black Image in the White Mind: The Debate on Afro-American Character and Destiny, 1817–1914* (New York: Harper & Row, 1971); John S. Haller, Jr., *Outcasts from Evolution: Scientific Attitudes of Racial Inferiority, 1859–1900* (Urbana: Univ. of Illinois Press, 1971); Burton W. Peretti, *The Creation of Jazz: Music, Race, and Culture in Urban America* (Urbana: Univ. of Illinois Press, 1992); Joseph Boskin, *Sambo: The Rise and Decline of an American Jester* (New York: Oxford Univ. Press, 1986); Sterling Stuckey, *Slave Culture: Nationalist Theory and the Foundations of Black America* (New York: Oxford Univ. Press, 1987); and Roger D. Abrahams, *Singing the Master: The Emergence of African American Culture in the Plantation South* (New York: Pantheon, 1992).

The overviews of African Americans in sport are generally not so impressive as the works mentioned above. However, there are some good (in several cases, excellent) works that provide important information and insights about African American athletes. I have found some useful information (and many photographs) on the history of African American athletes in such popular books as Jack Orr, *The Black Athlete: His Story in American History* (New York: Lion Books, 1969); Jack Olsen, *The Black Athlete: A Shameful Story* (New York: Time-Life Books, 1968); Wally Jones and Jim Washington, *Black Champions Challenge American Sports* (New York: David McKay, 1972); Andrew S. "Doc"

279

Young, *Negro Firsts in Sports* (Chicago: Johnson Publishing, 1963); Stephen Fox, *Big Leagues: Professional Baseball, Football, and Basketball in National Memory* (New York: William Morrow, 1994); Arna Bontemps, *Famous Negro Athletes* (New York: Dodd, Mead, 1964); Ocania Chalk, *Pioneers of Black Sport: The Early Days of the Black Professional Athlete in Baseball, Basketball, Boxing, and Football* (New York: Dodd, Mead, 1975); Art and Edna Rust, *Art Rust's Illustrated History of the Black Athlete* (Garden City, N.Y.: Doubleday, 1985); Arthur R. Ashe, Jr., *A Hard Road to Glory: A History of the African-American Athlete*, 3 vols. (New York: Warner Books, 1988); and George L. Lee, *Interesting Athletes: Black American Sports Heroes* (New York: Ballantine, 1976).

Two books by Gerald Early provide extremely well-written and stimulating interpretative essays on African Americans in sport, particularly boxing: *Tuxedo Junction: Essays on American Culture* (New York: Ecco Press, 1989) and *The Culture of Bruising: Essays on Prizefighting, Literature, and Modern American Culture* (New York: Ecco Press, 1994). Four lesser known but informative surveys are William W. MacDonald, "The Black Athlete in American Sports," in William J. Baker and John M. Carroll, *Sports in Modern America* (St. Louis: River City Publishers, 1981), 88–98; John P. Davis, "The Negro in American Sports," in John P. Davis, ed., *The American Negro Reference Book* (Englewood Cliffs, N.J.: Prentice-Hall, 1966), 775–825; Barry D. McPherson, "Minority Group Involvement in Sport: The Black Athlete," *Exercise and Sport Science Reviews* 2 (1974): 71–101; and David K. Wiggins, "Critical Events Affecting Racism in Athletics," in Dana Brooks and Ronald Althouse, eds., *Racism in College Athletics: The African-American Athlete's Experience* (Morgantown, W.Va.: Fitness Information Technology, 1993), 23–49.

Virtually all the survey texts on the history of sport include materials on African American athletes. The best of these, as far as the coverage of black athletes is concerned, are William J. Baker, *Sports in the Western World* (Urbana: Univ. of Illinois Press, 1988); Allen Guttmann, *A Whole New Ball Game: An Interpretation of American Sports* (Chapel Hill: Univ. of North Carolina Press, 1988); John A. Lucas and Ronald A. Smith, *Saga of American Sport* (Philadelphia: Lea & Febiger, 1978); Benjamin G. Rader, *American Sports: From the Age of Folk Games to the Age of Spectators* (Englewood Cliffs, N.J.: Prentice-Hall, 1983); Randy Roberts and James Olson, *Winning Is the Only Thing: Sports in America Since 1945* (Baltimore: Johns Hopkins Univ. Press, 1989); and Elliott J. Gorn and Warren Goldstein, *A Brief History of American Sports* (New York: Hill & Wang, 1993).

The survey texts in sport sociology all include chapters on "Sport and Race" that provide a more contemporary overview on African American athletes. Harry Edwards, *Sociology of Sport* (Homewood, Ill.: Dorsey Press, 1973); Jay J. Coakley, *Sport in Society: Issues and Controversies* (St. Louis: Times Mirror/Mosby, 1994); Wilbert M. Leonard II, *A Sociological Perspective of Sport* (New York: MacMillan, 1993); Timothy J. Curry and Robert M. Jiobu, *Sports: A Social Perspective* (Englewood Cliffs, N.J.: Prentice-Hall, 1984); John W. Loy et al., eds., *Sport, Culture and Society* (Philadelphia: Lea & Febiger, 1981); Daniel M. Landers, *Social Problems in Athletics: Essays in the Sociology of Sport* (Urbana: Univ. of Illinois Press, 1976); John T. Talamini and Charles H. Page, *Sport and Society: An Anthology* (Boston: Little, Brown, 1973); and D. Stanley Eitzen and George H. Sage, *Sociology of North American Sport* (Dubuque, Iowa: Brown & Benchmark, 1993) are works of this genre that are especially good on the topic. Kenneth L. Shropshire, *In Black and White: Race and Sports in America* (New York: New York Univ. Press, 1996) is a work that touches on some of the same topics broached in the above mentioned sport sociology texts.

Scholars interested in the African American athlete's past would do well to consult Jeffrey T. Sammons, "'Race' and Sport: A Critical, Historical Examination," *Journal of Sport History* 21 (fall 1994): 203–98, the most thorough review essay on the subject. Other important bibliographic sources are Lenwood G. Davis and Belinda Daniels, comps., *Black Athletes in the United States: A Bibliography of Books, Articles, Autobiographies, and Biographies on Professional Black Athletes, 1880–1981* (Westport, Conn.: Greenwood, 1983); David L. Porter, ed., *African-American Sports Greats: A Biographical Dictionary* (Westport, Conn.: Greenwood, 1995); David K. Wiggins, "From Plantation to Playing Field: Historical Writings on the Black Athlete in American Sport," *Research Quarterly For Exercise and Sport* 57 (June 1986): 101–16; Manning Marable, "Black Athletes in White Men's Games, 1880–1920," *Maryland Historian* 4 (fall 1973): 143–49; Bruce L. Bennett, "Bibliography on the Negro in Sports," *Journal of Health, Physical Education, and Recreation* 41 (Jan. 1970): 77–78., "Supplemental Selected Annotated Bibliography on the Negro in Sports," *Journal of Health, Physical Education, and Recreation* 41 (Sept. 1970): 71; and Grant Henry, "A Bibliography Concerning Negroes in Physical Education, Athletics and Related Fields," *Journal of Health, Physical Education, and Recreation* 44 (May 1973): 65–70.

The involvement of African Americans in sport behind segregated walls during the late nineteenth century and the first half of the twentieth has received increasing attention from academicians. J. Thomas Jable, "Sport in Philadelphia's African-American Community, 1865–1900," in George Eisen and David K. Wiggins, eds., *Ethnicity and Sport in North American History and Culture* (Westport, Conn.: Greenwood, 1994), 157–76; Ralph Watkins, "Recreation, Leisure, and Charity in the Afro-American Community of Buffalo, New York: 1920–1925," *Afro-Americans in New York Life and History* 6 (July 1982): 7–15; Gerald R. Gems, "Blocked Shot: The Development of Basketball in the African-American Community of Chicago," *Journal of Sport History* 22 (summer 1995): 135–48; Dale Somers, *The Rise of Sports in New Orleans, 1850–1900* (Baton Rouge: Louisiana State Univ, Press, 1972); Stephen Hardy, *How Boston Played: Sport, Recreation, and Community, 1865–1915* (Boston: Northeastern Univ Press, 1982); Steven A. Riess, *City Games: The Evolution of American Urban Society and the Rise of Sports* (Urbana: Univ. of Illinois Press, 1990); James Roland Coates, Jr., "Recreation and Sport in the African-American Community of Baltimore, 1890–1920," (Ph.D. Diss., University of Maryland, 1991); and especially Rob Ruck, *Sandlot Seasons: Sport in Black Pittsburgh* (Urbana: Univ. of Illinois Press, 1987) are all works that examine various aspects of black sport in the urban setting.

Sport in historically black colleges, a topic largely ignored by scholars, has been nicely analyzed by Patrick B. Miller in "To 'Bring the Race Along Rapidly': Sport, Student Culture, and Educational Mission at Historically Black Colleges During the Interwar Years," *History of Education Quarterly* 35 (summer 1995): 111–133, and *The Playing Fields of American Culture: Athletics and Higher Education* (forthcoming, tentatively titled, Oxford Univ. Press). See also Leon Wright Bey, "Impact of Desegregation on Selected Aspects of the Athletic Programs of the Traditionally Black Institutions in the Central Intercollegiate Athletic Association" (Ph.D. diss., Temple University, 1985); Earl Henry Duval, Jr., "An Historical Analysis of the Central Intercollegiate Athletic Association" (Ph.D. diss., Kent State University, 1985); Hal A. Lawson, "Physical Education and Sport in the Black Community: The Hidden Perspective," *Journal of Negro Education* 48 (spring 1979): 187–95; O. K. Davis, *Grambling's Gridiron Glory: Eddie Robinson and the Tigers Success Story* (Ruston, La.: M & M Printing, 1983); Michael Hurd, *Black College Football, 1892–1992: One Hundred Years of History, Education, and Pride* (Virginia Beach, Va.: 1992); and Ted Chambers, *The History of Athletics and Physical Education at Howard University* (Washington, D.C.: Vantage, 1986).

Information on early black professional basketball, most specifically the Harlem Globetrotters and the New York Renaissance Five, can be found in Robert W. Peterson, *Cages to Jump Shots: Pro Basketball's Early Years* (New York: Oxford Univ. Press, 1990); Nelson George, *Elevating the Game: Black Men and Basketball* (New York: Harper Collins, 1992); and Susan J. Rayl, "The New York Renaissance Professional Black Basketball Team, 1923–1950," (Ph.D. diss., Penn State Univ., 1996). Studies on all-black professional football teams are virtually non-existent, with the notable exception of Rob Ruck, "Soaring above the Sandlots: The Garfield Eagles," *Pennsylvania Heritage* 8 (summer 1982): 13–18, an essay that serves as the basis for a chapter in his *Sandlot Seasons: Sport in Black Pittsburgh*, mentioned earlier. The most closely examined of the all-black sporting organizations are the negro baseball leagues. Robert W. Peterson, *Only the Ball Was White* (Englewood Cliffs, N.J.: Prentice-Hall, 1970); Donn Rogosin, *Invisible Men: Life in Baseball's Negro Leagues* (New York: Atheneum, 1987); John Holway, *Blackball Stars: Negro League Pioneers* (Westport, Conn.: Meckler, 1988); Janet Bruce, *The Kansas City Monarchs: Champions of Black Baseball* (Lawrence: University Press of Kansas, 1985); Bruce Chadwick, *When the Game Was Black and White: The Illustrated History of Baseball's Negro Leagues* (New York: Abberville Press, 1992); Phil Dixon and Patrick J. Hannigan, *The Negro Baseball Leagues: A Photographic History* (Mattituck, N.Y.: Ameron 1992); and Mark Ribowsky, *The Power and the Darkness: The Life of Josh Gibson in the Shadows of the Game* (New York: Simon & Schuster, 1996), are important works on this topic. For personal reminiscences, see Leroy "Satchel" Paige, as told to David Lipman, *Maybe I'll Pitch Forever* (Garden City, N.Y.: Doubleday, 1962); Roy Campanella, *It's Good to be Alive* (Boston: Little, Brown, 1959); John B. Holway, *Voices from the Great Negro Baseball Leagues* (New York: Dodd, Mead, 1975); Buck O'Neil, with Steve Wulf and David Conrads, *I Was Right on Time* (New York: Simon & Schuster, 1996); and Monte Irvin, with James A. Riley, *Monte Irvin: Nice Guys Finish First* (New York: Carroll & Graf, 1996).

Studies of elite African American athletes who found success in predominantly white organized sport during the nineteenth century and the first half of the twentieth have increased substantially over the last few years. Among the noteworthy studies of nineteenth-century black athletes are Michael H. Goodman, "The Moor vs. Black Diamond," *Virginia Cavalcade* 29 (spring 1980): 164–73; Carl B. Cone, "The Molineaux-Cribb Fight, 1810: Wuz Tom Molineaux Robbed?" *Journal of Sport History* 9 (winter 1982): 83–91; Jerome Zuckerman et al., "The Black Athlete in Post-Bellum 19th Century," *Physical Educator* 29 (Oct. 1972): 142–46; David W. Zang, *Fleet Walker's Divided Heart: The Life of Baseball's First Black Major Leaguer* (Lincoln: Univ. of Nebraska Press, 1995); Andrew Ritchie, *Major Taylor: The Extraordinary Career of a Champion Bicycle Racer* (San Francisco: Bicycle Books, 1988); Jack W. Berryman, "Early Black Leadership in Collegiate Football: Massachusetts as a Pioneer," *Historical Journal of Massachusetts* 9 (June 1981): 17–28; and G. B. McKinney, "Negro Professional Baseball Players in the Upper South in the Gilded Age," *Journal of Sport History* 3 (winter 1976): 273–80. Marshall "Major" Taylor, *The Fastest Bicycle Rider in the World* (1928; reprint, Battleboro, Vt.: Green-Stephen Press, 1971) and M. F. Walker, *Our Home Colony: A Treatise on the Past, Present, and Future of the Negro Race in America* (Steubenville, Ohio: Herald, 1908) are fascinating personal accounts by two of the most famous African American athletes of the period.

Jack Johnson, America's first black heavyweight champion and one of the most controversial athletes in history, wrote an equally controversial autobiography, *Jack Johnson Is a Dandy: An Autobiography* (New York: Chelsea House, 1969). For secondary works on Johnson's life and career, see William H. Wiggins, "Jack Johnson as Bad Bigger: The Folklore of His Life," *Black Scholar* 2 (Jan. 1971): 4–19, and, "Boxing's Sambo Twins: Racial Stereotypes in Jack Johnson and Joe Louis Newspaper Cartoons, 1908 to 1938," *Journal of Sport History* 15 (winter 1988): 242–54; Al-Tony Gilmore, *Bad Nigger: The National Impact of Jack Johnson* (New York: Kennikat, 1975); and Randy Roberts, *Papa Jack: Jack Johnson and the Era of White Hopes* (New York: Free Press, 1983).

The careers of Jesse Owens and Joe Louis, two of the most prominent African American athletes of the first half of the twentieth century, are covered very well. On Owens, see William J. Baker, *Jesse Owens: An American Life* (New York: Free Press, 1986); and Owens's autobiographies: with Paul Neimark, *Blackthink: My Life as Black Man and White Man* (New York: William Morrow, 1970); [With Paul Neimark], *The Jesse Owens Story* (New York: Putnams, 1970); [With Paul Neimark], *I Have Changed* (New York: William Morrow, 1972); [With Paul Neimark], *Jesse: A Spiritual Autobiography* (Plainfield, N.J.: Logos, 1978). On Louis, see Jeffrey T. Sammons, "Boxing as a Reflection of Society: The Southern Reaction to Joe Louis," *Journal of Popular Culture* 16 (spring 1983): 23–33.; Dominic J. Capeci, Jr., and Martha Wilkerson, "Multifarious Hero: Joe Louis, American Society and Race Relations During World Crisis, 1935–1945," *Journal of Sport History;* 10 (winter 1983): 5–25; Al-Tony Gilmore, "The Myth, Legend and Folklore of Joe Louis: The Impression of Sport on Society," *South Atlantic Quarterly* 82 (summer 1983): 256–268; Anthony O. Edmonds, *Joe Louis* (Grand Rapids: William B. Erdman, 1976); Chris Mead, *Champion: Joe Louis, Black Hero in White America* (New York: Scribner's, 1985); and Joe Louis Barrow, Jr. and Barbara Munder, *Joe Louis: 50 Years An*

American Hero (New York: McGraw-Hill, 1988). Louis's autobiography is *Joe Louis, My Life* (New York: Harcourt Brace Jovanovich, 1978).

The experiences of African American athletes who competed in college sport at predominantly white institutions during the first half of the twentieth century can be gleaned from Donald Spivey and Tom Jones, "Intercollegiate Athletic Servitude: A Case Study of the Black Illinois Student-Athletes, 1931–1967," *Social Science Quarterly* 55 (Mar. 1975): 939–47; Donald Spivey, "Sport, Protest, and Consciousness: The Black Athlete in Big-Time Intercollegiate Sports, 1941–1968," *Phylon* 44 (June 1983): 116–25, and "End Jim Crow in Sports: The Protest at New York University, 1940–1941," *Journal of Sport History* 15 (winter 1988): 282–303; David K. Wiggins, "Prized Performers, but Frequently Overlooked Students: The Involvement of Black Athletes in Intercollegiate Sports on Predominantly White University Campuses, 1890–1972," *Research Quarterly for Exercise and Sport* 62 (June 1991): 164–77; Patrick B. Miller, "Harvard and the Color Line: The Case of Lucien Alexis," in Ronald Story, ed., *Sports in Massachusetts: Historical Essays* (Westfield, Mass.: 1991), 137–58, and *The Playing Fields of American Culture: Athletics and Higher Education;* John M. Carroll, *Fritz Pollard: Pioneer in Racial Advancement* (Urbana: Univ. of Illinois Press, 1992); and John Behee, *Hail to the Victors! Black Athletes at the University of Michigan* (Ann Arbor: Swink-Tuttle Press, 1974). In addition to the Jesse Owens and Joe Louis autobiographies, see Woody Strode and Sam Young, *Goal Dust: The Warm and Candid Memoirs of a Pioneer Black Athlete and Actor* (New York: Madison Books, 1990); Jimmy Brown, *Off My Chest* (New York: Doubleday, 1964); and Paul Robeson, *Here I Stand* (London: Dennis Dobson, 1958), for personal accounts of black athletes who participated in predominantly white college sport.

The shattering of the color line in major league baseball and other predominantly white organized sports at various levels of competition in the mid-twentieth century has been chronicled by a number of scholars. For the integration of intercollegiate sport in the South, see Joan Paul et al., "The Arrival and Ascendence of Black Athletes in the Southeastern Conference, 1966–1980," *Phylon* 45 (Dec. 1984): 284–97; Ronald E. Marcello, "The Integration of Intercollegiate Athletics in Texas: North Texas State College as a Test Case, 1956," *Journal of Sport History* 14 (winter 1987): 286–316; Charles H. Martin, "Jim Crow in the Gymnasium: The Integration of College Basketball in the American South," *International Journal of the History of Sport* 10 (Apr. 1993): 68–86; Richard Pennington, *Breaking the Ice: The Racial Integration of Southwest Conference Football* (Jefferson, N.C.: McFarland, 1987). The integration of professional football is examined in Thomas G. Smith, "Civil Rights on the Gridiron: The Kennedy Administration and the Desegregation of the Washington Redskins," *Journal of Sport History* 14 (summer 1987): 189–208, and "Outside the Pale: The Exclusion of Blacks From the National Football League, 1934–1946," *Journal of Sport History* 15 (winter 1988): 255–81; and Gerald R. Gems, "Shooting Stars: The Rise and Fall of Blacks in Professional Football," *Professional Football Research Association Annual Bulletin* (1988): pp. 1–16.

Information on the desegregation of professional basketball, while far less extensive than that found on football and baseball, can be gleaned from Robert W. Peterson, *Cages to Jump Shots: Pro Basketball's Early Years* (New York:

Oxford Univ. Press, 1990); Nelson George, *Elevating the Game: Black Men and Basketball* (New York: Simon & Schuster, 1992); and Charles Salzberg, *From Set Shot to Slam Dunk: The Glory Days of Basketball in the Words of Those Who Played It* (New York: Dutton, 1987). For the desegregation of professional golf, see Charlie Sifford, with James Gullo, *Just Let Me Play: The Story of Charlie Sifford, The First Black PGA Golfer* (Latham, N.Y.: British American Publishing, 1992). Most of the research on the desegregation of sport has focused, not surprisingly, on major league baseball. The definitive study on Jackie Robinson and the desegregation of America's "National Pastime" is Jules Tygiel, *Baseball's Great Experiment: Jackie Robinson and His Legacy* (New York: Oxford Univ. Press, 1983). Tygiel and other scholars have been helped tremendously by Robinson's autobiography, *I Never Had It Made* (New York: Putnam's, 1972). Other notable studies on the desegregation of baseball are William Simons, "Jackie Robinson and the American Mind: Journalistic Perceptions of the Reintegration of Baseball," *Journal of Sport History* 12 (spring 1985): 39–64; Jack E. Davis, "Baseball's Reluctant Challenge: Desegregating Major League Spring Training Sites, 1961–1964," *Journal of Sport History* 19 (summer 1992): 144–62; Ronald A. Smith, "The Paul Robeson-Jackie Robinson Saga and a Political Collision," *Journal of Sport History* 6 (summer 1979): 5–27; and Joseph Thomas Moore, *Pride Against Prejudice: The Biography of Larry Doby* (Westport, Conn.: Greenwood, 1988).

The role of African American Athletes in the civil rights struggle of the late 1960s and the 1970s has not yet received a great deal of attention from academicians. There are a number of studies, however, that provide important insights on the topic. Anyone interested in Muhammad Ali should consult his autobiography, written with Richard Durham, *The Greatest: Muhammad Ali* (New York: Random House, 1976). Two excellent secondary works that focus on his life and boxing career are Thomas Hauser, *Muhammad Ali: His Life and Times* (New York: Simon & Schuster, 1991), and Elliott J. Gorn, ed., *Muhammad Ali: The People's Champ* (Urbana: Univ. of Illinois Press, 1995). Other important studies that discuss aspects of Ali's career are Jeffrey T. Sammons, *Beyond the Ring: The Role of Boxing in American Society* (Urbana: Univ. of Illinois Press, 1988); Jose Torres, *Sting Like A Bee: The Muhammad Ali Story* (New York: Abelard-Schuman, 1971); Ali A. Mazuri, "Boxer Muhammad Ali and Soldier Idi Amin as International Political Symbols: The Bioeconomics of Sports and War," *Comparative Studies in Society and History* 19 (Apr. 1977): 189–215. The best personal treatments of the black athletic revolt are Harry Edwards, *The Revolt of the Black Athlete* (New York: Free Press, 1970), and *The Struggle That Must Be: An Autobiography* (New York: Macmillan, 1980); Bill Russell, *Go Up For Glory* (New York: Coward McCann, 1966), and with Taylor Branch, *Second Wind: The Memoirs of an Opinionated Man* (New York: Random House, 1974); and Vincent Matthews, with Neil Amdur, *My Race Be Won* (New York: Charterhouse, 1974). Additional information about African American athletes and the Black Power movement can be gained from reading William VanDeburg, *A New Day in Babylon: The Black Power Movement and American Culture, 1965–1975* (Chicago: Univ. of Chicago Press, 1992); Richard Lapchick, *Broken Promises: Racism in American Sports* (New York: St. Martin's, 1984); Adolph H. Grundman, "Image of Intercollegiate Sports and the

Civil Rights Movement: A Historian's View," *Arena Review* 3 (Oct. 1979): 17–24; and Donald Spivey, "Black Consciousness and Olympic Protest Movement, 1964–1980," in Donald Spivey, ed., *Sport in America: New Historical Perspetives* (Westport, Conn.: Greenwood, 1985), 239–59. An autobiography that does not focus specifically on the black athletic revolt but is indispensable for understanding one African American athlete's struggle for equal opportunity both within and outside of sport is Arthur Ashe and Arnold Rampersad, *Days of Grace, A Memoir* (New York: Knopf, 1993).

Studies of African American women athletes are about as limited as those completed on sport and the Black Power movement. Until recently, it has been a subject in search of historians. Ellen W. Gerber et al. *The American Woman in Sport* (Reading, Mass.: Addison-Wesley, 1974), was one of the first works to raise questions concerning the involvement of black women in sport. Linda D. Williams's, "Sportswomen in Black and White: Sports History From an Afro-American Perspective," in Pamela J. Creeden, ed., *Women, Media and Sport: Challenging Gender Values* (Thousand Oaks, Calif.: Sage, 1994), 45–66, provides an examination of African American women athletes from the perspective of the black press. Michael B. Davis, in *Black American Women in Olympic Track and Field: A Complete Illustrated Reference* (Jefferson, N.C.: MacFarland, 1992), recounts the exploits of African American women athletes in Olympic Track and Field Competition. Yevonne R. Smith's, "Women of Color in Society and Sport," *Quest* 44 (summer 1992): 228–50, furnishes an analysis of African American women both within and outside of sport. Cindy Himes Gissendanner, in both "African-American Women and Competitive Sport, 1920–1960," in Susan Birrell and Cheryl Cole, eds., *Women, Sport and Culture* (Champaign Ill.: Human Kinetics, 1993), 81–92, and "African American Women Olympians: The Impact of Race, Gender, and Class Ideologies, 1932–1968," *Research Quarterly for Exercise and Sport* 67 (June 1996): 172–82 provides interesting and cogent analyses of African American women athletes in Olympic competition. Gwendolyn Captain's, "Enter Ladies and Gentlemen of Color: Gender, Sport, and the Ideal of African American Manhood and Womanhood During the Late Nineteenth Century and Early Twentieth Centuries," *Journal of Sport History* 18 (spring 1991): 81–102, examines the intersection of race, gender, class, and sport at the turn of the century. Susan Cahn furnishes one of the fullest and most insightful accounts of African American women and sport in her *Coming On Strong: Gender and Sexuality in Twentieth-Century Women's Sport* (New York: Free Press, 1994); Tina Sloan-Green et al., *Black Women in Sport* (Reston, Va.: American Alliance for Health, Physical Education, Recreation, and Dance, 1981) furnishes some interesting data on African American women athletes. Susan Birrell explores the connection between various sociological theories, African American women, and sport in her "Women of Color, Critical Autobiography, and Sport," in Michael A. Messner and Donald F. Sabo, eds., *Sport, Men, and the Gender Order: Critical Feminist Perspectives* (Champaign, Ill.: Human Kinetics, 1990), 185–99. Two well-known personal memoirs that provide insights are Althea Gibson's, *I Always Wanted To Be Somebody* (New York: Harper, 1958) and Wilma Rudolph's, *Wilma* (New York: New American Library, 1977).

There is a vast amount of literature focusing more specifically on racial ideology, sport, and African American athletes in contemporary society. One of the most popular areas of research over the last few years has been the relationship between race, social structure, and sport orientation. David L. Andrews, *Deconstructing Michael Jordan: Popular Culture and the Politics of Race and Ethnicity in Postmodern America* (Albany: State University of New York Press, forthcoming); William J. Rudman, "The Sport Mystique in Black Culture," *Sociology of Sport Journal* 3 (1986): 305–19; Michael Eric Dyson "Be Like Mike? Michael Jordan and 'The Pedagogy of Desire,'" in Michael Eric Dyson, *Reflecting Black African-American Cultural Criticism* (Minneapolis: Univ. of Minnesota Press, 1993), 64–75 and "Crossing over Jordan," in *Between God and Gangster Rap: Bearing Witness to Black Culture* (New York: Oxford University Press, 1996), 56–60; Michael A. Messner, *Power at Play: Sports and the Problem of Masculinity* (Boston: Beacon Press, 1992), and "Masculinities and Athletic Careers: Bonding and Status Differences," in Messner and Sabo, eds., *Sport, Men, and the Gender Order*, 97–108; Richard Majors, "Cool Pose: Black Masculinity and Sports," in Messner and Sabo, 109–14; Richard Lapchick, *Five Minutes to Midnight: Race and Sport in the 1990s* (Lanham, M.D.: Madison Books, 1991); James LeFlore, "Athleticism Among American Blacks," in Robert M. Pankin, ed., *Social Approaches to Sport* (Toronto: Associated University Presses, 1982), 104–21; and Larry E. Jordan, "Black Markets and Future Superstars: An Instrumental Approach to Opportunity in Sport Forms," *Journal of Black Studies* 11 (Mar. 1981): 289–306, are just a few studies dealing with the topic.

Two topics that have received special attention from academicians are "stacking" in sport (the overrepresentation of African Americans in particular playing positions) and the question over racial differences and sport performance. For studies on stacking, see John W. Loy and Joseph F. McElvoque, "Racial Segregation in American Sport," *International Review of Sport Sociology* 5 (1970): 5–23; Donald W. Ball, "Ascription and Position: A Comparative Analysis of 'Stacking' in Professional Football," *Canadian Review of Sociology and Anthropology* 10 (May 1973): 97–113; Gregg Jones et al., "A Log-Linear Analysis of Stacking in College Football," *Social Science Quarterly* 68 (Mar. 1987): 70–83; Wilbert M. Leonard II, "Stacking in College Basketball: A Neglected Analysis," *Sociology of Sport Journal* 4 (1987): 403–9; and Mark Lavoie, "The Economic Hypothesis of Positional Segregation: Some Further Comments," *Sociology of Sport Journal* 6 (1989): 163–66. For insights into the question of racial differences and sport performance, see Harry Edwards, "The Sources of the Black Athlete's Superiority," *Black Scholar* 3 (Nov. 1971): 32–41, and "The Myth of the Racially Superior Athlete," *Intellectual Digest* 2 (Mar. 1972): 58–60; Gary Sailes, "Myth of Black Sports Supremacy," *Black Scholar* 21 (June 1991): 480–87; Laurel R. Davis, "The Articulation of Difference: White Preoccupation with the Question of Racially Linked Genetic Differences Among Athletes," *Sociology of Sport Journal* 7 (1990): 179–87; Philip M. Hoose, *Necessities: Racial Barriers in American Sports* (New York: Random House, 1989); John Hoberman, *Mortal Engines: The Science of Performance and the Dehumanization of Sport* (New York: Free Press, 1992), and *Darwin's Athletes: How Sport Has Damaged Black America and Preserved the Myth of Race* (Boston: Houghton Mifflin, forthcoming).

Index

Index